T0207354

Lecture Notes in Computer Science 13816

More information about this series at https://link.springer.com/bookseries/558

Jun Ma · Bo Wang (Eds.)

Fast and Low-Resource Semi-supervised Abdominal Organ Segmentation

MICCAI 2022 Challenge, FLARE 2022
Held in Conjunction with MICCAI 2022
Singapore, September 22, 2022
Proceedings

 Springer

Editors
Jun Ma ⓘ
University of Toronto
Toronto, ON, Canada

Bo Wang ⓘ
University of Toronto
Toronto, ON, Canada

ISSN 0302-9743   ISSN 1611-3349 (electronic)
Lecture Notes in Computer Science
ISBN 978-3-031-23910-6   ISBN 978-3-031-23911-3 (eBook)
https://doi.org/10.1007/978-3-031-23911-3

This Springer imprint is published by the registered company Springer Nature Switzerland AG
The registered company address is: Gewerbestrasse 11, 6330 Cham, Switzerland

Preface

This volume contains the proceedings of the international challenge on Fast and Low-resource Semi-supervised Abdominal Organ Segmentation in CT Scans (FLARE 2022), held in conjunction with the International Conference on Medical Image Computing and Computer Assisted Intervention (MICCAI) in 2022. By "proceedings", we mean to say that this volume contains the papers written by participants in the FLARE challenge to describe their solutions for automatic abdominal organ segmentation using the official training dataset released for this purpose.

Abdominal organ segmentation has many important clinical applications, such as organ quantification, surgical planning, and disease diagnosis. However, manually annotating organs from CT scans is time-consuming and labor-intensive. Thus, we usually cannot obtain a huge number of labeled cases. As a potential alternative, semi-supervised learning can explore useful information from unlabeled cases.

This challenge focuses on how to use unlabeled data to improve model performance. Specifically, we provide a small number of labeled cases (50) and a large number of unlabeled cases (2000) in the training set, 50 visible cases for validation, and 200 hidden cases for testing. The segmentation targets include 13 organs: liver, spleen, pancreas, right kidney, left kidney, stomach, gallbladder, esophagus, aorta, inferior vena cava, right adrenal gland, left adrenal gland, and duodenum. In addition to the typical Dice Similarity Coefficient (DSC) and Normalized Surface Dice (NSD), our evaluation metrics also focus on the inference speed and resources (GPU, CPU) consumption. Compared to the previous FLARE 2021 challenge, the dataset is 4x larger and the segmentations targets are increased to 13 organs. Moreover, the resource-related metrics are changed to the area under the GPU memory-time curve and the area under the CPU utilization-time curve rather than the maximum GPU memory consumption.

We finally received 48 successful Docker container submissions during the testing phase. Participants also submitted their methodology papers on openreview platform. Each paper received three to seven reviews. Based on the initial reviews and the authors' revisions and responses, we accepted 28 papers. This proceedings provides the state-of-the-art methods for semi-supervised abdominal organ segmentation in CT scans. We thank all the participants, reviewers, and program committee whose incredible work made this possible.

November 2022

Jun Ma
Bo Wang

Organization

Organizing Committee

Jun Ma   University of Toronto, Canada
Bo Wang   University of Toronto, Canada

Program Committee

Yao Zhang   Institute of Computing Technology, Chinese
                          Academy of Sciences; University of Chinese
                          Academy of Sciences, China
Song Gu   Nanjing Anke Medical Technology, China
Cheng Ge   Ocean University of China, China
Shihao Ma   University of Toronto, Canada
Adamo Young   University of Toronto, Canada

Contents

Self-training with Selective Re-training Improves Abdominal Organ Segmentation in CT Image

Fan Zhang[1], Meihuan Wang[2], and Hua Yang[1(✉)]

[1] Department of Radiological Algorithm, Fosun Aitrox Information Technology Co., Ltd., Shanghai, China
yanghua@fosun.com
[2] College of Medicine and Biological Information Engineering, Northeastern University, Shenyang, China

Abstract. Inspired by self-training learning via pseudo labeling, we construct self-training framework with selective re-training pseudo labels to improve semi-supervised abdominal organ segmentation. In this work, we carefully design the strong data augmentations (SDA) and test-time augmentations (TTA) to alleviate overfitting noisy labels as well as decouple similar predictions between the teacher and student models. For efficient segmentation learning (ESL), knowledge distillation is adopted to transfer larger teacher model to smaller student model for compressing model. In addition, we propose the single-label based connected component labelling (CCL) for post processing. Compared to one-hot CCL of $O(n)$ time complexity, which on the single-label based method is reduced to $O(1)$. Quantitative evaluation on the FLARE2022 validation cases, this method achieves the average dice similarity coefficient (DSC) of 0.8813 on semi-supervised model, it achieves significant improvement compared to 0.7711 on full-supervised model. Code is available at https://github.com/Shanghai-Aitrox-Technology/EfficientSegLearning.

Keywords: Self-training · Efficient segmentation learning · Abdominal organ segmentation

1 Introduction

Automatic segmentation of abdominal organs is confronted with main difficulties stem from three aspects: 1) It is costly, laborious, and even infeasible to annotate multi-organs at pixel-wise level in a large dataset. 2) The limited consumption resource and segmentation efficiency are required. 3) The variations in size, morphology and texture of different organs lead to class imbalance problem.

To avert the labor-intensive procedure for voxel-wise manual labeling, semi-supervised semantic segmentation has been proposed to learn a model from a handful of labeled images along with abundant unlabeled images. The self-training is commonly regarded as a form of entropy minimization in semi-supervised learning (SSL), since the re-trained student is supervised with pseudo

© The Author(s), under exclusive license to Springer Nature Switzerland AG 2022
J. Ma and B. Wang (Eds.): FLARE 2022, LNCS 13816, pp. 1–10, 2022.
https://doi.org/10.1007/978-3-031-23911-3_1

labels produced by the teacher which is trained on labeled data. However, potential performance degradation when iteratively optimizing the model with those ill-posed pseudo labels.

For efficient segmentation learning (ESL), self-training and self-supervised as the label-efficient approaches are used to boost the model representation capacity. Moreover, the common model compression and acceleration methods including pruning, distillation and quantization are adopted to produce light-weight models for efficient inference. The main concern of these method is to avoid the potential performance degradation on compressed model.

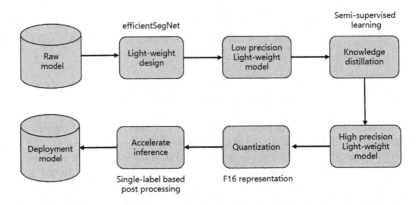

Fig. 1. A schematic diagram of the proposed efficient segmentation learning framework.

In this work, we empirically present four simple and effective techniques to alleviate the potential performance degradation as follows:

- We adopt an advanced self-training framework performs selective re-training via prioritizing reliable images based on holistic prediction-level stability in the entire training course.
- We design strong data augmentations (SDA) and test-time augmentations (TTA) on unlabeled images to alleviate overfitting noisy labels as well as decouple similar predictions between the teacher and student.
- We adopt knowledge distillation to transfer the knowledge from larger teacher model to smaller student model.
- We convert the one-hot based connected component labelling (CCL) to single-label based CCL for post processing.

2   Method

The pipeline of the proposed efficient segmentation framework is depicted in Fig. 1. We adopt the whole-volume-based coarse-to-fine framework as proposed in efficientSegNet [8] for abdominal multi-organ segmentation. The self-training is adopted for semi-supervised semantic segmentation. In addition, post quantization and single-label based CCL are designed to accelerate the inference. A detail description of the method is as follows.

2.1 Preprocessing

The proposed method includes the following preprocessing steps:

- Reorienting images to the right-anterior-inferior (RAI) view by linear resampling.
- Background removal by threshold segmentation. Cropping the bounding box of target, and resampling image to fixed size. The sizes of coarse and fine input are [160, 160, 160] and [160, 192, 192], respectively.
- Intensity normalization: First, the image is clipped to the range [-500, 500]. Then a z-score normalization is applied based on the mean and standard deviation of the intensity values.

2.2 Proposed Method

The proposed method is derived from self-training framework [7] (namely ST++) in semi-supervised semantic segmentation task. We employ 3D UNet with residual block (ResUNet) for both teacher and student models. The self-training from is as follows (Table 1):

1) Strong data augmentations

Table 1. The framework of self-training with selective re-training.

Step 1. Supervised Learning: Train a teacher model T with higher input resolution on labeled image with weak data augmentation
Step 2. Pseudo Labeling: Predict un-labeled image on three model checkpoints with T to obtain reliable scores. Select R highest scored images to generate pseudo labels with test-time-augmentation
Step 3. Re-training: Re-train a student model S with equal or larger model on the jointed labeled and 50% of highest reliable pseudo labels. Where the labeled image in training phase with weak data augmentation, while pseudo labels with strong data augmentation
Step 4. Re-labelling: Putting back the S as a T to obtain pseudo labels on un-labelled image
Step 5. Re-training: Re-train a student model S on the jointed labeled and all of pseudo labels which reliable scores exceed the 0.9
Step 6. Update: Return to step. 4 and employ the S model as the T model until reaching desired number of iterations

The weak or basic augmentations adopted in regular fully-supervised semantic segmentation, including random rotating, resizing, brightness, cropping and flipping. We inject SDA on unlabeled images to alleviate overfitting noisy labels as well as decouple similar predictions between the teacher and student, including color, noise and painting jitter. In the pseudo labeling phase, all unlabeled images are predicted with test-time augmentations, which contains rotating, cropping and fliping.

2) Selective re-training

We adopt a selective re-training scheme via prioritizing reliable unlabeled samples to safely exploit the whole unlabeled set in an easy-to-hard curriculum learning manner. The measurement for the reliability or uncertainty of an unlabeled image is to compute the holistic stability of the evolving pseudo masks in different iterations during the entire training course. Therefore, the more reliable and better predicted unlabeled images can be selected based on their evolving stability during training.

Concretely, several model checkpoints are saved in the first stage supervised training, and the discrepancy of their predictions on the unlabeled image serves as a measurement for reliability. Since training model tends to converge and achieve the best performance in the late training stage, we evaluate the mean Dice between each earlier pseudo mask and the final mask. Obtaining the stability score of all unlabeled images, we sort the whole unlabeled set based on these scores, and select the top R images with the highest scores for the first retraining phase.

3) Knowledge distillation

The teacher model has higher input resolution and wider initial channels by giving the teacher model enough capacity and difficult environments in terms of noise to learn through. In the last iteration phase, we train a small and fast student model for inference via knowledge distillation.

2.3   Post-processing

We convert full precision to half precision models on the inference phase. The CCL is applied on the coarse and fine model output to remove outlier and isolated objects. The one-hot labels are converted into single-label mask, and small isolated object removal is performed on the single-label mask. Compared to $O(n)$ time complexity of one-hot processing, this method reduces the time complexity to $O(1)$.

3   Experiments

3.1   Dataset and Evaluation Measures

The FLARE 2022 is an extension of the FLARE 2021 [4] with more segmentation targets and more diverse abdomen CT scans. The dataset is curated from more than 20 medical groups under the license permission, including MSD [6], KiTS [2,3], AbdomenCT-1K [5], and TCIA [1].

The training set includes 50 labelled CT scans with pancreas disease and 2000 unlabelled CT scans with liver, kidney, spleen, or pancreas diseases. The validation set includes 50 CT scans with liver, kidney, spleen, or pancreas diseases. The testing set includes 200 CT scans where 100 cases has liver, kidney, spleen, or pancreas diseases and the other 100 cases has uterine corpus endometrial, urothelial bladder, stomach, sarcomas, or ovarian diseases. All the CT scans only have image information and the center information is not available.

The evaluation measures consist of two accuracy measures: Dice Similarity Coefficient (DSC) and Normalized Surface Dice (NSD), and three running efficiency measures: running time, area under GPU memory-time curve, and area under CPU utilization-time curve. All measures will be used to compute the ranking. Moreover, the GPU memory consumption has a 2 GB tolerance.

3.2   Implementation Details

1) Data Augmentations
For weak data augmentations, the training images are randomly rotating on the x-y plane, flipping along each axis, resizing scale from 0.8 to 1.2, brightness from -200 to 200 and cropping. For the SDA on the unlabeled images, we use color jitter with random brightness, contrast and gamma, noise jitter with gaussian noise and blur, image in-painting with random values filled.

2) Test Time Augmentation
In the pseudo labeling phase, all unlabeled images are predicted with TTA, which contains rotating 180° along the z axis and cropping with central coordinates. The single-label based CCL is adopted to remove small isolated objects and the images are evaluated on their original resolution.

3) Selective Re-Training
The reliable images are measured with three checkpoints that are evenly saved at 1/3, 2/3, 3/3 total iterations during training. We simply treat the top 50% highest scored images with meanDice score larger than 0.9 as reliable ones and the remaining ones as unreliable. We oversampling labelled image to around the same scale as un-labelled image and then sampling uniformly from the combined dataset.

4) Environments and Requirements
The environments and requirements of the proposed method is shown in Table 2.

5) Training Procedure
We maintain the same optimizer strategy to train the teacher and student model. Specifically, the batch size is set as 1 with single NVIDIA 2080Ti GPU on distributed training. We use the adamW optimizer for training, where the initial base learning rate is set as 0.001. We use the step scheduling at 2/3, 6/7 epochs to decay the learning rate as 1e-4 and 5e-5 during the training process. The model is trained for 1000 epochs on the labelled image, 100 epochs on the labelled and

Table 2. Environments and requirements.

Ubuntu version	16.04.10
CPU	Intel(R) Xeon(R) Gold 5218 CPU @ 2.30 GHz (×4)
RAM	502G
GPU	NVIDIA 2080Ti (×8)
CUDA version	11.0
Programming language	Python 3.6
Deep learning framework	Pytorch (torch 1.5.0, torchvision 0.8.0)
Code is publicly available at	Shanghai-Aitrox-Technology/EfficientSegLearning

pseudo labelled image in the first iteration phase, and 60 epochs in the subsequent iteration phase. Empirically, the 5 times of iterative training could reach the satisfying result.

The training protocols of the proposed method is shown in Table 3.

Table 3. Training protocols.

Basic network	ResUNet with initial channels of 16
Network initialization	Kaiming normal initialization
Batch size	8
Patch size	Coarse: 160, 160, 160
	Fine: 160, 192, 192
Optimizer	Adam with betas(0.9, 0.99), L2 penalty: 0.00001
Loss	Dice loss
Dropout rate	0.2
Initial learning rate (lr)	0.001
Learning rate decay schedule	epoch <= epochs * 0.66: initLR
	epochs * 0.66 < epoch <= epochs * 0.86: initLR * 0.1
	epochs * 0.86 < epoch: initLR * 0.05
Training time per iteration	20 h

4   Results and Discussion

4.1   Quantitative Results on Validation Set

Quantitative result is illustrated in Table 4, it can be found that the proposed method can achieve very promising results on large organs, such as the liver, spleen, kidney, stomach. But for small organs, it remains very challenging and also desires to pay more attention, especially for some extremely small and unclear boundary organs, such as adrenal and duodenum. Compared to full-supervised model, the proposed semi-supervised method achieves the significant improvement.

Table 4. Quantitative results of validation set in terms of DSC.

Organs	Full-supervised	Semi-supervised
Liver	0.9198	0.9771
RK	0.8620	0.9253
Spleen	0.8777	0.9762
Pancreas	0.7452	0.8839
Aorta	0.9286	0.9667
IVC	08512	0.9172
RAG	0.6779	0.7791
LAG	0.5352	0.7415
Gallbladder	0.5769	0.7971
Esophagus	0.7706	0.8497
Stomach	0.7896	0.9120
Duodenum	0.6494	0.7954
LK	0.8397	0.9361
Mean	0.7711	0.8813

4.2 Qualitative Results on Validation Set

Figure 2 presents some easy and hard examples on validation set, and quantitative result is illustrated Table 5. For Case #21 and Case #35, our method successfully identify all organs with high DSC scores. For Case #2 and Case #44, Our method also performed well on large organs with clear boundaries, such as the spleen, but performed poorly on some organs with unclear boundaries or small organs, and even failed to segment, such as the stomach in Case #2.

4.3 Segmentation Efficiency Results on Validation Set

The average running time is 13.0 s per case in inference phase, and average used GPU memory is 2478 MB. The area under GPU memory-time curve is 13658.8 and the area under CPU utilization-time curve is 246.8.

4.4 Results on Final Testing Set

Quantitative result is illustrated in Table 6, it can be found that in the final test set, our test results are an average DSC of 0.8860 and an average NSD of 0.9335, and the average variance is very small, which proves that our model has excellent generalization.

Table 5. The DSC scores of easy and hard examples.

Organs	0021		0035		0002		0044	
	Full	Semi	Full	Semi	Full	Semi	Full	Semi
Liver	0.9797	0.9862	0.9757	0.9833	0.8927	0.9844	0.9175	0.9807
RK	0.9834	0.9791	0.9798	0.9833	0.8731	0.9510	0.0000	0.0000
Spleen	0.9871	0.9906	0.9885	0.9891	0.9754	0.9876	0.9650	0.9873
Pancreas	0.9254	0.9405	0.8618	0.9149	0.6832	0.8199	0.5878	0.8093
Aorta	0.9698	0.9721	0.9689	0.9729	0.9089	0.9574	0.8642	0.9464
IVC	0.9412	0.9491	0.9120	0.9368	0.8452	0.8524	0.8832	0.9449
RAG	0.8662	0.8525	0.6510	0.7973	0.5388	0.7670	0.0000	0.0000
LAG	0.6821	0.8503	0.6899	0.8464	0.7880	0.7540	0.5391	0.8424
Gallbladder	1.0000	1.0000	0.9358	0.9626	0.3066	0.2166	0.4060	0.9323
Esophagus	0.9073	0.9218	0.8539	0.9057	0.0000	0.0000	0.7171	0.8899
Stomach	0.9548	0.9705	0.8736	0.9669	0.5553	0.9624	0.4528	0.9168
Duodenum	0.9052	0.9333	0.8755	0.8910	0.7173	0.8500	0.0682	0.5606
LK	0.9830	0.9806	0.9847	0.9894	0.9344	0.9700	0.9257	0.9739
Mean	**0.9296**	**0.9482**	**0.8885**	**0.9338**	**0.6938**	**0.7748**	**0.5636**	**0.7526**

Table 6. Quantitative results on final testing set.

Organs	DSC	NSD
Liver	0.9786 ± 0.0259	0.9859 ± 0.0306
RK	0.9477 ± 0.1685	0.9507 ± 0.1718
Spleen	0.9517 ± 0.1435	0.9560 ± 0.1496
Pancreas	0.8536 ± 0.0647	0.9488 ± 0.0569
Aorta	0.9648 ± 0.0227	0.9831 ± 0.0294
IVC	0.9193 ± 0.0625	0.9319 ± 0.0757
RAG	0.8276 ± 0.1130	0.9404 ± 0.1118
LAG	0.8126 ± 0.1221	0.9106 ± 0.1261
Gallbladder	0.7792 ± 0.3339	0.7894 ± 0.3386
Esophagus	0.8166 ± 0.1166	0.9056 ± 0.1182
Stomach	0.9352 ± 0.0471	0.9631 ± 0.0555
Duodenum	0.7788 ± 0.1049	0.9139 ± 0.0818
LK	0.9519 ± 0.1363	0.9562 ± 0.1429
Mean	**0.8860 ± 0.0755**	**0.9335 ± 0.0501**

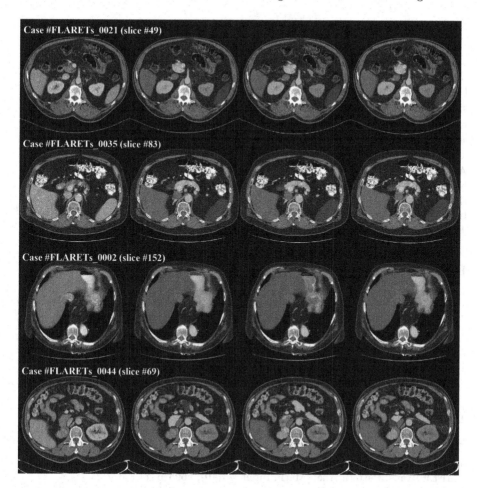

Fig. 2. Qualitative results of full-supervised and semi-supervised model on easy (case FLARETs #0021 and #0035) and hard (case FLARETs #0002 and #0044) examples. First column is the image, second column is the ground truth, third column is the predicted results by full-supervised model and forth column is the predicted results by semi-supervised model.

4.5   Limitation and Future Work

More verification experiments could be performed to reduce resource consumption: 1) Lower dimension input, such as multi-views or 2.5D images. 2) Lower precision representation, such as 8 bit-widths numerical precision. 3) Training-aware pruning and quantization methods may recover the performance.

5   Conclusion

The proposed method achieves the highly generation ability for large organs. The main challenge in this task lies in complex anatomical structures, the unclear boundary of soft tissues, high resolution of images, and extremely unbalanced sizes among large and small organs, etc. The proposed SSL method with low-resource consumption achieves the significant improvement compared to the full-supervised method.

Acknowledgements. We sincerely appreciate the organizers with the donation of FLARE2022 dataset. The authors of this paper declare that the segmentation method they implemented for participation in the FLARE 2022 challenge has not used any pre-trained models nor additional datasets other than those provided by the organizers. The proposed solution is fully automatic without any manual intervention.

References

1. Clark, K., et al.: The cancer imaging archive (TCIA): maintaining and operating a public information repository. J. Digit. Imaging **26**(6), 1045–1057 (2013)
2. Heller, N., et al.: The state of the art in kidney and kidney tumor segmentation in contrast-enhanced CT imaging: results of the kits19 challenge. Med. Image Anal. **67**, 101821 (2021)
3. Heller, N., et al.: An international challenge to use artificial intelligence to define the state-of-the-art in kidney and kidney tumor segmentation in CT imaging. Proc. Am. Soc. Clin. Oncol. **38**(6), 626–626 (2020)
4. Ma, J., et al.: Fast and low-GPU-memory abdomen CT organ segmentation: the flare challenge. Med. Image Anal. **82**, 102616 (2022). https://doi.org/10.1016/j.media.2022.102616
5. Ma, J., et al.: AbdomenCT-1K: is abdominal organ segmentation a solved problem? IEEE Trans. Pattern Anal. Mach. Intell. **44**(10), 6695–6714 (2022)
6. Simpson, A.L., et al.: A large annotated medical image dataset for the development and evaluation of segmentation algorithms. arXiv preprint arXiv:1902.09063 (2019)
7. Yang, L., Zhuo, W., Qi, L., Shi, Y., Gao, Y.: ST++: make self-training work better for semi-supervised semantic segmentation (2021)
8. Zhang, F., Wang, Y., Yang, H.: Efficient context-aware network for abdominal multi-organ segmentation (2021)

Unlabeled Abdominal Multi-organ Image Segmentation Based on Semi-supervised Adversarial Training Strategy

YuanKe Pan(ID), Jinxin Zhu(ID), and Bingding Huang$^{(\boxtimes)}$(ID)

College of Big Data and Internet, Shenzhen Technology University,
Shenzhen 518188, China
huangbingding@sztu.edu.cn

Abstract. The unlabeled images are helpful to generalize segmentation models. To make full use of the unlabeled images, we develop a generator-discriminator training pipeline based on the EfficientSegNet, which has achieved the best performance and efficiency in previous FLARE 2021 challenge. For the generator, a coarse-to-fine strategy is used to produce segmentations of abdominal organs. Then the labeled image and the ground truth are applied to optimize the generator. The discriminator receives the original unlabeled image or the relevant noised image, together with their generated segmentation results to determine which segmentation is better for the unlabeled image. After the adversarial training, the generator is used to segment the unlabeled images. On the FLARE 2022 final testing set of 200 cases, our method achieved an average dice similarity coefficient (DSC) of 0.8497 and a normalized surface dice (NSD) of 0.8915. In the inference stage, the average inference time is 11.67 s per case, and the average GPU (MB) and CPU (%) consumption per case are 311 and 225.6, respectively. The source code is freely available at https://github.com/Yuanke-Pan/Adversarial-Efficient SegNet.

Keywords: Unlabeled image segmentation · Semi-supervised learning · Adverarial training

1 Introduction

The lack of labeled images is a great burden in medical imaging tasks. In the past five years, there are many researches [1,10,12] show the potential of semi-supervised algorithms in medical applications. In this paper, we focus on building an abdominal multi-organ segmentation model with only 50 labeled and 2000 unlabeled abdominal CT scans. There are two main difficulties in this task: 1) how to use those 2000 unlabeled CT scans to obtain more generalized results. 2) how to keep GPU memory and computation cost at a low level.

Y. Pan and J. Zhu—These authors contributed equally to this work.

© The Author(s), under exclusive license to Springer Nature Switzerland AG 2022
J. Ma and B. Wang (Eds.): FLARE 2022, LNCS 13816, pp. 11–22, 2022.
https://doi.org/10.1007/978-3-031-23911-3_2

The EfficientSegNet [11] has shown excellent performance and efficiency in FLARE 2021 challenge [6]. The basic idea of our method is inheriting the network architecture of EfficientSegNet and applying semi-supervised learning algorithms to improve the generalizability of the inference model. In this work, we propose a novel adversarial strategy to use the unlabeled CT images which can improve the segmentation results. The main contributions of this work are:

1. We propose an adversarial semi-supervised learning pipeline for segmentation of medical images.
2. We design an image-label fusion discriminator to make full use of unlabeled images.

2 Method

2.1 Preprocessing

We use the same preprocessing strategy in both training and prediction. The details are described as follows:

– Reorienting the images to the left-posterior-inferior (LPI) view by flipping and reordering.
– Resampling the images to the fixed sizes. The sizes of coarse and fine input are [160, 160, 160] and [192, 192, 192], respectively.

For labeled images, we implement the following preprocessing steps:

– Reorienting the masks to the LPI view by flipping and reordering.
– Cropping the images according to the masks with a margin of [20, 20, 20].

2.2 Proposed Method

In this work, we combined efficient context-aware network as generator and image-label fusion discriminator to make cross learning between labeled CT images and unlabeled images. The whole workflow of our method is illustrated in Fig. 1.

The training phase of our proposed adversarial semi-supervise learning workflow consists of three steps in every iterations:

– In step 1, we use the generator to produce segmentation result of the original image. Then we train the discriminator with the original image, the generated segmentation and the ground truth. Here we assume that the ground truth is always the best segmentation of the original image.
– In step 2, we train the generator with original image and the ground truth as supervised learning.

– In step 3, we first add the Gaussian noise to the unlabeled image to get the relevant noised image. Then we input the unlabeled image and the noised image into the generator to produce segmentation-Unlabeled and segmentation-Noised, respectively. After that, we input the unlabeled image and the noised image separately with the two generated segmentation results (segmentation-Unlabeled and segmentation-Noised) into the discriminator to determine which segmentation is better. The better segmentation will be used as the pseudo label and will be used to train the generator.

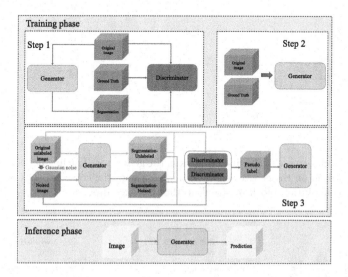

Fig. 1. The whole workflow of our proposed method. The first step is used to train the discriminator, the second step is used to train the generator, and the third step is used to process unlabeled data. Loop through three steps over multiple iterations.

It is important to emphasize that for the first 50 and the last 50 training iterations, we only use step 2 to fine-tune the network. After the training process, the final generator is used to segment the unlabeled images.

Generator. For the coarse-to-fine training strategy, there are two different networks to extract global and local information. The coarse model is a typical 5-layer U-net structure which is employed to locate target organs. The fine model is the EfficientSegNet shown in Fig. 2, which receives the coarse segmentation results from the coarse model for further refinement.

Discriminator. The input of the discriminator includes the original image and two segmentation results. For the labeled images, these two segmentation results are the generated segmentation and the ground truth. For the unlabeled images, these two segmentation results are derived from the unlabeled image and

14   Y. Pan et al.

the relevant noised unlabeled image. The discriminator is used to decide which segmentation is better for the original image.

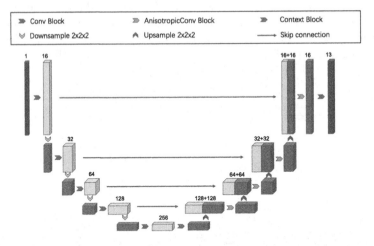

Fig. 2. The architecture of the fine network in the generator. The fine network performs fine segmentation on the coarse segmentation results of the corse network, and applies anisotropic convolution block to speed up the inference process.

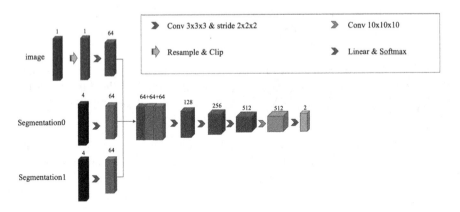

Fig. 3. The architecture of the discriminator network. Discriminator can be regarded as a condition-based binary classification model, which judges which segmentation is better according to the image.

As shown in Fig. 3, the image-label fusion discriminator fuses the original image with the two segmentation labels to output which label is better.

Optional Operation. In order to improve the discriminator's performance, we apply an augmentation to the ground truth called mask poisoning. This augmentation step adds a random noise to the ground truth, which can make the discriminator more concentrate on the data distribution.

Accelerate Strategy. The same as the EfficientSegNet, the anisotropic convolution, anisotropic pooling and coarse-to-fine strategy are used to reduce inference time and GPU memory usage.

2.3 Post-processing

In the last step of the coarse-to-fine model, we apply a connected components analysis [8] to get the final segmentation results.

3 Experiments

3.1 Dataset and Evaluation Metrics

The FLARE 2022 dataset is curated from more than 20 medical groups under the license permission, including MSD [9], KiTS [3,4], AbdomenCT-1K [7], and TCIA [2]. The training set includes 50 labeled CT scans with pancreas disease and 2000 unlabeled CT scans with liver, kidney, spleen, or pancreas diseases. The validation dataset includes 50 CT scans with liver, kidney, spleen, or pancreas diseases. The test dataset includes 200 CT scans where 100 cases with liver, kidney, spleen, or pancreas diseases and the other 100 cases with uterine corpus endometrial, urothelial bladder, stomach, sarcomas, or ovarian diseases. All the CT scans only have image information and the center information is not available.

The evaluation metrics are two accuracy measurements: Dice Similarity Coefficient (DSC) and Normalized Surface Dice (NSD), and three running efficiency measurements: running time, area under GPU memory-time curve, and area under CPU utilization-time curve. All measurements will be used to compute the ranking. Moreover, the GPU memory consumption has a tolerance of 2 GB.

3.2 Implementation Details

Environment Settings. The development environments and requirements are shown in Table 1.

Training Protocols. During the training process, we apply random shift and brightness to the whole dataset, and Gaussian noise to the unlabeled images. The details of the training protocols are shown in Table 2 and Table 3.

Table 1. Development environments and requirements.

Windows/Ubuntu version	Ubuntu 20.04.1 LTS
CPU	AMD EPYC 7742 64-Core Processor
RAM	16 × 4 GB
GPU	coarse: 2*NVIDIA A100 40G refine: 4*NVIDIA A100 40G
CUDA version	11.2
Programming language	Python 3.9
Deep learning framework	Pytorch (Torch 1.11, torchvision 0.12.0)

Table 2. Training protocols for the coarse model.

Network initialization	"he" normal initialization
Batch size	Labelled data: 4 UnLabelled data: 2
Patch size	160 × 160 × 160
Total epochs	300
Optimizer	Adam ($\mu = 0.99$)
Initial learning rate (lr)	0.001
Lr decay schedule	Halved by 200 epochs
Training time	6 h
Loss function	$\mathbf{L} = 1 - \frac{2*\sum p_{\text{true}}*p_{\text{pred}}}{\sum p_{\text{true}}^2 + \sum p_{\text{pred}}^2}$

Table 3. Training protocols for the fine model.

Network initialization	"he" normal initialization
Batch size	Labelled data: 8 UnLabelled data: 4
Patch size	192 × 192 × 192
Total epochs	500
Optimizer	Adam ($\mu = 0.99$)
Initial learning rate (lr)	0.001
lr decay schedule	Halved by 200 epochs
Training time	3.4 h
Loss function	$\mathbf{L} = 1 - \frac{2*\sum p_{\text{true}}*p_{\text{pred}}}{\sum p_{\text{true}}^2 + \sum p_{\text{pred}}^2}$

4 Results and Discussion

4.1 Qualitative Results on the Validation Dataset

We compare our proposed method with the baseline model on 20 cases of validation set. The qualitative results are shown in Table 4.

Table 4. Qualitative results of baseline and baseline+SS(semi-supervised) on 20 cases of validation set.

Organ	Baseline		Baseline+SS	
	DSC	NSD	DSC	NSD
Liver	0.936	0.915	0.961	0.955
RK	0.818	0.796	0.838	0.815
Spleen	0.920	0.899	0.941	0.932
Pancreas	0.762	0.848	0.816	0.892
Aorta	0.945	0.977	0.958	0.986
IVC	0.835	0.825	0.891	0.892
RAG	0.709	0.820	0.660	0.745
LAG	0.709	0.798	0.821	0.900
Gallbladder	0.676	0.658	0.753	0.751
Esophagus	0.798	0.884	0.806	0.877
Stomach	0.731	0.752	0.864	0.883
Duodenum	0.675	0.829	0.718	0.811
LK	0.889	0.879	0.893	0.893
Average	0.800	0.837	0.840	0.872

In the case of comparison with the ground truth, Fig. 4 and Fig. 5 show two examples with good segmentation results and two examples with poor segmentation results, respectively. Table 5 and Table 6 shows the corresponding DSC and NSD scores. For all 20 cases in the validation dataset, the average of DSC and NSD of our model are 0.840 and 0.872, respectively. At the same time, we observe that the segmentation results of our proposed model on Right Adrenal Gland (RAG) is the worst in all organs, with the average DSC and average NSD of 0.660 and 0.745, respectively. One reason may be that there are too many organs around it.

Meanwhile, we compare our proposed method with the baseline model on 50 cases of validation set based on DSC. The qualitative results are shown in Table 7.

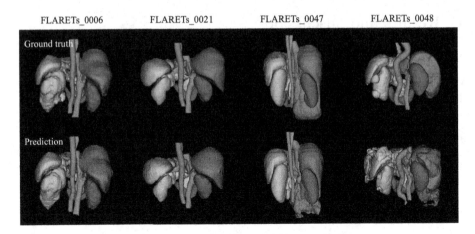

Fig. 4. Comparison of 3D segmentation in two good segmentation results (No. 6 and No. 21) and two poor segmentation results (No. 47 and No. 48).

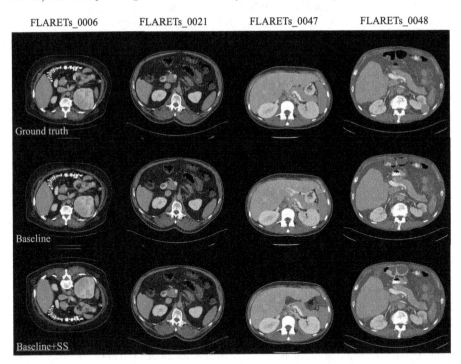

Fig. 5. Comparison of section segmentation of a layer in two good segmentation results (No. 6 and No. 21) and two poor segmentation results (No. 47 and No. 48).

Table 5. DSC of each organ in the two good segmentation results (No. 6 and No. 21) and two poor segmentation results (No. 47 and No. 48).

Organ	No. 6	No. 21	No. 47	No. 48
Liver	0.983	0.978	0.917	0.860
RK	0.979	0.978	0.984	0.738
Spleen	0.986	0.989	0.769	0.613
Pancreas	0.894	0.927	0.700	0.800
Aorta	0.976	0.972	0.938	0.828
IVC	0.970	0.951	0.734	0.523
RAG	0.898	0.807	0.000	0.788
LAG	0.926	0.888	0.860	0.921
Gallbladder	1.000	1.000	0.557	0.000
Esophagus	0.907	0.951	0.841	0.260
Stomach	0.938	0.977	0.734	0.297
Duodenum	0.826	0.939	0.000	0.708
LK	0.968	0.986	0.984	0.920
Average	0.942	0.949	0.694	0.635

Table 6. NSD of each organ in the two good segmentation results (No. 6 and No. 21) and two poor segmentation results (No. 47 and No. 48).

Organ	No. 6	No. 21	No. 47	No. 48
Liver	0.982	0.991	0.812	0.781
RK	0.988	0.986	0.998	0.658
Spleen	0.989	1.000	0.638	0.510
Pancreas	0.947	0.991	0.758	0.851
Aorta	0.998	0.999	0.988	0.850
IVC	0.996	0.962	0.688	0.581
RAG	0.968	0.918	0.000	0.888
LAG	0.989	0.972	0.944	0.984
Gallbladder	1.000	1.000	0.610	0.000
Esophagus	0.988	1.000	0.892	0.335
Stomach	0.948	0.999	0.772	0.373
Duodenum	0.871	0.999	0.001	0.836
LK	0.934	0.998	0.985	0.876
Average	0.969	0.986	0.699	0.656

Table 7. Qualitative DSC results of baseline and baseline+SS (semi-supervised) on 50 cases in the validation dataset.

Organ	Baseline+SS	Baseline
Liver	0.9555	0.9150
RK	0.9021	0.8586
Spleen	0.9341	0.8603
Pancreas	0.8069	0.7422
Aorta	0.9487	0.9180
IVC	0.8762	0.8065
RAG	0.6678	0.6842
LAG	0.7297	0.6511
Gallbladder	0.7644	0.6652
Esophagus	0.8018	0.7412
Stomach	0.8800	0.7279
Duodenum	0.7298	0.6588
LK	0.9066	0.8663
Average	0.8387	0.7766

4.2 Segmentation Efficiency Results on Validation Set

Our docker was validated with NVIDIA QUADRO RTX5000 (16G) and 32G RAM on 50-case validation set. The mean running time per case is 11.6 s, the mean maximum GPU memory is 2423MB, the mean area under GPU memory-time curve is 12287 and the mean area under CPU utilization-time curve is 224.

4.3 Results on Final Testing Set

On the final testing set of 200 cases with undisclosed ground truth, the average DSC and NSD of our method were 84.97 and 89.15, respectively. In terms of segmentation efficiency, the mean running time per case is 11.67 s, the mean area under GPU memory-time curve is 12155 and the mean area under CPU utilization-time curve is 226. The average DSC and NSD for these 13 organs are shown in Table 8.

4.4 Limitation and Future Work

In this work, we separate the training pipeline into three steps. In each step, the parameters of the discriminator and the generator are not updated at the same time, it might cost additional training time. An end-to-end semi-supervised learning algorithm will be our goal in the future. Due to the time limitations, we do not find a way to perform the proper analysis of the dataset. Considering the success of nn-UNet [5], we believe that a proper analysis might improve our final segmentation results.

Table 8. Average DSC and NSD of 13 organs on the final test set.

Organ	DSC	NSD
Liver	0.9650	0.9653
RK	0.9166	0.9075
Spleen	0.9307	0.9329
Pancreas	0.7721	0.8708
Aorta	0.9583	0.9796
IVC	0.8688	0.8727
RAG	0.7698	0.8804
LAG	0.7838	0.8794
Gallbladder	0.7705	0.7740
Esophagus	0.7590	0.8405
Stomach	0.8840	0.9040
Duodenum	0.7280	0.8474
LK	0.9396	0.9346
Average	0.8497	0.8915

5 Conclusion

In this paper, in order to use the large amount of unlabeled data, we develop an adversarial generator-discriminator training pipeline based on EfficientSegNet. For the generator, we employ the coarse-to-fine strategy to generate segmentation results. The labeled images and their ground truth are used to optimize the generator. For the discriminator, we first add noise to the original unlabeled images, then the discriminator receives the original unlabeled image or the relevant noised image together with their generated segmentation results. The better segmentation is determined by the discriminator as the pseudo label of the unlabeled image. On the FLARE 2022 validation dataset, our method achieved an average DSC of 0.840 and a NSD of 0.872 with an average process time of 11.6 s per case in the inference phase.

Acknowledgements. This work was supported by the Project of Educational Commission of Guangdong Province of China (No. 2022ZDJS113). The authors of this paper declare that the segmentation method implemented for participation in the FLARE 2022 challenge has not used any pre-trained models nor additional datasets other than those provided by the organizers. The proposed solution is fully automatic without any manual intervention.

References

1. Chen, X., Yuan, Y., Zeng, G., Wang, J.: Semi-supervised semantic segmentation with cross pseudo supervision. In: Proceedings of the IEEE/CVF Conference on Computer Vision and Pattern Recognition, pp. 2613–2622 (2021)

2. Clark, K., et al.: The cancer imaging archive (TCIA): maintaining and operating a public information repository. J. Digit. Imaging **26**(6), 1045–1057 (2013)

3. Heller, N., et al.: The state of the art in kidney and kidney tumor segmentation in contrast-enhanced CT imaging: results of the kits19 challenge. Med. Image Anal. **67**, 101821 (2021)

4. Heller, N., et al.: An international challenge to use artificial intelligence to define the state-of-the-art in kidney and kidney tumor segmentation in CT imaging. Proc. Am. Soc. Clin. Oncol. **38**(6), 626–626 (2020)

5. Isensee, F., et al.: nnU-Net: self-adapting framework for u-net-based medical image segmentation. arXiv preprint arXiv:1809.10486 (2018)

6. Ma, J., et al.: Fast and low-GPU-memory abdomen CT organ segmentation: the flare challenge. Med. Image Anal. **82**, 102616 (2022). https://doi.org/10.1016/j.media.2022.102616

7. Ma, J., et al.: AbdomenCT-1K: is abdominal organ segmentation a solved problem? IEEE Trans. Pattern Anal. Mach. Intell. **44**(10), 6695–6714 (2022)

8. Silversmith, W., cc3d: Connected components on multilabel 3D & 2D images. (3.2.1). Zenodo (2021). https://doi.org/10.5281/zenodo.571953

9. Simpson, A.L., et al.: A large annotated medical image dataset for the development and evaluation of segmentation algorithms. arXiv preprint arXiv:1902.09063 (2019)

10. Tarvainen, A., Valpola, H.: Mean teachers are better role models: weight-averaged consistency targets improve semi-supervised deep learning results. In: Advances in Neural Information Processing Systems, vol. 30 (2017)

11. Zhang, F., Wang, Y.: Efficient context-aware network for abdominal multi-organ segmentation. arXiv abs/2109.10601 (2021)

12. Zhang, Y., Yang, L., Chen, J., Fredericksen, M., Hughes, D.P., Chen, D.Z.: Deep adversarial networks for biomedical image segmentation utilizing unannotated images. In: Descoteaux, M., Maier-Hein, L., Franz, A., Jannin, P., Collins, D.L., Duchesne, S. (eds.) MICCAI 2017. LNCS, vol. 10435, pp. 408–416. Springer, Cham (2017). https://doi.org/10.1007/978-3-319-66179-7_47

Abdominal CT Organ Segmentation by Accelerated nnUNet with a Coarse to Fine Strategy

Shoujin Huang[1,2]⬤, Lifeng Mei[1], Jingyu Li[3], Ziran Chen[1], Yue Zhang[2],
Tan Zhang[4], Xin Nie[2], Kairen Deng[5], and Mengye Lyu[1(✉)]⬤

[1] College of Health Science and Environmental Engineering,
Shenzhen Technology University, Shenzhen, China
lvmengye@sztu.edu.cn
[2] Tencent Music Entertainment, Shenzhen, China
[3] College of Big Data and Internet, Shenzhen Technology University,
Shenzhen, China
[4] Sino-German College of Intelligent Manufacturing,
Shenzhen Technology University, Shenzhen, China
[5] First Clinical Medical College, Guangdong Medical University, Zhanjiang, China

Abstract. Abdominal CT organ segmentation is known to be challenging. The segmentation of multiple abdominal organs enables quantitative analysis of different organs, providing invaluable input for computeraided diagnosis (CAD) systems. Based on nnUNet, we develop an abdominal organ segmentation method applicable to both abdominal CT and whole-body CT data. The proposed new training pipeline combines the Kullback-Leibler semi-supervised learning and fully supervised learning, and employs a coarse to fine strategy and GPU accelerated interpolation. Our method achieves a mean Dice Similarity Coefficient (DSC) of 0.873/0.870 and a Normalized Surface Dice (NSD) of 0.911/0.915 on the FLARE 2022 validation/test dataset, with an average process time of 12.27 s per case. Overall, we ranked the fifth place in the FLARE 2022 Challenge. The code is available at https://github.com/Solor-pikachu/Infer-MedSeg-With-Low-Resource.

Keywords: FLARE 2022 · CT segmentation · Deep learning

1 Introduction

As a basic subject of medical image analysis, automatic and accurate abdominal organ segmentation from medical images is an essential step for computerassisted diagnosis, surgery navigation, visual augmentation, radiation therapy, and biomarker measurement systems [9]. In various recent competitions, nnUNet [4] have shown great performance consistently, but its memory consumption and GPU usage lead to huge demand of computing resources, which brings great difficulties on the industrial deployment of this method.

In this paper, we propose an improved training and inference scheme based on nnUNet, and a coarse to fine strategy is added to reduce the computing resources.

J. Ma and B. Wang (Eds.): FLARE 2022, LNCS 13816, pp. 23–34, 2022.
https://doi.org/10.1007/978-3-031-23911-3_3

The main contributions of this work are summarized as follows:

- A semi-supervised learning algorithm is used to train the model, and 2000 unlabeled CT samples are used to calculate pseudo-labels through the four decoders of the model. Pseudo-labels are used to calculate Kullback-Leibler (KL) divergence loss, and real labels are used to calculate cross entropy and dice loss.
- A coarse to fine strategy based on nnUNet is developed. Compared with the original nnUNet implementation, it achieved significant acceleration with almost no loss of accuracy.
- Unlike the common practice that resizes the CT data to a fixed size, a coarse model with a slide window approach [4] is used to roughly locate abdominal organs in whole-body CT, half-body CT, and abdominal CT, and a fine model is used to perform fine segmentation subsequently.
- The interpolation algorithm of nnUNet is optimized and highly accelerated. For interpolation of large samples of whole-body CT, the time is reduced from 90s to 1s, and the memory consumption is small.

2   Method

We propose a method as shown in Fig. 1. We use the coarse model by step=1, to obtain approximate segmentation results from the input CT scan, and then obtain the region of interest(ROI) coordinates of the abdomen from the coarse segmentation. Then we crop the area, and use the fine model for Step=0.5 inference, and finally restore the inference results to the original cropped area according to the ROI coordinates.

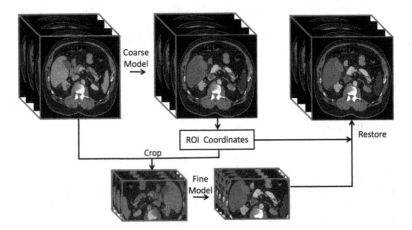

Fig. 1. Coarse-to-fine segmentation framework. Coarse and Fine are model inference processes. Crop means cutting the approximate position of the organ from the original image according to the result of coarse segmentation, and Restore means place the result back to the position before cropping.

2.1   Preprocessing

We regroup the 50 labeled samples and 2000 unlabeled samples to form two datasets. The first dataset containing all 2050 samples is used to train the model for coarse segmentation, and the second dataset containing only the 50 labeled samples is used to train the model for fine segmentation.

1. In the first dataset, we clip the foreground of the 2050 samples using threshold, and calculate their respective space, max intensity, and min intensity individually. All spaces are resampled to $[3.0, 2, 2]$, and the window width is adjusted to $[-325, 325]$. Last, the intensities of each CT sample are normalized to have a mean of 0 and a variance of 1 using the individual mean and standard deviation.
2. In the second dataset, we adjust the window width to $[-325, 325]$, and resample the spaces to $[2, 1.5, 1.5]$. The original CT data and label are cropped with a reserved 40 mm voxel position, and then the mean and standard deviation are calculated for the population of all samples, and the global mean and standard deviation are used to normalize the intensity of all CT data samples.

2.2   Network Architecture

We use a UNet [7] as our model as shown in Fig. 2. The model hyper-parameters and the input patch size of $[96, 128, 160]$ are chosen to satisfy the GPU memory requirement by the FLARE 2022 competition.

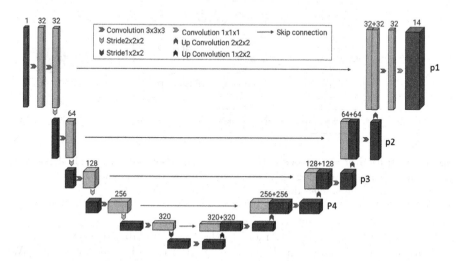

Fig. 2. Network architecture. A UNet is used and the outputs of four decoders (P1 to P4) are used to compute loss (see Sect. 2.3 for details).

2.3   Training

Coarse Model Training. During the training of the coarse model, we use a semi-supervised algorithm. This idea comes from Xiangde Luo et al. [5], who propose a new uncertainty correction module that enables the framework to gradually learn from meaningful and reliable consensus regions at different scales. For the 50 labeled data, we use cross entropy loss and dice loss to perform supervised learning on four outputs of the decoders (i.e., P1 to P4 shown in Fig. 2).

For the 2000 unlabeled data, we apply the following steps to calculate the loss as shown in Fig. 3:

1. we feed the patch into the model for inference and get four outputs (P1, P2, P3, and P4) from the UNet;
2. we add these four outputs and average them to get the pseudo-label P;
3. the four outputs P1, P2, P3, and P4 of the model are compared with the pseudo-label P to calculate the loss function.

We anticipate that the decoding heads of these four outputs can provide a relatively good pseudo-label by voting on the pseudo-mask. KL-divergence loss is used between the average prediction and the prediction at four scales as the uncertainty measurement.

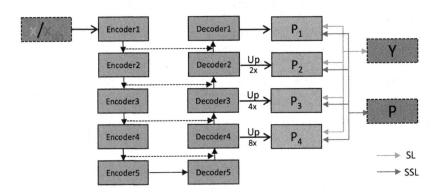

Fig. 3. Illustration of the proposed training strategy. Both semi-supervised learning (SSL) and supervised learning (SL) are used. Xun is the unlabeled data, P is the pseudo-label, X is the labeled data, and Y is the label of X.

We give the loss weight of sigmoid to the loss of unlabeled data, so that it can learn less pseudo-labels in the early stage and more in the later stage. We randomly select 40 samples as the training set and 10 samples as the validation set. Here we use Stochastic Gradient Descent (SGD) optimizer with momentum, and set the initial learning rate at 0.01 with poly learning rate decay. A total of 500 epochs of training is done.

Fine Model Training. To train the fine model, we initialize the model parameters with the pretrained coarse model. Compared with the randomly initialization, the coarse model has seen more data and improves the convergence speed. As above-mentioned, the cropped 50 gold-standard data are used to fine-tune the model. The optimizer and learning rate decay strategy are the same as in the coarse model training, but the initial learning rate is adjusted to 0.001. A total of 150 epochs of training are done, and in the last 10 epochs, all data augmentations are turned off.

2.4 Post-processing

Without post-processing, we found that the model may often mistake bladder and uterus as liver, kidney and stomach, and that the dice scores of the aorta and inferior vena cava were not high, yet the neural network can often predict the approximate correct location. Thus we perform the post-processing as follows: We find the largest connected area of the aorta and inferior vena cava, then calculate their centroids, and then find the center of these two centroids. We iterate all the connected regions, so to find the distance between the centroid and the center of each connected region. If the centroid is far away beyond a threshold, we delete the connected region. We preserve the largest connected area for all organs separately.

2.5 Acceleration on Resize and Argmax Operation

After the neural network finish inference, we need to interpolate the prediction results and restore the original size as input. We find that most of the CT scans are very large in the matrix size, and using the traditional CPU implementation, such as Skimage resize function, is slow, consuming CPU and memory resources. Thus, we change it to Torch's GPU interpolation function, using the trilinear interpolation method. Note that sending the CT array to the GPU at one time may exceed the maximum GPU memory. Therefore, we propose a slice interpolation procedure as shown in Fig. 4. When the output dimension of the sample is [14, z, x, y], it needs to be interpolated to [14, z*2, x*2, y*2], we divide the z-axis into N points, then each slice is [14, z/N, x, y], then we perform GPU-based interpolation on each slice, and finally merge the results of each slice on the Z axis. Similarly, when Argmax operates on the [14, z, x, y] array, we divide the z-axis into N parts again, and then perform the Argmax operation. According to our test, this slicing operation hardly affects the accuracy. Dramatically, the time here is reduced from 90 s to 1 s after switching to such GPU-based implementation.

3 Experiments

3.1 Dataset and Evaluation Measures

The FLARE 2022 dataset is curated from more than 20 medical groups under the license permission, including MSD [8], KiTS [2,3], AbdomenCT-1K [6], and

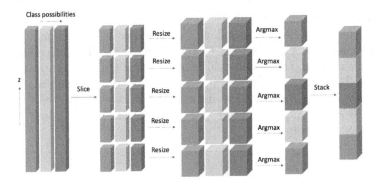

Fig. 4. Optimized resize and argmax operation based on slicing. The left represents the low-resolution output of the neural network's likelihood for each organ, and the right represents the segmentation result at the original resolution of the image.

TCIA [1]. The training set includes 50 labeled CT scans with pancreas disease and 2000 unlabelled CT scans with liver, kidney, spleen, or pancreas diseases. The validation set includes 50 CT scans with liver, kidney, spleen, or pancreas diseases. The testing set includes 200 CT scans where 100 cases has liver, kidney, spleen, or pancreas diseases and the other 100 cases has uterine corpus endometrial, urothelial bladder, stomach, sarcomas, or ovarian diseases. All the CT scans only have image information and the center information is not available.

3.2   Data Augmentation

During our training process, we introduce the following data augmentation. Gamma change, random Scale change between [0.6, 1.8], random enhancement of contrast, Gaussian blur, random rotation.

3.3   Implementation Details

Environment Settings. The development environments and requirements are presented in Table 1.

Training Protocols. The Training protocols and details (e.g., batchsize, epoch, optimizer) are presented in Table 2 and Table 3.

Table 1. Development environments and requirements.

Windows/Ubuntu version	Ubuntu 20.04.5 LTS
CPU	AMD EPYC 7H12 64-Core Processor
RAM	16 × 4 GB; 2.67MT/s
GPU (number and type)	One NVIDIA A100 40G
CUDA version	11.1
Programming language	Python 3.8
Deep learning framework	Pytorch (Torch 1.11.1)
Specific dependencies	
Link to code	github code

Table 2. Training protocols for the coarse model.

Network initialization	"he" normal initialization
Batch size	2
Patch size	96 × 128 × 160
Total epochs	500
Optimizer	SGD with nesterov momentum ($\mu = 0.99$)
Initial learning rate (lr)	0.01
Lr decay schedule	Halved by 200 epochs
Training time	8.5 h
Number of model parameters	30.79M
Number of flops	225.68G

Table 3. Training protocols for the refine model.

Network initialization	pre-train model
Batch size	2
Patch size	96 × 128 × 160
Total epochs	150
Optimizer	SGD with nesterov momentum ($\mu = 0.99$)
Initial learning rate (lr)	0.001
Lr decay schedule	Halved by 150 epochs
Training time	2.5 h
Number of model parameters	30.79M
Number of flops	225.68G

4   Results and Discussion

4.1   Quantitative Results on Validation Set

Overall, as shown in Table 4, our method achieves a mean Dice Similarity Coefficient (DSC) of 0.8725 and a Normalized Surface Dice (NSD) of 0.9109 on the FLARE 2022 validation dataset, with an average inference time of 15 s per case.

Table 4. DSC and NSC score in Validation dataset. Liv: liver, RKid: right kidney, Spl: spleen, Pan: pancreas, Aor: aorta, IVC: inferior vena cava, RAG: right adrenal gland, LAG: left adrenal gland, Gall: gallbladder, Eso: esophagus, Sto: stomach, Duo: Duodenum, LKid: left kidney.

Metric	Liv	RK	Spl	Pan	Aorta	IVC	RAG	LAG	Gall	Eso	Sto	Duo	LKid	Avg.
DSC	0.977	0.916	0.958	0.870	0.953	0.870	0.793	0.770	0.800	0.866	0.912	0.762	0.897	0.873
NSD	0.972	0.911	0.955	0.949	0.969	0.863	0.898	0.867	0.806	0.934	0.931	0.881	0.902	0.911

4.2   Quantitative Results on Final Test Set

As shown in Table 5, our method achieves a mean DSC of 0.870 and a NSD of 0.915 on the FLARE 2022 test dataset, with an average inference time of 12.27 s per case.

Table 5. DSC and NSC score in test dataset. Liv: liver, RKid: right kidney, Spl: spleen, Pan: pancreas, Aor: aorta, IVC: inferior vena cava, RAG: right adrenal gland, LAG: left adrenal gland, Gall: gallbladder, Eso: esophagus, Sto: stomach, Duo: Duodenum, LKid: left kidney.

Metric	Liv	RK	Spl	Pan	Aorta	IVC	RAG	LAG	Gall	Eso	Sto	Duo	LKid	Avg.
DSC	0.981	0.946	0.948	0.821	0.958	0.867	0.8340	0.823	0.7860	0.796	0.888	0.727	0.924	0.870
NSD	0.981	0.948	0.954	0.913	0.977	0.868	0.950	0.924	0.794	0.882	0.904	0.868	0.931	0.915

4.3   Qualitative Results on Validation

We analyze the samples with relatively good predictions and those with poor predictions. Figures 6 and 7 show the results. Samples No. 21 and 23 are good cases, it can be observed that the well-segmented cases have clear organ boundaries. Samples No. 42 and 48 are bad cases, they are often with heterogeneous lesions.

1. It can be seen from the 3D images in Fig. 5 that our neural network can extract masks for most normal organs, but it is difficult to identify the organs with the lesions. In the good cases, the neural network can predict most healthy organs very well, but in the bad cases, the organs with lesions such as kidney tumors are poorly predicted.
2. In Table 4, Table 6 and Tabel 7, our DSC scores are generally lower than the NSD scores on the validation set. Our algorithm misjudges very few regions when predicting, and has high confidence in the segmentation of each organ.

3. From the experimental results in Table 6 and Tabel 7, it can be seen that the duodenum, left and right adrenal glands, and inferior venacava have poor DSC scores in the bad cases, but the NSD scores are generally higher than DSC scores. We note that due to deformation and lesions of these organs, the CT HU values of these organs have changed greatly, to which our algorithm is not sensitive. The solution to this deserves further study in the future.

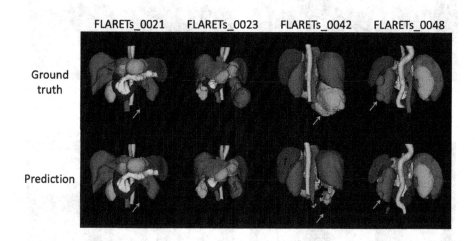

Fig. 5. Some representative segmentation results visualized by 3D Viewer

Table 6. NSD score of the samples shown in Figs. 6 and 7. Liv: liver, RKid: right kidney, Spl: spleen, Pan: pancreas, Aor: aorta, IVC: inferior vena cava, RAG: right adrenal gland, LAG: left adrenal gland, Gall: gallbladder, Eso: esophagus, Sto: stomach, Duo: Duodenum, LKid: left kidney.

Case	Liv	RK	Spl	Pan	Aorta	IVC	RAG	LAG	Gall	Eso	Sto	Duo	LKid	Avg.
FLARES21	0.994	0.998	1	0.999	1	0.959	0.988	0.995	1	0.999	0.999	0.997	0.998	0.994
FLARES23	0.994	0.906	1	0.998	1	0.895	0.937	0.965	0.896	0.991	0.974	0.915	0.611	0.930
FLARES42	0.968	0.062	0.869	0.881	0.951	0.926	0.738	0.743	0.974	0.999	0.916	0.606	0.956	0.815
FLARES48	0.9774	0.987	0.736	0.905	0.999	0.005	0.645	0.989	0	0.531	0.570	0.806	0.833	0.691

Table 7. DSC score of the samples shown in Figs. 6 and 7. Liv: liver, RKid: right kidney, Spl: spleen, Pan: pancreas, Aor: aorta, IVC: inferior vena cava, RAG: right adrenal gland, LAG: left adrenal gland, Gall: gallbladder, Eso: esophagus, Sto: stomach, Duo: Duodenum, LKid: left kidney.

Case	Liv	RK	Spl	Pan	Aorta	IVC	RAG	LAG	Gall	Eso	Sto	Duo	LKid	Avg.
FLARES21	0.990	0.985	0.991	0.931	0.982	0.951	0.911	0.900	1	0.947	0.970	0.931	0.985	0.959
FLARES23	0.986	0.919	0.992	0.925	0.983	0.919	0.849	0.871	0.932	0.932	0.968	0.812	0.547	0.895
FLARES42	0.975	0.121	0.910	0.795	0.932	0.933	0.570	0.644	0.938	0.899	0.925	0.432	0.967	0.772
FLARES48	0.980	0.980	0.817	0.841	0.973	0	0.589	0.910	0	0.480	0.524	0.546	0.897	0.657

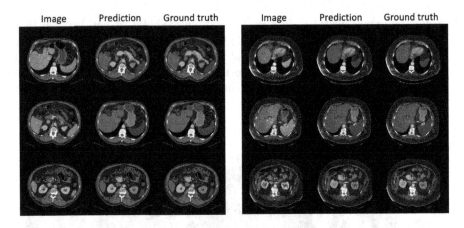

Fig. 6. Well segmented cases. Left is sample No. 21, and right is sample No. 23

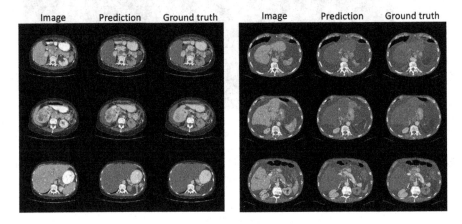

Fig. 7. Poorly segmented cases. Left is sample No. 42, and right is sample No. 48

4.4 Tricks for Improvement

As show in Tabel 8, our segmentation baseline is submitted based on plain nnUNet, and achieves DSC of 0.855 on the validation set. By adding unlabeled data, the DSC reaches 0.866. Further with the proposed coarse-to-fine segmentation, the DSC reaches 0.873 and NSD 0.915 on the validation set.

4.5 Two Normalization Strategies

In the first dataset (for coarse segmentation), we normalize the data using the individual normalization method. Because when locating the abdomen on CT scans, there will be full-body CT, half-body CT, and abdominal CT, leading to a big difference between samples. If global normalization is used, information may be erased from the CT intensities of some samples. So we use individual

Table 8. Effect of semi-supervised learning and coarse to fine strategy

Method	Val DSC
Baseline	0.855
Baseline+Unlabeled Data	0.866
Baseline+Unlabeled Data+Coarse to Fine	0.873

normalization to normalize the data to have a mean of 0 and a variance of 1. In the second dataset (for refining the segmentation), we use global normalization. Because in the first Coarse segmentation, we already obtained the approximate location of the abdomen, we crop the abdomen in the sample.

4.6 Effects of Sliding Windows

In the coarse segmentation, we use sliding windows instead of all voxels as input. In fact, we tested performing coarse segmentation without sliding windows in a way similar to the top 1 solution of FLARE 2021 [10], and found that the results of half-body CT and whole-body CT were very poor. Through visualization, we noticed that the coarse model didn't segment the approximate position of the abdomen well, due to the fact that whole-body CT and half-body CT are very scarce in the training data. So, it's difficult to improve the segmentation quality even using semi-supervised algorithms in whole-body CT and half-body CT. If the inference was performed in the coarse model without sliding windows, the model usually misidentified a large area as liver or kidney, and these samples were easily connected together, resulting in wrong abdomen locating, and the subsequent fine segmentation may be even worse. The method of using patch sliding window inference can reduce the occurrence of this problem.

5 Conclusion

In this paper, we propose an algorithm based on nnUNet to develop an abdominal organ segmentation method that can handle both abdominal CT and whole-body CT, through coarse-to-fine segmentation scheme, using semi-supervised algorithms. Quantitatively evaluated, the method achieves an average DSC of 0.873, and a NSD of 0.911 with an average process time of 15 s per case in the validation dataset. Also we achieve an average DSC of 0.870, and a NSD of 0.915 with an average process time of 12.27 s per case in the test dataset.

Acknowledgements. The authors of this paper declare that the segmentation method they implemented for participation in the FLARE 2022 challenge has not used any pre-trained models nor additional datasets other than those provided by the organizers. The proposed solution is fully automatic without any manual intervention. We thank to the timely help given by Bingding Huang in supporting GPU machine, Sixin Liu in supporting word spelling and grammar correction. This study is supported in part by Natural Science Foundation of Top Talent of Shenzhen Technology University (Grants No. 20200208 to Lyu, Mengye and No. GDRC202134 to Li, Jingyu), and the National Natural Science Foundation of China (Grant No. 62101348 to Lyu, Mengye).

References

1. Clark, K., et al.: The cancer imaging archive (TCIA): maintaining and operating a public information repository. J. Digit. Imaging **26**(6), 1045–1057 (2013)
2. Heller, N., et al.: The state of the art in kidney and kidney tumor segmentation in contrast-enhanced CT imaging: results of the KiTS19 challenge. Med. Image Anal. **67**, 101821 (2021)
3. Heller, N., et al.: An international challenge to use artificial intelligence to define the state-of-the-art in kidney and kidney tumor segmentation in CT imaging. Proc. Am. Soc. Clin. Oncol. **38**(6), 626–626 (2020)
4. Isensee, F., Jaeger, P.F., Kohl, S.A., Petersen, J., Maier-Hein, K.H.: nnU-Net: a self-configuring method for deep learning-based biomedical image segmentation. Nat. Methods **18**(2), 203–211 (2021)
5. Luo, X., et al.: Efficient semi-supervised gross target volume of nasopharyngeal carcinoma segmentation via uncertainty rectified pyramid consistency. In: de Bruijne, M., et al. (eds.) MICCAI 2021. LNCS, vol. 12902, pp. 318–329. Springer, Cham (2021). https://doi.org/10.1007/978-3-030-87196-3_30
6. Ma, J., et al.: AbdomenCT-1K: is abdominal organ segmentation a solved problem? IEEE Trans. Pattern Anal. Mach. Intell. **44**(10), 6695–6714 (2022)
7. Ronneberger, O., Fischer, P., Brox, T.: U-Net: convolutional networks for biomedical image segmentation. In: Navab, N., Hornegger, J., Wells, W.M., Frangi, A.F. (eds.) MICCAI 2015. LNCS, vol. 9351, pp. 234–241. Springer, Cham (2015). https://doi.org/10.1007/978-3-319-24574-4_28
8. Simpson, A.L., et al.: A large annotated medical image dataset for the development and evaluation of segmentation algorithms. arXiv preprint arXiv:1902.09063 (2019)
9. Van Ginneken, B., Schaefer-Prokop, C.M., Prokop, M.: Computer-aided diagnosis: how to move from the laboratory to the clinic. Radiology **261**(3), 719–732 (2011)
10. Zhang, F., Wang, Y., Yang, H.: Efficient context-aware network for abdominal multi-organ segmentation. arXiv preprint arXiv:2109.10601 (2021)

Semi-supervised Detection, Identification and Segmentation for Abdominal Organs

Mingze Sun, Yankai Jiang, and Heng Guo[✉]

Alibaba DAMO Academy, Beijing, China
gh205191@alibaba-inc.com

Abstract. Abdominal organ segmentation is an important prerequisite in many medical image analysis applications. Methods based on U-Net have demonstrated their scalability and achieved great success in different organ segmentation tasks. However, the limited number of data and labels hinders the training process of these methods. Moreover, traditional U-Net models based on convolutional neural networks suffer from limited receptive fields. Lacking the ability to model long-term dependencies from a global perspective, these methods are prone to produce false positive predictions. In this paper, we propose a new semi-supervised learning algorithm based on the vision transformer to overcome these challenges. The overall architecture of our method consists of three stages. In the first stage, we tackle the abdomen region location problem via a lightweight segmentation network. In the second stage, we adopt a vision transformer model equipped with a semi-supervised learning strategy to detect different abdominal organs. In the final stage, we attach multiple organ-specific segmentation networks to automatically segment organs from their bounding boxes. We evaluate our method on MICCAI FLARE 2022 challenge dataset. Experimental results demonstrate the effectiveness of our method. Our segmentation results currently achieve 0.897 mean DSC on the leaderboard of FLARE 2022 validation set.

Keywords: Semi-supervised · Organ detection · Organ segmentation

1 Introduction

Learning feature representations from a few labeled data is a fundamental problem in medical image analysis. It has attracted the interest of academia and industry because acquiring enough annotated medical images is tedious, time-consuming, and expensive. Compared to supervised methods, semi-supervised methods mainly focus on using labeled and large amounts of unlabeled data efficiently and properly [3,5,14]. Nowadays, semi-supervised methods are becoming the standard choice for data label shortage regimes.

Deep learning has been very popular in the field of medical image analysis. Modern deep learning-based strong baselines for medical image analysis are mostly trained on a large amount of manually labeled data and tailored for

J. Ma and B. Wang (Eds.): FLARE 2022, LNCS 13816, pp. 35–46, 2022.
https://doi.org/10.1007/978-3-031-23911-3_4

specific tasks. Abdominal organ segmentation is one of the most common tasks in this subject, which has many important clinical applications, such as organ quantification, surgical planning, and disease diagnosis. However, the shortage of labeled data hinders the development of deep learning models in this scenario since segmentation tasks often require enough dense annotations which come from domain experts' concentration and are hard to access. In addition, the diversity of data sources also challenges the robustness of existing state-of-the-art (SOTA) methods. As a potential alternative, semi-supervised learning can explore useful information from unlabeled cases. Therefore, exploiting unlabeled medical data in a semi-supervised learning scheme has become extremely important to improve the performance of medical image segmentation models and has attracted increasing research attention.

In this paper, we propose a new semi-supervised learning algorithm based on the vision transformer to overcome the aforementioned challenges. The architecture of our method consists of three stages. In the first stage, we build a lightweight segmentation network to locate the abdomen region. Then, in the second stage, we adopt a vision transformer model equipped with a semi-supervised learning strategy to detect different abdominal organs. In the third stage, we attach multiple organ-specific segmentation networks to automatically segment organs from their bounding boxes. We evaluate our method on MICCAI FLARE 2022 challenge dataset. Experimental results demonstrate the effectiveness of each network component in our method. The contributions of our method are threefold: (1) We propose a semi-supervised learning scheme that adopts multiple models' consistent predictions to produce high-quality pseudo labels to train the student network. (2) We propose a vision transformer-based detection model to detect different organs which has large variations in shape and texture. (3) Combining a semi-supervised training strategy and a vision transformer architecture with several segmentation heads, we build a strong segmentation inference framework which currently achieves 0.897 mean DSC on the leaderboard of FLARE 2022 validation set.

2   Method

In order to leverage the unlabeled data, we first train a teacher model using labeled data and then predict segmentation results for unlabeled data with the trained teacher model. Considering that many new network structures may not have good generalization ability in the unseen dataset, we choose a strong and general baseline, nnU-Net [7], as the standard choice for the teacher model. In previous deep learning works, network structure and parameters often need to be adjusted according to practical application [8,10]. It relies on users' experience and usually needs many experiments. If the whole training process can be properly designed, U-Net can achieve good results in most cases [12]. So it seems that the most straightforward way to build a student model is initializing another nn-UNet model with different initial parameters. However, training nnU-Net cost a lot of time, and its inference efficiency may not meet practical demands, we do not use it as our final choice. Despite this, from the well-trained nnU-Net model, we can get strong pseudo labels of the unlabeled data. We use these pseudo labels and unlabeled data as a new training set to modulate a new student model built with the vision transformer. In this section, we first introduce nnU-Net briefly and then bring out our new student model.

2.1   nnU-Net

Isensee et al. proposed nnU-Net [7], which can adapt to many datasets in a supervised training process. nnU-Net adjusts the network structure according to the characteristics of the training set. It can process images with various shapes and textures, so as to achieve SOTA results in multiple medical segmentation tasks [1]. Specifically, for different datasets, nnU-net defines adaptive adjustment strategies from four perspectives, including preprocessing, training procedure, inference, and postprocessing.

Network Structure. nnU-Net consists of 2D U-Net, 3D U-Net, and U-Net Cascade. In these architectures, ReLU is replaced with Leaky ReLU and batch normalization is replaced with instance normalization. While the network structure remains almost the same as the default U-Net and it did not adopt additional modules such as attention mechanisms.

3D U-Net is usually used for training on 3D medical images, including CT and MRI. However, it occupies a large amount of GPU memory. In order to improve training speed and reduce resource consumption, the patch-based 3D U-Net can be adopted to reduce the cost of network computing. 3D U-Net is mainly to solve the problem of the poor effect of 2D U-Net in anisotropic data. On the other hand, the patch-based 3D U-Net may have a poor effect on large image sizes due to a limited global view. 3D U-Net Cascade is used to solve this problem.

The network topologies adjust adaptively according to the image size. It considers the image geometry and balances the GPU memory occupation which corresponds to the adjustment of the network capacity and batch size. The initial network configuration is as follows:

2D U-Net: An input patch size is set to 256×256, a batch size of 42, and the number of feature maps of the highest layer is set to 30 (the number of feature maps will be doubled with each downsampling). The network parameters are automatically adjusted to the median plane size of each dataset so that the network can effectively train the whole slice.

3D U-Net: An input patch size is set to $128 \times 128 \times 128$, a batch size of 2, and the number of feature maps at the highest level is 30. Due to the GPU memory limitation, the resolution of the image size beyond 128^3 voxels is not increased but matches the median voxel size of the input image. If the median shape of the dataset is smaller than 128^3, we use the median shape as the input image size and add batch size.

U-Net Cascade: The first level 3D U-Net is firstly trained on the down-sampled image and then the results are up-sampled to the original resolution. These results are fed into the second level 3D U-Net.

Preprocessing. Image preprocessing is a very important part of training. For nnU-Net teacher models, this process is divided into three steps: (1) Cropping: Crop all data to the non-zero area. (2) Resampling: In order to enable the network to learn spatial semantics, images are resampled to the median voxel spacing of the dataset, and third order spline interpolation and nearest neighbor interpolation methods are used for data and segmentation mask respectively. (3) Normalization: For CT images, pixel values within the segmentation mask are collected, and all data is truncated to [0.5, 99.5] percentiles of these pixel values, followed by a z-score normalization. If the average size is decreased by more than 1/4, normalization is only applied to non-zero elements of the mask, and values outside the mask are set to 0.

2.2 Semi-supervised Cascaded Organ Detection, Identification and Segmentation

The overall architecture of our inference pipeline, i.e., the student part in the whole semi-supervised framework, is shown in Fig. 1. It consists of three stages. First, we adopt a lightweight U-Net to obtain the abdomen region-of-interest (RoI). Then we locate each organ with a new detection network built upon a vision transformer. Finally, we segment organs according to the detection bounding boxes. In the following context, we first describe the pseudo label preparation process, then we will introduce our inference architecture stage-by-stage according to Fig. 1.

Pseudo Label Preparation. The quality of pseudo labels is the key to determining whether the use of unlabeled data in semi-supervised training is effective. Poor quality pseudo labels may mislead the student model to learn wrong semantic information. In order to acquire high-quality pseudo labels, we adopt a consistency voting strategy that measures the consistency between pseudo labels generated by different teachers for the same case. The insight in our strategy is straightforward. For example, simple cases should be easy for most teacher models whereas hard cases may cause most models to fail. If a case causes different models to produce very inconsistent prediction outputs, we think that the distribution of this example is likely to be outside the distribution of most examples. We, therefore, reject examples with inconsistent pseudo labels, as they are likely to mislead the student network.

We choose nnU-Net as the teacher model. In order to enhance consistency between different teacher models, We build multiple different nnU-Net models with different initialization parameters. The same architecture of these teacher models ensures better consistency. Then we train these teacher models using 50 labeled data, and the models obtained are not used for the final testing stage, but only for generating pseudo labels. The mean DSC of the results on the validation set exceeds 0.89. We believe that the nnU-Net models have been able to generate pseudo labels of good quality. We take 2000 unlabeled data as input and use trained nnU-Net models to generate corresponding pseudo labels. Finally, we measure the consistency between these pseudo labels and screen high-quality pseudo labels. After a segmentation results ensemble, we obtain our framework's final pseudo labels as input labels.

Abdomen RoI Extraction. Given labels and pseudo labels, we train a simplified U-Net model to identify organ regions, then the proper RoI can be inferred by calculating the weighted average coordinates and distribution scope of the predicted organ voxels. This step helps us filter irrelevant background regions.

Organ Detection and Identification. We propose a new detection framework based on DETR [2] to detect each organ. DETR handles object detection as a direct set prediction problem through the conjunction of the bipartite matching loss and transformer with parallel decoding of queries. In abdomen CTs, the number and relative position of organs are stable. We intend to estimate a bounding box for each organ to obtain an accurate and compact RoI. To this end, we estimate bounding boxes, based on the comprehensively annotated instance-level organ segmentation mask (ground-truth label and pseudo label), as supervision signal. For queries matched to the background class, only classification loss is accounted for.

Organ Segmentation. To get high accuracy instance segmentation results, we adopt multiple stand-alone U-Net [12] models to segment each organ independently with a finer spatial resolution but in a locally cropped patch based on the detected bounding boxes from the second stage. The segmentation heads perform a binary segmentation for all 3D patches. After this, all predicted binary masks are merged back with their corresponding labels and spatial locations to form the final instance segmentation results of organs.

Preprocessing. Before training the student model, we conduct preprocessing similar to the preprocessing used for the teacher model (nnU-Net). We perform cropping, resampling and normalization.

Training Procedure. The model is trained from scratch and evaluated by five-fold cross-validation on the training set. The total loss for segmentation is Dice loss [4] combined with cross-entropy.

$$\mathscr{L}_{total} = \mathscr{L}_{dice} + \mathscr{L}_{CE} \tag{1}$$

For the teacher model, Adam is selected as the optimizer in the training process, with an initial learning rate of 3×10^{-4} and 250 batches of each epoch.

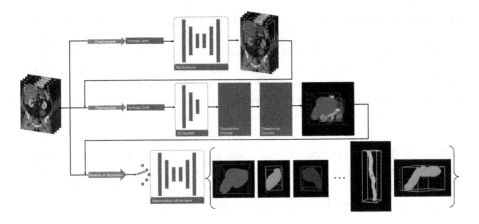

Fig. 1. Schematic of our inference architecture.

A Learning rate adjustment strategy is used which calculates the exponential moving average loss of the training set and validation set. If the training set loss decreases less than 5×10^{-3} within 30 epochs, then the learning rate decreases by 5 times. When the learning rate is larger than 10^{-6} and the exponential moving average loss of the validation set decreases less than 5×10^{-3} within 60 epochs, the training is terminated. Random rotations, Random scaling, Random elastic deformations, Gamma correction augmentation, and Mirroring are adopted as data augmentation. If the maximum side length of the image patch size of 3D U-Net is more than twice the minimum side length, then 2D data augmentation methods are used. For the student model, readers are referred to Table 2 for stage-specific training details.

Inference. All inferences are performed by the student model. In our implementation, we dynamically clear the memory footprint to release the redundant memory occupancy in time and reduce resource consumption. The inference speed of our method is very fast thanks to the cascaded detection-then-segmentation strategy which significantly reduces the computation cost of redundancy regions.

Postprocessing. For the teacher model, we adopt commonly used postprocessing methods such as removing small connected components. It is generally considered that a certain class is within a simply connected domain, which means that there is only one such domain within a case. So only the largest connected domain is retained, and the other small connected domains are removed. For the student model, we omit the postprocessing step for the sake of inference efficiency.

3   Experiments

3.1   Dataset and Evaluation Measures

The FLARE 2022 dataset is curated from more than 20 medical groups under the license permission, including KiTS [6] and AbdomenCT-1K [9]. The training set includes 50 labeled CT scans with pancreas disease and 2000 unlabeled CT scans with liver, kidney, spleen, or pancreas diseases. The validation set includes 50 CT scans with liver, kidney, spleen, or pancreas diseases. The testing set includes 200 CT scans where 100 cases have liver, kidney, spleen, or pancreas diseases and the other 100 cases have uterine corpus endometrial, urothelial bladder, stomach, sarcomas, or ovarian diseases. All the CT scans only have image information and the center information is not available.

The evaluation measures consist of two accuracy measures: Dice Similarity Coefficient (DSC) and Normalized Surface Dice (NSD), and three running efficiency measures: running time, area under GPU memory-time curve, and area under CPU utilization-time curve. All measures will be used to compute the ranking. Moreover, the GPU memory consumption has a 2 GB tolerance.

3.2   Implementation Details

Environment Settings. We develop our cascaded model based on PyTorch [11]. All models are trained from scratch. We train the segmentation networks with a combination of dice and cross-entropy loss. We use the AdamW optimizer in the detection part and the Adam optimizer in the RoI extractor and segmentation part. An initial learning rate of 1×10^{-4} is used in RoI extractor, 4×10^{-4} and 1×10^{-3} are used respectively in detection and segmentation. Training batches are set as 8, 8, and 4 respectively. The development environments and requirements are presented in Table 1.

Table 1. Development environments and requirements.

Windows/Linux version	AliOS 7
CPU	Intel(R) Xeon(R) Platinum 8163 CPU @ 2.50 GHz
RAM	724 GB
GPU (number and type)	Eight Tesla V100 32G
CUDA version	11.4
Programming language	Python 3.7.3
Deep learning framework	PyTorch (torch 1.7.0, torchvision 0.8.1)

Training Protocols. All images are automatically normalized based on statistics of the entire respective dataset. During training, in order to help networks properly learn spatial semantics, all patients are resampled to the median voxel spacing of their respective dataset, where third-order spline interpolation is used for image data and nearest-neighbor interpolation for the corresponding segmentation mask. The detailed training protocols are shown in Table 2.

Table 2. Training protocols. "roi" means the RoI extraction in stage 1. "det" means the organ detection network in stage 2. "seg" means the segmentation head in stage 3.

Network initialization	Kaiming normal initialization
Batch size	roi: 8 | det: 8 | seg: 4
Patch size	seg only: organ-specific patch size
Total epochs	roi: 1000 | det: 1000 | seg: 500
Optimizer	roi: Adam | det: AdamW | seg: Adam
Initial learning rate (lr)	roi: 0.0001 | det: 0.0004 | seg: 0.001
Lr decay schedule	warmup 200 epochs and ×0.1 at 800th epoch
Training time	roi: 52h | det: 20h | seg: organ-specific
Number of model parameters	roi: 4.8M | det: 9.6M | seg: 4.8M
Loss function	seg: Dice loss and cross entropy

4 Results and Discussion

4.1 Quantitative Results on Validation Set

We compare our method with two state-of-the-art segmentation models including CNN-based methods and vision transformer-based methods. As shown in Table 3, our results currently obtain 0.897 mean DSC on the leaderboard of FLARE 2022 validation set. Compared with nnU-Net and Swin-UNETR [13], which are also trained from scratch, our method exceeds these two methods in terms of DSC on most abdominal organs. Moreover, our model is even better than the Swin-UNETR model with pre-training on FLARE unlabeled part. This emphasizes the significance of our semi-supervised method. Last but not least, our method even outperforms the ensembled nnU-Net, which ensemble the segmentation results of 12 different initialized nnU-Net models, and has much less training and inference time than the nnU-Net with the ensemble. The segmentation results of these methods are shown in Fig. 2. Our method can obtain better segmentation results than all the other methods. For hidden testing set, our method obtains 0.889 mean DSC and 0.933 mean NSD as shown in Table 4.

4.2 DSC Comparisons Between with and Without Unlabeled Images

Due to the long training and inference time of nnU-Net, we only use it to generate pseudo labels of 2000 unlabeled images. Then we use these unlabeled images and their pseudo labels to train our model. In order to validate the effectiveness of the unlabeled images and the pseudo labels, we conduct an ablation study on

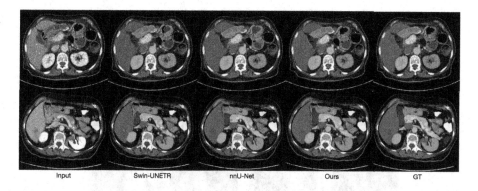

Fig. 2. Comparison between segmentation results of different methods.

Table 3. DSC values on different organs. Abbreviations: "Liv."-Liver, "RK"-Right Kidney, "Spl."-Spleen, "Pan."-Pancreas, "Aor."-Aorta, "IVC"-Inferior Vena Cava, "RAG"-Right Adrenal Gland, "LAG"-Left Adrenal Gland, "Gall."-Gallbladder, "Eso."-Esophagus, "Sto."-Stomach, "Duo."-Duodenum, "LK"-Left Kidney.

Methods	Liv.	RK	Spl.	Pan.	Aor.	IVC	RAG	LAG	Gall.	Eso.	Sto.	Duo.	LK	mDSC
Swin-UNETR	0.965	0.912	0.942	0.846	0.930	0.865	0.758	0.742	0.771	0.790	0.886	0.765	0.887	0.850
Swin-UNETR pre.	0.964	0.921	0.952	0.881	0.937	0.862	0.794	0.791	0.792	0.818	0.895	0.790	0.879	0.867
nnU-Net	0.977	0.941	0.958	0.872	0.968	0.878	0.830	0.801	0.765	0.892	0.899	0.771	0.911	0.882
nnU-Net ens.	0.979	**0.948**	0.960	0.886	**0.969**	0.897	**0.838**	**0.819**	0.787	**0.901**	0.907	**0.792**	0.920	0.892
Ours	**0.980**	0.945	**0.972**	**0.890**	0.966	**0.903**	0.824	0.806	**0.861**	0.874	**0.915**	0.787	**0.937**	**0.897**

our organ detection module, which is relatively more sensitive to the amount of data due to its task attribute and transformer component. As shown in Table 5, the effect of using unlabeled cases is significant. If we remove the training of unlabeled images with pseudo labels, we observe a significant performance drop in our final results. Since there are few labeled images, the distribution of labeled images is very different from the real data distribution. So if we do not use the unlabeled images, the model will have no chance to learn unseen cases in the target data distribution. This adds huge difficulties to regress 3D boxes and segment accurate boundaries for organs, especially for relatively small organs such as gallbladder and adrenal glands.

4.3 Visualized Examples of Successful and Failed Cases

Figure 3 shows the segmentation results of our method. It clearly reveals that our method can obtain excellent segmentation results on most organs. However, we find that sometimes the model failed especially when some organs have larger size and shape variations due to the appearance of tumors. For example, the trained models can't generalize well when the patient has a kidney tumor, which makes the size of the kidney much larger than usual. One possible solution is adding more supervised cases which have a similar distribution to those hard cases.

Table 4. Final results on the hidden test set.

Methods	DSC(%)	NSD(%)	Time(s)	GPU(MB)	CPU(%)
Ours	0.889	0.933	27.32	6028	533.1

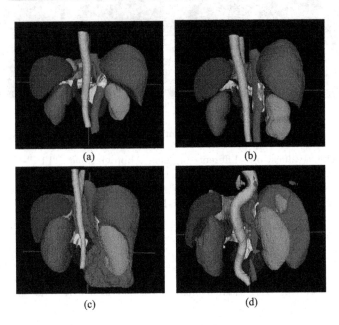

(a) (b)

(c) (d)

Fig. 3. (a) to (b): Plots of good results visualization and (c) to (d): Plots of bad results visualization.

4.4 Segmentation Efficiency Analysis

We perform segmentation efficiency analysis on validation set, the results are shown in Table 6. Our method is significantly faster than other methods in terms of inference time. To be noted, our inference time measurement does not include Docker launching stage and model initialization, because there may exist large variance among different configurations. Besides, we start the Docker only once at the start of the evaluation, and get the average inference time of all evaluation cases. Therefore, the measurement of our method in Table 6 is smaller than that in Table 4.

4.5 Limitations and Future Work

The proposed method works well on most cases. However, there are still some misclassification failures on some organs. Perhaps adding organ shape-related prior knowledge will help solve the limitations, which is left for future work.

Table 5. DSC comparisons between with and without using unlabeled images. *wo.* means without using unlabeled images and *w.* means using unlabeled images.

Methods	Liv.	RK	Spl.	Pan.	Aor.	IVC	RAG	LAG	Gall.	Eso.	Sto.	Duo.	LK	mDSC
Ours *wo.*	0.975	0.885	0.879	0.876	0.952	0.898	0.809	0.753	0.594	0.855	0.862	0.770	0.881	0.845
Ours *w.*	0.980	0.945	0.972	0.890	0.966	0.903	0.824	0.806	0.861	0.874	0.915	0.787	0.937	0.897

Table 6. Efficiency analysis of different methods.

Methods	Inference time (s)	GPU memory footprint (MB)
Swin-UNETR	18.00	22284
nnU-Net	126.40	4639
Ours	3.10	3208

5 Conclusion

In this paper, we propose a novel three-stage instance segmentation network for the abdominal organ segmentation task. We develop and test the whole framework on the FLARE 2022 challenge dataset. The network consists of a vision transformer-based detection model and several lightweight segmentation heads. We adopt a semi-supervised learning strategy to leverage a large amount of unlabeled data. We use nnU-Net as the teacher model and design a consistency measuring strategy to generate high-quality pseudo labels. The whole framework of our method acquires 0.897 mean DSC on the FLARE 2022 challenge validation dataset.

Acknowledgements. The authors of this paper declare that the segmentation method they implemented for participation in the FLARE 2022 challenge has not used any pre-trained models nor additional datasets other than those provided by the organizers. The proposed solution is fully automatic without any manual intervention.

References

1. Antonelli, M., et al.: The medical segmentation decathlon. arXiv abs/2106.05735 (2021)
2. Carion, N., Massa, F., Synnaeve, G., Usunier, N., Kirillov, A., Zagoruyko, S.: End-to-end object detection with transformers. In: Vedaldi, A., Bischof, H., Brox, T., Frahm, J.-M. (eds.) ECCV 2020. LNCS, vol. 12346, pp. 213–229. Springer, Cham (2020). https://doi.org/10.1007/978-3-030-58452-8_13
3. Chen, X., Yuan, Y., Zeng, G., Wang, J.: Semi-supervised semantic segmentation with cross pseudo supervision. In: Proceedings of the IEEE/CVF Conference on Computer Vision and Pattern Recognition, pp. 2613–2622 (2021)
4. Drozdzal, M., Vorontsov, E., Chartrand, G., Kadoury, S., Pal, C.: The importance of skip connections in biomedical image segmentation. In: Carneiro, G., et al. (eds.) LABELS/DLMIA -2016. LNCS, vol. 10008, pp. 179–187. Springer, Cham (2016). https://doi.org/10.1007/978-3-319-46976-8_19

5. French, G., Laine, S., Aila, T., Mackiewicz, M., Finlayson, G.: Semi-supervised semantic segmentation needs strong, varied perturbations. arXiv preprint arXiv:1906.01916 (2019)
6. Heller, N., et al.: An international challenge to use artificial intelligence to define the state-of-the-art in kidney and kidney tumor segmentation in ct imaging. Proc. Am. Soc. Clin. Oncol. **38**(6), 626–626 (2020)
7. Isensee, F., et al.: nnU-Net: a self-configuring method for deep learning-based biomedical image segmentation. Nat. Methods **18**, 203–211 (2021)
8. Li, X., Chen, H., Qi, X., Dou, Q., Fu, C.W., Heng, P.A.: H-DenseUNet: hybrid densely connected UNet for liver and tumor segmentation from CT volumes. IEEE Trans. Med. Imaging **37**(12), 2663–2674 (2018)
9. Ma, J., et al.: AbdomenCT-1K: is abdominal organ segmentation a solved problem. IEEE Trans. Pattern Anal. Mach. Intell. **44**(10), 6695–6714 (2022)
10. Oktay, O., et al.: Attention U-Net: learning where to look for the pancreas. arXiv preprint arXiv:1804.03999 (2018)
11. Paszke, A., et al.: Pytorch: an imperative style, high-performance deep learning library, vol. 32 (2019)
12. Ronneberger, O., Fischer, P., Brox, T.: U-Net: convolutional networks for biomedical image segmentation. In: Navab, N., Hornegger, J., Wells, W.M., Frangi, A.F. (eds.) MICCAI 2015. LNCS, vol. 9351, pp. 234–241. Springer, Cham (2015). https://doi.org/10.1007/978-3-319-24574-4_28
13. Tang, Y., et al.: Self-supervised pre-training of swin transformers for 3D medical image analysis. In: Proceedings of the IEEE/CVF Conference on Computer Vision and Pattern Recognition, pp. 20730–20740 (2022)
14. Wua, Y., et al.: Mutual consistency learning for semi-supervised medical image segmentation. arXiv preprint arXiv:2109.09960 (2021)

An Efficiency Coarse-to-Fine Segmentation Framework for Abdominal Organs Segmentation

Cancan Chen, Weixin Xu, and Rongguo Zhang[(⊠)]

Infervision Advanced Research Institute, Beijing, China
{ccancan,xweixin,zrongguo}@infervision.com

Abstract. U-Net has been proved as the most successful segmentation architecture for medical image processing in recent years. Based on this, ResUNet imported ResBlock with skip connection focuses more on the contextual information. In this work, we adopt the 3D ResUNet to build a whole-volume-based coarse-to-fine segmentation framework for the abdominal multi-organs segmentation task, and the mean Dice Similarity Coefficient (DSC) of the segmentation results has achieved 87.67%, the mean Normalized Surface Dice (NSD) has achieved 93.16% on the FLARE2022 validation set. Besides, for each case on the FLARE2022 validation set, the average running time is 19.5614 s, and the max gpu memory consumption is 2657 MB.

Keywords: Abdominal organs · Segmentation · FLARE

1 Introduction

Abdominal organ segmentation plays an important role in clinical practice. In recent years, with the development of deep learning, many methods have been proposed to accomplish the segmentation task automatically. In this paper, we focus on multi-organ segmentation from abdominal CT scans. According to the Fast and Low GPU Memory Abdominal Organ Segmentation challenge which required develop segmentation methods that can segment 13 kinds of abdominal organs like the liver, kidney, spleen, pancreas, aorta, IVC, adrenal glands, gallbladder, esophagus, stomach and duodenum simultaneously, we attempted to design our method based on the original ResUNet [5].

In this paper, based on the original ResUNet, we propose a whole-volume-based coarse-to-fine framework. In the first stage, i.e., coarse segmentation, we directly use whole volume CT images and resample it to $128 \times 128 \times 128$ as the input. In the fine stage, 13 organs are split into 2 groups: big organs and small organs. For the big organs, we crop the areas containing the organs based on the coarse segmentation results, and resample the cropped volumes to $160 \times 160 \times 160$ as fine stage input. For the other group, volumes are cropped to $64 \times 256 \times 256$ or $128 \times 128 \times 128$. Specifically, LAG, RAG, Gallbladder and Esophagus are regarded as small organs. Backbones for both stages are 3D ResUNet with 4 down-sample

J. Ma and B. Wang (Eds.): FLARE 2022, LNCS 13816, pp. 47–55, 2022.
https://doi.org/10.1007/978-3-031-23911-3_5

layers encoder and 4 up-sample layers decoders. Notably, the ASPP [1] module maybe be used to supply the info-loss caused by the multi down-sample on top level.

The main contributions of this work are summarized as follows:

- We propose a whole-volume-based coarse-to-fine framework, which can effectively complete abdominal organs segmentation.
- Based on our proposed framework, we fully utilize the relative position information between big organs by group neighbour organs, which can better locate and segment these organs, especially for stomach, pancreas, duodenum and oesophagus.
- We evaluate our proposed framework on FLARE2022 challenge dataset. The effectiveness and efficiency can be well demonstrated.

2   Method

Our proposed method is a whole-volume-based coarse-to-fine framework. Details about the method are described as follows.

2.1   Preprocessing

Our proposed method includes the following preprocessing steps:

- Reorientation image to target direction.
- Cropping strategy: None
- Resampling method for anisotropic data:
  Constrained by hardware conditions, the original images are resampled to $128 \times 128 \times 128$ for both coarse segmentation and small organs' fine segmentation task. For the fine segmentation of big organs, images are resampled to $160 \times 160 \times 160$.
- Intensity normalization method:
  Considering that volumes from different centers have different HU values, and this phenomenon appears on the different organs. Therefore, images are clipped to range $[-100, 300]$ and normalized to range $[0, 1]$.
- Others:
  To improve the training and testing efficiency, mixed precision is adopted in the whole process of our framework working.

2.2   Proposed Method

The process of our framework is shown in Fig. 1. In our proposed framework, coarse segmentation always leads to the error location of small organs, so the 3D ResUNet is cascaded to realize the relocation of small organs. And 8 large organs are divided into 3 groups since that more relative position information can be captured. Figure 2 illustrates the applied 3D ResUNet [5], where a U-Shape architecture is adopted.

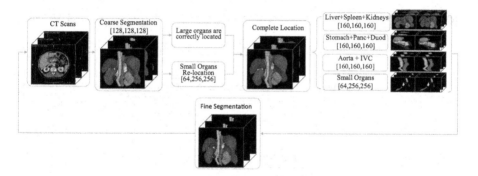

Fig. 1. Process of our proposed framework.

Network architecture details: our proposed method is a whole-volume-based coarse-to-fine segmentation framework. For both coarse and fine segmentation stages, the network consists of 4 down-sample layers, 4 up-sample layers for the final segmentation results, and ASPP module.

Loss function: we use the summation between Dice loss and Cross-Entropy loss because compound loss functions have been proved to be robust in various medical image segmentation tasks [9].

2.3 Post-processing

To avoid the impact of noise, the connected component analysis [13] is used, and we choose the maximum connected component as the final segmentation results.

3 Experiments

3.1 Dataset and Evaluation Measures

The FLARE2022 dataset is curated from more than 20 medical groups under the license permission, including MSD [12], KiTS [6,7], AbdomenCT-1K [10], and TCIA [4]. The training set includes 50 labelled CT scans with pancreas disease and 2000 unlabelled CT scans with liver, kidney, spleen, or pancreas diseases. The validation set includes 50 CT scans with liver, kidney, spleen, or pancreas diseases. The testing set includes 200 CT scans where 100 cases has liver, kidney, spleen, or pancreas diseases and the other 100 cases has uterine corpus endometrial, urothelial bladder, stomach, sarcomas, or ovarian diseases. All the CT scans only have image information and the center information is not available.

The evaluation measures consist of two accuracy measures: Dice Similarity Coefficient (DSC) and Normalized Surface Dice (NSD), and three running efficiency measures: running time, area under GPU memory-time curve, and area

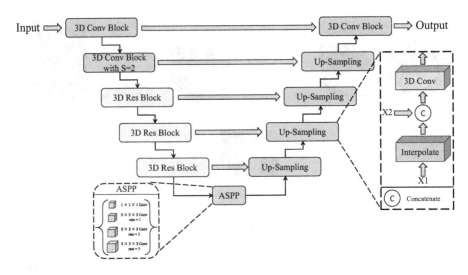

Fig. 2. Our proposed network architecture. For the Res Block layer, the stride of the final $1 \times 1 \times 1$ conv is set as 2, that's how we downsample the volumes.

under CPU utilization-time curve. All measures will be used to compute the ranking. Moreover, the GPU memory consumption has a 2 GB tolerance.

3.2 Implementation Details

Environment Settings. The development environments and requirements are presented in Table 1.

Table 1. Development environments and requirements.

Windows/Ubuntu version	Ubuntu 18.04.06 LTS
CPU	Intel(R) Xeon(R) Silver 4210R CPU @ 2.40 GHz
RAM	4×32 GB; 3200MT/s
GPU (number and type)	Four NVIDIA RTX A6000 48G
CUDA version	11.4
Programming language	Python 3.7
Deep learning framework	Pytorch (Torch 1.7.1+cu110, torchvision 0.8.2)
Specific dependencies	
(Optional) Link to code	

Training Protocols. In our training process, we performed the following data augmentation with project MONAI [11]: 1). randomly crop the volumes from range -0.5 to 0.5; 2). add brightness and contrast on the volumes from range

−0.4 to 0.4. 3). random elastic transform with prob = 0.5 with sigma from range 3 to 5 and magnitude from range 100 to 200; 4). clip volumes from range 0 to 1. Details of our training protocols are shown in Table 2 and Table 3.

Different organs combination will bring different localization information, which is helpful for fine segmentation. Therefore, we divided the large organs into three groups: (liver, spleen, left and right kidneys); (stomach, pancreas and duodenum); (aorta and IVC). The other four small organs (LAG, RAG, gallbladder, esophagus) are localized by the 3D ResUNet firstly and then refined by another 3D ResUNet respectively.

Table 2. Training protocols.

Network initialization	"he" normal initialization
Batch size	8
Patch size	$128 \times 128 \times 128$
Total epochs	100
Optimizer	ADAMW [8] ($weightdecay = 1e - 4$)
Initial learning rate (lr)	1e-4
Lr decay schedule	halved by 20 epochs
Training time	18 h
Loss function	Summation of cross entropy and dice loss
Number of model parameters	15.17M
Number of flops	93.43G

Table 3. Training protocols for the refine model.

Network initialization	"he" normal initialization
Batch size	8
Patch size	$160 \times 160 \times 160$
Total epochs	120
Optimizer	ADAMW [8] ($weightdecay = 1e - 4$)
Initial learning rate (lr)	1e-4
Lr decay schedule	halved by 20 epochs
Training time	18 h
Loss function	Summation of cross entropy and dice loss
Number of model parameters	15.17M
Number of flops	182.49G

4   Results and Discussion

4.1   Quantitative Results on Validation Set

As shown in Table 4, our proposed method has achieved mean DSC as 0.8767 and mean NSD as 0.9316 on validation set. The segmentation performance is quite well, especially for the organs with big-size, such as liver, spleen, aorta and kidneys.

With Unlabelled Data. In the process of our experiments, we tried to training our model by self-supervised learning with those unlabelled 2000 cases. In summary, we have tried classical methods like MOCOV2 [2], SimSam [3], etc. We also tried to random crop from the original volumes and segment the unlabelled cases by our trained coarse segmentation network and then masked RAG by the segmentation results, then using pix2pix GAN to restore the original volumes, the generator of the pix2pix GAN is utilized as pretrained model. However, all these methods have little effect, and have consumed us much time to attempt these methods. The best mean DSC value on validation set derived from our method, masked RAG and then utilized generator of the pix2pix GAN as pretrained model, with unlabelled data is 0.8416. Moreover, we have tried to combined predicted pseudo label from unlabeled 2000 images with the labeled 50 images, results show that pseudo labels are helpful.

Table 4. Results of our proposed method on validation set.

Organ	DSC	NSD
Liver	0.9695 ± 0.0211	0.9832 ± 0.0350
RK	0.9203 ± 0.1899	0.9448 ± 0.1956
Spleen	0.9420 ± 0.0197	0.9807 ± 0.0421
Pancreas	0.8711 ± 0.0459	0.9643 ± 0.0442
Aorta	0.9426 ± 0.0248	0.9813 ± 0.0312
IVC	0.9049 ± 0.0825	0.9272 ± 0.0885
RAG	0.7703 ± 0.2240	0.8807 ± 0.2313
LAG	0.8009 ± 0.2352	0.8948 ± 0.2315
Gallbladder	0.8070 ± 0.2417	0.7943 ± 0.2475
Esophagus	0.8482 ± 0.1205	0.9315 ± 0.1207
Stomach	0.9122 ± 0.1430	0.9553 ± 0.1245
Duodenum	0.8102 ± 0.1023	0.9424 ± 0.0611
LK	0.8977 ± 0.1746	0.9302 ± 0.1799
Average	0.8767 ± 0.1250	0.9316 ± 0.1256

4.2   Qualitative Results on Validation Set

Figure 3 shows some failed and successful examples on validation set. It can be found that our proposed method cannot segment gallbladder well on case #2 since that size of gallbladder on this case is too small. Besides, for case #3, because that the stomach is squeezed and displaced, in this caes, stomach was mistakenly segmented as esophagus. Moreover, in case #31, some lesions like tumors in liver may look like gallbladder, this also will influence gallbladder segmentation performance. In case #6, 8 and 35, no lesion in volumes look like neighbour organs, sizes of organs are normal, therefore organs in abdominal can achieve satisfactory segmentation performance.

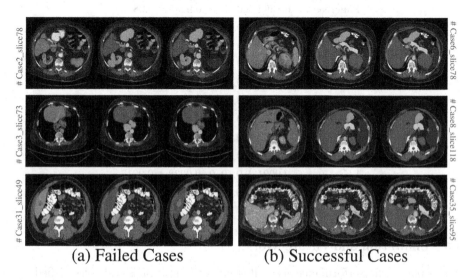

(a) Failed Cases   (b) Successful Cases

Fig. 3. Some failed and successful examples. Columns from left to right are original volumes, ground truth and our predicted results, respectively.

4.3   Segmentation Efficiency Results on Validation Set

Our segmentation efficiency results on the validation set is shown in Table 5. The average running time of each case in validation set is 19.5614 s, the max gpu memory consumption is 2657 MB. The total AUC of GPU time and CPU time are 1,597,650 and 18,215.44, respectively.

4.4   Results on Final Testing Set

Our test phase results are shown in Table 6, the average DSC and NSD value of 13 organs is 0.8774 and 0.9358, respectively.

Table 5. Segmentation efficiency results of our proposed method on validation set.

Average running time	Max Gpu memory	AUC of GPU time	AUC of CPU time
19.5614 s	2657 MB	1,597,650	18,215.44

Table 6. Results of our proposed method on test set.

Organ	DSC	NSD
Liver	0.9722 ± 0.0105	0.9893 ± 0.0181
RK	0.8979 ± 0.2279	0.9240 ± 0.2359
Spleen	0.9175 ± 0.1520	0.9587 ± 0.1616
Pancreas	0.8394 ± 0.0866	0.9485 ± 0.0886
Aorta	0.9218 ± 0.0638	0.9621 ± 0.0632
IVC	0.9099 ± 0.0777	0.9400 ± 0.0919
RAG	0.8471 ± 0.1237	0.9488 ± 0.1324
LAG	0.8484 ± 0.1604	0.9429 ± 0.1646
Gallbladder	0.8034 ± 0.2629	0.7977 ± 0.2683
Esophagus	0.8292 ± 0.1157	0.9277 ± 0.1132
Stomach	0.9175 ± 0.0983	0.9553 ± 0.0964
Duodenum	0.8020 ± 0.1063	0.9376 ± 0.0955
LK	0.9001 ± 0.1950	0.9338 ± 0.2017
Average	0.8774 ± 0.1292	0.9358 ± 0.1331

4.5   Limitation and Future Work

In this paper, the performance of small organ segmentation is still not satisfied. In the future, we will focus on the segmentation of those organs, such as gallbladder and adrenal gland. Moreover, self-supervised learning with unlabelled data will also be considered as our future work, and the careful adjustment will further improve the segmentation performance.

5   Conclusion

The proposed method can work well on abdominal organs, especially for the organs with big-size, such as liver, spleen and kidneys. Disappointing performance is obtained for AGs and gallbladder because the blurred edges and small-size.

Acknowledgements. The authors of this paper declare that the segmentation method they implemented for participation in the FLARE 2022 challenge has not used any pre-trained models nor additional datasets other than those provided by the organizers. The proposed solution is fully automatic without any manual intervention.

References

1. Chen, L.C., Zhu, Y., Papandreou, G., Schroff, F., Adam, H.: Encoder-decoder with atrous separable convolution for semantic image segmentation. In: Proceedings of the European Conference on Computer Vision (ECCV), pp. 801–818 (2018)
2. Chen, X., Fan, H., Girshick, R., He, K.: Improved baselines with momentum contrastive learning. arXiv preprint arXiv:2003.04297 (2020)
3. Chen, X., He, K.: Exploring simple siamese representation learning. In: Proceedings of the IEEE/CVF Conference on Computer Vision and Pattern Recognition, pp. 15750–15758 (2021)
4. Clark, K., et al.: The cancer imaging archive (TCIA): maintaining and operating a public information repository. J. Digit. Imaging **26**(6), 1045–1057 (2013)
5. Diakogiannis, F.I., Waldner, F., Caccetta, P., Wu, C.: ResUNet-a: a deep learning framework for semantic segmentation of remotely sensed data. ISPRS J. Photogramm. Remote. Sens. **162**, 94–114 (2020)
6. Heller, N., et al.: The state of the art in kidney and kidney tumor segmentation in contrast-enhanced CT imaging: results of the KiTS19 challenge. Med. Image Anal. **67**, 101821 (2021)
7. Heller, N., et al.: An international challenge to use artificial intelligence to define the state-of-the-art in kidney and kidney tumor segmentation in CT imaging. Proc. Am. Soc. Clin. Oncol. **38**(6), 626–626 (2020)
8. Loshchilov, I., Hutter, F.: Decoupled weight decay regularization. arXiv preprint arXiv:1711.05101 (2017)
9. Ma, J., et al.: Loss odyssey in medical image segmentation. Med. Image Anal. **71**, 102035 (2021)
10. Ma, J., et al.: AbdomenCT-1K: is abdominal organ segmentation a solved problem. IEEE Trans. Pattern Anal. Mach. Intell. (2021)
11. Nic, M., Wenqi, L., Richard, B., Yiheng, W., Behrooz, H.: MONAI, [Version 0.8.1]. https://github.com/Project-MONAI/MONAI
12. Simpson, A.L., et al.: A large annotated medical image dataset for the development and evaluation of segmentation algorithms. arXiv preprint arXiv:1902.09063 (2019)
13. William, S., Nico, K., Odidev: CC3D, [Version 3.10.1]. https://github.com/seung-lab/connected-components-3d

Semi-supervised Augmented 3D-CNN for FLARE22 Challenge

Zining Chen[✉], Tianyi Wang, Shihao Han, Yinan Song, and Shichao Li

Beijing University of Posts and Telecommunications, Beijing, China
chenzn@bupt.edu.cn

Abstract. Abdominal organ segmentation has been used in many important clinical applications, however, cases with accurate labels require huge manual labour and financial resources. As a potential alternative, semi-supervised learning can explore useful information from unlabeled cases, with only few labeled cases involved. Therefore, we propose our baseline model using augmented 3D-UNet and adopt semi-supervised method–Mean Teacher, to make quantitative evaluation on the FLARE2022 validation cases. Our method achieves average dice similarity coefficient (DSC) of 62.16%, Normalized Surface Distance (NSD) of 62.27%, running time of 9.58 s, and AUC of GPU and CPU is only 7424 and 199 respectively, which surpasses almost all other teams on resource consumption, demonstrating the effectiveness of our methods.

Keywords: Abdominal organ segmentation · Semi-supervised learning

1 Introduction

Computed Tomography (CT) has long been regarded as an effective therapeutic method in clinical workflow and is capable of improving patient treatment by visualization of abnormal organs. With the rapid development of deep learning, semantic segmentation in medical image plays an important role in clinical practice and is used in radiotherapy to accurately delineate tumors and treat certain cancers [9].

However, huge amount of labeled medical image are required for fully-supervised segmentors, which is not only laborious and time-consuming, but also cost-intensive and conse-quently. Thus, semi-supervised learning is proposed to explore useful information from unlabeled cases, which is a combination of supervised learning and unsupervised learning. The basic process uses the existing labeled cases to pseudolabel the remaining unlabeled data, so as to effectively help increase the information in training data, which can strengthen the consistency of the prediction of unlabeled data and labeled data through the regularization in loss function. For semantic segmentation, convolutional neural

---

Z. Chen and T. Wang—Equal contribution

J. Ma and B. Wang (Eds.): FLARE 2022, LNCS 13816, pp. 56–63, 2022.
https://doi.org/10.1007/978-3-031-23911-3_6

network(CNN) has achieved a dominant position in the field of medical image segmentation, especially Unet and its various modified versions by adjusting the network structure, e.t.c. adding various attention mechanisms and feature fusion structures, aiming to fit a more powerful model on the limited data.

However, the performance of semi-supervised learning methods in medical image segmentation is still limited, most of which are only able to process 2D images while FLARE2022 challenges focus on 3D volumes in clinical practice. Difficulties mainly stem from four aspects: 1) Variations in field-of-views, shape and size of different organs. 2) Difficulty in using unlabeled data. 3) Diversity of data source in term of multi-center, multi-phase and multi-vendor cases. 4) Limited GPU memory size and high computation.

In this stage, we develop a semi-supervised baseline composed of backbone network 3D-UNet [2] and semi-supervised method Mean Teacher [11] to effectively and efficiently tackle FLARE2022 challenges. The model aims to obtain the rough location of target organs from the whole CT volume. In this way, the background can be preferentially screened, which is more conducive to the identification of target organs. To overcome Temporal Ensembling, a common semi-supervised potential problem, we use Mean Teacher method which effectively update teacher model weights instead of hard label predictions.

2 Method

This whole-volume-based semi-supervised segmentation framework is composed of backbones network 3D-UNet and semi-supervised method Mean Teacher. A detail description of the method is as follows.

2.1 Preprocessing

The baseline method includes the following preprocessing steps:

- Delete abnormal data.
- Reorientation image to target direction.
- Resample image to fixed size: [160, 160, 160].
- Intensity normalization: Apply a z-score normalization based on the mean and standard deviation of the intensity values.
- Clip image in range of [−600, 600].
- Convert mask labels into one-hot coding formation.

2.2 Proposed Method

As mentioned in Fig. 1 and Fig. 2, our framework uses Mean Teacher method on semi-supervised learning, and apply a two-stage coarse-and-fine segmentation method based on 3D-UNet to extract abdominal features. A detail description of our method is as follows.

First, based on the winning solution in FLARE 2021, we accordingly adopt the applied 3D-UNet, as illustrated in Fig. 1. The proposed backbone can learn

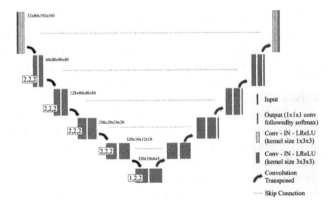

Fig. 1. 3D U-Net [2]

from sparse annotations and provides a dense 3D segmentation mask corresponding to the 3D image, showing great robustness on various abdominal organ segmentation tasks.

Second, method used on semi-supervised learning is Mean Teacher, illustrated in Fig. 2, which is composed of a student and teacher network. Input a batch of labeled and unlabeled cases with random noise to student network, and calculate the supervised loss on labeled cases to update student network, after which the teacher network weights are updated as an exponential moving average of the student network weights. Also, input batch to teacher and student network to calculate the comparative loss on unlabeled cases, then two losses are summed as the final loss for gradient descent to update student network.

Third, to improve inference speed and reduce resource consumption, we recommend using ONNX or TensorRT to speed up the inference process.

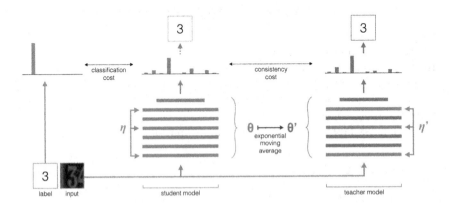

Fig. 2. Mean teacher method

2.3   Post-processing

We tend to use a connected component analysis of segmentation mask applied on model output in next stage.

3   Experiments

3.1   Dataset and Evaluation Measures

The FLARE2022 dataset is curated from more than 20 medical groups under the license permission, including MSD [9], KiTS [4,5], AbdomenCT-1K [8], and TCIA [3]. The training set includes 50 labelled CT scans with pancreas disease and 2000 unlabelled CT scans with liver, kidney, spleen, or pancreas diseases. The validation set includes 50 CT scans with liver, kidney, spleen, or pancreas diseases. The testing set includes 200 CT scans where 100 cases has liver, kidney, spleen, or pancreas diseases and the other 100 cases has uterine corpus endometrial, urothelial bladder, stomach, sarcomas, or ovarian diseases. All the CT scans only have image information and the center information is not available.

The evaluation measures consist of two accuracy measures: Dice Similarity Coefficient (DSC) and Normalized Surface Dice (NSD), and three running efficiency measures: running time, area under GPU memory-time curve, and area under CPU utilization-time curve. All measures will be used to compute the ranking. Moreover, the GPU memory consumption has a 2 GB tolerance.

3.2   Implementation Details

Environment Settings. The environments and requirements are presented in Table 1.

Table 1. Environments and requirements.

Windows/Ubuntu version	Ubuntu 18.04.5 LTS
CPU	Intel(R) Xeon(R) Gold 5218R CPU@2.10 GHz
RAM	32×4 GB; 3200MT/s
GPU (number and type)	Two Nvidia Tesla T4 16G
CUDA version	10.2
Programming language	Python 3.7
Deep learning framework	Pytorch (Torch 1.8.0, torchvision 0.9.0)

Training Protocols. Training protocols are listed in Table 2. First, due to limited GPU resources and speed requirements, we set patch size as [160, 160, 160]. Furthermore, imbalance on field-of-views, shape and size of different organs further render difficulty on hard samples. Therefore, we design DiceLoss-based MultiDiceLoss, utilizing segmentation mask distribution to calculate weights on different organs. Also, two sets of indices are designed to be iterated in single iteration, during which we sample from both the primary indices and secondary indices, and labeled cases are iterated as many times as needed. Finally, we use loss value and visulization on training and validation set to select optimal model hyperparameters. Visulization is shown in Fig. 3 and 4.

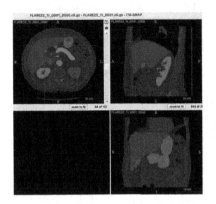
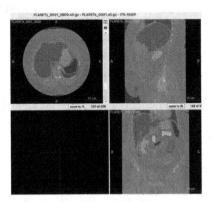

Fig. 3. Test on train set   Fig. 4. Test on validation set

Table 2. Training protocols.

Network initialization	"he" normal initialization
Batch size	4
Patch size	$160 \times 160 \times 160$
Loss	MultiDiceLoss and FocalLoss [7]
Total iterations	8000
Optimizer	AdamW with weight decay =1e-4 and $\beta = 0.9$
Initial learning rate (lr)	0.002
Training time	15.5 h
Number of model parameters	1.50M[a]
Number of flops	73.09G[b]

[a] https://github.com/sksq96/pytorch-summary
[b] https://github.com/facebookresearch/fvcore

4   Results and Discussion

Unlabeled cases enrich image information and effectively reduce overfitting. Ablation study is used to verify the necessity of unlabeled cases. According to visualization in Fig. 3, if labeled images are only input to the whole network, loss decreases fast but prones to overfitting. The use of unlabeled cases can effectively tackle the overfitting problem with more feature information, meanwhile pseudolabel can be obtained through training.

To solve the above problems, method used on semi-supervised learning–Mean Teacher works well. It is composed of a student and teacher network. The whole process includes, input a batch of labeled and unlabeled cases with random noise to student network, and calculate the supervised loss on labeled cases to update student network, after which the teacher network weights are updated as an exponential moving average of the student network weights. Then, input batch to teacher and student network to calculate the comparative loss on unlabeled cases, and two losses are summed as the final loss for gradient descent to update student network.

Our mean DSC scores is relatively low, especially on abnormal cases and lesion-affected organs, e.t.c. RAG, LAG, Gallbladder. Reasons can be categorized into insufficient training, ordinary one-stage coarse framework, few processing strategies. Therefore, in next stage, we will make improvements on accurate extraction of image features by designing two-stage coarse-and-fine framework. Also, we will use other semi-supervised methods, e.t.c pseudolabel on unlabeled cases [1], data augmentation method [10]. Last but not least, we will try different training strategies and preprocessing/postprocessing methods.

4.1   Quantitative Results on Validation Set

Table 3 illustrates the results on validation set. Only using labeled data results in quick overfitting. With the design of Mean Teacher method, our model can effectively alleviate this problem.

4.2   Segmentation Efficiency Results

The running time is 9.58 s and maximum used GPU memory is 2011 MB. To accelerate inference process, we tend to use ONNX or TensorRT. To further decrease the use of GPU memory, we attempt to design lighter network architecture and other data processing methods. Finally, our method achieves average dice similarity coefficient (DSC) of 62.16%, Normalized Surface Distance (NSD) of 62.27%, running time of 9.58 s, and AUC of GPU and CPU is only 7424 and 199 respectively.

Table 3. Quantitative results.

Mean DSC	0.60
Liver	0.84
RK	0.72
Spleen	0.74
Pancreas	0.48
Aorta	0.81
IVC	0.69
RAG	0.44
LAG	0.40
Gallbladder	0.22
Esophagus	0.60
Stomach	0.69
Duodenum	0.44
LK	0.75

5   Conclusion

Our method performs high generalization and robustness on most organs, such as liver, kidney and spleen in terms of DSC scores. Also, our AUC of GPU and CPU is only 7424 and 199 respectively, which surpasses almost all other teams on resource consumption, demonstrating the effectiveness of our methods. However, RAG, LAG and Gallbladder performs relatively bad as a result of the inter-patient and anatomical variability of volume and shape. Meanwhile, lesion-affected organ is also a critical reason for the poor segmentation performance. Therefore, we consider investigations on fine-stage segmentation network, e.t.c nn-UNet [6], preprocessing methods on certain organs, and postprocessing strategies for future work, to obtain a more accurate boundary segmentation to increase DSC scores.

Acknowledgements. The authors of this paper declare that the segmentation method they implemented for participation in the FLARE 2022 challenge has not used any pre-trained models nor additional datasets other than those provided by the organizers.

References

1. Chen, X., Yuan, Y., Zeng, G., Wang, J.: Semi-supervised semantic segmentation with cross pseudo supervision. In: Proceedings of the IEEE/CVF Conference on Computer Vision and Pattern Recognition, pp. 2613–2622 (2021)

2. Çiçek, Ö., Abdulkadir, A., Lienkamp, S.S., Brox, T., Ronneberger, O.: 3D U-Net: learning dense volumetric segmentation from sparse annotation. In: Ourselin, S., Joskowicz, L., Sabuncu, M.R., Unal, G., Wells, W. (eds.) MICCAI 2016. LNCS, vol. 9901, pp. 424–432. Springer, Cham (2016). https://doi.org/10.1007/978-3-319-46723-8_49

3. Clark, K., et al.: The cancer imaging archive (TCIA): maintaining and operating a public information repository. J. Digit. Imaging **26**(6), 1045–1057 (2013)

4. Heller, N., et al.: The state of the art in kidney and kidney tumor segmentation in contrast-enhanced CT imaging: results of the KiTS19 challenge. Med. Image Anal. **67**, 101821 (2021)

5. Heller, N., et al.: An international challenge to use artificial intelligence to define the state-of-the-art in kidney and kidney tumor segmentation in CT imaging. Proc. Am. Soc. Clin. Oncol. **38**(6), 626 (2020)

6. Isensee, F., Jaeger, P.F., Kohl, S.A., Petersen, J., Maier-Hein, K.H.: nnU-Net: a self-configuring method for deep learning-based biomedical image segmentation. Nat. Methods **18**(2), 203–211 (2021)

7. Lin, T.Y., Goyal, P., Girshick, R.: Focal loss for dense object detection. In: Proceedings of the IEEE International Conference on Computer Vision, pp. 2980–2988 (2017)

8. Ma, J., et al.: AbdomenCT-1K: is abdominal organ segmentation a solved problem? IEEE Trans. Pattern Anal. Mach. Intell. **44**(10), 6695–6714 (2022)

9. Simpson, A.L., et al.: A large annotated medical image dataset for the development and evaluation of segmentation algorithms. arXiv preprint arXiv:1902.09063 (2019)

10. Souly, N., Spampinato, C., Shah, M.: Semi supervised semantic segmentation using generative adversarial network. In: 2017 IEEE International Conference on Computer Vision (ICCV) (2017)

11. Tarvainen, A., Valpola, H.: Mean teachers are better role models: weight-averaged consistency targets improve semi-supervised deep learning results. In: Advances in Neural Information Processing Systems (2017)

DLUNet: Semi-supervised Learning Based Dual-Light UNet for Multi-organ Segmentation

Haoran Lai[✉], Tao Wang, and Shuoling Zhou

Guangdong Provincial Key Laboratory of Medical Image Processing,
Southern Medical University, Guangzhou 510515, China
haoranlai@163.com, wangtao_9802@sina.com

Abstract. The manual ground truth of abdominal multi-organ is labor-intensive. In order to make full use of CT data, we developed a semi-supervised learning based dual-light UNet. In the training phase, it consists of two light UNets, which make full use of label and unlabeled data simultaneously by using consistent-based learning. Moreover, separable convolution and residual concatenation was introduced light UNet to reduce the computational cost. Further, a robust segmentation loss was applied to improve the performance. In the inference phase, only a light UNet is used, which required low time cost and less GPU memory utilization. The average DSC of this method in the validation set is 0.8718. The code is available in https://github.com/laihaoran/Semi-Supervised-nnUNet.

Keywords: Semi-supervised learning · UNet · Robust segmentation loss

1 Introduction

Fast automatic abdominal multi-organs segmentation can greatly improve the labeling speed of radiologists. However, there are still a series of challenges for automatic abdominal multi-organ segmentation: 1) Manual labeling of ground truth requires significant labor cost. 2) There is a large amount of unlabeled data that can be used to improve performance. 3) Medical image segmentation suffers from unclear boundaries. 4) Integrated automatic segmentation algorithms need to meet the requirements of low time cost and less GPU memory utilization.

Semi-supervised learning can be achieved by combining a small amount of labeled data and a large amount of unlabeled data, thus enabling training on small labeled datasets. The current major semi-supervised learning algorithms can be categorized into 1) pseudo-labeling-based learning [1,6] and 2) consistency-based learning [2,10]. The prospects of abdominal multi-organ segmentation have multiple categories and dense distribution (multiple categories may exist in a region), which is suitable for consistency-based learning.

J. Ma and B. Wang (Eds.): FLARE 2022, LNCS 13816, pp. 64–73, 2022.
https://doi.org/10.1007/978-3-031-23911-3_7

Therefore, we propose a semi-supervised learning based dual-light UNet to achieve fast automatic abdominal multi-organs segmentation. First, consistency learning strategy was introduced in to the proposed network to effectively utilize the large amount of unlabeled data. Second, a light UNet was proposed to achieve efficient and fast automatic segmentation. Then, a robust segmentation loss function was applied to overcome the challenge of tiny foreground. Finally, this proposed method achieves fast and accurate automatic abdominal multi-organ segmentation.

The main contributions of this work are as follows.

- We use a network consistency-based semi-supervised learning strategy to leverage large amounts of unlabeled data.
- We propose a light UNet for fast and efficient automatic abdominal multi-organs segmentation.
- We adopt a robust segmentation loss function to effectively overcome the challenge of tiny foreground.

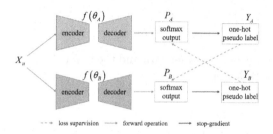

Fig. 1. Illustrating the architectures for consistent learning.

2   Method

2.1   Consistency-based Learning

As shown in Fig. 1, let the $X_l = \{x_{li}, i \in N\}$ and $X_u = \{x_{ui}, i \in M\}$ be the labeled and unlabeled data, respectively, where N and M are the number of labeled and unlabeled data, respectively. In our experiment, the condition of $\ll M$ is established for semi-supervised learning. First, dual identical networks $f(\theta_A)$ and $f(\theta_B)$ are built with different parameter initialization methods. Then, dual identical networks $f(\theta_A)$ and $f(\theta_B)$ are trained by using the labeled data for abdominal organ segmentation, respectively.

$$f(x_{li}; \theta_A) = p_{A,li}$$
$$f(x_{li}; \theta_B) = p_{B,li} \tag{1}$$

where p is the probability map. Next, the trained network is used to obtain different probability map of unlabeled data and their pseudo-labels.

$$f(x_{ui}; \theta_A) = p_{A,ui}, f(x_{uj}; \theta_A) = p_{A,uj}$$
$$f(x_{ui}; \theta_B) = p_{B,ui}, f(x_{uj}; \theta_B) = p_{B,uj} \tag{2}$$

$$y_{A,ui} = \text{argmax}(p_{A,ui}), y_{A,uj} = \text{argmax}(p_{A,uj})$$
$$y_{B,ui} = \text{argmax}(p_{A,ui}), y_{B,uj} = \text{argmax}(p_{B,uj}) \tag{3}$$

CutMix operation [14] is implemented on different unlabeled data and pseudo labels:

$$x_{uij} = \mathbf{H} \odot x_{ui} + (1 - \mathbf{H}) \odot x_{uj}$$
$$y_{A,uij} = \mathbf{H} \odot y_{A,ui} + (1 - \mathbf{H}) \odot y_{A,uj} \tag{4}$$
$$y_{B,uij} = \mathbf{H} \odot y_{B,ui} + (1 - \mathbf{H}) \odot y_{B,uj}$$

In this situation, the outputs of the two networks can be used to supervise for each other, which achieves the network consistency-based learning.

$$f(x_{uij}; \theta_A) = p_{A,uij} \longrightarrow y_{B,uij}$$
$$f(x_{uij}; \theta_B) = p_{B,uij} \longrightarrow y_{A,uij} \tag{5}$$

During each iteration, the label data and the unlabel data are simultaneously input to the network for optimization.

2.2   Light UNet

To accelerate inference speed and reduce the GPU memory utilization, we modify the UNet in nnU-Net [9]. A light UNet was presented in Fig. 2.

– We replace the original convolution with depthwise separable convolution [3], thus reducing the number of trainable parameters.
– Residual connection [5] was introduced between all convolution layers, including encoder and decoder, thus improving the representational ability of the UNet.

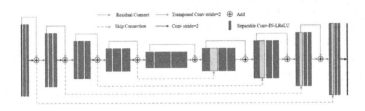

Fig. 2. The architecture of Light UNet.

2.3 Robust Segmentation Loss

In the segmentation task, the commonly used segmentation loss is a combination of Dice loss and cross entropy (CE) loss, which have been proved be robust in various medical image segmentation task [11]. In this paper, based on the previous segmentation loss, the idea of mean absolute error (MAE) loss was introduced into Dice and CE loss respectively. Therefore, a robust segmentation loss fuction $\mathcal{L}_{RS}$ was proposed, which consists of noise robust dice loss $\mathcal{L}_{NRD}$ and taylor cross entropy loss $\mathcal{L}_{TCE}$.

$$\mathcal{L}_{RS} = \mathcal{L}_{NRD} + \mathcal{L}_{TCE} \tag{6}$$

$$\mathcal{L}_{NRD} = \frac{\sum_{n=1}^{DWH} |\mu_n - v_n|^{\gamma}}{\sum_{n=1}^{DWH} \mu_n^2 + \sum_{n=1}^{DWH} v_n^2 + \epsilon} \tag{7}$$

$$\mathcal{L}_{TCE} = \sum_{n=1}^{DWH} (1 - \mu_{n,v=1}) + \frac{\sum_{n=1}^{DWH} (1 - \mu_{n,v=1})^2}{2} \tag{8}$$

where D, W and H are the depth, width and height of input, respectively. μ and v are the voxels of softmax output and ground truth, respectively.

2.4 Preprocessing and Inference

The dataset was preprocessed by nnU-Net configuration [9], including HU value clipping, HU values normalization, and resolution uniformity. In order to achieve category-balanced cropping for unlabeled data in training stage, a nnU-Net model was trained in advance using a small amount of labeled data. Then, a pseudo-label for unlabeled data is generated, which is only involved in achieving category-balanced cropping and not in other utilization.

In the inference phase, a patch shift-based approach was used to generate mask outputs for the entire 3D CT. We used 0.5 shift steps for each patch to alleviate the misclassification of the results by local information. Moreover, all patchs were flipped along three axes to generate robust performance.

3 Experiments

3.1 Dataset and Evaluation Measures

The FLARE2022 dataset is curated from more than 20 medical groups under the license permission, including MSD [13], KiTS [7,8], AbdomenCT-1K [12], and TCIA [4]. The training set includes 50 labelled CT scans with pancreas disease and 2000 unlabelled CT scans with liver, kidney, spleen, or pancreas diseases. The validation set includes 50 CT scans with liver, kidney, spleen, or pancreas diseases. The testing set includes 200 CT scans where 100 cases has liver, kidney, spleen, or pancreas diseases and the other 100 cases has uterine corpus endometrial, urothelial bladder, stomach, sarcomas, or ovarian diseases. All the CT scans only have image information and the center information is not available.

The evaluation measures consist of two accuracy measures: Dice Similarity Coefficient (DSC) and Normalized Surface Dice (NSD), and three running efficiency measures: running time, area under GPU memory-time curve, and area under CPU utilization-time curve. Only DSC score was presented in the experiments. All measures will be used to compute the ranking. Moreover, the GPU memory consumption has a 2 GB tolerance.

3.2   Implementation Details

Environment Settings. The development environments and requirements are presented in Table 1.

Table 1. Development environments and requirements.

Windows/Ubuntu version	Ubuntu 18.04.5 LTS
CPU	Intel(R) Xeon(R) Gold 5218 CPU @ 2.30GHz
RAM	503 GB
GPU (number and type)	Two NVIDIA RTX 2080Ti 11G
CUDA version	11.0
Programming language	Python 3.7
Deep learning framework	Pytorch (Torch 1.11, torchvision 0.2.2)

Training Protocols. Ther training protocols are presented in Table 2.

Table 2. Training protocols.

Network initialization	"he" normal initialization
Batch size	1
Patch size	$56 \times 160 \times 160$
Target resolution	$2.5 \times 1.5 \times 1.5$
Total epochs	1000
Optimizer	SGD with nesterov momentum ($\mu = 0.99$)
Initial learning rate (lr)	0.01
Lr decay schedule	Halved by 200 epochs
Training time	276 h
Loss function	RRD + TCE
Number of model parameters	5.59M
Number of flops	33.81G

4 Results and Discussion

A public unlabeled validation set was used to evaluate the experiment results, which can be uploaded to the online[1] for metrics.

4.1 Ablation of Semi-supervised Learning

Table 3 shows the effects of introducing semi-supervised learning in the nnU-Net and light unet on the final segmentation performance, respectively. Two conclusions can be found from Table 3: (1) The segmentation performance of the light unet is inferior to the nnU-Net due to the less parameters, but the light unet can speed up the inference and reduce the GPU memory utilization. (2) The introduction of semi-supervised learning has greatly improved the segmentation performance for both. Further, the performance improvement is greater for the light unet with a smaller number of parameters than nnU-Net, which may be caused by model with few parameters has strong potential for improvement.

Table 3. Ablation of semi-supervised learning (SSL). LV, RK, SL, PC, AT, IVC, RAG, LAG, GB, EH, SM, DD, and LK are short for Liver, Right Kidney, Spleen, Pancreas, Aorta, Inferior Vena Cava, Right Adrenal Gland, Left Adrenal Gland, Gallbladder, Esophagus, Stomach, and Left kidney, respectively.

Method	Mean	LV	RK	SL	PC	AT	IVC	RAG	LAG	GB	EH	SM	DD	LK
nnU-Net w/o SSL	0.869	0.967	0.880	0.941	0.841	0.949	0.882	0.822	0.819	0.821	0.877	0.885	0.748	0.871
nnU-Net w SSL	**0.895**	0.978	0.897	0.973	0.909	0.973	0.922	0.839	0.826	0.779	0.900	0.914	0.838	0.888
Light UNet w/o SSL	0.837	0.965	0.869	0.932	0.830	0.945	0.860	0.766	0.731	0.731	0.837	0.858	0.717	0.843
Light UNet w SSL	**0.878**	0.976	0.910	0.969	0.894	0.960	0.896	0.807	0.763	0.764	0.865	0.915	0.799	0.891

Table 4. Comparison of loss function.

Loss	Mean	LV	RK	SL	PC	AT	IVC	RAG	LAG	GB	EH	SM	DD	LK
Dice+CE	0.869	**0.972**	**0.915**	**0.954**	**0.861**	**0.958**	**0.884**	**0.823**	0.814	0.720	0.867	**0.888**	**0.751**	**0.889**
NRD+TCE	**0.870**	0.967	0.880	0.941	0.841	0.949	0.882	0.822	**0.819**	0.821	**0.877**	0.885	0.748	0.871

4.2 Comparison of Loss Function

From Table Table 4, it can be found that the robust segmentation loss is superior to the combination of dice and CE loss in terms of overall performance. Moreover, it can be noticed that although the robust segmentation loss is inferior to the combination of dice and CE loss for the segmentation of most organs from the segmentation performance of different organs, the robust segmentation loss has a great advantage for the segmentation of the gallbladder. The gallbladder belongs to the small target segmentation region, therefore, we conclude that robust segmentation loss has some advantages for the small target region.

[1] https://flare22.grand-challenge.org/evaluation/challenge/submissions/create/.

4.3   Segmentation Efficiency Results

Considering the balance between segmentation performance and inference speed, we reduce the original 7 times flips in nnU-net to 3 tmes flips (tta). Moreover, in order to address the phenomenon that particularly large samples in the image will be out of memory during the inference process, we only keep the final generated labels and do not keep the intermediate network output (RAM). The result was performed in Table 5.

We did not upload docker to test computational efficiency issues. However, we tested on our own platform to test the optimization of computational efficiency. In the end, we achieved a test time of 0.67 h on 50 validation samples, maximum ram is 18G, and GPU memory is 2045MB.

Table 5. Extra Processing for fianl result. IS(H) is short for inference speed, with hour as unit.

Method	Mean	IS(H)	LV	RK	SL	PC	AT	IVC	RAG	LAG	GB	EH	SM	DD	LK
DLUNet	0.878		0.976	0.910	0.969	0.894	0.960	0.896	0.807	0.763	0.764	0.865	0.915	0.799	0.891
DLUNet+tta	**0.884**	2.00	0.977	0.910	0.972	0.899	0.962	0.901	0.816	0.762	0.801	0.873	0.917	0.800	0.895
DLUNet+tta+RAM	0.872	**0.67**	0.973	0.903	0.964	0.890	0.948	0.888	0.789	0.741	0.792	0.857	0.911	0.795	0.885

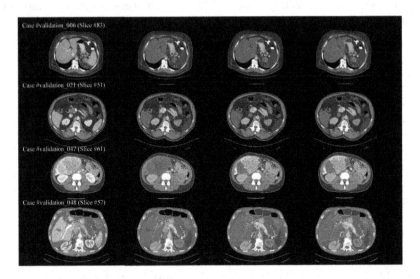

Fig. 3. Qualitative results on easy (case 06 and 21) and hard (case 47 and 48) examples. First column is the image, second column is the ground truth, third column is the predicted results by Light U-Net without ssl, third column is the predicted results by DLUNet with ssl.

4.4   Qualitative Results

Fig. 3 presents some easy and hard examples on validation set, and quantitative result is illustrated in Table 6. Comparing (Case 06 and Case 21) and (Case 47 and Case 48), we can find that our proposed method does not work well for lesion-affected organs. For example, the liver cancer region is wrongly identified in Case 47 and Case 48, especially Case 48. This situation may be due to our proposed method is implemented by a patch-based training strategy, which lacks global information.

Table 6. The DSC scores of easy and hard examples.

Example	Method	Mean	LV	RK	SL	PC	AT	IVC	RAG	LAG	GB	EH	SM	DD	LK
Case 06	w/o ssl	0.915	0.983	0.974	0.978	0.924	0.965	0.944	0.899	0.894	1.000	0.908	0.936	0.756	0.729
	w ssl	**0.924**	0.985	0.983	0.983	0.929	0.977	0.955	0.927	0.920	1.000	0.922	0.940	0.760	0.725
Case 21	w/o ssl	0.946	0.985	0.972	0.983	0.926	0.966	0.937	0.869	0.864	1.000	0.935	0.969	0.926	0.973
	w ssl	**0.957**	0.988	0.980	0.989	0.932	0.980	0.946	0.894	0.897	1.000	0.949	0.973	0.936	0.981
Case 47	w/o ssl	0.798	0.885	0.978	0.866	0.798	0.936	**0.665**	**0.677**	0.818	**0.676**	0.807	0.904	**0.395**	0.977
	w ssl	**0.805**	0.882	0.986	0.868	0.805	0.954	**0.682**	**0.676**	0.833	**0.707**	0.815	0.918	**0.358**	0.983
Case 48	w/o ssl	0.716	0.971	0.971	0.667	0.841	0.958	**0.461**	**0.679**	0.856	**0.000**	0.693	0.598	0.796	0.811
	w ssl	**0.729**	0.972	0.978	0.702	0.861	0.970	**0.456**	**0.747**	0.869	**0.000**	0.692	0.623	0.795	0.812

4.5 The Performance of Testing Set

As shown in Table 7, our method shows a competitive segmentation performance on the testing set. Moreover, we find that all metrics of case 97 are 0. This may be caused by the fact that the view of case 97 is flipped, which leads to the misjudgment of the inference optimization algorithm and terminates the inference in advance, resulting in not generating the correct segmentation output. Since the focus of our method is on segmentation performance improvement, the optimization of inference speed is neglected, resulting in the lack of advantage of our method in the final composite score.

Table 7. The performance of testing set.

Metric	Mean	LV	RK	SL	PC	AT	IVC	RAG	LAG	GB	EH	SM	DD	LK
DSC	0.881	0.968	0.941	0.949	0.854	0.949	0.900	0.815	0.805	0.809	0.805	0.924	0.797	0.937
NSD	0.940	0.969	0.960	0.961	0.954	0.982	0.923	0.953	0.939	0.828	0.913	0.951	0.926	0.958
Times(s)	73.92													
AUC GPU	138831													
AUC CPU	1195													

4.6 Limitation and Future Work

In this paper, we do not use existing deep learning model packaging techniques (e.g., TensorRT) to package the model, reduce computational memory, and increase inference speed. Therefore, the implementation of the operation can be considered in the future work.

5   Conclusion

The FLARE2022 competition aims to design an efficient and accuracy abdominal multi-organ segmentation network by using a small amount of labeled data and a large amount of unlabeled data. In this paper, we proposed DLUNet for this task. First, consistent-based learning was introduced to achieve semi-supervised learning. Second, separable convolution and residual connection were used to greatly reduce the computational cost. Moreover, a robust segmentation loss was applied to improve segmentation performance. Experiments prove that the DLUNet achieves a certain balance in terms of model parameters, computation time, GPU memory utilization, and segmentation performance. The method is promising for the task.

Acknowledgements. The authors of this paper declare that the segmentation method they implemented for participation in the FLARE 2022 challenge has not used any pre-trained models nor additional datasets other than those provided by the organizers. The proposed solution is fully automatic without any manual intervention.

References

1. Arazo, E., Ortego, D., Albert, P., O'Connor, N.E., McGuinness, K.: Pseudo-labeling and confirmation bias in deep semi-supervised learning. In: 2020 International Joint Conference on Neural Networks (IJCNN), pp. 1–8. IEEE (2020)
2. Chen, X., Yuan, Y., Zeng, G., Wang, J.: Semi-supervised semantic segmentation with cross pseudo supervision. In: IEEE Conference on Computer Vision and Pattern Recognition, CVPR 2021, virtual, 19–25 June 2021, pp. 2613–2622. Computer Vision Foundation/IEEE (2021). https://openaccess.thecvf.com/content/CVPR2021/html/Chen_Semi-Supervised_Semantic_Segmentation_With_Cross_Pseudo_Supervision_CVPR_2021_paper.html
3. Chollet, F.: Xception: deep learning with depthwise separable convolutions. In: Proceedings of the IEEE Conference on Computer Vision and Pattern Recognition, pp. 1251–1258 (2017)
4. Clark, K., et al.: The cancer imaging archive (TCIA): maintaining and operating a public information repository. J. Digit. Imaging **26**(6), 1045–1057 (2013)
5. He, K., Zhang, X., Ren, S., Sun, J.: Deep residual learning for image recognition. In: Proceedings of the IEEE Conference on Computer Vision and Pattern Recognition, pp. 770–778 (2016)
6. He, R., Yang, J., Qi, X.: Re-distributing biased pseudo labels for semi-supervised semantic segmentation: a baseline investigation. In: Proceedings of the IEEE/CVF International Conference on Computer Vision, pp. 6930–6940 (2021)
7. Heller, N., et al.: The state of the art in kidney and kidney tumor segmentation in contrast-enhanced CT imaging: results of the kits19 challenge. Med. Image Anal. **67**, 101821 (2021)
8. Heller, N., et al.: An international challenge to use artificial intelligence to define the state-of-the-art in kidney and kidney tumor segmentation in ct imaging. Proc. Am. Soc. Clin. Oncol. **38**(6), 626–626 (2020)
9. Isensee, F., Jaeger, P.F., Kohl, S.A., Petersen, J., Maier-Hein, K.H.: NNU-net: a self-configuring method for deep learning-based biomedical image segmentation. Nat. Methods **18**(2), 203–211 (2021)

10. Luo, X., Chen, J., Song, T., Wang, G.: Semi-supervised medical image segmentation through dual-task consistency. CoRR abs/2009.04448 (2020). arxiv.org:abs/2009.04448
11. Ma, J., et al.: Loss odyssey in medical image segmentation. Med. Image Anal. **71**, 102035 (2021)
12. Ma, J., et al.: Abdomenct-1k: is abdominal organ segmentation a solved problem? IEEE Trans. Pattern Anal. Mach. Intell. **44**(10), 6695–6714 (2022)
13. Simpson, A.L., et al.: A large annotated medical image dataset for the development and evaluation of segmentation algorithms. arXiv preprint arXiv:1902.09063 (2019)
14. Yun, S., Han, D., Oh, S.J., Chun, S., Choe, J., Yoo, Y.: Cutmix: regularization strategy to train strong classifiers with localizable features. In: Proceedings of the IEEE/CVF International Conference on Computer Vision, pp. 6023–6032 (2019)

Multi-organ Segmentation Based on 2.5D Semi-supervised Learning

Hao Chen, Wen Zhang, Xiaochao Yan, Yanbin Chen, Xin Chen, Mengjun Wu, Lin Pan, and Shaohua Zheng(✉)

Intelligent Image Processing and Analysis Laboratory, Fuzhou University, Fuzhou 350108, Fujian, China
sunphen@fzu.edu.cn

Abstract. Automatic segmentation of multiple organs is a challenging topic. Most existing approaches are based on 2D network or 3D network, which leads to insufficient contextual exploration in organ segmentation. In recent years, many methods for automatic segmentation based on fully supervised deep learning have been proposed. However, it is very expensive and time-consuming for experienced medical practitioners to annotate a large number of pixels. In this paper, we propose a new two-dimensional multi slices semi-supervised method to perform the task of abdominal organ segmentation. The network adopts the information along the z-axis direction in CT images, preserves and exploits the useful temporal information in adjacent slices. Besides, we combine Cross-Entropy Loss and Dice Loss as loss functions to improve the performance of our method. We apply a teacher-student model with Exponential Moving Average (EMA) strategy to leverage the unlabeled data. The student model is trained with labeled data, and the teacher model is obtained by smoothing the student model weights via EMA. The pseudo-labels of unlabeled images predicted by the teacher model are used to train the student model as the final model. The mean DSC for all cases we obtained on the validation set was 0.5684, the mean NSD was 0.5971, and the total run time was 783.14 s.

Keywords: Semi-supervised · Deep learning · Organ segmentation

1 Introduction

Automatic segmentation of multiple organs is a challenging topic. The main problems in medical segmentation can be outlined as follows: (1) Manual annotation of organs from CT scans is time-consuming and laborious. (2) Medical data involves patient privacy issues. In recent years, many proposed fully supervised deep learning automatic segmentation methods rely on a large number of pixel-level annotations, but the annotation of multiple organs is very expensive and time-consuming. In addition, existing 2D methods cannot fully utilize spatial information, and 3D methods consume a lot of computational resources.

J. Ma and B. Wang (Eds.): FLARE 2022, LNCS 13816, pp. 74–86, 2022.
https://doi.org/10.1007/978-3-031-23911-3_8

This paper proposes a novel 2.5D multi-slice semi-supervised approach to perform abdominal organ segmentation. Considering the limited labeled data, semi-supervised learning is applied to explore useful information from unlabeled data.

Integrated learning and other power-hungry algorithms can achieve wonderful segmentation results. However, it will eventually lead to a very bloated model. In contrast, the lightweight model needs low requirements on device. It is easier to be deployed in real-world applications. The main theme of the Fast and Low-resource semi-supervised Abdominal Organ Segmentation in CT 2022(FLARE2022) Challenge is to propose a solution with high efficiency and high accuracy as the benchmark while occupying low GPU and CPU resources. It is important to have both lightweight model and low resource usage, as well as high accuracy and efficiency. A representative of the current state-of-the-art approaches is nnU-Net [5], which provides a fully automated end-to-end segmentation method and comes out top in several competitions. The model has good performance on segmentation, but it is also not light enough and requires a lot of GPU memory.

In this paper, our contributions are listed as follows:

1. We propose a 2.5D semi-supervised multi-organ segmentation framework. It introduces connected adjacent slices as input [7] to improve the utilization of 3D information with only a few increase in computational resources. It employs a teacher-student semi-supervised strategy to use unlabeled data.
2. We use 2D U-Net [5] as the main network framework. The attention module of Convolutional Block Attention Module (CBAM) [14] is added to improve the data information mining.
3. EMA [6] is applied to optimize the teacher model, which makes the performance of model more robust.

2 Method

2.1 Preprocessing

Threshold Truncation. According to our observation of CT files, the contrast between organ tissues is more obvious when the threshold is taken near $[-250,300]$, so we truncate the CT threshold on this basis.

Cropping Strategy. In the training phase, the images and labels are cropped according to the slices containing labels and the slices without the labels are discarded. In the inference phase, the area to be segmented in the CT image is concentrated in the middle of z-axis. The larger the image size is, the more unrelated areas exist in the CT. So we use center cropping to cut the number of z-axis slices to the nearest power 2. For example, a CT image size is $809 \times 512 \times 512 (Z \times H \times W)$, we can cut it to $512 \times 512 \times 512$ to speed up the subsequent data reading.

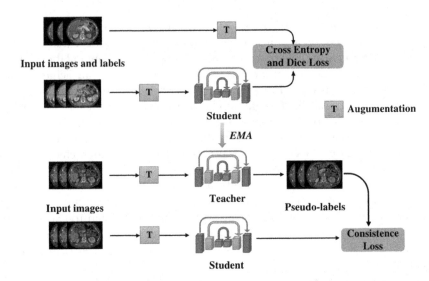

Fig. 1. The workflow of our method. The labeled data are fed into the student network after data augmentation. The student network is passed through EMA to obtain a more robust teacher model. The unlabeled data are pseudo-labeled by the teacher network after data augmentation. The pseudo-labels are sent to the student network with the corresponding unlabeled data.

Resampling Method for Anisotropic Data. We adjust the slice size during data loading to reduce GPU memory usage. After testing with different sizes, the 2D slice size of 128×128 has an impact on model performance, while 256×256 takes up more memory without much performance improvement. So we resample the 2D slice from the original 512×512 to a size of 192×192. Meanwhile, during the scaling process, we use trilinear sampling to ensure that the variation of image texture features is as small as possible. We use nearest neighbor sampling on labels to ensure that the label values remain unchanged.

Intensity Normalization Method. To make the data more easily compute and improve the performance of model, we normalize and standardize the threshold value to $[0, 1]$.

2.2 Proposed Method

Figure 1 illustrates the general workflow of our semi-supervised segmentation network.

Firstly, we train the student model on labeled data.

Secondly, we use the EMA method to obtain teacher model by smoothing the student model weights. The loss curve of the model using EMA is smoother and has less jitter on the image [6]. The model does not fluctuate significantly due to some abnormal loss values. So the robustness of the model after EMA optimization is better.

Thirdly, the teacher model predicts the unlabeled data to generate pseudo-labels. Then we continue to train the student model on the unlabeled data with pseudo-labels. Finally, we get the final student model.

The teacher-student model uses the U-Net-CBAM network architecture. Figure 2 illustrates the Network architecture of our method.

We apply the attention mechanism to the U-Net segmentation network. The CBAM allows better focus on prominent areas and suppress irrelevant background regions. It can be well embedded in the CNN framework. Compared with other attention modules, the model performance can be improved without adding too much computational effort [14].

Number Setting of Adjacent Slices. We investigated some papers [13]. It is best to use 3 adjacent slices, while making full use of context information. In terms of details, 3 adjacent slices are connected on the channel, fed into the model for training and inference. It makes the best possible use of 3D information while slightly increasing the GPU memory footprint.

Relevant Principles of EMA. In depth learning, the weight of the model will shake at the actual best point in the last n steps of each training, and there will be an abnormal value relative to the best point. Therefore, we take the average of the last n steps to make the model more robust. Since the value of n is a decreasing process, it is equivalent to a sliding average process.

Strategies to Use the Unlabelled Cases. We use the teacher model to predict unlabeled data to get pseudo-labels and use consistency loss to allow student models to learn the content of unlabeled data. We believe that too much unlabeled data will magnify the error information in the pseudo-labels and bring greater impact on the model. Therefore, only part of the unlabeled data is used for training. We randomly selected 100 data before the start of the training.

Network Architecture Details Description. In Fig. 2, our proposed U-Net-CBAM network consists of a combination of U-Net network and CBAM. CBAM includes the spatial attention module and the channel attention module. The network input first goes through 5 convolution modules and 4 max pooling layers to complete the downsampling process, and then passes through 5 convolution modules and four upsampling to get the output. The output of each layer of the downsampling path is connected by the features of the skip connection and the upsampling path, respectively. The skip connection performs channel-wise and spatial-wise feature correction via the CBAM.

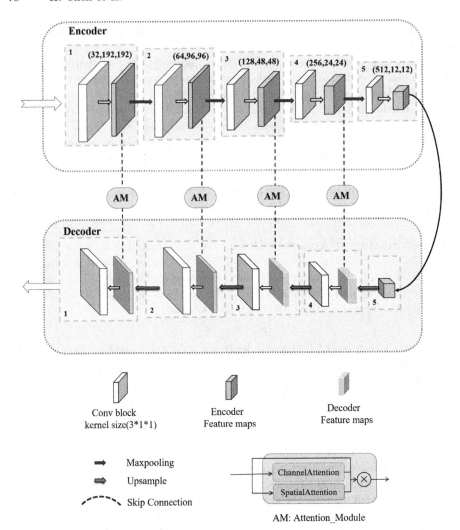

Fig. 2. Network architecture. U-Net-CBAM is based on U-Net with additional CBAM in the jump connection can better extract the image features and details.

Loss Function. [8] We set up two loss functions on our method. They are Supervised loss function and Unsupervised loss function.

1) Supervised loss function: It consists of Cross-Entropy Loss(L_{ce}) [2] and Dice Loss(L_{dice}) [11] with weights, and the percentages of both are α and $1-\alpha$, respectively. The L_{dice} comes with weights to facilitate the adjustment of the percentages between different categories.

$$Loss = \alpha * L_{ce}(g,p) + (1-\alpha) * L_{dice}(g,p) \tag{1}$$

where g is ground truth, p is prediction, we use α to balance the L_{ce} and L_{dice}. α is a constant weight to balance the L_{ce} and L_{dice}. Here we set it to 0.5.

$$L_{dice} = 1 - \sum_{i=0}^{k-1} \beta_i * Dice(g_i, p_i) \qquad (2)$$

where g_i is ground truth, p_i is prediction, β_i represents weight of every class. The ratio between any two categories is set to 1:1.

$$Dice(g, p) = \frac{2g \cap p|}{|g| + |p|} \qquad (3)$$

where g and p is what we want to compare by using dice.

$$L_{ce}(g, p) = - \sum_{i=1}^{C} g_i \log(p_i) \qquad (4)$$

where C denotes the number of classes, g_i is ground truth, p_i is prediction.

2) Unsupervised loss function: we use consistency loss(L_{csst}) [6], which directly measures the consistency between prediction and pseudo-label.

$$L_{csst} = \|M_s(A_1(x)) - M_t(A_2(x))\|_2^2 \qquad (5)$$

where x is input image, $A_1(\cdot)$ and $A_2(\cdot)$ are different noise addition functions, $M_s(\cdot)$ and $M_t(\cdot)$ denotes output of model of student and teacher.

Strategies to Improve Inference Speed and Reduce Consumption. Firstly, we use U-Net network architecture and combine it with CBAM. Compared with other attention modules, it has less parameters and consumes less computational resources.

Secondly, we use multiple slices to avoid losing 3D information. Besides, we resize the image as shown in the preprocessing stage to reduce the GPU memory consumption without affecting the model performance.

2.3   Post-processing

Operation 1: We perform a median filtering operation with a convolution kernel of $5 \times 5 \times 5$ on the image. It can optimize the edges of the segmentation results.

Operation 2: We resize the image in preprocessing. After obtaining the segmentation results, we scale the predicted values to the original size in postprocessing based on the nearest neighbor interpolation operation.

When we perform operation 1, some of the segmentation results disappear, even if reducing the size of the convolution kernel. We finally abandon operation 1.

3 Experiments

3.1 Dataset and Evaluation Measures

The FLARE 2022 is an extension of the FLARE 2021 [9] with more segmentation targets and more diverse abdomen CT scans. The dataset is curated from more than 20 medical groups under the license permission, including MSD [12], KiTS [3,4], AbdomenCT-1K [10], and TCIA [1]. The training set includes 50 labelled CT scans with pancreas disease and 2000 unlabelled CT scans with liver, kidney, spleen, or pancreas diseases. The validation set includes 50 CT scans with liver, kidney, spleen, or pancreas diseases. The testing set includes 200 CT scans where 100 cases have liver, kidney, spleen, or pancreas diseases and the other 100 cases have uterine corpus endometrial, urothelial bladder, stomach, sarcomas, or ovarian diseases. All the CT scans only have image information, while the center information is not available.

The evaluation measures consist of two accuracy measures: Dice Similarity Coefficient (DSC) and Normalized Surface Dice (NSD), and three running efficiency measures: running time, area under GPU memory-time curve, and area under CPU utilization-time curve. All measures will be used to compute the ranking. Moreover, the GPU memory consumption has a 2 GB tolerance.

3.2 Implementation Details

Environment Settings. We performed the training and inference process based on the environment of Table 1.

Table 1. Development environments and requirements.

Windows/Ubuntu version	Ubuntu 18.04.6 LTS
CPU	Intel(R) Core(TM) i5-7500 CPU@3.40 GHz
RAM	4×4 GB; 2400MT/s
GPU (number and type)	1 NVIDIA RTX 2080 (8G)
CUDA version	11.4
Programming language	Python 3.8
Deep learning framework	Pytorch (Torch 1.7.0, torchvision 0.8.2)
Specific dependencies	Medicaltorch, pandas, scipy, collections
(Optional) Link to code	

Training Protocols. In training the teacher and student models, we optimized the models using the Adam optimizer with an initial learning rate of 0.001 and a learning rate reduction strategy using CosineAnnealingLR. The training protocols are presented in Table 2 and Table 3.

Data Augmentation. In training teacher and student model, we used elastic transformation, random horizontal and vertical flipping and random rotation for data enhancement.

The elastic transformation is to generate a random standard deviation for each dimension of the pixel in the $(-1,1)$ interval. It filters the deviation matrix of each dimension with a Gaussian filter $(0, \sigma)$. The final amplification factor α is used to control the deviation range. We set σ to fluctuate between $(10.0, 20.0)$ and α to fluctuate between $(2.0, 4.0)$. We set the random possibility to 0.3.

Random horizontal and vertical flipping is to randomly rotate the image vertically and horizontally. We set the random possibility to 0.5.

Random Rotation is to randomly select an angle $(0, 90, 180, 270)$ to rotate the image.

Table 2. Training protocols.

Network initialization	Teacher Net
Batch size	16
Patch size	$3 \times 192 \times 192$
Total epochs	150
Optimizer	Adam
Initial learning rate (lr)	0.001
Lr decay schedule	CosineAnnealingLR
Training time	3.25 h
Number of model parameters	74.1M[a]
Number of flops	8.22G[b]
CO_2eq	1 Kg[c]
Loss function	Cross-Entropy Loss and Dice Loss[b]

[a] https://github.com/sksq96/pytorch-summary
[b] https://github.com/facebookresearch/fvcore
[c] https://github.com/lfwa/carbontracker/

4   Results and Discussion

4.1   Quantitative Results on Validation Set

On the provided validation dataset, we perform ablation experiments and the results are shown in Table 4. The purpose is to compare the model performance on the validation set using only labeled data and using both labeled and unlabeled data. When using only labeled dataset, the DSC reaches 0.5454, while when using both labeled and unlabeled dataset, the DSC reaches 0.5684.

Table 3. Training protocols for the refine model.

Network initialization	Student Net
Batch size	8
Patch size	$3 \times 192 \times 192$
Total epochs	100
Optimizer	Adam
Initial learning rate (lr)	0.001
Lr decay schedule	CosineAnnealingLR
Training time	16 h
Number of model parameters	74.1M[a]
Number of flops	8.65G[b]
CO_2eq	1 Kg[c]
Loss function	Consistence Loss[b]

[a] https://github.com/sksq96/pytorch-summary
[b] https://github.com/facebookresearch/fvcore
[c] https://github.com/lfwa/carbontracker/

After using unlabeled data, the segmentation results improve, and the previously under-segmented organs can be initially segmented. The improvement in the DSC illustrates that using pseudo-labels to exploit unlabeled data can improve model performance.

In this paper, the performance of the proposed method is evaluated using the provided validation set with ground truth. The evaluation metrics are DSC and NSD. The results are shown in Table 4. The average value of DSC is 0.5684 and the average value of NSD is 0.5971.

We can find that the model performs better in the segmentation of three organs, the Liver, Spleen, and Aorta, but is slightly weak in the other organs.

4.2   Qualitative Results on Validation Set

The segmentation excellence results are shown in the Fig. 3 and the results of the poor segmentation are shown in the Fig. 4.

Our method makes excellent segmentation results on case #08 and #21, but makes poorer segmentation results on case #30 and #48. The supervised method on case #08, #21, #30, #48 have over-segmentation results than the semi-supervised method.

We demonstrate ablation experiments in a visual manner. The experiment results verity the effectiveness of semi-supervised method. They are all from the provided validation set with ground truth.

Possible reasons for the failure of cases or organ segmentation are listed as follows:

1) We use fewer adjacent slices for training and inference.

2) Some of the organ segments are lost in the preprocessing because some information is lost in the scaling of the images.
3) The pseudo-labels from the teacher model may contain error information, which the student model may have learned in training.

Table 4. Overview of DSC and NSD metrics on validation set.

Name Method	Mean(DSC) w/o ssl	Mean(DSC) w ssl	Mean(NSD) w/o ssl	Mean(NSD) w ssl
Liver	0.8079	0.8496	0.7320	0.7718
RK	0.4590	0.4816	0.3773	0.4022
Spleen	0.7169	0.7073	0.6400	0.6475
Pancreas	0.5177	0.5463	0.6109	0.6447
Aorta	0.8525	0.8703	0.8578	0.8811
IVC	0.6561	0.6671	0.6219	0.6424
RAG	0.4057	0.3968	0.5415	0.5458
LAG	0.3045	0.3750	0.4236	0.5130
Gallbladder	0.2460	0.3540	0.1918	0.3026
Esophagus	0.5981	0.5638	0.7202	0.6917
Stomach	0.5650	0.5890	0.5580	0.5736
Duodenum	0.3685	0.3957	0.5475	0.5911
LK	0.5916	0.5931	0.5307	0.5544
Average	0.5454	0.5684	0.5656	0.5971

4.3   Segmentation Efficiency Results on Validation Set

The segmentation efficiency results of the validation set are shown in Table 5. It mainly includes various metrics such as CPU, GPU and runtime. The GPU-Memory usage is 1455 MB, which is smaller than 2048 MB. The model has a good level in Time, AUC-GPU-Time, and AUC-CPU-Time metrics, and the average values are 15.66 s, 17140.12, and 348.15 respectively. We can see that the model fully meets the minimum requirements of the Challenge in terms of resource usage and consumption.

Table 5. Overview of segmentation efficiency on validation set.

	Time/s	GPU-Memory/MB	AUC-GPU-Time	AUC-CPU-Time
Lowest	8.53	1455	94932	1661.84
Average	15.66	1455	17140.12	348.15
Highest	74.56	1455	7644	181.96

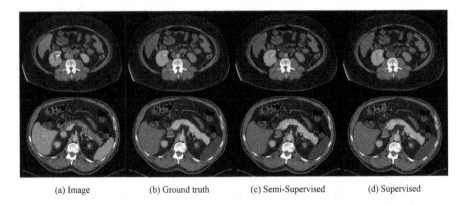

(a) Image   (b) Ground truth   (c) Semi-Supervised   (d) Supervised

Fig. 3. Excellent segmentation results on case #08(up) and #21(down)

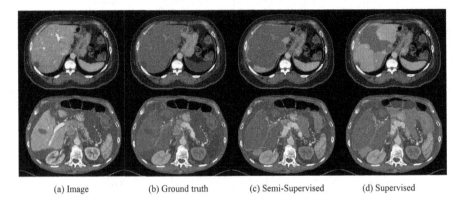

(a) Image   (b) Ground truth   (c) Semi-Supervised   (d) Supervised

Fig. 4. Poorer segmentation results on case #30(up) and #48(down)

4.4   Results on Final Testing Set

Our final results on the test set are shown in Table 6. The final average DSC value is 0.6153, and the average NSD value is 0.6484. We can find that the model performs better in the segmentation of three organs, the Liver, Spleen, and Aorta, but is slightly weak in the other organs. The results on the test set are consistent with those of the validation set.

4.5   Limitation and Future Work

The limitation of our method is whether we can obtain good teacher models. If the teacher model cannot be well pseudo-labeled for unlabeled data, it will affect the results of semi-supervised training. This eventually leads to poor segmentation. In future work, we can improve the effect of pseudo-labeling by optimizing our method, such as improving the network architecture, post-processing the pseudo-labeling, etc.

Table 6. Overview of DSC and NSD metrics on test set.

Name	Mean(DSC)	Mean(NSD)
Liver	0.8723	0.8086
RK	0.4932	0.3722
Spleen	0.7976	0.7418
Pancreas	0.5579	0.6685
Aorta	0.8312	0.8506
IVC	0.7037	0.6813
RAG	0.4885	0.6723
LAG	0.4295	0.5873
Gallbladder	0.5232	0.4530
Esophagus	0.6180	0.7568
Stomach	0.6626	0.6699
Duodenum	0.3868	0.5915
LK	0.6350	0.5753
Average	0.6153	0.6484

5 Conclusion

In the work of abdominal multi-organ segmentation, we propose a 2.5D-based semi-supervised segmentation method to achieve effective use of unlabeled data and reduce the occupation of computing resources.

Findings. The main findings are listed as follows:

1) The performance of the model is improved after using pseudo-labels to exploit unlabelled data.
2) In some cases, it is able to segment each organ very well. However, in some other cases, the segmentation of the corresponding organs is poor. After observation, we found that in these cases, there was more noise in the CT images.
3) The quality of the pseudo-label depends on the supervised training phase.

Results. The main results are listed as follows:

1) We believe that only a part of the data distribution of some cases is learned during training. The generalization performance of the model is not very good.
2) The quality of the CT image files themselves is also important, i.e. the equipment used to take the CT images should also be checked.
3) Our teacher-student model strategy is feasible, it improves the performance of our model to some extent.

Acknowledgements. The authors of this paper declare that the segmentation method they implemented for participation in the FLARE 2022 challenge has not used any pre-trained models nor additional datasets other than those provided by the organizers. The proposed solution is fully automatic without any manual intervention.

References

1. Clark, K., et al.: The cancer imaging archive (TCIA): maintaining and operating a public information repository. J. Digit. Imaging **26**(6), 1045–1057 (2013)
2. de Boer, P.T., Kroese, D., Mannor, S., Rubinstein, R.: A tutorial on the cross-entropy method. Ann. Oper. Res. **134**(1), 19–67 (2005). https://doi.org/10.1007/s10479-005-5724-z
3. Heller, N., et al.: The state of the art in kidney and kidney tumor segmentation in contrast-enhanced CT imaging: results of the kits19 challenge. Med. Image Anal. **67**, 101821 (2021)
4. Heller, N., et al.: An international challenge to use artificial intelligence to define the state-of-the-art in kidney and kidney tumor segmentation in CT imaging. Proc. Am. Soc. Clin. Oncol. **38**(6), 626–626 (2020)
5. Isensee, F., Jaeger, P.F., Kohl, S.A., Petersen, J., Maier-Hein, K.H.: nnU-Net: a self-configuring method for deep learning-based biomedical image segmentation. Nat. Methods **18**(2), 203–211 (2021)
6. Li, X., Yu, L., Chen, H., Fu, C.W., Xing, L., Heng, P.A.: Transformation-consistent self-ensembling model for semisupervised medical image segmentation. IEEE Trans. Neural Networks Learn. Syst. **32**(2), 523–534 (2020)
7. Lv, P., Wang, J., Wang, H.: 2.5 d lightweight RIU-net for automatic liver and tumor segmentation from CT. Biomed. Signal Process. Control **75**, 103567 (2022)
8. Ma, J., et al.: Loss odyssey in medical image segmentation. Med. Image Anal. **71**, 102035 (2021)
9. Ma, J., et al.: Fast and low-GPU-memory abdomen CT organ segmentation: the flare challenge. Med. Image Anal. **82**, 102616 (2022). https://doi.org/10.1016/j.media.2022.102616
10. Ma, J., et al.: AbdomenCT-1K: is abdominal organ segmentation a solved problem? IEEE Trans. Pattern Anal. Mach. Intell. **44**(10), 6695–6714 (2022)
11. Milletari, F., Navab, N., Ahmadi, S.A.: V-net: fully convolutional neural networks for volumetric medical image segmentation. In: 2016 Fourth International Conference on 3D Vision (3DV), pp. 565–571. IEEE (2016)
12. Simpson, A.L., et al.: A large annotated medical image dataset for the development and evaluation of segmentation algorithms. arXiv preprint arXiv:1902.09063 (2019)
13. Wardhana, G., Naghibi, H., Sirmacek, B., Abayazid, M.: Toward reliable automatic liver and tumor segmentation using convolutional neural network based on 2.5 d models. Int. J. Comput. Assis. Radiol. Surg. **16**(1), 41–51 (2021)
14. Woo, S., Park, J., Lee, J.Y., Kweon, I.S.: CBAM: convolutional block attention module. In: Proceedings of the European Conference on Computer Vision (ECCV), pp. 3–19 (2018)

3D Cross-Pseudo Supervision (3D-CPS): A Semi-supervised nnU-Net Architecture for Abdominal Organ Segmentation

Yongzhi Huang[1,3], Hanwen Zhang[1,3], Yan Yan[1,3],
and Haseeb Hassan[1,2,3]

[1] College of Big Data and Internet, Shenzhen Technology University,
Shenzhen 518188, China
haseeb@sztu.edu.cn
[2] Guangdong Key Laboratory for Biomedical Measurements and Ultrasound
Imaging, National-Regional Key Technology Engineering Laboratory for Medical
Ultrasound, School of Biomedical Engineering, Shenzhen University Medical School,
Shenzhen 518060, China
[3] College of Applied Sciences, Shenzhen University, Shenzhen 518060, China

Abstract. Large curated datasets are necessary, but annotating medical images is a time-consuming, laborious, and expensive process. Therefore, recent supervised methods are focusing on utilizing a large amount of unlabeled data. However, to do so, is a challenging task. To address this problem, we propose a new 3D Cross-Pseudo Supervision (3D-CPS) method, a semi-supervised network architecture based on nnU-Net with the Cross-Pseudo Supervision method. We design a new nnU-Net based preprocessing. In addition, we set the semi-supervised loss weights to expand linearity with each epoch to prevent the model from low-quality pseudo-labels in the early training process. Our proposed method achieves an average dice similarity coefficient (DSC) of 0.881 and an average normalized surface distance (NSD) of 0.913 on the 2022-MICCAI-FLARE validation set (20 cases).

Keywords: Abdominal organ segmentation · Semi-supervised learning · 3D Cross-Pseudo Supervision

1 Introduction

With the advancement of medical technology, more and more medical imaging devices are being used in clinical diagnosis [1]. Nowadays, the analysis of medical images by physicians to diagnose any possible disease has become the basis of clinical diagnosis [2]. Therefore, image segmentation is the first step in the process of many clinical diagnoses and plays a key role in the quantitative analysis of medical images [3]. With the rapid development of deep learning

---

Y. Huang and H. Zhang—These two authors are contributed equally to this work.

© The Author(s), under exclusive license to Springer Nature Switzerland AG 2022
J. Ma and B. Wang (Eds.): FLARE 2022, LNCS 13816, pp. 87–100, 2022.
https://doi.org/10.1007/978-3-031-23911-3_9

in recent years, various U-Net-based network models have achieved excellent results in different medical image segmentation competitions [4]. Among them, the nnU-Net performs significantly well with its excellent adaption to different datasets and achieves excellent segmentation results under fully supervised medical datasets using a plain U-Net network [5]. However, the manual annotation for segmentation is time-consuming and needs expert experience, especially in medical images. Thus, recent trends have focused on automatically using a large amount of unlabeled medical images. For instance, a semi-supervised approach has been introduced to construct a teacher-student model with dropout or uncertainty to generate stable segmentations automatically over unlabeled images [6,7]. Likewise, Li et al. and Luo et al. proposed a model for different tasks, and then this model can be trained with consistency losses on unlabeled data [8,9].Above all, these inspired semi-supervised-based approaches still have the following challenges.

1. Data preprocessing pipelines and algorithms that rely on labeled data can not be applied directly to unlabeled data.
2. Semi-supervised strategies for processing data are often used only in binary tasks, while multi-class 3D medical tasks will take more time and memory consumption in the data processing.
3. To deal with the imbalance problem in the number of labeled and unlabeled data, an appropriate training strategy is required to learn from different losses.

To address the above challenges, we design a semi-supervised method based on nnU-Net by improving the Cross Pseudo-label algorithm. The proposed method applies the preprocessing of nnU-Net to unlabeled data and further adapts the Cross Pseudo-label algorithm(CPS) [10] to 3D CT images. The proposed method is validated on Fast and Low-resource semi-supervised Abdominal oRgan sEgmentation in CT challenge (2022-MICCAI-FLARE). The main contributions of our work are summarized as follows.

1. Modified the nnU-Net architecture for semi-supervised tasks.
2. Adopted a semi-supervised strategy called Cross-Pseudo Supervision for 3D medical images.

2   Method

2.1   Preprocessing

Training. In the training stage, we use the same preprocessing pipeline generated from the heuristic rules as in the nnU-Net on labeled data, including intensity transformation, spatial transformation, and data augmentation. The only difference is that when analyzing the distribution of CT intensity, nnU-Net analyzes the intensity of the foreground so that the label is required. However, we obtain the intensity distribution of unlabeled data by unifying a statistical method for calculating the intensity of the whole image by collecting global pixels information instead of foreground pixels.

Inference. We follow the nnU-Net in the inference stage: adopting the TTA inference, setting the step size of the sliding window 0.7 and using "normal mode" in nnU-Net.

2.2   Proposed Method

Semi-supervised Learning on nnU-Net Architecture. Our proposed framework is shown in Fig. 1, which is adopted from the nnU-Net. For segmentation tasks on a specific dataset, the pipeline of the nnU-Net framework mainly includes the following steps:

1. Collect and analyze the data information, and generate rule-based parameters using its heuristic rules.
2. Train the network based on fixed parameters and rule-based parameters.
3. Perform ensemble selection and post-processing methods based on empirical parameters.

Our proposed framework keeps the pipeline of the nnU-Net but modifies some of their components such as for data fingerprint collection. We replaced the distribution of foreground pixels with global pixels to analyze the intensity distribution of unlabeled data, as mentioned in Sect. 2.1. Secondly, we doubled the U-Net network architecture and optimizer generated from the heuristic rules of the nnU-Net. The sibling networks have the same architecture but with different initialization. Correspondingly, the two sibling networks have their optimizer to update the weights. Then, the proposed semi-supervised method trains the

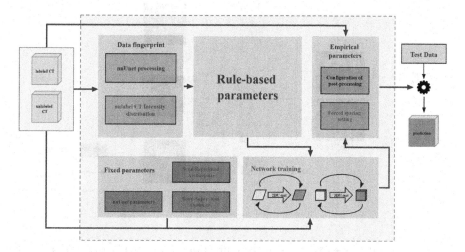

Fig. 1. The 3D CPS framework: a semi-supervised learning framework based on nnU-Net architecture. The proposed framework entirely follows nnU-Net and we modified their respective blocks including intensity distribution analysis, network architecture, optimizer, training policy, and inference preprocessing in the framework which is marked as red. The forced spacing settings is only used in experiments of the final test. (Color figure online)

network in the training stage, which will be discussed in detail in the next section. Since the model ensembling module is of no use for comparing the plain 2D and 3D U-Net architectures with or without the CPS, so it is removed from the proposed framework. Additionally, in the inference stage, the enforced spacing settings is used before preprocessing to improve the segmentation efficiency.

Proposed Semi-supervised Method. The proposed semi-supervised method is mainly derived from CPS. Though the CPS is a 2D semi-supervised semantic segmentation method, this method can be adopted for 3D CT images. A semi-supervised semantic segmentation task aims to learn a segmentation network by exploring labeled and unlabeled data. For instance, given a set D_l of labeled images and a set D_u of unlabeled images. The proposed method consists of two parallel segmentation networks T_1 and T_2, with the same network architecture but were initialized with different weights θ_1 and θ_2. The input X can be either a 2D patch with the shape of [C, H, W] or a 3D patch with the shape of [C, S, H, W].

The semi-supervised training strategy is shown in Fig. 2, where the input X is preprocessed with the same pipeline as the nnU-Net. Then, the default data augmentation in nnU-Net is applied for the input X. $T_1(X)$ and $T_2(X)$ represent the predicted one-hot confidence map from the two parallel T_1 and T_2 networks, respectively. $Y_1(X)$ and $Y_2(X)$ represent the predicted one-hot label map generated from $T_1(X)$ and $T_2(X)$, respectively.

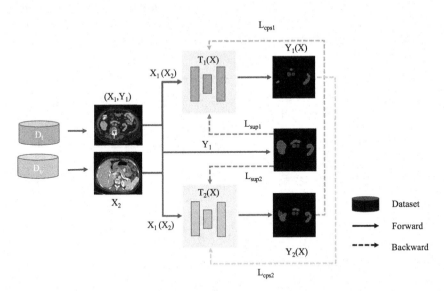

Fig. 2. Modified semi-supervised architecture from cross-pseudo supervision(CPS). Labeled data (X_1, Y_1) and unlabeled data X_2 are sampled randomly as input for both networks $T_1(\cdot)$ and $T_2(\cdot)$. For any input X, the output is a pair of branches, i.e., $T_1(X)$ and $T_2(X)$. Labeled data and unlabeled data are calculated based on cross-pseudo supervision loss. Moreover, the labeled data also requires calculation of supervision loss.

Furthermore, our training objective contains two losses: supervision loss L_{sup} and cross-pseudo supervision loss L_{cps}. The supervision loss L_{sup} can only be calculated for the labeled data and is given as follows.

$$L_{sup}^l = l_{sup}(T_1(x), Y) + l_{sup}(T_2(x), Y) \tag{1}$$

where Y is the ground truth, and l_{sup} is dice and cross-entropy loss configured by default in nnU-Net, which is proved to be robust in medical image segmentation tasks [11].

The cross-pseudo supervision loss L_{cps} is defined as $L_{cps} = L_{cps}^l + L_{cps}^u$, which is combined with the CPS loss on labeled dataset L_{cps}^l and on unlabeled dataset L_{cps}^u. The two parallel networks view the output of the other one as own pseudo-labels and the L_{cps} can be calculated as L_{sup}. The cross-pseudo supervision loss on the unlabeled data is written as:

$$L_{cps}^u = l_{cps}(T_1(x), Y_2) + l_{cps}(T_2(x), Y_1) \tag{2}$$

where l_{cps} is dice and cross-entropy loss like l_{sup} in our experiments. Given Eq. 2, the definition of CPS loss on labeled data is the same as the loss on unlabeled data. The overall training objective is given as:

$$L = L_{sup} + \lambda L_{cps} \tag{3}$$

where λ is a hyper-parameter that needs to be set in advance, determining the weight of cross supervision loss. We set the λ to increase linearity with epoch from 0 to 0.5, and keep that fixed after the specific epoch instead of the fixed value as in CPS.

Network Architecture. Our network is a U-Net [12] like Encoder-Decoder architecture, and its backbone is based on residual blocks [13]. Following the configurations of nnU-Net, two different U-Net architectures (2D and 3D) are generated from heuristic rules of nnU-Net. Their detailed structures are provided in Figs. 3 and 4, respectively.

The 2D CPS U-Net can only take one slice as input. During the training and inference stage, each slice needs to be resized to 512×512. The network is an 8-layers U-Net, and the encoding process downsamples images to 4×4. The implementation of residual blocks is as follows: conv-instnorm-ReLU, and each encoder contains two residual blocks, where the first residual block performs the downsampling task (except encoder1). The decoder has a similar structure to the encoder, except that it adds a transposed convolution at the end for upsampling.

Regarding 3D CPS U-Net, 3D data can be used as input (i.e., a sliding window). During our training and inference stage, each input needs to be resized to $112 \times 160 \times 128$ (S $\times$ H $\times$ W). The 3D network is a 6-layers U-Net, and the encoding process downsamples images to $7 \times 5 \times 4$. The residual blocks' structure is similar to 2D CPS U-Net, except that 3D convolutions replace the 2D convolutions.

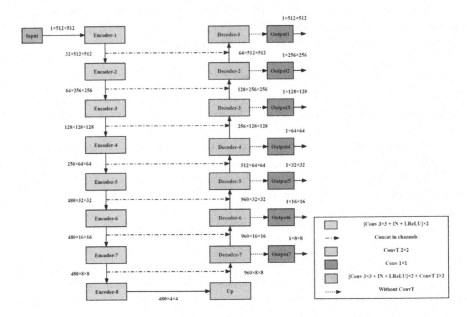

Fig. 3. A 2D U-Net like Encoder-Decoder architecture generated by heuristic rules of nnU-Net. The network further entails residual encoder blocks (containing conv-instnorm-ReLU), residual decoder blocks (containing conv-instnorm-ReLU and transpose convolution), and output blocks. The output blocks generate segmentations at different resolutions.

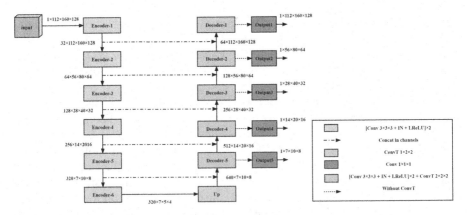

Fig. 4. A 3D U-Net like Encoder-Decoder architecture generated by heuristic rules of nnU-Net. The 3D network further entails residual encoder blocks (including conv-instnorm-ReLU), residual decoder blocks (containing conv-instnorm-ReLU and transpose convolution), and output blocks. Same as in the 2D network, the output blocks generate segmentations at different resolutions.

Inference Speed and Resources Consumption Trade-Offs. Generally, the performance of the segmentation network is contrary to inference speed and resource consumption. Most methods improve performance at the expense of inference speed or more resource consumption, such as Test Time Augmentation(TTA) inference or sliding window inference.

Due to the limitation of the evaluation platform in the FLARE2022, e.g., the memory limit of 28 GB, we propose enforced spacing settings when making our test submission to reduce resource consumption and speed up the inference time. So, by modifying its spacing parameters before preprocessing, the input patch size is constrained to an optimal value for the inference stage. It is worth mentioning that this strategy is not applied in our experiments except for results on the final test set, which is discussed furthermore in Sect. 4.3.

2.3 Post-processing

The spacing of the segmentation output needs to be modified back to its original spacing in the post-processing stage if the enforced spacing settings is used in the preprocessing stage. The remaining post-processing method is consistent with the pipeline of the nnU-Net.

3 Experiments

3.1 Dataset and Evaluation Measures

The FLARE 2022 is an extension of the FLARE 2021 [14] with more segmentation targets and more diverse abdomen CT scans. The FLARE 2022 dataset is curated from more than 20 medical groups under the license permission including MSD [15], KiTS [16,17], AbdomenCT-1K [18], and TCIA [19]. The training set includes 50 labeled CT scans with pancreas disease and 2000 unlabelled CT scans with liver, kidney, spleen, or pancreas diseases. The validation set includes 50 CT scans with liver, kidney, spleen, or pancreas diseases. The testing set includes 200 CT scans where 100 cases have liver, kidney, spleen, or pancreas diseases and the other 100 cases have uterine corpus endometrial, urothelial bladder, stomach, sarcomas, or ovarian diseases. All the CT scans only have image information and the center information is not available. The evaluation measures are Dice Similarity Coefficient (DSC) and Normalized Surface Dice (NSD), and three running efficiency measures: running time, area under GPU memory-time curve, and area under CPU utilization-time curve. All measures are used to compute the ranking score. Moreover, the GPU memory consumption has a 2 GB performance. For the FLARE2022 challenge, we use 50 labeled CT scans and the first 1000 unlabeled CT scans.

3.2   Environments and Requirements

The configured environments and requirements are provided in Table 1.

3.3   Training and Inference Protocols

The protocols are basically calculated by the heuristic rules of nnU-Net, while data-independent parameters are consistent with nnU-Net. The training and inference protocols of our experiments are provided in Table 2.

Table 1. Development environments and requirements.

Windows/Ubuntu version	Ubuntu 20.04.1 LTS
CPU	AMD EPYC 7742 64-Core Processor
RAM	1.8TB
GPU (number and type)	8 NVIDIA A100 (40G)
CUDA version	11.4
Programming language	Python 3.9
Deep learning framework	Pytorch (1.10), nnU-Net

Table 2. Training and inference protocols.

Mode	2D+CPS	3D+CPS
Network initialization	"he" normal initialization	"he" normal initialization
Batch size	12 in D_l and 12 in D_u	2 in D_l and 2 in D_u
Patch size	512×512	$112 \times 160 \times 128$
Total epochs	1000	1000
Optimizer	SGD	SGD
Weight decay	3e-5	3e-5
Initial learning rate (lr)	0.01	0.01
Lr scheduler	ReduceLROnPlateau	ReduceLROnPlateau
Training time	47 h	97 h
Loss function	Dice and Cross-Entropy	Dice and Cross-Entropy
Number of model parameters	41.29M[a]	30.79M
Number of flops	65.55G[b]	585.43G

[a] https://github.com/sksq96/pytorch-summary.
[b] https://github.com/facebookresearch/fvcore.

4   Results and Discussions

4.1   Quantitative Results on Validation Set

For the ablation study to analyze the effect of unlabeled data and semi-supervised learning, we use 2D and 3D supervised training strategies (previously deployed by nnU-Net) as the baseline in our experiments. Furthermore, our experiments adopt the same preprocessing method and training protocol. In a semi-supervised scheme, we employ two parallel models with the same structure but different initialization weights, while in a supervised scheme, only a single model is required. Note that the loss function for the semi-supervised scheme is based on Eq. 3, while the experiments in a supervised scheme are performed without L_{cps}.

The quantitative results are provided in Table 3, showing the DSC for 13 organs and mean DSC (mDSC) for all classes. The baseline method refers to fully supervised learning on nnU-Net, while Baseline + CPS are the results of 3D-CPS. Table 3 shows baseline+CPS slightly outperforming baseline for both 2D and 3D networks, by +0.0223 and +0.0167 mDSC respectively.

Table 3. Quantitative results on 50 cases of validation set.

Method	2D		3D	
	Baseline	Baseline+CPS	Baseline	Baseline+CPS
Liver	0.9623	0.9733	0.9717	0.9745
RK	0.7699	0.8042	0.8863	0.8851
Spleen	0.8936	0.9202	0.9311	0.9559
Pancreas	0.7646	0.7865	0.8619	0.8769
Aorta	0.9392	0.9630	0.9584	0.9617
IVC	0.8230	0.8545	0.8851	0.8992
RAG	0.7124	0.7362	0.8196	0.8354
LAG	0.6479	0.7196	0.8060	0.8236
Gallbladder	0.6137	0.6993	0.7228	0.8067
Esophagus	0.8357	0.8461	0.8637	0.8644
Stomach	0.8377	0.7414	0.8800	0.9059
Duodenum	0.6119	0.6363	0.7586	0.7753
LK	0.7880	0.8091	0.8699	0.8672
mDSC	0.7846	0.8069	0.8627	0.8794

4.2   Qualitative Results

The qualitative analysis of 20 cases of the validation set released officially is shown in Tables 4 and 5, including both the score of DSC and NSD. Exemplary segmentation results generated by nnU-Net(baseline) and 3D-CPS (baseline+CPS) are shown in Fig. 5, where case2 and case42 are challenging and case21 and case28 are easy cases. In easy cases, both 2D and 3D networks performed marginally better and improved overall performance. In the challenging cases, the performance of 3D CPS seems to be struggling. Although the overall performance of baseline+CPS is better than the baseline in 20 released cases, the DSC score of baseline+CPS has dropped in these cases(2D model of case2 and 3D model of case42).

Table 4. Quantitative analysis of 2D model on 20 cases of validation set.

Metrics	DSC		NSD	
	Baseline	Baseline+CPS	Baseline	Baseline+CPS
Liver	0.9725	0.9769	0.9487	0.9587
RK	0.7595	0.7946	0.7225	0.7690
Spleen	0.9374	0.9413	0.9151	0.9355
Pancreas	0.8043	0.8052	0.8858	0.8944
Aorta	0.9661	0.9717	0.9832	0.9881
IVC	0.8403	0.8575	0.8280	0.8615
RAG	0.7768	0.7625	0.8782	0.8596
LAG	0.6867	0.7817	0.7958	0.8839
Gallbladder	0.5034	0.6345	0.4929	0.6328
Esophagus	0.7690	0.8231	0.8322	0.8980
Stomach	0.8575	0.7217	0.8668	0.7736
Duodenum	0.6817	0.6580	0.8329	0.8212
LK	0.8210	0.8495	0.7749	0.8545
Mean	0.7982	0.8137	0.8274	0.8562

Table 5. Quantitative analysis of 3D model on 20 cases of validation set.

Metrics	DSC		NSD	
	Baseline	Baseline+CPS	Baseline	Baseline+CPS
Liver	0.9790	0.9754	0.9736	0.9707
RK	0.8063	0.8483	0.7927	0.8479
Spleen	0.9436	0.9581	0.9386	0.9434
Pancreas	0.8737	0.8862	0.9538	0.9589
Aorta	0.9713	0.9730	0.9864	0.9899
IVC	0.8897	0.8958	0.8926	0.8937
RAG	0.8596	0.8651	0.9568	0.9527
LAG	0.8386	0.8521	0.9228	0.9301
Gallbladder	0.6626	0.7998	0.6553	0.7946
Esophagus	0.8752	0.8861	0.9411	0.9438
Stomach	0.8891	0.8869	0.9082	0.9182
Duodenum	0.7682	0.7727	0.8930	0.8733
LK	0.8651	0.8537	0.8453	0.8490
Mean	0.8632	0.8810	0.8969	0.9128

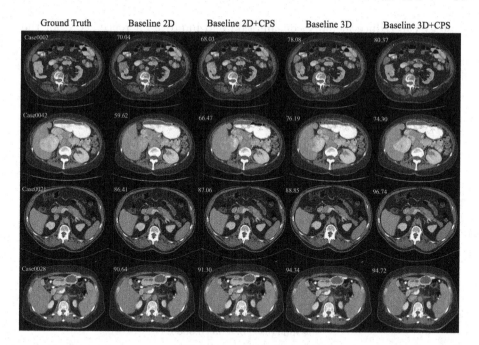

Fig. 5. Qualitative results on challenging (case 0002 and 0042) and easy (case 0021 and 0028) cases. Mean DSC scores (%) are attached to the top left. The first column is the ground truth released by the official. The second and fourth columns are the segmentation mask generated from the 2D model and 3D model in nnU-Net, respectively, and the third and fifth columns are generated from 3D-CPS (baseline+CPS).

4.3   Results on Test Dataset

To adapt evaluation platform for our model, we apply the enforced spacing settings strategy in the inference stage. The enforced spacing settings is an empirical parameter strategy that needs to be set manually. For this purpose, we consider the number of slices (S) of CT images for spacing settings, where s_x,s_y and s_z represent spacing on the x, y, and z axes, respectively. In our experiments, default settings for s_x,s_y and s_z are 0.75, 0.75, 0.5. So, if S is less than 150, only the spacing of s_x and s_y are modified, and s_z will be set as the original spacing. If S is between 150 and 600, the spacing will be modified as the default spacing, and if S is greater than 600, s_x and s_y will be modified as default settings, and s_z will be set to $max(0.8, 600/S) * s_z$.

Other Specific parameters of inference of test submission are set as follows: the TTA inference and post-processing are disabled, whereas the step size of the sliding window is set to 0.7, and the inference mode is set to "fastest mode" as in nnU-Net.

The evaluation of test submission is shown in Table 6. Applying the strategy of enforced spacing settings to the 3D-CPS causes a dramatic drop in DSC and NSD for all types of organs by about ten to twenty percent. Although this strategy can reduce memory consumption and improve inference speed for the nnU-Net based framework, it proves brute-forced for trade-off accuracy and efficiency, especially for the training set and testing set with different distributions like FLARE 2022 [18].

Table 6. Quantitative analysis of test set with the enforced spacing settings.

Metrics	DSC	NSD
Liver	0.8729	0.8384
RK	0.7073	0.7074
Spleen	0.7366	0.7345
Pancreas	0.6301	0.7018
Aorta	0.8200	0.8316
IVC	0.8135	0.8115
RAG	0.6587	0.7413
LAG	0.6586	0.7031
Gallbladder	0.6153	0.6143
Esophagus	0.6063	0.6855
Stomach	0.6147	0.6299
Duodenum	0.5584	0.6842
LK	0.7341	0.7433
Mean	0.6920	0.7251

5   Conclusion

Our anticipated model aims to take part in FLARE 2022 competition. For this purpose, a co-training-based semi-supervised method is developed. The proposed method incorporated a semi-supervised architecture based on Cross-Pseudo Supervision (CPS) and nnU-Net, extending to 2D and 3D medical images for segmentation tasks. The proposed method yields better quantitative results with marginally better qualitative predictions than the baseline(nnU-Net). Moreover, introducing enforced spacing settings in the inference stage leads to low-memory consumption and faster inference. It makes nnU-Net based model available with the limitation of the evaluation platform.

Our future work aims two folds. As a first instance, generating more robust pseudo-labels for semi-supervised learning. As our proposed method's generated pseudo-labels are weak at some iterations, and due to no filter module for these low-quality pseudo-labels, our proposed model's accuracy can be affected for some organs. To address this, morphological methods, such as level set representation and edge detection by generating patch-level confidence scores rather than image-level scores, may potentially remedy this anomaly. Secondly, we plan to optimize resource consumption and improve the efficiency of the nnU-Net-based framework in the inference stage. So, a better method that can trade off accuracy and efficiency is needed, e.g., a two-stage framework with a coarse-to-fine network proposed in the top-10 works of the FLARE2021 challenge.

Acknowledgements. We would like to thank the School-Enterprise Graduate Student Cooperation Fund of Shenzhen Technology University and the Project of Educational Commission of Guangdong Province of China (No. 2022ZDJS113).

References

1. Liu, X., Song, L., Liu, S., Zhang, Y.: A review of deep-learning-based medical image segmentation methods. Sustainability **13**(3), 1224 (2021)
2. Shen, D., Guorong, W., Suk, H.-I.: Deep learning in medical image analysis. Annu. Rev. Biomed. Eng. **19**, 221 (2017)
3. Monteiro, M., et al.: Multiclass semantic segmentation and quantification of traumatic brain injury lesions on head CT using deep learning an algorithm development and multicentre validation study. Lancet Digital Health **2**(6), e314–e322 (2020)
4. Getao, D., Cao, X., Liang, J., Chen, X., Zhan, Y.: Medical image segmentation based on u-net: a review. J. Imaging Sci. Technol. **64**, 1–12 (2020)
5. Isensee, F., et al.: nnU-net: Self-adapting framework for u-net-based medical image segmentation. arXiv preprint arXiv:1809.10486 (2018)
6. Li, X., Lequan, Yu., Chen, H., Chi-Wing, F., Xing, L., Heng, P.-A.: Transformation-consistent self-ensembling model for semisupervised medical image segmentation. IEEE Trans. Neural Netw. Learn. Syst. **32**(2), 523–534 (2020)
7. Yu, L., Wang, S., Li, X., Fu, C.-W., Heng, P.-A.: Uncertainty-aware self-ensembling model for semi-supervised 3D left atrium segmentation. In: Shen, D., et al. (eds.) MICCAI 2019. LNCS, vol. 11765, pp. 605–613. Springer, Cham (2019). https://doi.org/10.1007/978-3-030-32245-8_67
8. Li, S., Zhang, C., He, X.: Shape-aware semi-supervised 3D semantic segmentation for medical images. In: Martel, A.L., et al. (eds.) MICCAI 2020. LNCS, vol. 12261, pp. 552–561. Springer, Cham (2020). https://doi.org/10.1007/978-3-030-59710-8_54
9. Luo, X., Chen, J., Song, T., Wang, G.: Semi-supervised medical image segmentation through dual-task consistency. Proc. AAAI Conf. Artif. Intell. **35**, 8801–8809 (2021)
10. Chen, X., Yuan, Y., Zeng, G., Wang, J.: Semi-supervised semantic segmentation with cross pseudo supervision. In: Proceedings of the IEEE Computer Society Conference on Computer Vision and Pattern Recognition, pp. 2613–2622 (2021)
11. Ma, J., et al.: Loss odyssey in medical image segmentation. Med. Image Anal. **71**, 102035 (2021)
12. Ronneberger, O., Fischer, P., Brox, T.: U-net: Convolutional networks for biomedical image segmentation. arXiv:1505.04597
13. He, K., Zhang, X., Ren, S., Sun, J.: Deep residual learning for image recognition. In: Proceedings of the IEEE Computer Society Conference on Computer Vision and Pattern Recognition, 2016-December, pp. 770–778 (2016). (ISBN: 9781467388504 _eprint: 1512.03385)

14. Ma, J., et al.: Fast and low-GPU-memory abdomen CT organ segmentation: the flare challenge. Med. Image Anal. **82**, 102616 (2022)
15. Simpson, A.L., et al.: A large annotated medical image dataset for the development and evaluation of segmentation algorithms. arXiv preprint arXiv:1902.09063 (2019)
16. Heller, N., et al.: The state of the art in kidney and kidney tumor segmentation in contrast-enhanced CT imaging: results of the kits19 challenge. Med. Image Anal. **67**, 101821 (2021)
17. Heller, N., et al.: An international challenge to use artificial intelligence to define the state-of-the-art in kidney and kidney tumor segmentation in CT imaging. Am. Soc. Clin. Oncol. **38**(6), 626–626 (2020)
18. Ma, J., et al.: Abdomenct-1k: is abdominal organ segmentation a solved problem? IEEE Trans. Pattern Anal. Mach. Intell. **44**(10), 6695–6714 (2022)
19. Clark, K., et al.: The cancer imaging archive (TCIA): maintaining and operating a public information repository. J. Digit. Imaging **26**(6), 1045–1057 (2013)

Knowledge Distillation from Cross Teaching Teachers for Efficient Semi-supervised Abdominal Organ Segmentation in CT

Jae Won Choi[1,2(✉)]

[1] Department of Radiology, Armed Forces Yangju Hospital, Yangju, South Korea
[2] College of Medicine, Seoul National University, Seoul, South Korea
jhoci@snu.ac.kr

Abstract. For more clinical applications of deep learning models for medical image segmentation, high demands on labeled data and computational resources must be addressed. This study proposes a coarse-to-fine framework with two teacher models and a student model that combines knowledge distillation and cross teaching, a consistency regularization based on pseudo-labels, for efficient semi-supervised learning. The proposed method is demonstrated on the abdominal multi-organ segmentation task in CT images under the MICCAI FLARE 2022 challenge, with mean Dice scores of 0.8429 and 0.8520 in the validation and test sets, respectively. The code is available at https://github.com/jwc-rad/MISLight.

Keywords: Knowledge distillation · Semi-supervised learning · Medical image segmentation

1 Introduction

Organ segmentation has been one of the most popular applications of artificial intelligence in abdominal radiology [29]. As more high-quality imaging data are becoming available and advanced deep learning methods are being developed, many recent studies on automated abdominal organ segmentation have achieved promising results [2,8,15]. However, these methods are based on supervised learning that depends on large-scale, carefully labeled data. Also, current segmentation methods often require high computation costs. Therefore, for practical application in the clinical workflow, demands on labeled data and computational resources must be reduced.

Acquiring labeled data for medical image segmentation is especially expensive as it requires expert-level voxel-wise labeling and clinical data is innately heterogeneous. In this context, to utilize unlabeled data, various semi-supervised learning (SSL) in medical imaging have been studied, including Uncertainty-aware Mean Teacher [34], Uncertainty Rectified Pyramid Consistency [20], and Dual-task Consistency [18]. Among them, we adopt cross teaching, a simple consistency regularization based on pseudo-labels, which recently showed promising

J. Ma and B. Wang (Eds.): FLARE 2022, LNCS 13816, pp. 101–115, 2022.
https://doi.org/10.1007/978-3-031-23911-3_10

results in semi-supervised medical image segmentation on cardiac MR data [19]. Also, we use models with slightly different decoders to boost the consistency regularization, following Mutual Consistency Training [33].

The main strategies to address the high computational cost of deep learning methods include (1) efficient building blocks and (2) model compression and acceleration techniques [7]. The latter has not gained as much interest as the former, especially in medical image segmentation [26], while there are many studies on lightweight networks [1,35]. Among model compression and acceleration techniques, knowledge distillation (KD), which refers to knowledge transfer from a larger teacher model to a smaller student model [10], has been applied increasingly in recent research [7,32]. The target knowledge to transfer can be the response of the last output layer, outputs of intermediate feature layers, or relationships between different feature maps [7]. Here, we apply the response-based KD because it is simple and can be implemented regardless of network architectures.

The current study proposes a coarse-to-fine framework (Fig. 1) with two teacher models and a student model that combines KD and cross teaching, a consistency regularization based on pseudo-labels, for efficient semi-supervised medical image segmentation. Labeled data are used in all three models to train supervised segmentation. Pseudo-labels from unlabeled data are used to perform cross teaching between the two teachers and pseudo-supervision of the student. Meanwhile, outputs of the teachers on both labeled and unlabeled data are used to guide the student model through KD. Only the student model is used for efficient inference. The proposed method is developed and evaluated on the abdominal multi-organ segmentation task in CT images under the MICCAI FLARE 2022 challenge[1].

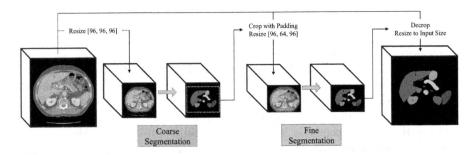

Fig. 1. An overview of the coarse-to-fine segmentation framework. For the coarse segmentation, the whole-volume input is resampled to $96 \times 96 \times 96$. For the fine segmentation, cropping with 10% padding around the coarse mask is first performed, and the cropped volume is resampled to $96 \times 64 \times 96$. The resultant fine segmentation mask is resized and padded back to the original input size.

---

[1] https://flare22.grand-challenge.org/.

2   Method

2.1   Preprocessing

The following preprocessing steps are performed in all experiments:

– Reorienting images to the right-anterior-inferior (RAI) view.
– For coarse segmentation, whole-volume resampling to fixed size $96 \times 96 \times 96$ with trilinear interpolation. For fine segmentation, cropping with 10% padding around the coarse mask (ground truth, if present), then resampling to fixed size $96 \times 64 \times 96$ with trilinear interpolation.
– Clipping based on the Hounsfield units to $[-300, 300]$.
– Patch-wise intensity normalization with z-score normalization based on the mean and standard deviation of the voxel values.

2.2   Proposed Method

The proposed method is a coarse-to-fine framework, where coarse segmentation is first yielded from whole-volume input and then refined by fine segmentation (Fig. 1). Such a two-stage framework lowers computation costs, especially in terms of memory use and running time, compared to the sliding window approach, which is a more common solution in medical image segmentation [31,35]. Empirically, a single-stage segmentation led to poor segmentation results and long inference time in large field-of-view or whole-body CT images. Each stage of the proposed framework consists of two teacher models T_1 and T_2 and a smaller student model S which are trained simultaneously (Fig. 2). At inference, only the student model is used.

Supervised Segmentation. Labeled data are used to train supervised segmentation for all models. Recently, compound losses have been suggested as the most robust losses for medical image segmentation tasks [21]. For model prediction P and label Y, we apply the sum of Dice loss [25] and focal loss [16] as the supervised segmentation loss:

$$L_{seg} = Dice(P,Y) + Focal(P,Y)$$

Cross Teaching and Pseudo-supervision. For SSL of the teacher models T_1 and T_2, we use the cross teaching strategy adopted from Cross Teaching between CNN and Transformer [19] and inspired by Cross Pseudo-supervision [4] and Mutual Consistency Training [33]. These methods all train two models with network-level perturbations that supervise each other with pseudo-labels to encourage consistent outputs on the same input. They differ in the perturbation targets (initialization [4], upsampling method for decoder [33], and learning paradigm [19]). Here, to distinguish using pseudo-labels for training between teacher models from using them to train the student model, we refer to the former as cross teaching and the latter as pseudo-supervision. With predictions of

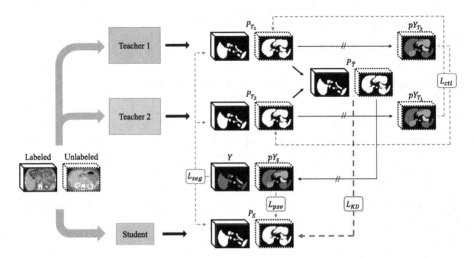

Fig. 2. An overview of KD from Cross Teaching Teachers. Each stage of the coarse-to-fine framework consists of two teacher models and a smaller student model. While labeled data are used in all three models to train supervised segmentation, the unlabeled data are used for cross teaching between the two teachers and pseudo-supervision of the student. All data are used for KD from the teacher models to the student model.

the student model P_S, teacher models P_{T_1} and P_{T_2}, and teachers' mean $P_{\bar{T}}$, the cross teaching and pseudo-supervision losses for the unlabeled data are defined as:

$$L_{ctl} = Dice(P_{T_1}, argmax(P_{T_2})) + Dice(P_{T_2}, argmax(P_{T_1}))$$
$$L_{psv} = Dice(P_S, argmax(P_{\bar{T}}))$$

Knowledge Distillation. The main idea of response-based KD is training the student model to directly mimic the final prediction of the teacher model. Following Hinton et al. [10], we apply the Kullback-Leibler (KL) divergence loss between P_S and $P_{\bar{T}}$ on both labeled and unlabeled data. A weight factor λ_{dis} is applied to balance distillation loss with the supervised segmentation loss for labeled data and the cross teaching and pseudo-supervision losses for unlabeled data:

$$L_{labeled} = L_{seg} + \lambda_{dis} KL(P_S, P_{\bar{T}})$$
$$L_{unlabeled} = L_{ctl} + L_{psv} + \lambda_{dis} KL(P_S, P_{\bar{T}})$$

Moreover, the proposed method is an online distillation where both the teachers and student models are updated simultaneously [7].

Overall Objective. The overall training objective of the proposed method is the weighted sum of $L_{labeled}$ and $L_{unlabeled}$ with a weight factor λ_{ssl} defined as:

$$Loss = L_{labeled} + \lambda_{ssl} L_{unlabeled}$$

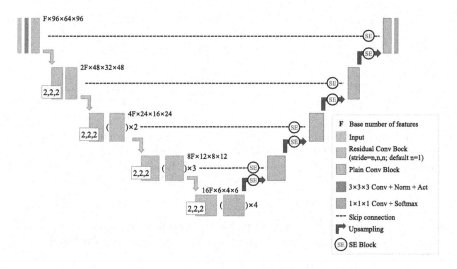

Fig. 3. Residual-USE-Net architecture. Mobile-Residual-USE-Net uses depthwise separable convolutions for residual and plain convolution blocks.

Network Architecture. An overview of the network architecture is shown in Fig. 3.

Inspired by the residual variant of the nnU-Net framework [13,14] and USE-Net [27], we employ Residual-USE-Net, a 3D U-Net [5] with an encoder with residual convolution blocks and a decoder with plain convolution blocks incorporated with residual squeeze-and-excitation (SE) blocks [12]. A convolution block is implemented as two sets of convolution, normalization, and nonlinear activation layers, and for the residual block, the residual summation takes place before the last activation. We set $r = 8$ for the reduction ratio of SE blocks [12,27] (Fig. 4).

The teacher models T_1 and T_2 are Residual-USE-Nets with 32 base features and 4 skip connections. Following mutual consistency training [33], while T_1 and T_2 share the same encoder structure, their decoders use different upsampling methods where T_1 uses transposed convolutions and T_2 uses trilinear interpolation followed by regular convolutions.

The student and teacher models share the same overall network structure, but we apply depthwise separable convolutions as in MobileNets [11] to build a lighter neural network for the student model. The student model S is Mobile-Residual-USE-Net, a Residual-USE-Net with depthwise separable convolutions

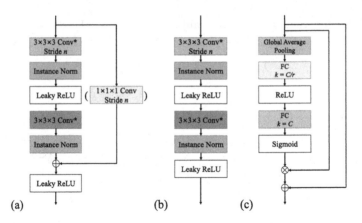

Fig. 4. (a) Residual convolution block. If stride $n = 1$ and the number of input and output channels are the same, the residual connection uses an identity layer instead of $1 \times 1 \times 1$ convolution. (b) Plain convolution block. (c) Residual SE block. *These layers are replaced with depthwise separable convolutions for Mobile-Residual-USE-Net.

instead of regular convolutions except for the initial convolution layer, with 32 base features, 4 skip connections, and transposed convolutions for the decoder.

2.3   Post-processing

The largest connected component of the segmentation mask is extracted per each class for both coarse and fine outputs. The connected component analysis is performed using Python connected-components-3d[2] and fastremap[3] packages [35].

3   Experiments

3.1   Dataset and Evaluation Measures

The MICCAI FLARE 2022 is an extension of the FLARE 2021 [22] with more segmentation targets and more diverse images. The dataset is curated from more than 20 medical groups under the license permission, including MSD [28], KiTS [8,9], AbdomenCT-1K [23], and TCIA [6]. The training set includes 50 labeled CT scans with pancreas disease and 2000 unlabeled CT scans with liver, kidney, spleen, or pancreas diseases. The validation set includes 50 CT scans with liver, kidney, spleen, or pancreas diseases. The testing set includes 200 CT scans where 100 cases has liver, kidney, spleen, or pancreas diseases and the other 100 cases has uterine corpus endometrial, urothelial bladder, stomach, sarcomas, or ovarian diseases. All the CT scans only have image information and the center information is not available.

---

[2] https://github.com/seung-lab/connected-components-3d.
[3] https://github.com/seung-lab/fastremap.

The evaluation measures consist of two accuracy measures: Dice Similarity Coefficient (DSC) and Normalized Surface Dice (NSD), and three running efficiency measures: running time, area under GPU memory-time curve, and area under CPU utilization-time curve. All measures will be used to compute the ranking. Moreover, the GPU memory consumption has a 2 GB tolerance.

3.2   Implementation Details

Environment Settings. The environments and requirements are presented in Table 1.

Table 1. Environments and requirements.

Windows/Ubuntu version	Ubuntu 20.04
CPU	AMD Ryzen Threadripper PRO 3975WX
RAM	251G
GPU (number and type)	NVIDIA GeForce RTX 3090 (24G, ×1)
CUDA version	11.4
Programming language	Python 3.9
Deep learning framework	PyTorch (torch 1.10.0, torchvision 0.11.1)
Code available at	https://github.com/jwc-rad/MISLight

Training Protocols. The training protocols are shown in Table 2. Except for the preprocessing, coarse and fine segmentation training are performed with the same protocols. During training, the labeled and unlabeled data are randomly sampled alternatively at a ratio of 1:1. An epoch is defined as an iteration over all the labeled data. Therefore, each epoch includes a random subset of the unlabeled data.

The weight factors λ_{dis} and λ_{ssl} are time-dependent Gaussian warming-up functions [34] $\lambda(t) = \lambda_0 \cdot e^{-5(1-t/t_{max})^2}$ where t denotes the current training epoch and t_{max} is the total epoch number. We use $\lambda_0 = 10$ for λ_{dis} [17] and $\lambda_0 = 0.1$ for λ_{ssl} [34].

The coarse segmentation is first trained using the whole-volume inputs. Then, the trained student model is applied to all the unlabeled data to acquire coarse masks. For the fine segmentation, cropping is performed around the coarse masks and the ground truth masks for the unlabeled and labeled data, respectively. Using the cropped volumes as inputs, the fine segmentation training is performed.

Testing Protocols. Only the student is used at inference, with the number of model parameters 5.2M and the number of flops 21.7G.

Table 2. Training protocols.

Data augmentation	Elastic deformation, scaling, rotation, crop, Gaussian noise, brightness
Network initialization	Xavier normal initialization
Batch size	1
Patch size	$96 \times 64 \times 96$
Total epochs	1000
Optimizer	SGD with nesterov momentum ($\mu = 0.99$, $decay = 3e - 5$)
Loss	Dice + Focal ($\alpha = 0.5$, $\gamma = 2$)
Initial learning rate	0.01
Learning rate decay schedule	$(1 - epoch/epoch_{max})^{0.9}$ [3]
Training time	7.5 h
Number of model parameters	189.3 M (5.2 M in test)[a]
Number of flops	443.1 G (21.7 G in test)[b]

[a] https://github.com/PyTorchLightning/pytorch-lightning.
[b] https://github.com/sovrasov/flops-counter.pytorch.

The same preprocessing as the training protocols except for data augmentation is applied for the testing. For coarse segmentation, inference is performed with a sliding window approach with overlap by half of the size of a patch where the resulting prediction is a weighted sum of sliding windows. To reduce the influence of predictions close to boundaries, a Gaussian importance weighting is applied for each predicted patch [13]. For fine segmentation, since the image is cropped with 10% padding around the coarse mask and resampled to the size same as the input size of the model, inference is only performed once without the sliding window approach.

3.3 Ablation Study

In the ablation study, as the baseline, fully supervised learning (FSL) is performed to train both coarse and fine segmentation models using only the labeled data. In other experiments, the coarse segmentation is fixed to the proposed method, and different training pipelines are used for the fine segmentation. First, FSL is applied to the fine segmentation using only the student model. Also, we conduct experiments with a single teacher and a student framework: FSL with KD, SSL with KD, SSL with pseudo-supervision, and SSL with KD and pseudo-supervision. We investigate the isolated effect of cross-teaching by training two cross-teaching students. Moreover, the proposed method's variants with no KD, no pseudo-supervision, and teachers sharing the same architecture, respectively, are performed. In all experiments, the network architectures of teacher and student models and training protocols are the same as in the proposed method. For experiments with two models of the same size for inference, we choose the one with transposed convolutions. Otherwise, the student model is used for inference.

4   Results and Discussion

All DSC results for the experiments are obtained via the validation leaderboard of the MICCAI FLARE 2022 challenge. Also, detailed results, including efficiency analysis, are processed privately and provided by the challenge organizers based on submissions using Docker containers.

4.1   Ablation Study

Table 3 shows the results of the ablation study. The baseline FSL shows a mean DSC of 0.7712, which slightly increases to 0.7812 when the proposed method is performed for the coarse segmentation. Applying KD to the basic FSL model yields an improved mean DSC of 0.8261 from 0.7812. This is better than the experiments on SSL with a single teacher and a student, which implies that ineffective use of unlabeled data only hinders the training of the student model. When unlabeled data is effectively exploited by the cross-teaching strategy, it shows better results than the FSL with KD even without the teacher model. Although there is little performance gain with pseudo-supervision from cross teaching teachers only, KD and combined use of KD and pseudo-supervision improve results. Moreover, teachers with slightly different decoders achieve better results than those with the same decoders, which is consistent with the results in Mutual Consistency Training [33].

Table 3. Ablation study results on the MICCAI FLARE 2022 validation set. The baseline uses only the labeled data to train both coarse and fine segmentations, whereas, in the rest of the experiments, the proposed method is used for training the coarse segmentation and each row shows the training settings for the fine segmentation. CTS and CTT mean cross teaching between two students and two teachers, respectively. CTT_{SD} uses teachers with decoders with the same architecture. *The one with transposed convolutions out of two models is used for inference.

# of T	# of S	SSL	KD	PSV	Cross teaching	Mean DSC
0	1					0.7712 ± 0.1193 (baseline)
0	1					0.7812 ± 0.1121
1	1		✓			0.8261 ± 0.1107
1	1	✓	✓			0.8227 ± 0.1122
1	1	✓		✓		0.8234 ± 0.1101
1	1	✓	✓	✓		0.8173 ± 0.1149
0	2	✓			CTS	$0.8296 \pm 0.1092^*$
2	1	✓		✓	CTT	0.8297 ± 0.1111
2	1	✓	✓		CTT	0.8407 ± 0.1075
2	1	✓	✓	✓	CTT_{SD}	0.8394 ± 0.1086
2	1	✓	✓	✓	CTT	$\mathbf{0.8429 \pm 0.1043}$ (**proposed**)

4.2   Quantitative Results on Validation Set

The proposed method shows a mean DSC of 0.8429±0.1043 and a mean NSD of 0.8990±0.0755 in the MICCAI FLARE 2022 validation set (Table 4). While large organs such as the liver or spleen are well segmented with DSC higher than 0.9, the proposed method works relatively poorly for adrenal glands and gallbladder. This may be attributed to the weakness of overlap-based metrics, including DSC, to small objects, since the proposed method depends on the Dice loss [30].

Table 4. Segmentation results on the MICCAI FLARE 2022 validation set.

Organ	DSC	NSD
Liver	0.9711 ± 0.0214	0.9762 ± 0.0406
RK	0.9095 ± 0.2092	0.9177 ± 0.2221
LK	0.8975 ± 0.2163	0.9053 ± 0.2240
Spleen	0.9593 ± 0.0417	0.9704 ± 0.0663
Pancreas	0.8575 ± 0.0529	0.9468 ± 0.0526
Aorta	0.9383 ± 0.0249	0.9744 ± 0.0544
IVC	0.8781 ± 0.0963	0.8855 ± 0.1254
RAG	0.6907 ± 0.1533	0.8383 ± 0.1684
LAG	0.6578 ± 0.2009	0.7876 ± 0.2228
Gallbladder	0.7165 ± 0.3546	0.7225 ± 0.3632
Esophagus	0.8189 ± 0.1200	0.9199 ± 0.1187
Stomach	0.8959 ± 0.1647	0.9288 ± 0.1563
Duodenum	0.7672 ± 0.1281	0.9139 ± 0.0872
Mean	0.8429 ± 0.1043	0.8990 ± 0.0755

4.3   Qualitative Results on Validation Set

Figure 5 illustrates the example segmentation results of the baseline FSL model and the proposed method from the MICCAI FLARE 2022 validation set. Whereas baseline and proposed methods yield satisfactory results for routine contrast-enhanced CT images and healthy organs, the proposed method shows better results for CT with noise and non-portal contrast phases and lesion-affected organs. However, the proposed fails in some cases with large lesions or out-of-distribution diseases such as hiatal hernia or large amounts of ascites.

4.4   Segmentation Efficiency Results on Validation Set

The segmentation efficiency results are acquired in the private testing environment of the MICCAI FLARE 2022 challenge (Table 5). In the validation set, the mean running time of the proposed method is 28.89 s with a range of 24.77–48.43 s. The maximum GPU memory usage is 2025 MB for all cases. The areas

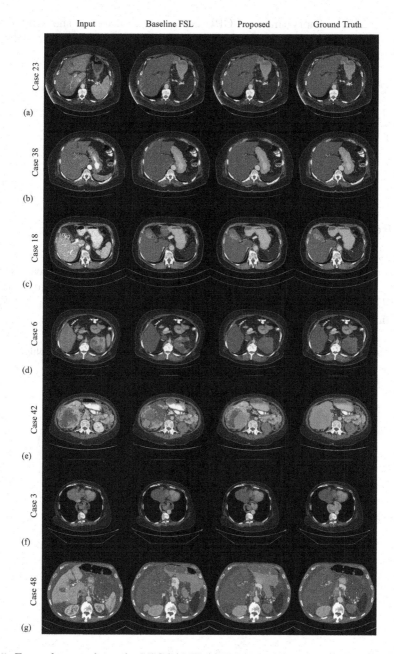

Fig. 5. Example cases from the MICCAI FLARE 2022 validation set. The first column is the CT image, the last column is the ground truth, and the second and third columns show the segmentation by the baseline fully supervised model and the proposed method, respectively. Descriptions for each row are as follows: (a) noisy image, (b) arterial phase contrast CT, (c) gallstones, (d) left kidney tumor, (e) large right kidney tumor, (f) hiatal hernia, and (g) large amounts of ascites.

under the GPU memory-time and CPU utilization-time curves shows a mean of 27167 MB·s and 596.95 %·s, respectively, and a range of 25890–37132 MB·s and 466.76-990.31 %·s, respectively.

Table 5. Testing environments in MICCAI FLARE 2022 challenge.

Windows/Ubuntu version	Ubuntu 20.04
CPU	Intel® Xeon(R) W-2133 CPU @ 3.60 GHz × 12
RAM	32G (Available memory 28G)
GPU	NVIDIA QUADRO RTX5000 (16G)

4.5   Results on Test Set

The proposed method ranked 10th in the MICCAI FLARE 2022 test phase. The segmentation results showed a mean DSC of 0.8520 ± 0.0987 and a mean NSD of 0.9137 ± 0.0666 (Table 6). The mean running time was 28.16 s. The areas under the GPU memory-time and CPU utilization-time curves showed a mean of 23092 MB·s and 575 %·s, respectively.

Table 6. Segmentation results in the MICCAI FLARE 2022 test phase.

Organ	DSC	NSD
Liver	0.9763 ± 0.0154	0.9859 ± 0.0244
RK	0.9332 ± 0.1672	0.9471 ± 0.1742
LK	0.9420 ± 0.1179	0.9542 ± 0.1306
Spleen	0.9471 ± 0.1386	0.9634 ± 0.1445
Pancreas	0.8204 ± 0.1002	0.9281 ± 0.0961
Aorta	0.9375 ± 0.0469	0.9748 ± 0.0634
IVC	0.8850 ± 0.0858	0.9050 ± 0.0991
RAG	0.7338 ± 0.1200	0.8808 ± 0.1429
LAG	0.7135 ± 0.1361	0.8559 ± 0.1488
Gallbladder	0.7312 ± 0.3493	0.7370 ± 0.3567
Esophagus	0.7721 ± 0.1398	0.8777 ± 0.1554
Stomach	0.9254 ± 0.0947	0.9569 ± 0.0982
Duodenum	0.7587 ± 0.1177	0.9109 ± 0.1021
Mean	0.8520 ± 0.0987	0.9137 ± 0.0666

4.6   Limitations and Future Work

Although the idea of KD from SSL-based teachers can be applied to any kind of SSL design, this study only uses the cross teaching method, but there are other state-of-the-art SSL methods, including uncertainty-aware strategies [20,34]. Also, for KD, other losses than the KL divergence loss and other distillation methods such as feature-based or relation-based KD can be utilized [7]. Moreover, we only use depthwise separable convolutions to build a student model, but other efficient building blocks such as the spatial pyramid module in ESPNet [24] may be a better choice. Comparisons of different SSL designs, KD methods, and efficient network architectures should be addressed in future work.

5   Conclusion

This study combines several methods for efficient semi-supervised abdominal organ segmentation in CT. A whole-volume-based coarse-to-fine framework and depthwise separable convolutions contribute to efficiency. Cross teaching and pseudo-supervision are applied to utilize unlabeled data. Also, models with slightly different decoders further enhance the effect of cross teaching. Finally, knowledge distillation enables the joint use of model compression and semi-supervised learning. The proposed method showed mean Dice scores of 0.8429 and 0.8520 in the MICCAI FLARE 2022 validation and test sets, respectively.

Acknowledgements. The author of this paper declares that the segmentation method implemented for participation in the FLARE 2022 challenge has not used any pre-trained models or additional datasets other than those provided by the organizers. Also, the proposed solution is fully automatic without any manual intervention.

References

1. Alalwan, N., Abozeid, A., ElHabshy, A.A., Alzahrani, A.: Efficient 3d deep learning model for medical image semantic segmentation. Alex. Eng. J. **60**(1), 1231–1239 (2021)
2. Bilic, P., et al.: The liver tumor segmentation benchmark (LITS). arXiv preprint arXiv:1901.04056 (2019)
3. Chen, L.C., Papandreou, G., Kokkinos, I., Murphy, K., Yuille, A.L.: DeepLab: Semantic image segmentation with deep convolutional nets, Atrous convolution, and fully connected CRFs. IEEE Trans. Pattern Anal. Mach. Intell. **40**(4), 834–848 (2017)
4. Chen, X., Yuan, Y., Zeng, G., Wang, J.: Semi-supervised semantic segmentation with cross pseudo supervision. In: Proceedings of the IEEE/CVF Conference on Computer Vision and Pattern Recognition, pp. 2613–2622 (2021)
5. Çiçek, Ö., Abdulkadir, A., Lienkamp, S.S., Brox, T., Ronneberger, O.: 3D U-net: learning dense volumetric segmentation from sparse annotation. In: Ourselin, S., Joskowicz, L., Sabuncu, M.R., Unal, G., Wells, W. (eds.) MICCAI 2016. LNCS, vol. 9901, pp. 424–432. Springer, Cham (2016). https://doi.org/10.1007/978-3-319-46723-8_49
6. Clark, K., et al.: The cancer imaging archive (TCIA): maintaining and operating a public information repository. J. Digit. Imaging **26**(6), 1045–1057 (2013)
7. Gou, J., Yu, B., Maybank, S.J., Tao, D.: Knowledge distillation: a survey. Int. J. Comput. Vision **129**(6), 1789–1819 (2021)
8. Heller, N., et al.: The state of the art in kidney and kidney tumor segmentation in contrast-enhanced CT imaging: results of the kits19 challenge. Med. Image Anal. **67**, 101821 (2021)

9. Heller, N., et al.: An international challenge to use artificial intelligence to define the state-of-the-art in kidney and kidney tumor segmentation in ct imaging. Proc. Am. Soc. Clin. Oncol. **38**(6), 626–626 (2020)

10. Hinton, G., Vinyals, O., Dean, J., et al.: Distilling the knowledge in a neural network. arXiv preprint arXiv:1503.02531 2(7) (2015)

11. Howard, A.G., et al.: Mobilenets: Efficient convolutional neural networks for mobile vision applications. arXiv preprint arXiv:1704.04861 (2017)

12. Hu, J., Shen, L., Sun, G.: Squeeze-and-excitation networks. In: Proceedings of the IEEE Conference on Computer Vision and Pattern Recognition, pp. 7132–7141 (2018)

13. Isensee, F., Jaeger, P.F., Kohl, S.A., Petersen, J., Maier-Hein, K.H.: NNU-net: a self-configuring method for deep learning-based biomedical image segmentation. Nat. Methods **18**(2), 203–211 (2021)

14. Isensee, F., Maier-Hein, K.H.: An attempt at beating the 3d u-net. arXiv preprint arXiv:1908.02182 (2019)

15. Kavur, A.E., et al.: Chaos challenge-combined (CT-MR) healthy abdominal organ segmentation. Med. Image Anal. **69**, 101950 (2021)

16. Lin, T.Y., Goyal, P., Girshick, R., He, K., Dollár, P.: Focal loss for dense object detection. In: Proceedings of the IEEE International Conference on Computer Vision, pp. 2980–2988 (2017)

17. Liu, Y., Chen, K., Liu, C., Qin, Z., Luo, Z., Wang, J.: Structured knowledge distillation for semantic segmentation. In: Proceedings of the IEEE/CVF Conference on Computer Vision and Pattern Recognition, pp. 2604–2613 (2019)

18. Luo, X., Chen, J., Song, T., Wang, G.: Semi-supervised medical image segmentation through dual-task consistency. In: Proceedings of the AAAI Conference on Artificial Intelligence, vol. 35, pp. 8801–8809 (2021)

19. Luo, X., Hu, M., Song, T., Wang, G., Zhang, S.: Semi-supervised medical image segmentation via cross teaching between cnn and transformer. arXiv preprint arXiv:2112.04894 (2021)

20. Luo, X., et al.: Efficient semi-supervised gross target volume of nasopharyngeal carcinoma segmentation via uncertainty rectified pyramid consistency. In: de Bruijne, M., et al. (eds.) MICCAI 2021. LNCS, vol. 12902, pp. 318–329. Springer, Cham (2021). https://doi.org/10.1007/978-3-030-87196-3_30

21. Ma, J., et al.: Loss odyssey in medical image segmentation. Med. Image Anal. **71**, 102035 (2021)

22. Ma, J., et al.: Fast and low-GPU-memory abdomen CT organ segmentation: the flare challenge. Med. Image Anal. **82**, 102616 (2022). https://doi.org/10.1016/j.media.2022.102616

23. Ma, J., et al.: Abdomenct-1k: is abdominal organ segmentation a solved problem? IEEE Trans. Pattern Anal. Mach. Intell. **44**(10), 6695–6714 (2022)

24. Mehta, S., Rastegari, M., Caspi, A., Shapiro, L., Hajishirzi, H.: ESPNet: efficient spatial pyramid of dilated convolutions for semantic segmentation. In: Ferrari, V., Hebert, M., Sminchisescu, C., Weiss, Y. (eds.) ECCV 2018. LNCS, vol. 11214, pp. 561–580. Springer, Cham (2018). https://doi.org/10.1007/978-3-030-01249-6_34

25. Milletari, F., Navab, N., Ahmadi, S.A.: V-net: Fully convolutional neural networks for volumetric medical image segmentation. In: 2016 Fourth International Conference on 3D Vision (3DV), pp. 565–571. IEEE (2016)

26. Qin, D., et al.: Efficient medical image segmentation based on knowledge distillation. IEEE Trans. Med. Imaging **40**(12), 3820–3831 (2021)

27. Rundo, L., et al.: Use-net: incorporating squeeze-and-excitation blocks into u-net for prostate zonal segmentation of multi-institutional mri datasets. Neurocomputing **365**, 31–43 (2019)

28. Simpson, A.L., et al.: A large annotated medical image dataset for the development and evaluation of segmentation algorithms. arXiv preprint arXiv:1902.09063 (2019)

29. Soffer, S., Ben-Cohen, A., Shimon, O., Amitai, M.M., Greenspan, H., Klang, E.: Convolutional neural networks for radiologic images: a radiologist's guide. Radiology **290**(3), 590–606 (2019)

30. Taha, A.A., Hanbury, A.: Metrics for evaluating 3d medical image segmentation: analysis, selection, and tool. BMC Med. Imaging **15**(1), 1–28 (2015)

31. Thaler, F., Payer, C., Bischof, H., Stern, D.: Efficient multi-organ segmentation using spatial configuration-net with low GPU memory requirements. arXiv preprint arXiv:2111.13630 (2021)

32. Wang, L., Yoon, K.J.: Knowledge distillation and student-teacher learning for visual intelligence: a review and new outlooks. IEEE Trans. Pattern Anal. Mach. Intell. **44**, 3048–3068 (2021)

33. Wu, Y., Xu, M., Ge, Z., Cai, J., Zhang, L.: Semi-supervised left atrium segmentation with mutual consistency training. In: de Bruijne, M., et al. (eds.) MICCAI 2021. LNCS, vol. 12902, pp. 297–306. Springer, Cham (2021). https://doi.org/10.1007/978-3-030-87196-3_28

34. Yu, L., Wang, S., Li, X., Fu, C.-W., Heng, P.-A.: Uncertainty-aware self-ensembling model for semi-supervised 3d left atrium segmentation. In: Shen, D., et al. (eds.) MICCAI 2019. LNCS, vol. 11765, pp. 605–613. Springer, Cham (2019). https://doi.org/10.1007/978-3-030-32245-8_67

35. Zhang, F., Wang, Y., Yang, H.: Efficient context-aware network for abdominal multi-organ segmentation. arXiv preprint arXiv:2109.10601 (2021)

Uncertainty-Guided Self-learning Framework for Semi-supervised Multi-organ Segmentation

Natália Alves$^{(\boxtimes)}$ and Bram de Wilde

Diagnostic Image Analysis Group, Department of Medical Imaging, Radboud University Medical Center, 6500 HB Nijmegen, The Netherlands
{natalia.alves,bram.dewilde}@radboudumc.nl

Abstract. Automatic multi-organ segmentation in medical imaging has important clinical applications, but manual voxel-level annotations are time and labour-consuming, limiting the annotated data available for training. We propose an uncertainty-guided framework for multi-organ segmentation on CT scans that uses a small labelled dataset to leverage a large unlabelled dataset in a semi-supervised setting. First, we train five models to segment 13 abdominal organs using 50 manually labelled training cases and 5-fold cross-validation. Then, we use these models to generate pseudo-labels for 2000 unlabelled cases and estimate the uncertainty associated with the pseudo-labels by calculating the pairwise Dice score (DSC) for the five individual predictions. Cases with pairwise mean DSC>0.9 for all organs are included in the training set at the next iteration, together with the respective pseudo-labels. This process is repeated for four iterations. All selected cases are combined in the last iteration, and a single model is trained to reduce the computational costs associated with ensembling. The self-configuring method for biomedical image segmentation nnU-Net was used to train the segmentation models. We obtained a mean DSC of 0.8388 on the validation set with the network trained using the labelled data alone. The Dice score improved to 0.8874 in the final iteration of the model, trained with the 50 labelled cases and 1813 unlabelled cases with pseudo-labels. On the final test set, the mean DSC was 0.8685, and the mean inference time per case was 42 s. All code is open-source and available on GitHub (https://github.com/DIAGNijmegen/flare22-brananas).

Keywords: Semi-supervised learning · Uncertainty · Pseudo-labeling

1 Introduction

Abdominal organ segmentation on medical images has many important applications, such as organ quantification, surgical planning, and disease diagnosis. Recently, deep learning models, in particular convolutional neural networks (CNNs), have shown outstanding performance at abdominal organ segmentation across different datasets and image modalities [5]. CNNs require large-scale

J. Ma and B. Wang (Eds.): FLARE 2022, LNCS 13816, pp. 116–127, 2022.
https://doi.org/10.1007/978-3-031-23911-3_11

labelled datasets for model training to generalise well to unseen cohorts. However, the manual voxel-level annotation of multiple abdominal organs is time-consuming and labour-intensive, limiting the number of samples available for training.

Semi-supervised learning (SSL) is a training strategy that uses a small amount of labelled data to leverage a large amount of unlabelled data [11]. In the medical domain, popular SSL techniques include transfer learning from a distant or related task, contrastive learning, and self-supervised representation learning with automatically generated labels [1]. A common approach for semi-supervised medical image segmentation is self-training, which consists of generating automatic pseudo-labels for the unlabelled data using the available annotated cases [1]. In particular, a segmentation CNN is first trained on the labelled samples, the trained model then segments the unlabelled samples, and finally, these samples, or a subset of these samples, are added to the training set. This process can be repeated several times, improving the pseudo-labels generated for the unlabelled data.

An inherent risk of the self-training method is the generation of low-quality pseudo-labels, which can lead to noisy training and poor generalisation. In order to lower this risk, only the most accurate pseudo-labels should be added to the training set at each iteration. This can be done, for example, by selecting the unlabelled cases with the most confident softmax output predictions. However, due to poor calibration of neural networks, wrong predictions can have high confidence, leading to the selection of low-quality pseudo-labels [9]. A more robust method also incorporates uncertainty quantification into the selection method. In a recent study, Rizve et al. propose an uncertainty-aware pseudo-label selection framework for natural image classification tasks, which improves pseudo-labelling accuracy by drastically reducing the amount of noise encountered in the training process [9].

In this work, we combine the state-of-the-art self-configuring method for biomedical image segmentation nnU-Net [5] with deep-ensemble uncertainty estimation [6] to build a self-learning framework that leverages prediction uncertainty to guide the pseudo-label selection procedure.

2 Method

2.1 Preprocessing

The proposed solution is based on the nnU-Net self-configuring framework for medical image segmentation [5]. All images are resampled to a resolution of $1.2 \times 1.2 \times 4$ mm^3. No other preprocessing is performed before training with the nnU-Net framework [5]. The framework calculates the global mean and standard deviation of the training dataset and applies z-score normalization to each instance, followed by clipping to the 0.5 and 99.5 percentiles. This framework applies its own cropping and intensity normalization strategies. The framework zero-pads patches to $40 \times 224 \times 192$ if needed.

2.2   Proposed Method

The network architecture is the 3D full resolution variant of the nnU-Net framework [5], which is illustrated in Fig. 1. The loss function is the sum of Dice and Cross Entropy loss, as employed by default by nnU-Net.

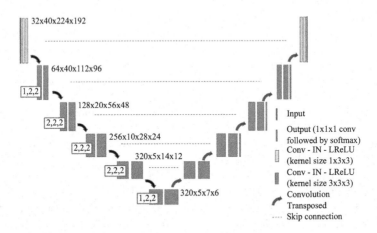

Fig. 1. 3D U-Net variant automatically selected by the nnU-Net framework, when applying it to the labelled data (see Sect. 3.1) resampled to $1.2 \times 1.2 \times 4$ mm^3.

For training, we propose an iterative uncertainty-guided process to generate pseudo-labels for the 2000 unlabelled cases in the dataset. Initially, we train 5 models for 1000 epochs each with the 50 labelled cases using 5-fold cross validation. All models do individual inference on the 2000 unlabelled cases, which allows us to evaluate uncertainty for each case. The uncertainty metric we use is the mean pairwise DSC per organ considering the 5 individual models, $\overline{DSC_i}$, given by Equation (1). Here, i is the organ index and S_{ig} is a segmentation of organ i by model g. Instead of using all 2000 cases for the next training iteration, we discard cases where the mean pairwise DSC is below 0.9 for at least one organ ($\min_i \overline{DSC_i} < 0.9$). In the next iteration, we train 5 models again using 5-fold cross validation, but now combining the 50 annotated cases with the pseudo-labelled cases that passed the uncertainty criterion. These pseudo-labels are the ensemble of the predictions generated by the 5 individual models. This process is continued for three iterations, after which we train a single model on all cases which pass the uncertainty threshold. The framework is depicted in Fig. 2.

$$\overline{DSC_i} = \frac{1}{10} \sum_{g=1}^{4} \sum_{h=g+1}^{5} DSC(S_{ig}, S_{ih}) \tag{1}$$

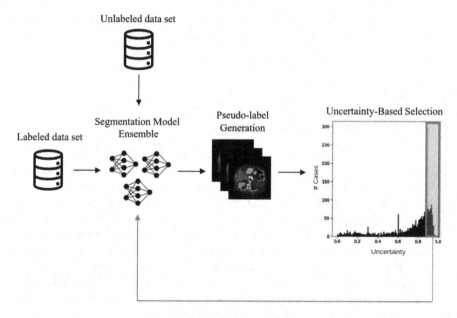

Fig. 2. Overview of the uncertainty-guided self-learning framework. A segmentation model ensemble is trained with a labeled data set. The ensemble generates pseudo-labels and using uncertainty all cases are ranked. A subset of cases which pass an uncertainty criterion (green rectangle) are used in a new training iteration, along with their pseudo-labels. (Color figure online)

2.3 Post-processing

The inference is performed with a modified version of the nnU-Net framework. In particular, we increase the step size of strided inference from 0.5 to 0.9. This reduces the amount of 3D patches that have to pass through the network, reducing GPU time by a factor of 2. Additionally, we disable test-time augmentation to reduce GPU time by a factor of 2.5, as we observed modest gains in performance.

For post-processing, we start by correcting small noisy segmentations by removing all structures with a volume lower than the minimum volume for that organ in the labelled training set multiplied by 0.5. Then, we perform binary closing to the left and right adrenal gland masks with a $5 \times 5 \times 5$ kernel to connect any separate components on these small structures. We then mask the whole multi-organ segmentation based on the aorta, inferior vena cava and esophagus predictions to remove noisy labels outside the abdominal region. All slices above the first slice containing at least one of these structures and all slices below the last slice containing at least one of these structures are set to 0. We observed that lesions in the liver were often wrongly segmented as gallbladder, driving down the Dice for both structures. To correct this issue, we check every separate connected component segmented as gallbladder and if it is completely contained within the liver on any 2D slice (in the axial plane), we set the component to liver. Finally, to further remove smaller noisy structures, for every organ we remove any connected component with a volume smaller than 10 % of the whole segmented volume for that organ.

3   Experiments

3.1   Dataset and Evaluation Measures

The FLARE 2022 challenge is an extension of the FLARE 2021 [7] with more segmentation targets and more diverse abdomen CT scans. The dataset is curated from more than 20 medical groups under the license permission, including MSD [10], KiTS [3,4], AbdomenCT-1K [8], and TCIA [2]. The training set includes 50 labelled CT scans with pancreas disease and 2000 unlabelled CT scans with liver, kidney, spleen, or pancreas diseases. The validation set includes 50 CT scans with liver, kidney, spleen, or pancreas diseases. The testing set includes 200 CT scans where 100 cases have liver, kidney, spleen, or pancreas diseases and the other 100 cases have uterine corpus endometrial, urothelial bladder, stomach, sarcomas, or ovarian diseases. All the CT scans only have image information and the center information is not available.

The evaluation measures consist of two accuracy measures: Dice Similarity Coefficient (DSC) and Normalized Surface Dice (NSD), and three running efficiency measures: running time, area under GPU memory-time curve, and area under CPU utilization-time curve. All measures will be used to compute the ranking. Moreover, the GPU memory consumption has a 2 GB tolerance.

3.2   Implementation Details

Environment Settings. The development environments and requirements are presented in Table 1.

Table 1. Development environments and requirements.

Ubuntu version	20.04
CPU	Intel(R) Xeon(R) Gold 6152 CPU @ 2.10 GHz (9 cores)
RAM	30 GB
GPU (number and type)	1 NVIDIA RTX 2080 Ti
CUDA version	11.3 with cudnn 8
Programming language	Python 3.9
Deep learning framework	PyTorch (Torch 1.11, torchvision 0.12, apex 0.1)
Specific dependencies	nnunet

Training Protocols. The data augmentation strategy is determined automatically by the nnU-Net framework. Patch sampling during training is done randomly and the models we choose for inference are always the final checkpoints after 1000 training epochs. More details are provided in Table 2.

Table 2. Training protocol

Network initialization	"he" normal initialization
Batch size	2
Patch size	$40 \times 224 \times 192$
Total epochs	1000
Optimizer	SGD with nesterov momentum ($\mu = 0.99$)
Loss function	Dice + CE
Initial learning rate (lr)	0.01
Lr decay schedule	Exponentially decaying (poly lr)
Training time	1000 h hours

4 Results and Discussion

4.1 Quantitative Results on Validation and Test Set

The validation DSC scores for various experiments are shown in Table 3. The results from iterations 1–3 were obtained by ensambling the models trained with 5-fold cross-validation, while for iteration 4 only one model was trained using the selected training set. We can make a few observations regarding the use of the unlabelled data. Firstly, using all 2000 cases after training on only the annotated data improves performance by about 2%. Secondly, using uncertainty to select a subset of cases improves performance by an additional 1%. Lastly, continuing this iterative process leads to another 1% increase in performance.

Table 3. Validation DSC per iteration

Configuration	DSC
Iteration 0 (50)	0.8388
Unfiltered iteration 1 (50 + 2000)	0.8566
Iteration 1 (50 + 401)	0.8658
Iteration 2 (50 + 1213)	0.8769
Iteration 3 (50 + 1628)	0.8761
Iteration 4 (50 + 1813)	0.8784
Iteration 4 + post-processing	0.8874

No further iterations were performed, because no improvement in performance was observed that warranted spending extra computational resources.

The results for each organ in the best performing iteration are shown in Table 4, for both the validation and test set. The worst performing organs were the adrenal glands, followed by the duodenum and the gallbladder. One explanation for this could be that down-sampling to the chosen spacing of $1.2 \times 1.2 \times 4$ mm^3 was too aggressive for these small structures, removing necessary information for an accurate segmentation. In general, overall performance was a bit worse on the test set, with mainly the esophagus being segmented less accurately. Interestingly, both the adrenal glands have a slightly higher DSC in the test set.

Table 4. Validation and test DSC per organ for Iteration 4 with post-processing

Organ	Validation DSC	Test DSC
Liver	0.9721	0.9513
Right Kidney	0.9374	0.9188
Spleen	0.9565	0.9303
Pancreas	0.8825	0.8339
Aorta	0.9543	0.9333
Inferior Vena Cava	0.8988	0.8867
Right Adrenal Gland	0.7962	0.8051
Left Adrenal Gland	0.7933	0.8095
Gallbladder	0.8265	0.8303
Esophagus	0.8650	0.8085
Stomach	0.9141	0.9016
Duodenum	0.8059	0.7656
Left Kidney	0.9331	0.9149
Overall	0.8874	0.8685

4.2   Qualitative Results

Figure 3 shows the segmentations obtained across different model iterations and Fig. 4 depicts the effect of the post-processing step. From Fig. 3 we can see the clear improvement in segmentation quality for structures like the right kidney (Case 0002), the duodenum (Case 0042) and the left kidney (Case 0006) with the increasing model iterations. These improvements indicate that the model is generating better-quality pseudo-label for the unlabelled portion of the training set at each iteration, which in turn increases the model's generalization power and the performance on the separate validation set. There are however still structures that are incorrectly segmented or not detected at all after iteration 4. We observe that this is more often the case with small structures, due to the aggressive re-sampling performed in the pre-processing step. This can be seen in Fig. 3, where for case 0002 the gallbladder and duodenum are missed at every iteration, while large structures such as the liver, stomach and kidneys are accurately segmented. We also observe that the model has difficulties in defining the boundaries of abnormal organs, especially for cases with kidney and spleen disease. This is depicted in Fig. 3, where for case 0042 a significant portion of the enlarged, diseased right kidney gets classified as liver. One possible reason for these results is that the labelled training set only contains cases with pancreas disease, leading to the generation of noisy pseudo-labels for the cases with other diseases in the training set. Another common mistake we observed was the segmentation of liver lesions as gallbladder. To overcome this issue, at post-processing all liver-enclosed components segmented as gallbladder are re-classified as liver, as is shown in Fig. 4.

To give an impression of the cases that are excluded from new iterations by the uncertainty criterion, a few representative examples are shown in Fig. 5. In the left case, there is a big artifact, which explains the high uncertainty between models. In the right case, all organs are segmented well, except the gallbladder. In this case, it is segmented in two places and far outside the liver. In both these cases the uncertainty criterion works well, because pseudo-label quality is not sufficient for model training. The middle case is an example where there is no clear reason for high uncertainty, but which is still excluded by the criterion.

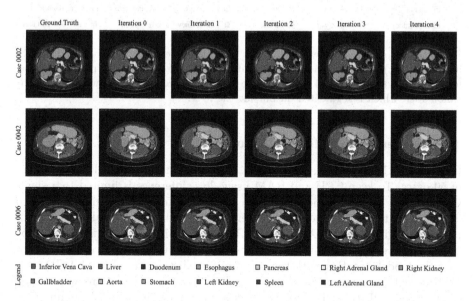

Fig. 3. Segmentation results across model iterations. Clear improvement in segmentation quality are visible for structures like the right kidney (Case 0002), the duodenum (Case 0042) and the left kidney (Case 0006) with the increasing model iterations. However, the model still struggles with the segmentation of small structures (gallbladder and duodenum for Case 0002) and diseased organs (right kidney for Case 0042).

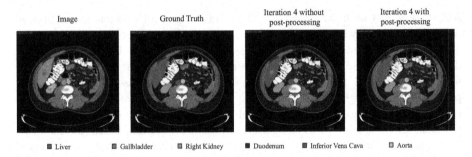

Image   Ground Truth   Iteration 4 without   Iteration 4 with
                                     post-processing   post-processing

■ Liver   ■ Gallbladder   ■ Right Kidney   ■ Duodenum   ■ Inferior Vena Cava   ☐ Aorta

Fig. 4. Effect of post-processing. After iteration 4 the model wrongly segments the liver lesion as gallbladder. This is corrected with the post-processing step.

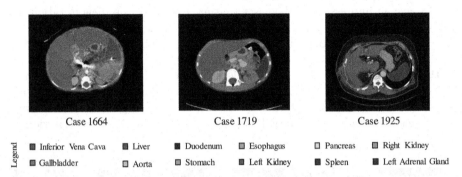

Case 1664   Case 1719   Case 1925

Legend

■ Inferior Vena Cava   ■ Liver   ■ Duodenum   ☐ Esophagus   ☐ Pancreas   ■ Right Kidney
■ Gallbladder   ☐ Aorta   ☐ Stomach   ■ Left Kidney ■ Spleen   ■ Left Adrenal Gland

Fig. 5. Examples of cases which did not pass the uncertainty criterion in the final iteration. (left) A case with a severe artifact, (middle) a case with no clear reason for high uncertainty, (right) a case where all organs are segmented well, except the gallbladder, which is segmented far outside the liver.

4.3   Segmentation Efficiency Results

CPU and RAM usage are shown in Fig. 6, for inference on the full validation set of 50 cases. To keep CPU and RAM usage low, inference is limited to a single CPU thread. The GPU memory usage for a single case is shown in Fig. 7 and is approximately 2.7 GB during inference. There is a short peak of 6 GB for the first predicted patch. About 1.3 GB on our testing machine is allocated by NVIDIA drivers, as is visible in the graph at the end of inference. This means that the model, together with the patches it predicts, takes about 1.4 GB.

Different combination of step size and test-time augmentations were tested to minimize GPU time. The ablation results are shown in Table 5. The minimum GPU time was achieved with a step size of 0.9 and no test-time augmentation, with minimal impact on the final segmentation accuracy. This was the selected configuration for the final model. Complete prediction of the validation set of 50 cases takes 22 min, meaning that on average the inference time per case is 26.4 s.

In the test cohort of 200 cases, the mean time per case was 42 s. The difference with the mean time on the validation set could be attributed to a different validation and test environment, or perhaps on average bigger CT volumes in the test set. The area under the GPU memory-time curve and CPU memory-time curve were 7958 and 783, respectively, on the test set.

4.4   Limitations and Future Work

Currently, inference is done with the standard nnU-Net framework. This framework is not optimized for low GPU (<2GB) and low RAM (<28GB) environments. This may be improved with a custom inference pipeline, for example including ONNX runtime.

Apart from inference, the training process is very expensive in terms of GPU compute. This is because every iteration requires 5 models to be trained, each consuming roughly 40 GPU hours. The easiest way to improve this is to train each iteration for fewer epochs than the standard 1000 epochs of nnU-Net. Especially for the earlier model iterations it may not be as crucial to train for many epochs, but this has to be explored.

In this paper, we use the mean pairwise DSC per organ as uncertainty metric and propose a threshold of 0.9. For both of these, alternatives are possible, but

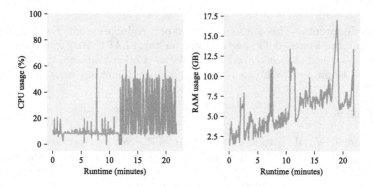

Fig. 6. The CPU utilization (left) and RAM (right) over time for a typical inference session.

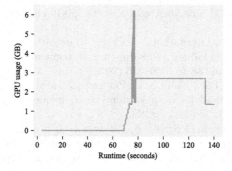

Fig. 7. The GPU memory usage over time a single case.

Table 5. Ablation study for inference step size and test-time augmentation.

Step size	TTA	DSC	GPU time (s)
0.9	No	0.8848	56
0.9	Yes	0.8860	102
0.5	No	0.8663	129
0.5	Yes	0.8874	284

have not been explored yet. Especially the threshold is interesting to investigate, as it determines the amount of samples per iteration.

5 Conclusion

Uncertainty-guided selection of pseudo-labels can improve the< performance of semi-supervised deep learning for multi-organ segmentation on CT. The proposed framework improves segmentation accuracy by 4% compared to not using unlabelled data at all and by 2% compared to using all unlabelled data without selection.

Acknowledgements. The authors of this paper declare that the segmentation method they implemented for participation in the FLARE 2022 challenge has not used any pre-trained models nor additional datasets other than those provided by the organizers. The proposed solution is fully automatic without any manual intervention.

References

1. Cheplygina, V., de Bruijne, M., Pluim, J.P.: Not-so-supervised: a survey of semi-supervised, multi-instance, and transfer learning in medical image analysis. Med. Image Anal. **54**, 280–296 (2019). https://doi.org/10.1016/j.media.2019.03.009, https://www.sciencedirect.com/science/article/pii/S1361841518307588
2. Clark, K., et al.: The cancer imaging archive (TCIA): maintaining and operating a public information repository. J. Digit. Imaging **26**(6), 1045–1057 (2013)
3. Heller, N., et al.: The state of the art in kidney and kidney tumor segmentation in contrast-enhanced CT imaging: results of the kits19 challenge. Med. Image Anal. **67**, 101821 (2021)
4. Heller, N., et al.: An international challenge to use artificial intelligence to define the state-of-the-art in kidney and kidney tumor segmentation in ct imaging. Proc. Am. Soc. Clin. Oncol. **38**(6), 626–626 (2020)
5. Isensee, F., Jaeger, P.F., Kohl, S.A., Petersen, J., Maier-Hein, K.H.: NNU-net: a self-configuring method for deep learning-based biomedical image segmentation. Nat. Methods **18**(2), 203–211 (2021)
6. Lakshminarayanan, B., Pritzel, A., Blundell, C.: Simple and scalable predictive uncertainty estimation using deep ensembles. In: Guyon, I., et al. (eds.) Advances in Neural Information Processing Systems, vol. 30. Curran Associates, Inc. (2017). https://proceedings.neurips.cc/paper/2017/file/9ef2ed4b7fd2c810847ffa5fa85bce38-Paper.pdf

7. Ma, J., et al.: Fast and low-GPU-memory abdomen CT organ segmentation: the flare challenge. Med. Image Anal. **82**, 102616 (2022). https://doi.org/10.1016/j.media.2022.102616

8. Ma, J., et al.: Abdomenct-1k: is abdominal organ segmentation a solved problem? IEEE Trans. Pattern Anal. Mach. Intell. **44**(10), 6695–6714 (2022)

9. Rizve, M.N., Duarte, K., Rawat, Y.S., Shah, M.: In defense of pseudo-labeling: an uncertainty-aware pseudo-label selection framework for semi-supervised learning. arXiv preprint arXiv:2101.06329 (2021)

10. Simpson, A.L., B., et al.: A large annotated medical image dataset for the development and evaluation of segmentation algorithms. arXiv preprint arXiv:1902.09063 (2019)

11. Zhou, Z.H.: A brief introduction to weakly supervised learning. Natl. Sci. Rev. **5**(1), 44–53 (2017). https://doi.org/10.1093/nsr/nwx106

A Noisy nnU-Net Student
for Semi-supervised Abdominal Organ Segmentation

Gregor Koehler[1,2(✉)] , Fabian Isensee[1,2,3] , and Klaus Maier-Hein[1,2]

[1] German Cancer Research Center (DKFZ), Heidelberg, Germany
g.koehler@dkfz.de
[2] Division of Medical Image Computing, German Cancer Research Center, Heidelberg, Germany
[3] HI Applied Computer Vision Lab, Heidelberg, Germany

Abstract. While deep learning methods have shown great potential in the context of medical image segmentation, it remains both time-consuming and expensive to collect sufficient data with expert annotations required to train large neural networks effectively. However, large amounts of unlabeled medical image data is available due to the rapid growth of digital healthcare and the increase in availability of imaging devices. This yields great potential for methods which can exploit large unlabeled image datasets to improve sample efficiency on downstream tasks with limited amounts of labeled data. At the same time, deploying such models in real-world scenarios poses some limitations in terms of model size and required compute resources during inference. The 2022 MICCAI FLARE Challenge tries to address both these aspects in a task where participants can make use of 2000 unlabeled, as well as 50 labeled images, while also measuring inference speed, CPU utilization and GPU memory as part of the evaluation metrics. In the context of this challenge, we propose a simple method to make use of unlabeled data: The noisy nnU-Net student. Here the unlabeled data is exploited through self-training, where a teacher model creates pseudo labels, which in turn are used to improve a student model of the same architecture. We show, based on results in a cross-validation and a separate held-out dataset, that this simple method yields improvements over even a strong baseline (+2 DSC), while simultaneously reducing inference time by an order of magnitude, from an average of over 500 s to roughly 50 s, and peak memory requirements by almost a factor of two.

Keywords: Organ segmentation · Self-training · Noisy student

1 Introduction

The MICCAI FLARE 2022 challenge is concerned with multi-organ segmentation from abdominal CT scans. The dataset consists of 2000 unlabeled CT

© The Author(s), under exclusive license to Springer Nature Switzerland AG 2022
J. Ma and B. Wang (Eds.): FLARE 2022, LNCS 13816, pp. 128–138, 2022.
https://doi.org/10.1007/978-3-031-23911-3_12

scans and 50 labeled CT scans. This represents a challenge often faced in practice, where medical images are readily available, but expert annotations are scarce due to their expensive and time-consuming nature. A successful method in this context has to make efficient use of the unlabeled images in addition to the labeled set. Additionally, the FLARE 2022 challenge not only evaluates via established segmentation metrics, but also measures CPU utilization and GPU memory during inference. This poses limits on the model size and pre-/post-processing used. Being able to efficiently run inference for segmentation models is often a necessary step for their application in clinical practice, where long inference times can be prohibitive. We address the challenges of this efficiency-focused semi-supervised setting by choosing a moderate architecture size paired with self-training based on noisy student training [9].

The main contributions of this work can be summarized as follows:

– We propose a simple extension to the proven nnU-Net framework using self-training with an ensemble of teacher models and a noisy student model of the same network architecture.
– With some small architecture and preprocessing adaptations, we greatly reduce the memory footprint of the proposed method, while sacrificing only little performance compared with a larger model.
– Through a lightweight inference and resampling scheme, we greatly reduce the resource requirements and inference time compared to nnU-Net.
– We evaluate the effectiveness of the proposed method in the context of the FLARE 2022 challenge, where we achieve performance improvements over even a strong baseline.

2   Method

We propose a method based on the nnU-Net framework [5]. To make use of the large unlabeled dataset, we implement noisy student training, inspired by [9], with additional fine-tuning. Additionally, we propose several inference strategies detailed in Sect. 2.3 to reduce resource consumption during inference.

2.1   Preprocessing

Following [5], we make use of the following preprocessing steps:

– Cropping the individual scans to non-zero region.
– Global dataset intensity percentile clipping and z-score normalization with global foreground mean and standard deviation.
– Resampling to median spacing for each axis.

The intensity percentile clipping and normalization based on global foreground mean and standard deviation are employed due to the CT scan values representing physical properties, which should be retained in the preprocessed state.

2.2 Proposed Method

The proposed **noisy nnU-Net student** is inspired by noisy student training [4,9], based on the nnU-Net framework [5]. Here, we distill the knowledge of an ensemble of teacher models into the student by using pseudo labels created by the teacher ensemble. In knowledge distillation, the student model is often chosen to be of smaller capacity to aid in scenarios where the teacher model is too expensive to deploy in a real-world use-case. We instead opt to use the same architecture for both teacher and student. This was shown to yield performance improvements in the context of image classification [9]. A schematic overview of the U-Net architecture used is illustrated in Fig. 1. This architecture represents a slight adaptation from the full resolution 3D nnU-Net [5,7], where the base number of convolutional filters is reduced to achieve a smaller memory footprint.

We first train the teacher model in a standard nnU-Net training scheme on the labeled portion of the FLARE 2022 challenge dataset. This results in 5 different teacher models trained in a 5-fold cross-validation. To create robust pseudo labels for the following student training, we ensemble the predictions from all 5 teacher models by averaging the softmax outputs of the individual models before creating the hard pseudo labels. For simplicity reasons, we make use of hard pseudo labels to train the student model, instead of soft labels as proposed in [9]. The student model largely follows the same setup. However we sample the training batch by using both labeled samples, as well as unlabeled samples with pseudo labels, in the same minibatch. We balance the two datasets by using 3 times as many samples from the pseudo labeled set in every minibatch. To introduce additional noise for the student, we make use of a stronger data augmentation scheme for the student training, see Sect. 3.3. In a final stage, we fine-tune the resulting model using only the labeled training cases.

2.3 Inference Optimization

Apart from the Dice Similarity Coefficient and the Normalized Surface Dice, the 2022 MICCAI FLARE challenge tracks three additional metrics related to inference resource consumption and speed, which contribute to the overall ranking. These metrics are the area under GPU memory-time curve, the area under CPU utilization-time curve, as well as the running time per sample. On top of that, the challenge requires a hard memory limit of 28 GB.

Originally, nnU-Net was not designed with these resource consumption metrics in mind, and instead aims to make efficient use of a given GPU memory setup, optimizing for a maximum of GPU memory and utilization during training to increase segmentation performance. This also impacts nnU-Net's resource consumption during inference. To adapt nnU-Net for the resource consumption metrics used in this challenge, we propose several inference strategies detailed below.

As mentioned in Sect. 2.2, we adapt the 3D nnU-Net architecture to use fewer filters per convolutional layer. This achieves a smaller memory footprint during both training and inference.

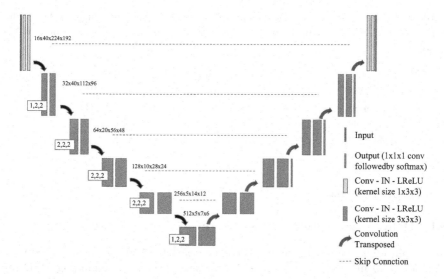

Fig. 1. Schematic of the U-Net architecture used for both the teacher and student model. It represents the network architecture proposed by nnU-Net [5], however with half the base number of features. The number of features is then progressively doubled up to the network's bottleneck.

Staying within the challenge's memory limit of 28 GB during inference on at times very large CT scans is a challenging task when using 3D segmentation networks, as the resampling of softmax outputs or segmentation maps to the desired target spacing requires a lot of memory. In this context, we switch the default order of operations usually employed by nnU-Net when creating the final segmentation maps from the network's softmax outputs. Instead of resampling the softmax outputs directly, we instead first create segmentation maps before resampling to the target spacing, as this represents a more computationally efficient operation. Additionaly, we only make use of nearest neighbor interpolation during resampling. While this might come at a segmentation performance cost, this greatly reduces the memory footprint during inference, while simultaneously reducing inference time by roughly an order of magnitude on average. The resulting resource consumption improvements are shown in Table 1. We note that without these adaptations, for 7 out of 50 validation cases, the memory limit would be surpassed. However, these improvements in resource consumption and inference time come at a small cost of increased CPU utilization.

2.4 Post-processing

We do not make use of any post-processing in the context of this challenge.

Table 1. Comparison of resource consumption metrics during inference on the validation dataset. Best results are highlighted in bold. *Seven cases resulted in peak RAM above 28 GB.

Inference metric	nnU-Net	Low-footprint nnU-Net	Noisy nnU-Net student
Mean Peak RAM	22.69 GB*	23.07 GB*	**13.78 GB**
Mean GPU memory	5.911 GB	1.834 GB	**1.722 GB**
Mean CPU utilization	**3.87%**	3.9%	4.38%
Mean inference time	535.4 s	122.3 s	**53.5 s**

3 Experiments

3.1 Dataset and Evaluation Measures

As per official challenge documentation, the FLARE2022 dataset is curated from more than 20 medical groups under the license permission, including MSD [8], KiTS [2,3], AbdomenCT-1K [6], and TCIA [1]. The training set includes 50 labeled CT scans with pancreas disease and 2000 unlabeled CT scans with liver, kidney, spleen, or pancreas diseases. The validation set includes 50 CT scans with liver, kidney, spleen, or pancreas diseases. The testing set includes 200 CT scans, where 100 cases show liver, kidney, spleen, or pancreas diseases and the other 100 cases has uterine corpus endometrial, urothelial bladder, stomach, sarcomas, or ovarian diseases. All the CT scans only have image information and the center information is not available.

The evaluation measures consist of two accuracy measures: Dice Similarity Coefficient (DSC) and Normalized Surface Dice (NSD), and three running efficiency measures: running time, area under GPU memory-time curve, and area under CPU utilization-time curve. All measures will be used to compute the ranking. Moreover, the GPU memory consumption has a 2 GB tolerance.

3.2 Dataset Splits

For model selection, we make use of a 5-fold cross-validation split, resulting in 40 training cases in each fold in the case of the labeled dataset. During the training with the joint labeled and pseudo labeled dataset, we re-use the same cross-validation splits for the labeled samples and add all pseudo labeled scans to each respective fold's training set.

3.3 Implementation Details

Environment Settings. The environments and requirements are presented in Table 2. We note that while development was done in this environment, the training runs were performed on a GPU cluster node with different hardware.

Table 2. Development environment and requirements.

Ubuntu version	Ubuntu 20.04.2 LTS
CPU	AMD Ryzen 9 3900X 12-Core CPU@3.80 GHz
RAM	4 × 16 DDR4@3.60 GHz
GPU (number and type)	1 Nvidia GeForce RTX 2080Ti 11G
CUDA version	11.3
Programming language	Python 3.9.7
Deep learning framework	Pytorch (Torch 1.10.2)
Specific dependencies	nnU-Net

Training Protocols. For training both the teacher and student model, we follow the general training protocol detailed in Table 3. However, the training protocols differ in terms of data augmentation strategies employed. For the initial teacher models, we use the data augmentation strategy described in Table 4. We make use of nnUNet's deep supervision loss based on equally weighted dice and cross-entropy loss terms.

After training the 5 teacher models to convergence, we ensemble their predictions on the unlabeled samples to create pseudo labels for the student model.

Table 3. Training protocol.

Network initialization	"he" normal initialization
Training mode	Mixed precision
Batch size	4
Patch size	40 × 224 × 192
Total epochs	1000
Optimizer	SGD with nesterov momentum ($\mu = 0.99$)
Initial learning rate (lr)	0.01
Lr decay schedule	Poly (exponent 0.9)
Training time (5 initial teacher models)	5 × 36 h
Training time (student model)	36 h
Training time (fine-tune)	2.7 h
Loss function	Combined dice and cross-entropy loss

Using the pseudo labels created by the teacher models, we then train the student model. For this training, we again follow the protocol from Table 3, but use more extensive data augmentation, as detailed in Table 5. We then select the best-performing student model based on a 5-fold cross-validation, and perform an additional fine-tuning using just the labeled training data, again following the protocol from Table 3. The resulting model is used as the final model for test set inference.

Table 4. Data augmentation strategy for the teacher model. p_{sample} refers to a probability to apply this augmentation on a sample level, while $p_{channel}$ and p_{axis} are used on a channel and axis level, respectively.

Rotation	Angle range: $[-30°, 30°]$
Scaling	Scale range: $[0.7, 1.4]$
Gaussian noise	$p_{sample} = 0.1$, $\sigma^2 = [0.0, 0.1]$
Gaussian blur	$p_{sample} = 0.2$, $p_{channel} = 0.5$, $\sigma = [0.5, 1.0]$
Brightness (multiplicative)	$p_{sample} = 0.15$, Multiplier range: $[0.75, 1.25]$
Contrast	$p_{sample} = 0.15$, Contrast range: $[0.75, 1.25]$
Simulate low resolution	$p_{sample} = 0.25$, $p_{channel} = 0.5$, Zoom range: $[0.5, 1.0]$
Gamma correction	$p_{sample} = 0.1$, Gamma range: $[0.7, 1.5]$
Mirroring	$p_{sample} = 1.0$, $p_{axis} = 0.5$

Table 5. Data augmentation strategy for the student model.

Rotation	Angle range: $[-30°, 30°]$
Scaling	Scale range: $[0.7, 1.4]$
Gaussian noise	$p_{sample} = 0.15$, $\sigma^2 = [0.0, 0.1]$
Gaussian blur	$p_{sample} = 0.2$, $p_{channel} = 0.5$, $\sigma = [0.5, 1.5]$
Brightness (multiplicative)	$p_{sample} = 0.15$, Multiplier range: $[0.7, 1.3]$
Contrast	$p_{sample} = 0.15$, Contrast range: $[0.65, 1.5]$
Simulate low resolution	$p_{sample} = 0.25$, $p_{channel} = 0.5$, Zoom range: $[0.5, 1.0]$
Gamma correction	$p_{sample} = 0.15$, Gamma range: $[0.7, 1.5]$
Mirroring	$p_{sample} = 1.0$, $p_{per_axis} = 0.5$

Testing Protocols. We use the same preprocessing as used during training and use the best student model, as determined in cross-validation, for test set inference. To reduce the memory footprint both for GPU VRAM and RAM, we predict using FP16 precision mode and don't use test-time augmentation, while also up-sampling segmentation maps using nearest neighbor interpolation, as detailed in Sect. 2.3.

4   Results and Discussion

4.1   Quantitative Results for 5-Fold Cross-Validation

We show ablation analysis results of using noisy student training for the low-footprint nnU-Net network in Table 6. In this cross-validation ablation, we can see a noticeable benefit of the proposed noisy student training regarding the mean foreground Dice score. This suggests that self-training with a noisy student can be an effective way to leverage unlabeled images in the context of medical image segmentation.

Table 6. Quantitative results for 5-fold cross-validation in terms of mean DSC. The low-footprint nnU-Net refers to the reduced architecture as shown in Fig. 1.

Training scheme	Mean foreground DSC (all classes)
Low-footprint nnU-Net	93.5 ± 0.4
Low-footprint nnU-Net (w. noisy student training)	**94.0 ± 0.4**

4.2 Quantitative Results on the Validation and Test Set

While cross-validation results yield first performance indicators, we perform a more thorough evaluation of the proposed method on 20 held-out cases. Table 7 illustrates the results on this validation set. As expected, we can observe a clear performance degradation when moving from the original architecture to the low-footprint model, which also represents one individual teacher model used for ensembling the pseudo labels. This is most likely due to the reduced capacity and lack of additional learning signal from the pseudo labeled data. We note that this low-footprint model was necessary to obtain the GPU memory consumption reported in Table 1.

However, the proposed noisy nnU-Net student is able to compensate for the reduced model capacity and even substantially improve upon the strong nnU-Net baseline. This is represented also in most individual class metrics, in both the DSC and NSD. Only the right adrenal gland shows performance which is markedly worse than the baseline.

This performance is also reflected in the held-out test set, where the proposed noisy nnU-Net student achieved 87.4 DSC and 91.68 NSD, which is in line with the validation results, if not slightly better. For this reason, we believe the validation results are a reliable indicator of general performance gains with the proposed method.

Table 7. Quantitative results on the validation dataset in terms of mean DSC/NSD per class and overall. The best results per metric are highlighted in bold.

Class	nnU-Net		Low-footprint nnU-Net		Noisy nnU-Net student	
	DSC	NSD	DSC	NSD	DSC	NSD
Liver	96.73	94.33	96.5	94.43	**97.58**	**97.43**
Right kidney	85.2	83.59	80.44	77.3	**86.61**	**85.88**
Spleen	93.87	92.25	92.45	91.16	**95.75**	**95.32**
Pancreas	82.11	91.04	83.86	92.4	**84.05**	**93.4**
Aorta	**97.13**	98.52	96.96	98.25	96.58	**98.8**
Inferior Vena Cava	87.64	87.25	87.22	87.02	**88.17**	**88.36**
Right Adrenal Gland	**85.43**	**94.95**	80.27	89.73	80.73	90.94
Left Adrenal Gland	**88.23**	96.96	82.7	91.71	88.13	**97.57**
Gallbladder	57.19	56.91	62.95	62.0	**67.18**	**66.31**
Esophagus	86.01	92.72	83.92	90.3	**88.56**	**96.16**
Stomach	87.82	88.41	80.82	84.68	**88.4**	**90.95**
Duodenum	71.94	84.83	74.07	86.74	**77.75**	**89.7**
Left Kidney	86.2	85.73	82.51	79.83	**91.13**	**91.01**
Mean	85.04	88.27	83.44	86.58	**86.97**	**90.91**

4.3   Qualitative Results

We present segmentation results on an easy, as well as a hard sample in Fig. 2. In the top row we can attest the proposed method a clear improvement over the low-footprint model without using the unlabeled data via noisy student training, while showing similar shortcomings as the original nnU-Net, as can be seen e.g. from the class confusion in the lower left side of the shown segmentation maps. As the example in the bottom row of Fig. 2 shows however, the model is still susceptible to confusing e.g. the left and right kidney. Such failure cases could potentially be decreased by more involved postprocessing and ensembling of multiple models, which in turn comes at the cost of slower inference speeds.

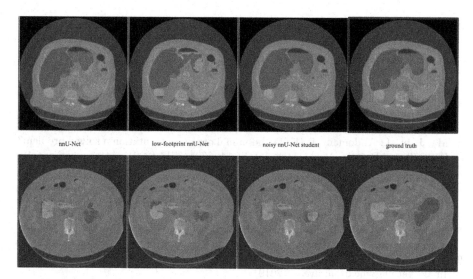

Fig. 2. Qualitative results on a rather easy (case #2, top) and a rather hard (case #23, bottom) example from the validation set. The first column shows the prediction by nnU-Net, the second column the prediction by the low-footprint model, the third column the proposed method's prediction and the fourth column shows the ground truth labels.

5   Conclusion

We conclude that the proposed method of self-training with a noisy student can lead to performance improvements even over strong baselines such as the nnU-Net [5]. While we restricted ourselves to a low memory footprint architecture, we note that performance improvements might be more pronounced when employing larger teacher and student models or longer schedules with stronger data augmentation. We also note that future work could incorporate segmentation confidence estimates in order to filter for high-confidence pseudo labels.

Acknowledgements. The authors of this paper declare that the segmentation method they implemented for participation in the FLARE 2022 challenge has not used any pre-trained models nor additional datasets other than those provided by the organizers.

References

1. Clark, K., et al.: The cancer imaging archive (TCIA): maintaining and operating a public information repository. J. Digit. Imaging **26**(6), 1045–1057 (2013)
2. Heller, N., et al.: The state of the art in kidney and kidney tumor segmentation in contrast-enhanced CT imaging: results of the kits19 challenge. Med. Image Anal. **67**, 101821 (2021)

3. Heller, N., et al.: An international challenge to use artificial intelligence to define the state-of-the-art in kidney and kidney tumor segmentation in CT imaging. Proc. Am. Soc. Clin. Oncol. **38**(6), 626–626 (2020)
4. Hinton, G., Vinyals, O., Dean, J.: Distilling the Knowledge in a Neural Network. arXiv (2015)
5. Isensee, F., Jaeger, P.F., Kohl, S.A., Petersen, J., Maier-Hein, K.H.: nnU-Net: a self-configuring method for deep learning-based biomedical image segmentation. Nat. Methods **18**(2), 203–211 (2021)
6. Ma, J., et al.: AbdomenCT-1K: Is abdominal organ segmentation a solved problem? IEEE Trans. Pattern Anal. Mach. Intell. **44**, 6695–6714 (2021). https://doi.org/10.1109/TPAMI.2021.3100536
7. Ronneberger, O., Fischer, P., Brox, T.: U-Net: convolutional networks for biomedical image segmentation. In: International Conference on Medical Image Computing and Computer-Assisted Intervention, pp. 234–241 (2015)
8. Simpson, A.L., et al.: A large annotated medical image dataset for the development and evaluation of segmentation algorithms. arXiv preprint arXiv:1902.09063 (2019)
9. Xie, Q., Luong, M.T., Hovy, E., Le, Q.V.: Self-training with Noisy Student improves ImageNet classification. arXiv (2019)

CLEF: Contrastive Learning of Equivariant Features in CT Images

Ilya Kuleshov[1]([✉]), Mikhail Goncharov[2], and Vera Soboleva[2]

[1] Moscow Institute of Physics and Technology, Dolgoprudny, Russia
kuleshov.ia@phystech.edu
[2] Skoltech Institute, Moscow, Russia

Abstract. This work focuses on developing a self-supervised method of pretraining on biomedical images. The pretrained models are then fine-tuned on a small labelled dataset. We show, that using contrastive learning along with an equivariance loss and a loss, designed by us to maximise the features' information, we manage to improve quality in comparison to a fully-supervised baseline. Our method of pretraining achieves an average dice score of 0.86, reducing the baseline error by 20%.

Keywords: Self-supervised learning · Biomedical image segmentation · Contrastive learning

1 Introduction

The biomedical datasets with labelled image are very limited due to high complexity of the process of labelling these images. This gives way to the idea of self-supervised pretraining on unlabelled images. We propose to force the learned features, corresponding to a voxel in the human body, to reflect it's anatomical location. This would guarantee high quality on the task of organ segmentation, which is the task at hand. To achieve said quality, we propose a compound, three-part loss, which would force the features to behave similarly to such a general anatomical system of coordinates.

2 Method

2.1 Preprocessing

In this section we will describe our preprocessing strategy. The transformations are as follows.

1. A mask of all voxels with intensities, greater than $-500\,\mathrm{HU}$ is generated.
2. The image is cropped to the smallest box, containing the mask, generated in the previous step.
3. The image is resized (via interpolation) to shape $(192, 192, 192)$.
4. If necessary, the axes are flipped, so that the resulting image has canonical orientation.
5. The intensities are clipped to the window $(-200, 300)$, the HU interval in which most soft tissues reside.
6. Finally, the intensities are scaled to the range $(-1, 1)$

J. Ma and B. Wang (Eds.): FLARE 2022, LNCS 13816, pp. 139–151, 2022.
https://doi.org/10.1007/978-3-031-23911-3_13

2.2 Proposed Method

Our key contribution lies in the self-supervised pretraining on the large unlabeled part of our dataset. The pretraining method utilises three losses, each accomplishing a different objective. We use the notation f_{enc} to depict the encoding part of our network, and X for the preprocessed input image.

Pretraining: Decoding Loss. Firstly, we want to ensure that the encoded features contain the information about the intensity of the original voxel. For that purpose we use the decoding head: two 1×1 convolutions, applied to the output features. We minimise the mean squared error between the output of our decoding head f_{dec} and our original image X:

$$L_{dec} = MSE(f_{dec}(f_{enc}(X)), X) = \frac{1}{N} \sum_{i,j,k} (f_{dec}(f_{enc}(X))[i, j, k] - X[i, j, k])^2$$

Pretraining: Discriminativeness Loss. We also aim to be able to guess the location of a voxel by it's features. Thus, we add a loss which forces the model to predict distinct features, such that voxels, located far apart from each other, have different representations. After getting the features of each voxel, we randomly sample a small subset of anchor voxels I_A and a large subset of leaf voxels I_L and compute the pairwise distance in feature space (negative inner product) between the anchors and the leaves D:

$$D[i_A, i_L] = -\langle X[i_A] \cdot X[i_L] \rangle; i_A \in I_A, i_L \in I_L$$

Next, for each anchor i_A, we compute the indices of the voxels which are far enough from it, $F(i_A)$. Typically, we considered voxels to be far enough from each other if the euclidean distance between them was $\geq 10\,\text{mm}$, so $F(i_A)$ can be computed as the following (we use $\|\cdot\|_{mm}$ to denote the physical distance in milimeters between voxels):

$$F(i_A) = \{i \in I_L : \|i - i_A\|_{mm} \geq 10\}$$

Finally, we apply the following activation function:

$$L_d = \sum_{i_A \in I_A} \sum_{i_L \in F(i_A)} \text{relu}(M - D[i_A, i_L]) \tag{1}$$

Here, M, margin, is a hyperpameter, we set it to -0.9 in our experiments. Such a loss forces the model to cluster features of close voxels together. The higher M is, the less is the amount of possible feature vectors, located from each other at a distance, greater than M. For example, if our feature space is a 3D sphere and $M = 0$, then there are at most 8 vectors $\{v_i\}_{i=1}^8$, which all satisfy the inequality $(v_i, v_j) \geq M$ (all of such vectors are either perpendicular to each other, or facing in opposite directions from each other).

Pretraining: Equivariance Loss. Finally, we also demand the equivariance property from our model. Although this accomplishes more or less the same task as our decoder, we decided to include this loss, as it is easily learned by the model. One of many strenghts of convolutional networks is that the object's representation is independent of it's location in the image, which implies equivariance, at least in relation to shifts. In addition to shifts, we also train our neural network to be equivariant in relation to zooming and rotation. The loss is the negative inner product between a randomly rotated, scaled and shifted representation of the original image, and the representation of the transformed image. In other words, if we denote T as our random affine transformation, X as our image, and f as our neural network, the loss is as follows:

$$L_e = -\langle T(f(X)) \cdot f(T(X)) \rangle \tag{2}$$

Finetuning. We fine-tune with a compound loss function, which is the summation between Dice loss and cross entropy loss. This kind of loss function has proven to be effective in biomedical image segmenation [4].

Architecture. We use a two-part architecture, consisting of a large, feature-extracting backbone and a small head. The backbone is a simple 3D U-Net. The head consists of two 1×1 convolutions, which we apply to the output features of the backbone. Figure 1 illustrates the applied 3D U-Net [6]. The number of channels the head outputs determines the dimensionality of our feature space in the case of pretraining, whereas in the case of fine-tuning it must be equal to the number of classes, thus when transferring weights from the pretraining model to the fine-tuning model, we transfer only the weights of the backbone U-Net, while the head is re-initialized with fresh random weights.

2.3 Post-processing

The fine-tuning predictions are passed through a sigmoid function, thus scaling to a $(0, 1)$ range. Then, for each voxel: if all of the resulting logits are less than .5, we deduce that voxel to be outside of any organs, which interest us in this task. Otherwise, that voxel is labelled with the index of the largest logit value in it's predicted vector.

3 Experiments

3.1 Dataset and Evaluation Measures

The FLARE2022 dataset is curated from more than 20 medical groups under the license permission, including MSD [7], KiTS [2,3], AbdomenCT-1K [5], and TCIA [1]. The training set includes 50 labelled CT scans with pancreas disease and 2000 unlabelled CT scans with liver, kidney, spleen, or pancreas diseases. The validation set includes 50 CT scans with liver, kidney, spleen, or pancreas

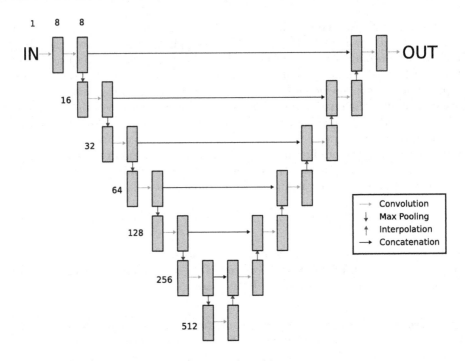

Fig. 1. Network architecture

diseases. The testing set includes 200 CT scans where 100 cases has liver, kidney, spleen, or pancreas diseases and the other 100 cases has uterine corpus endometrial, urothelial bladder, stomach, sarcomas, or ovarian diseases. All the CT scans only have image information and the center information is not available.

The evaluation measures consist of two accuracy measures: Dice Similarity Coefficient (DSC) and Normalized Surface Dice (NSD), and three running efficiency measures: running time, area under GPU memory-time curve, and area under CPU utilization-time curve. All measures will be used to compute the ranking. Moreover, the GPU memory consumption has a 2 GB tolerance.

3.2   Implementation Details

Environment Settings. The development environments and requirements are presented in Table 1.

Table 1. Development environments and requirements.

Windows/Ubuntu version	Ubuntu 18.04.5 LTS
CPU	Intel(R) Core(TM) i9-7900X CPU@3.30 GHz
RAM	16×4 GB; 2.67MT/s
GPU (number and type)	Four NVIDIA V100 16G
CUDA version	11.0
Programming language	Python 3.9
Deep learning framework	Pytorch (Torch 1.10, torchvision 0.2.2)
Specific dependencies	
(Optional) Link to code	

Training Protocols. We used no data augmentation, passing the whole $192 \times 192 \times 192$ image to the model without random cropping. The equivariance loss requires a random affine transform. We randomly sampled two of three axes, and applied a random transform in the corresponding plane. For the transform, we used a combination of a random scale in the range $(1, 1.5)$, a random shift in the range $(-0.1, 0.1)$ on each of the selected axes, and a random rotation in the range $(-30°, 30°)$ in the selected plane.

When fine-tuning, we randomly divide the 50 labeled samples into 5 folds. One of the five resulting subsets is used for validation the others are used for training. We use early stopping to stop our model from overfitting on the small dataset of labelled samples: when the loss on the validation set does not decrease for three epochs, the training stops. This results in the training being cut short after 18–22 epochs, depending on the chosen fold.

Table 2. Training protocols.

Network initialization	Default PyTorch initialization
Batch size	1
Total epochs	50
Optimizer	Adam
Initial learning rate (lr)	0.0004
Training time	15.5 h
Number of model parameters	33.0M[a]

[a] https://github.com/sksq96/pytorch-summary.

Table 3. Training protocols for the fine-tuning model (if using two-stage framework).

Network initialization	Default PyTorch initialization
Batch size	1
Total epochs	50/Early stopping
Optimizer	Adam
Initial learning rate (lr)	0.001
Training time	1–2 h
Number of model parameters	33.0M[a]

[a] https://github.com/sksq96/pytorch-summary.

4 Results and Discussion

4.1 Evaluation on the Validation Set

The self-supervised pretraining on unlabelled cases provided an improvement in comparison to a model, trained in a supervised fashion. The model works very well on clearly visible organs, which can be visually separated from their surroundings. Such organs include the liver, kidneys, the aorta and some others. Less visible organs, such as the duodenum (see Fig. 2), the pancreas (see Fig. 3), the left adrenal gland proved to be more complicated for our method, which is to be expected. But, according to Table 4, there are some isolated cases, in which highly-visible organs have lower quality. This is due to anomalies, as can be seen on Fig. 4. The average dice score after pretraining on the validation set is 0.87, which is a rather big improvement from the baseline average dice score (0.84).

Table 4. Segmentation results

	Liver	RK	Spleen	Pancreas	Aorta	IVC	RAG	LAG	GB	Esophagus	Stomach	Duodenum	LK
0	0.98	0.96	0.97	0.80	0.93	0.90	0.88	0.86	0.86	0.82	0.95	0.68	0.96
1	0.98	0.97	0.98	0.78	0.96	0.92	0.74	0.75	0.93	0.85	0.95	0.71	0.97
2	0.97	0.97	0.98	0.85	0.95	0.93	0.93	0.88	0.69	0.88	0.93	0.81	0.96
3	0.98	0.97	0.96	0.75	0.96	0.85	0.91	0.90	0.91	0.80	0.84	0.63	0.98
4	0.98	0.96	0.98	0.78	0.95	0.89	0.89	0.81	0.93	0.77	0.93	0.79	0.89
5	0.96	0.98	0.97	0.80	0.94	0.80	0.50	0.78	0.80	0.87	0.88	0.84	0.97
6	0.97	0.51	0.98	0.80	0.96	0.87	0.88	0.78	0.94	0.78	0.94	0.80	0.97
7	0.98	0.96	0.97	0.52	0.92	0.90	0.75	0.87	0.90	0.89	0.95	0.57	0.89
8	0.98	0.97	0.98	0.79	0.94	0.91	0.83	0.84	0.93	0.81	0.91	0.78	0.98
9	0.97	0.93	0.98	0.59	0.95	0.92	0.83	0.63	0.91	0.88	0.92	0.59	0.40
Mean	0.98	0.92	0.97	0.75	0.95	0.89	0.81	0.81	0.88	0.83	0.92	0.72	0.90

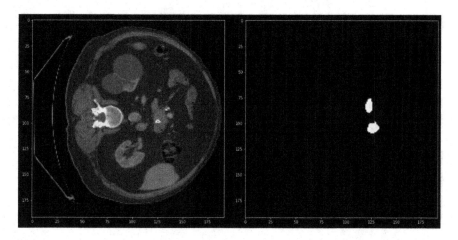

Fig. 2. A slice and the corresponding duodenum mask.

4.2 Validation Results

Here are some segmentation maps on the validation set: Subsect. 4.2, Fig. 6, Fig. 7, Fig. 8, Fig. 9. As instructed, all segmentation maps are presented in a window, centered at 40 HU, with a width of 400 HU.

4.3 Results on Final Testing Set

The results on the testing set can be seen in Table 5, they are worse than the results on the validation set, probably due to a slightly skewed distribution.

4.4 Limitation and Future Work

Our method shows great promise. Nevertheless, it can be modified in many ways. These include, but are not limited to the following.

– Adding preprocessing. This could help with artifacts that are visible on some predicted masks (see Fig. 10).
– This method could be improved by predicting several neighbouring image voxels by the MLP head, instead of a single voxel. This should help store information on the surrounding voxels in pretrained features, forcing our model to learn better features.

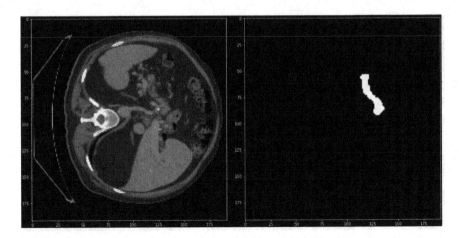

Fig. 3. A slice and the corresponding pancreas mask

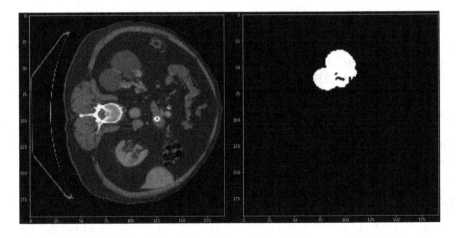

Fig. 4. An anomaly in the left kidney, image FLARE22_Tr_0045

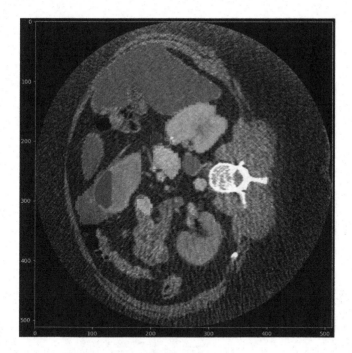

Fig. 5. Segmentation results on case 1

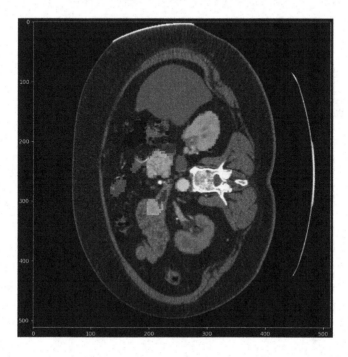

Fig. 6. Segmentation results on case 10

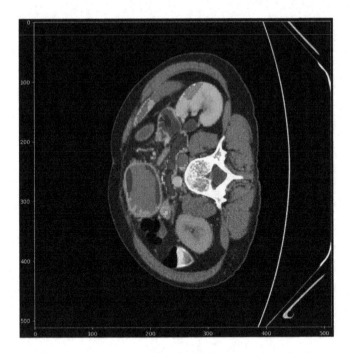

Fig. 7. Segmentation results on case 16

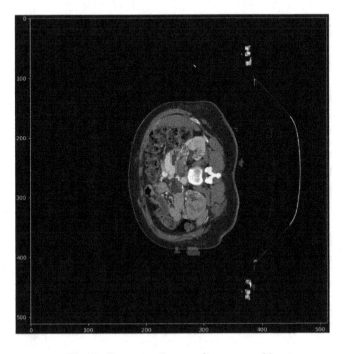

Fig. 8. Segmentation results on case 30

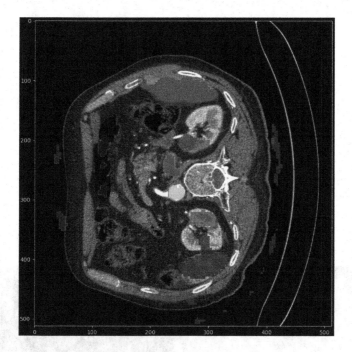

Fig. 9. Segmentation results on case 50

Table 5. Testing results

Name	Mean	STD
Liver_DSC	0.89	0.09
RK_DSC	0.84	0.21
Spleen_DSC	0.85	0.19
Pancreas_DSC	0.53	0.18
Aorta_DSC	0.81	0.12
IVC_DSC	0.73	0.12
RAG_DSC	0.02	0.04
LAG_DSC	0.01	0.1
Gallbladder_DSC	0.14	0.17
Esophagus_DSC	0.53	0.21
Stomach_DSC	0.66	0.2
Duodenum_DSC	0.47	0.19
LK_DSC	0.81	0.22
Liver_NSD	0.78	0.17
RK_NSD	0.81	0.23

(continued)

Table 5. (*continued*)

Name	Mean	STD
Spleen_NSD	0.83	0.22
Pancreas_NSD	0.61	0.17
Aorta_NSD	0.77	0.16
IVC_NSD	0.65	0.13
RAG_NSD	0.09	0.09
LAG_NSD	0.01	0.1
Gallbladder_NSD	0.16	0.17
Esophagus_NSD	0.65	0.22
Stomach_NSD	0.59	0.21
Duodenum_NSD	0.73	0.19
LK_NSD	0.76	0.24

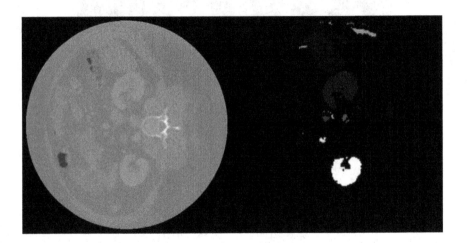

Fig. 10. Artifacts on predictions

5   Conclusion

Contrastive self-supervised pretraining helps improve quality of the resulting fine-tuned network. This means, that our pretraining method forces the backbone to learn informative features, which, at least in part, carry information on human organs.

Acknowledgements. The authors of this paper declare that the segmentation method they implemented for participation in the FLARE 2022 challenge has not used any pre-trained models nor additional datasets other than those provided by the organizers. The proposed solution is fully automatic without any manual intervention.

References

1. Clark, K., et al.: The cancer imaging archive (TCIA): maintaining and operating a public information repository. J. Digit. Imaging **26**(6), 1045–1057 (2013)
2. Heller, N., et al.: The state of the art in kidney and kidney tumor segmentation in contrast-enhanced CT imaging: results of the kits19 challenge. Med. Image Anal. **67**, 101821 (2021)
3. Heller, N., et al.: An international challenge to use artificial intelligence to define the state-of-the-art in kidney and kidney tumor segmentation in CT imaging. Proc. Am. Soc. Clin. Oncol. **38**(6), 626–626 (2020)
4. Ma, J., et al.: Loss odyssey in medical image segmentation. Med. Image Anal. **71**, 102035 (2021)
5. Ma, J., et al.: AbdomenCT-1K: Is abdominal organ segmentation a solved problem? IEEE Trans. Pattern Anal. Mach. Intell. (2021). https://doi.org/10.1109/TPAMI.2021.3100536
6. Ronneberger, O., Fischer, P., Brox, T.: U-Net: convolutional networks for biomedical image segmentation. In: International Conference on Medical Image Computing and Computer-Assisted Intervention, pp. 234–241 (2015)
7. Simpson, A.L., et al.: A large annotated medical image dataset for the development and evaluation of segmentation algorithms. arXiv preprint arXiv:1902.09063 (2019)

Teacher-Student Semi-supervised Approach for Medical Image Segmentation

Maria Baldeon Calisto$^{(\boxtimes)}$ (iD)

Departamento de Ingeniería Industrial and Instituto de Innovación en Productividad y Logística CATENA-USFQ, Universidad San Francisco de Quito, Diego de Robles s/n y Vía Interoceánica, Quito 170901, Ecuador
`mbaldeonc@usfq.edu.ec`

Abstract. Accurate segmentation of anatomical structures is a critical step for medical image analysis. Deep learning architectures have become the state-of-the-art models for automatic medical image segmentation. However, these models require an extensive labelled dataset to achieve a high performance. Given that obtaining annotated medical datasets is very expensive, in this work we present a two-phase teacher-student approach for semi-supervised learning. In phase 1, a three network U-Net ensemble, denominated the teacher, is trained using the labelled dataset. In phase 2, a student U-Net network is trained with the labelled dataset and the unlabelled dataset with pseudo-labels produced with the teacher network. The student network is then used for inference of the testing images. The proposed approach is evaluated on the task of abdominal segmentation from the FLARE2022 challenge, achieving a mean 0.53 dice, 0.57 NSD, and 44.97 prediction time on the validation set.

Keywords: Semi-supervised learning · Image segmentation · Medical image analysis

1 Introduction

Accurate segmentation of anatomical structures is a critical step for medical image analysis. Deep learning models have become the de-facto techniques for segmentation tasks given its state-of-the-art performance in various medical datasets [1,2]. However, without an extensive labelled dataset, neural networks can overfit the training data and perform poorly in unseen data points. In the case of medical image segmentation, this is an important limitation because annotating segmentation masks is an expensive and laborious process that requires of an experienced radiologists. Therefore it has become necessary to develop models that leverage unlabeled data information to aid the learning process.

A promising research direction is semi-supervised learning (SSL). SSL models aim to utilize information from unlabelled data to produce predictions that achieve a higher performance than if trained solely with labelled data [16]. Recently, important semi-supervised deep learning models have been proposed

J. Ma and B. Wang (Eds.): FLARE 2022, LNCS 13816, pp. 152–162, 2022.
https://doi.org/10.1007/978-3-031-23911-3_14

for medical image segmentation. Luo et al. [9] developed a dual-task network that predicts the pixel-wise segmentation map and level set function of the input image. The implemented loss function combines a supervised learning loss with an unsupervised dual-task-consistency loss function. Chen et al. [4] proposed a multi-task attention-based SSL model that combines an autoencoder with a U-Net-like network. The autoencoder is trained to reconstruct synthetic segmentation labels that encourages the segmentation model to learn discriminative latent representations from the unlabelled images. Nevertheless, previous approaches are tested in datasets where the number of classes is small, so when the numbers of classes increases, the complexity and size of the training framework rises importantly.

In this work, we propose a two-phase teacher-student semi-supervised training approach. In phase 1, a three network "teacher" ensemble is trained in a supervised manner using the labelled dataset. In phase 2, a "student" network is trained with the labelled images in a supervised manner, and the unlabelled images using the pseudo-labels provided by the teacher network. The model is tested on the FLARE2022 challenge dataset, that aims to segment 13 abdominal organs. Our model achieves a mean 0.53 dice, 0.57 NSD, and 44.97 prediction time on the validation set. Our experiments demonstrate that using the teacher-student approach increases a 5% the dice metric over using the model trained with only the labelled dataset.

2 Method

The proposed method is composed of two phases as displayed in Fig. 1. In phase one, three 2D U-Net [13] models are trained with 2D slices in a supervised manner with the labelled training set using a five fold cross validation division scheme. The teacher network is formed by uniting the networks through soft voting. In phase two, a student 2D U-Net is trained in a semi-supervised manner with the labelled and unlabelled images with pseudo-labels provided by the teacher ensemble. Details of each phase are provided next.

2.1 Phase One

The training dataset is divided into 5 folds, by assigning 80% of the observations for training and 20% observations for validation. A deeply supervised 2D U-Net, as presented in Fig. 2, is trained on each of the folds using the training protocols described in the following section. The 2D U-Net is composed of five down-sampling modules and four up-sampling modules. The modules are comprised of two convolutional blocks, each convolutional block has a 3×3 convolutional layer, batch normalization layer, and ReLU activation function. The last and second-last up-sampling modules are followed a 1×1 convolutional layer with a softmax activation function to produce the predicted segmentation. The objective function being minimized during training is a linear combination of the soft dice loss and cross entropy loss as presented in Eq. 1 as it has shown to provide robust results in various medical image segmentation tasks [10].

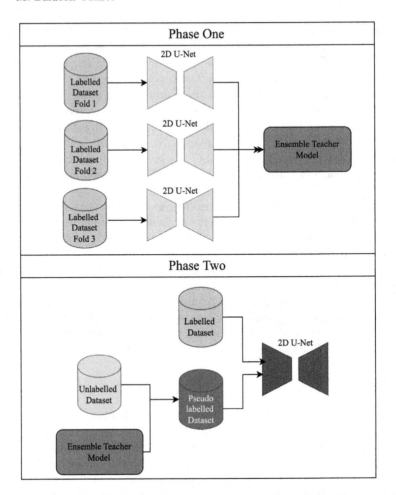

Fig. 1. Two-phase approach for semi-supervised learning. In Phase 1 a teacher ensemble is trained in a supervised manner. In Phase 2 a student network is trained in an semi-supervised manner using pseudo labels from the teacher.

$$\mathcal{L}_{seg} = \beta \sum_c 1 - \frac{2 \sum_i \widehat{y}_{ic} y_{ic}}{\sum_i \widehat{y}_{ic} + \sum_i y_{ic}} - (1 - \beta) \sum_c \sum_i (y_{ic} log(\widehat{y}_{ic}) \qquad (1)$$

where y_{ic} is the ground-truth label for pixel i in class c, and $\widehat{y}_{ic}$ the corresponding predicted probability. β is a weight parameter for the dice loss, which we set to 0.65. As previously mentioned, a deep supervised layer with an auxiliary segmentation loss [8] is located in the second-last up-sampling block to aid the model to learn rich hierarchical features. Therefore, the final loss function is comprised of the loss from the main output and the loss from the deep supervised layer with a weight of 0.1.

From the five networks trained, three were selected to form an ensemble as this combination provided the best performance on the challenge's validation set.

2.2   Phase Two

In phase two, a 2D U-Net architecture (refer to Fig. 2) is trained in a semi-supervised manner to segment the medical images. First, the teacher ensemble network formed in phase one is utilized to produce pseudo-labels for the unlabelled images. During a training iteration, the student 2D U-Net is trained with a batch of 2D labelled images using the same loss function displayed in Eq. 1, and later with a batch of unlabelled images with the psuedo-labels as ground truth with the loss shown in Eq. 2. Here $\tilde{y}_{ic}$ represents the pseudo-label for pixel i in class c. An L1 loss between the predicted segmentation and pseudo-label has been added to Eq. 2 as previous work has shown that it incentivizes the segmentations to be consistent [15].

$$\mathcal{L}_{pseudo-seg} = \beta \sum_c 1 - \frac{2 \sum_i \widehat{y}_{ic} \tilde{y}_{ic}}{\sum_i \widehat{y}_{ic} + \sum_i \tilde{y}_{ic}} - (1 - \beta) \sum_c \sum_i (\tilde{y}_{ic} log(\widehat{y}_{ic}) + \sum_c \sum_i ||\widehat{y}_{ic} - \tilde{y}_{ic}|| \tag{2}$$

The resulting 2D U-Net is used for inference on the validation and testing sets. This trick also allows the single 2D U-Net to learn all the information of the three-network ensemble, performing even better than the ensemble while reducing the size to 1/3.

3   Experiments

3.1   Dataset and Evaluation Measures

The FLARE2022 dataset is an extension of the FLARE 2021 [11] with more segmentation targets and more diverse images. The dataset is curated from more than 20 medical groups under the license permission, including MSD [14], KiTS [6,7], AbdomenCT-1K [12], and TCIA [5]. The training set includes 50 labelled CT scans with pancreas disease and 2000 unlabelled CT scans with liver, kidney, spleen, or pancreas diseases. The validation set includes 50 CT scans with liver, kidney, spleen, or pancreas diseases. The testing set includes 200 CT scans where 100 cases has liver, kidney, spleen, or pancreas diseases and the other 100 cases has uterine corpus endometrial, urothelial bladder, stomach, sarcomas, or ovarian diseases. All the CT scans only have image information and the center information is not available.

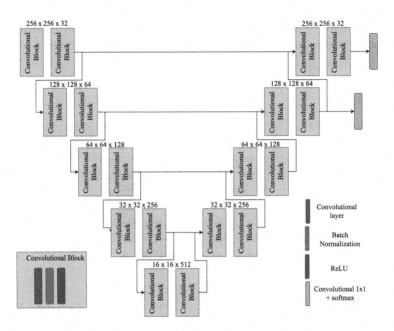

Fig. 2. 2D U-Net implemented to segment the abdominal structures. It is composed of five down-sampling modules and four up-sampling modules. The modules are comprised of two convolutional blocks, each convolutional block has a 3 × 3 convolutional layer, batch normalization layer, and ReLU activation function.

The evaluation measures consist of two accuracy measures: Dice Similarity Coefficient (DSC) and Normalized Surface Dice (NSD), and three running efficiency measures: running time, area under GPU memory-time curve, and area under CPU utilization-time curve. All measures will be used to compute the ranking. Moreover, the GPU memory consumption has a 2 GB tolerance.

3.2   Preprocessing

The images have a heterogeneous voxel spacing and shape. Hence, we first resample all images to have a voxel spacing of 1.5 mm × 1.5 mm × 2.5 mm and set to a fixed size of 256 × 256 × 123 voxels. Moreover, the pixel intensities are clipped to be inside the 3 standard deviations from the mean and rescaled to a [0, 1] range.

3.3   Post-processing

No post-processing operations are applied.

3.4   Implementation Details

Environment Settings. The environments and requirements are presented in Table 1.

Table 1. Environments and requirements.

Windows/Ubuntu version	Ubuntu 18.04
CPU	Intel Xeon E5-2698
RAM	256 GB
GPU (number and type)	Four Nvidia V100 32G
CUDA version	10.1.243
Programming language	Python 3.9
Deep learning framework	Pytorch (Torch 1.11, torchvision 0.12.0)
Specific dependencies	SimpleITK, nibabel, numpy, albumentation

Training Protocols. The training protocols for phase one and phase two are presented in Table 2 and Table 3 respectively. On both phases we implement data augmentation on the fly for the labelled dataset using the albumentations library [3]. The operations implemented are horizontal flip, vertical flip, random rotation to a maximum of $+/- 90$ °C, elastic transformation, grid distortion, and optical distortion.

Table 2. Training protocol phase one.

Network initialization	Kaiming uniform
Batch size	40
Patch size	256×256
Total epochs	3000
Optimizer	ADAM ($\beta_1 = 0.5$, $\beta_2 = 0.999$)
Initial learning rate (lr)	0.0002
Lr with polynomial decay	
Training time	216 h
Number of model parameters	6.98M each 2D U-Net network
Number of flops	9.07G each 2D U-Net network
Loss function	Dice loss + Cross-entropy loss

Table 3. Training protocols for phase two

Network initialization	Kaiming uniform
Batch size	20
Patch size	256×256
Total epochs	200
Optimizer	ADAM ($\beta_1 = 0.5$, $\beta_2 = 0.999$)
Initial learning rate (lr)	1×10^{-5}
Lr with polynomial decay	
Training time	48 h
Number of model parameters	6.98M
Number of flops	9.07G
Loss function	Dice loss + Cross-entropy loss

4   Results and Discussion

4.1   Quantitative Results on Validation Set

The proposed model is tested on the validation set and the evaluation metrics obtained through the challenge's website and displayed in Table 4. We first test the U-Net trained with all the labelled images, which obtained a mean dice of 0.4815. We also test the three U-Net network ensemble obtained in Phase 1, which achieved a 0.4973 mean dice. Finally, we test the proposed semi-supervised phase 1 and phase 2 approach, which increased in approximately 0.05 the mean dice over the single U-Net and 0.02 over the ensemble model. Due to computational limitations, we were not able to train with all the unlabelled images and had to selected a subset of 750 images for the implementation of phase 2. In Table 5, the validation scores for each substructure segmented are shown. The overall result of the model is not high in comparison to the competitor models. This might be caused by the use of 2D CNN instead of a 3D CNN, which does not exploits inter-slice information. Moreover, the testing dataset does not follow the same distribution as the training set. Hence, by not using all the unlabeled images, important information about the testing distribution might be excluded.

Table 4. Evaluation metrics on the validation set

Network	Mean DSC
U-Net (supervised training)	0.4815
Ensemble U-Net (supervised training)	0.4973
Phase 1 + Phase 2	0.5272

4.2   Qualitative Results on Validation Set

Figure 3 presents examples with good and poor segmentation results. The algorithm performs better in the segmentation of the liver, aorta, and inferior vena cava. Meanwhile, it has problems recognizing and segmenting the duodenum and esophagus. This might be caused by the contrast of the anatomical structures, where the liver and aorta can be differentiated from the other structures while the duodenum has a lower contrast with the surroundings.

4.3   Segmentation Efficiency Results on Validation Set

The average segmentation efficiency results on the validation set are presented in Table 6.

Table 5. Evaluation metrics per substructre on the validation set

Substructure	Mean DSC	Mean NSD
Liver	0.74 ± 0.25	0.66 ± 0.24
Right Kidney	0.56 ± 0.38	0.55 ± 0.35
Spleen	0.53 ± 0.35	0.51 ± 0.32
Pancreas	0.49 ± 0.30	0.62 ± 0.30
Aorta	0.67 ± 0.26	0.70 ± 0.25
Inferior Vena Cava	0.59 ± 0.28	0.58 ± 0.28
Right Adrenal Gland	0.46 ± 0.31	0.58 ± 0.36
Left Adrenal Gland	0.43 ± 0.32	0.53 ± 0.37
Gallbladder	0.46 ± 0.39	0.45 ± 0.38
Esophagus	0.37 ± 0.37	0.43 ± 0.42
Stomach	0.56 ± 0.29	0.57 ± 0.25
Duodenum	0.40 ± 0.27	0.62 ± 0.28
Left Kidney	0.58 ±0.37	0.56 ± 0.35

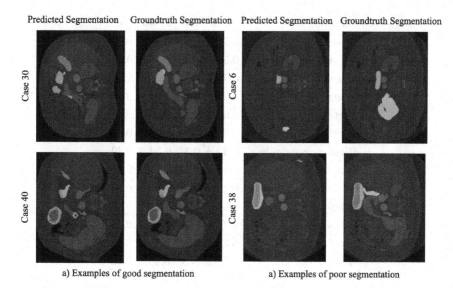

a) Examples of good segmentation   a) Examples of poor segmentation

Fig. 3. Examples of good and poor performing segmentations. The model produces the best segmentations for the liver, aorta, and inferior vena cava. Meanwhile it has problems recognizing the duodenum and esophagus.

Table 6. Average segmentation efficiency metrics on the validation set

Time	44.97
Max GPU memory	1405
AUC GPU time	49930.08
Max CPU utilization	95.10
AUC CPU time	785.13

4.4 Results on Final Testing Set

The model is evaluated on the test through a docker container submission to the challenge. The proposed framework is ranked 30 out of 47 submissions, the evaluation metrics per substructure are presented in Table 7. The model achieves an average 44.39 dice, 46.84 NSD, 44.87 inference time in seconds, 49706 AUC GPU, and 794 AUC CPU.

Table 7. Evaluation metrics per substructre on the test set

Substructure	Mean DSC	Mean NSD
Liver	0.62 ± 0.30	0.52 ± 0.30
Right Kidney	0.56 ± 0.35	0.51 ± 0.33
Spleen	0.45 ± 0.37	0.42 ± 0.36
Pancreas	0.37 ± 0.30	0.48 ± 0.35
Aorta	0.60 ± 0.24	0.64 ± 0.24
Inferior Vena Cava	0.50 ± 0.30	0.50 ± 0.29
Right Adrenal Gland	0.42 ± 0.34	0.52 ± 0.40
Left Adrenal Gland	0.40 ± 0.33	0.49 ± 0.39
Gallbladder	0.40 ± 0.40	0.39 ± 0.40
Esophagus	0.24 ± 0.31	0.28 ± 0.36
Stomach	0.41 ± 0.29	0.42 ± 0.28
Duodenum	0.28 ± 0.26	0.43 ± 0.37
Left Kidney	0.51 ±0.38	0.48 ± 0.36

4.5 Limitation and Future Work

A big limitation was the computational memory available. The computing infrastructure is shared between various users, so it was impossible to use all the unlabelled images during training. This was also the reason a 2D network is implemented instead of a 3D network. For future work, we will analyze the confidence of the pseudo labels and implement a GAN to encourage all segmentations to follow a similar distribution.

5   Conclusion

In the present work we propose a two-phase semi-supervised learning approach. In the first phase, a three network teacher ensemble is formed by using only the labelled training set. In the second phase, a segmentation network is trained in a semi-supervised scheme using the labelled dataset and unlabelled dataset with pseudo-labels provided by the teacher ensemble. Phase two improved in approximately 0.05 the mean dice from the single U-Net.

Acknowledgements. The authors of this paper declare that the segmentation method they implemented for participation in the FLARE 2022 challenge has not used any pre-trained models nor additional datasets other than those provided by the organizers.

References

1. Baldeon Calisto, M., Lai-Yuen, S.K.: AdaEn-Net?: an ensemble of adaptive 2D–3D fully convolutional networks for medical image segmentation. Neural Netw. **126**, 76–94 (2020). https://doi.org/10.1016/j.neunet.2020.03.007
2. Baldeon-Calisto, M., Lai-Yuen, S.K.: AdaResU-Net: Multiobjective adaptive convolutional neural network for medical image segmentation. Neurocomputing **392**, 325–340 (2020). https://doi.org/10.1016/j.neucom.2019.01.110
3. Buslaev, A., Iglovikov, V.I., Khvedchenya, E., Parinov, A., Druzhinin, M., Kalinin, A.A.: Albumentations: fast and flexible image augmentations. Information **11**(2) (2020). https://doi.org/10.3390/info11020125, https://www.mdpi.com/2078-2489/11/2/125
4. Chen, S., Bortsova, G., García-Uceda Juárez, A., van Tulder, G., de Bruijne, M.: Multi-task attention-based semi-supervised learning for medical image segmentation. In: Shen, D., et al. (eds.) MICCAI 2019. LNCS, vol. 11766, pp. 457–465. Springer, Cham (2019). https://doi.org/10.1007/978-3-030-32248-9_51
5. Clark, K., Vendt, B., Smith, K., Freymann, J., Kirby, J., Koppel, P., Moore, S., Phillips, S., Maffitt, D., Pringle, M., et al.: The cancer imaging archive (TCIA): maintaining and operating a public information repository. J. Digit. Imaging **26**(6), 1045–1057 (2013)
6. Heller, N., et al.: The state of the art in kidney and kidney tumor segmentation in contrast-enhanced CT imaging: results of the kits19 challenge. Med. Image Anal. **67**, 101821 (2021)
7. Heller, N., et al.: An international challenge to use artificial intelligence to define the state-of-the-art in kidney and kidney tumor segmentation in CT imaging. Proc. Am. Soc. Clin. Oncol. **38**(6), 626–626 (2020)
8. Lee, C.Y., Xie, S., Gallagher, P., Zhang, Z., Tu, Z.: Deeply-supervised nets. In: Proceedings of the Eighteenth International Conference on Artificial Intelligence and Statistics, PMLR 38 2015. pp. 562–570 (2015)
9. Luo, X., Chen, J., Song, T., Wang, G.: Semi-supervised medical image segmentation through dual-task consistency. In: Proceedings of the AAAI Conference on Artificial Intelligence, vol. 35, pp. 8801–8809 (2021)
10. Ma, J., et al.: Loss odyssey in medical image segmentation. Med. Image Anal. **71**, 102035 (2021)

11. Ma, J., et al.: Fast and low-GPU-memory abdomen CT organ segmentation: the flare challenge. Med. Image Anal. **82**, 102616 (2022). https://doi.org/10.1016/j.media.2022.102616
12. Ma, J., et al.: AbdomenCT-1K: Is abdominal organ segmentation a solved problem? IEEE Trans. Pattern Anal. Mach. Intell. **44**(10), 6695–6714 (2022)
13. Ronneberger, O., Fischer, P., Brox, T.: U-Net: convolutional networks for biomedical image segmentation. In: International Conference on Medical Image Computing and Computer-Assisted Intervention, pp. 234–241 (2015)
14. Simpson, A.L., et al.: A large annotated medical image dataset for the development and evaluation of segmentation algorithms. arXiv preprint arXiv:1902.09063 (2019)
15. Tomar, D., Lortkipanidze, M., Vray, G., Bozorgtabar, B., Thiran, J.P.: Self-attentive spatial adaptive normalization for cross-modality domain adaptation. IEEE Trans. Med. Imaging **40**(10), 2926–2938 (2021)
16. Van Engelen, J.E., Hoos, H.H.: A survey on semi-supervised learning. Mach. Learn. **109**(2), 373–440 (2020)

Semi-supervised Organ Segmentation with Mask Propagation Refinement and Uncertainty Estimation for Data Generation

Minh-Khoi Pham[1,2], Thang-Long Nguyen-Ho[1,2],
Thao Thi Phuong Dao[1,2,3,5], Tan-Cong Nguyen[1,2,4],
and Minh-Triet Tran[1,2,3(✉)]

[1] University of Science, Ho Chi Minh City, Vietnam
[2] Vietnam National University, Ho Chi Minh City, Vietnam
[3] John von Neumann Institute, Ho Chi Minh City, Vietnam
tmtriet@fit.hcmus.edu.vn
[4] University of Social Sciences and Humanities, Ho Chi Minh City, Vietnam
[5] Department of Otolaryngology, Thong Nhat Hospital, Ho Chi Minh City,
Tan Binh District, Vietnam

Abstract. We present a novel two-staged method that employs various 2D-based techniques to deal with the 3D segmentation task. In most of the previous challenges, it is unlikely for 2D CNNs to be comparable with other 3D CNNs since 2D models can hardly capture temporal information. In light of that, we propose using the recent state-of-the-art technique in video object segmentation, combining it with other semi-supervised training techniques to leverage the extensive unlabeled data. Moreover, we introduce a way to generate pseudo-labeled data that is both plausible and consistent for further retraining by using uncertainty estimation. Our code is publicly available at Github.

Keywords: 2D semi-supervised segmentation · Mask propagation · Uncertainty estimation

1 Introduction

Subclinical examination plays an important role in all medical treatment processes. With the help of deep learning algorithms, human abdominal organs can be identified automatically with effectiveness and efficiency; thus enabling doctors for faster diagnoses. For deep learning agents to achieve high performance, it often comes with a vast amount of high-quality labeled data for the training stage. However, obtaining a sufficient amount of medical data is quite expensive and time-consuming, not to mention the need for medical labels to be evaluated by experts to ensure accuracy for usability. Because of the lack of useful data

---

M.-K. Pham and T.-L. Nguyen-Ho—Equal contribution.

J. Ma and B. Wang (Eds.): FLARE 2022, LNCS 13816, pp. 163–177, 2022.
https://doi.org/10.1007/978-3-031-23911-3_15

and scarce medical experts, it makes the problem becomes more challenging to tackle for today's machines.

Since last year, the FLARE22 challenge has introduced a problem in a specific scenario where a shortage of labeled medical data occurs. The included dataset contains only 50 labeled CT volumes whereas 2000 unlabeled others are given. With the provision of an enormous quantity of non-annotated data, participants are required to utilize them to boost the accuracy of their methods for the segmentation task, as well as optimize their solution for practical applicability.

Past solutions mostly approached the problem by inheriting 3D techniques, which usually demand great computing resources. In fact, the original CT volumes must be resampled to a smaller size to fit these 3D-based approaches, then the prediction of these models must also be post-processed back to its preceding sizes, which can damage the precision of the prediction. In terms of that, other teams proposed 2D-based solutions which can leverage the ability to split the CT volumes into batches of slices for efficient processing. But in reality, these techniques face serious performance issues due to the incapability of capturing the temporal information of CT slices. Therefore, to overcome these drawbacks, we propose a novel pipeline, which works completely with only 2D image slices, that can comprehend information from all three planes of a volume.

Furthermore, to make use of a huge number of unlabeled data, two of the most common semi-supervised learning methods are consistency regularization and pseudo-labeling. Consistency-based methods train the model to produce the same pseudo-label for two different views (strong and weak augmentations) of an unlabeled sample, while pseudo-labeling converts model predictions on unlabeled samples into soft or hard labels as optimization targets. However, both of the methods suffer from the noise caused by the model trained on different data distribution (between labeled and unlabeled data). To address the above challenges, we propose a simple technique via modeling uncertainty that can be applied to filter out only potentially good pseudo labels for retraining.

Overall, our main contributions are as follows:

- We propose a 2D-based segmentation pipeline that can fully exploit information of all three dimensions of a CT volume by integrating temporal positional encoding and mask propagation.
- Simple enough, we come up with an uncertainty estimation technique to selectively choose which pseudo labels are useful for next cycle of training.

2   Method

2.1   Preprocessing

For preprocessing, we apply the Windowing technique [2] with different levels and widths to target specific parts of human organs. Windowing, also known as grey-level mapping, contrast stretching, histogram modification, or contrast enhancement is the process in which the CT image grayscale component of an

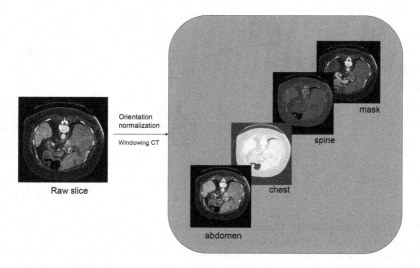

Fig. 1. Windowing CT

image is manipulated via the CT numbers; doing this will change the appearance of the picture to highlight particular structures. The brightness of the image is adjusted via the window level. The contrast is adjusted via the window width. In our experiments, we create 3 different versions of a single slice by highlighting the abdomen, chest, and spine groups and stacking them to one as a three-channel image (Fig. 1).

In addition, we choose the axial plane to cut the slices from the CT volumes since this plane has various dimension sizes. Due to some relatively small organs, it might be better to keep the original size of the slices without any cropping, resampling, or resizing methods. The image is rotated to a predefined angle, then divided by 255 for normalization before going through the next step.

2.2   Proposed Method

Our method composes of two main modules: the Reference module and the Propagation module, as can be seen in Fig. 2.

In the beginning, we uniformly select only k slices from the CT Volume to be our initial candidates. Next, these slices are processed by using the Windowing technique (described in Sect. 2.1). Afterward, these slices are put through the Reference module (described in Sect. 2.2), which performs the standard multi-class segmentation, then the preliminary k masks can be obtained. With these pairs of potential slices and masks as prior knowledge, the Propagation module (described in Sect. 2.2) can utilize them to propagate the objects' transformation information to the remaining slices across the CT volume length. The final output of this module is a 3D dense mask prediction, with each voxel indicating a class.

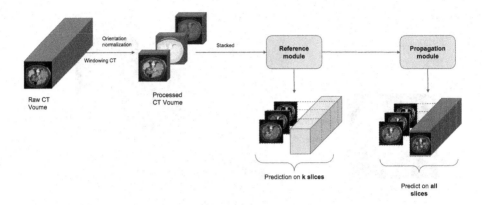

Fig. 2. Our overall proposed pipeline. Firstly, the entire CT Volume is processed using windowing CT to get a stack of three-channel slices. Then the slices progress through the Reference module to obtain a minimal number of preliminary masks. Lastly, the Propagation module refine these initial masks to finalize the result.

Reference Module. This module is expected to provide a suggestion of a minimal amount of slices and predicted masks that might contain the most information describing the entire CT Volume. Figure 3 describes the details of this module.

To utilize the enormous number of unlabeled data, we apply the recent semi-supervised method that performs effectively on several other datasets, which is called Cross Pseudo Supervision (CPS) [7] (yellow cube in Fig. 3). CPS enables the usage of unlabeled data by following the dual students technique, where two models are trained simultaneously on labeled data while generating pseudo data for their "peer" to learn. In the testing phase, two models predict the same image, and the result is aggregated by summing up.

We adopt two prominent state-of-the-arts 2D segmentation models with highly different learning paradigms for this CPS framework, which is TransUNet [5] and DeeplabV3+ [6]. While DeeplabV3+ traditionally focuses more on the local information, transformers model the long-range relation, so the cross training can help to learn a unified segmenter with these two properties at the same time. In short, we choose TransUNet and DeeplabV3+ due to their ability to compensate each other for better performance [13].

In addition, we also propose a both logical and specialist-based strategy to choose which slices can be further used to boost the performance of the Propagation module. The goal of this action is to preserve only some of the most useful information for the refinement stage.

To elaborate on these strategies, prior to being put into the CPS module for prediction, a small number of slices are uniformly sampled from the processed CT volume. After CPS produces segmentation masks for these slices, another selection step is performed to pick only some of the masks that contain the organs having the largest areas.

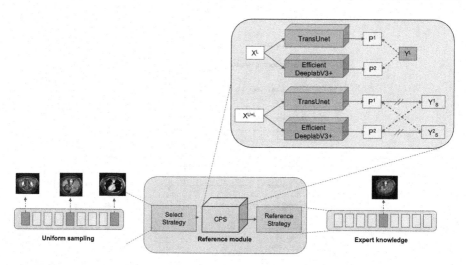

Fig. 3. The reference module. The semi-supervised technique CPS is applied in both the training and inference stage to enhance the precision of model prediction. Strategies are used to smartly choose slices that are informative for the next stage.

Although we have employed a semi-supervised learning technique for the Reference module, it still lacks information on the axial plane of the CT volume. Therefore, we simply resolve that by embedding the slices's relative position on the axial dimension as a feature vectors and input them to both networks TransUnet and DeeplabV3+ to learn. The rationale behind this is that, with additional temporal knowledge, models are expected to capture the position constraint for each organ's appearance, hence provide better prediction.

Positional Encoding. In order for the model to make use of the order of the sequence, we need to inject some information about the positions of the slices. For simplicity, we add an additional embedding layer to embed the relative position of each slice. Specifically, the embedded position index is concatenated with the hidden features before the final segmentation head. The relative position of kth frame of CT volume i with length T_i is calculated as:

$$PE(k) = \frac{k}{T_i} \tag{1}$$

We attach this layer to both DeeplabV3+ and TransUnet. Since they follow the conventional structure of segmentation models, which comprise of encoding and decoding phases, we manage to attach the layer in a similar way for both of them, as can be described in Fig. 4.

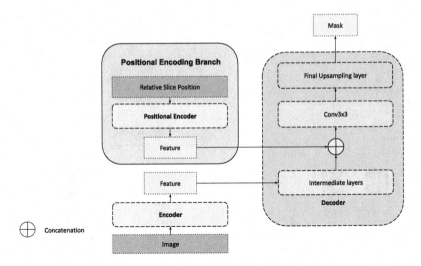

Fig. 4. A general and simple way to attach a Positional Encoding branch into segmentation models.

Propagation Module. This module aims to utilize prior knowledge of given annotated slices from the Reference module to make prediction on the remaining slices, this mechanism can be referred as mask (or label) propagation.

Intuitively, the conventional 2D CNNs cannot comprehend the third dimension information within a CT volume. Thus, in hope of the ability to capture the "temporal" information along the axial plane, we adapt the Space-Time Correspondence Networks (STCN) [8], which is a semi-supervised segmentation algorithm that has achieved promising results on Video object segmentation problem, to this 3D manner.

Basically, STCN proposes the use of a memory bank that stores information about previous frames and their corresponding masks and uses them later as prior knowledge. To generate the mask for the current frame, a pairwise affinity matrix is calculated between the query frame and memory frames based on negative squared Euclidean distance, then it is used for supporting the current mask generation [8].

Different from the original STCN, we slightly modify it to match the current problem. In the original work, they use only a single dense mask to propagate through the entire video, therefore for the model to perfectly work, that selected mask must contain information about all available classes. For our case to achieve that goal, we enable the usage of multiple masks for propagation, so that all of these masks should contain enough information about every organs. We also allow the STCN to work in a bidirectional way to enhance the refinement. Figure 5 illustrates this process.

Specially, STCN can be simply trained in the binary manner, meaning that each of the abdominal organs can be learned separately. Therefore, the knowledge can be transferred well between different organ classes.

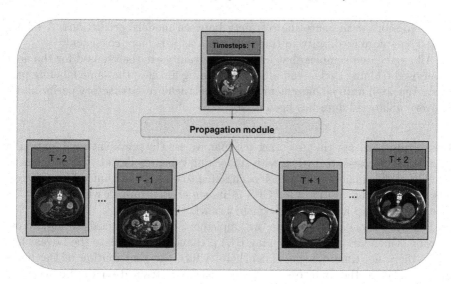

Fig. 5. The propagation module. From an annotated slice of CT, at timestep T, STCN can make use of that to spread the information through the entire defined range $[T - k_1, T + k_2]$.

Pseudo Labeling with Uncertainty Estimation. Given a vast amount of unlabeled CT volumes, we apply a uncertainty estimation technique to effectively maximize the utilization of the data.

Firstly, several CPS models are trained on the provided labeled data. Then, we use these trained CPS models to obtain pseudo masks on the unlabeled set. Inspired from [20], we calculate the dice scores between these pseudo masks and the aggregated one. The mean of these dice scores will be compared with a threshold to determine whether the aggregated pseudo masks are qualified. Simply speaking, consensus-based assessment is used to evaluate the quality of pseudo labels.

We determine a single score for the ith volume in the unlabeled set as the formulation below:

$$score_i = \frac{1}{K \times M} \sum_{k=1}^{K^i} \sum_{m=1}^{M} \mathrm{DSC}(\mathcal{Y}_m^{k,i}, \mathcal{Y}_{AVG}^{k,i}) \tag{2}$$

$$\mathrm{dsc} = \frac{2|X \cap Y|}{|X| + |Y|} \tag{3}$$

DSC represents the Dice Score evaluation metric calculating the overlapping area of prediction X and ground truth Y. Here $\mathcal{Y}_m^{k,i}$ indicates the mth model's output of the kth slice of volume i while $\mathcal{Y}_{AVG}^{k,i}$ is the mask averaged from all M models for the same slice. The easier the sample is, the more inclined the segmentation models are to get similar outputs. In contrast, hard samples are more likely to be segmented differently by different models. Hence, we use the proposed score to measure the certainty between models' predictions. A higher score gives more credibility to the prediction, as it is more consistent.

All aggregated samples that have high certainty are then reused for the next supervised training cycle. And after the training finishes, the same labeling process is repeated until all aforementioned models achieve satisfactory performance or every unlabeled data has been used.

Loss Function. For the Reference module, we use the prevalent combination of dice loss and cross-entropy loss with smoothing value to alleviate the imbalanced number of the small organs, which occurs due to our splitting into slices process. The same settings are used for CPS in its supervised branch whereas only the dice loss is set up for the unsupervised branch.

For the Propagation module, we implement the online hard example cross entropy (OhemCE or Bootstrapping CE) [21] and also calculate the Lovasz loss [3] at the same time. OhemCE can help reduce the contribution of the background label to the final loss. And since STCN is trained on the binary task, OhemCE can direct the model to focus on visible difficult objects. Meanwhile, Lovasz loss is commonly used in past research and competitions.

2.3   Post-processing

We do not use any post-processing techniques because no complex pre-processing ones are used, and we conduct all our experiments on the original-sized image volumes apart from the orientation settings. Thus, before submitting it to the evaluation system, the mask must be transformed back to the original orientation.

2.4   Inference Optimization

Unfortunately, we do not apply any engineering technique to reduce resource consumption nor speed up inference process.

3   Experiments

3.1   Dataset and Evaluation Measures

The FLARE2022 dataset is curated from more than 20 medical groups under the license permission, including MSD [19], KiTS [10,11], AbdomenCT-1K [15], and TCIA [9]. The training set includes 50 labelled CT scans with pancreas disease and 2000 unlabelled CT scans with liver, kidney, spleen, or pancreas diseases. The validation set includes 50 CT scans with liver, kidney, spleen, or pancreas diseases. The testing set includes 200 CT scans where 100 cases has liver, kidney, spleen, or pancreas diseases and the other 100 cases has uterine corpus endometrial, urothelial bladder, stomach, sarcomas, or ovarian diseases.

All the CT scans only have image information and the center information is not available.

The evaluation measures consist of two accuracy measures: Dice Similarity Coefficient (DSC) and Normalized Surface Dice (NSD), and three running efficiency measures: running time, area under GPU memory-time curve, and area under CPU utilization-time curve. All measures will be used to compute the ranking. Moreover, the GPU memory consumption has a 2 GB tolerance.

3.2 Implementation Details

Environment Settings. The development environments and requirements are presented in Table 1.

Table 1. Development environments and requirements.

Windows/Ubuntu version	Ubuntu 18.04.5 LTS
CPU	Intel(R) Xeon(R) Silver 4210R CPU @ 2.40 GHz
RAM	1 × 32 GB;
GPU (number and type)	One Quadro RTX 5000 16G
CUDA version	11.6
Programming language	Python 3.10
Deep learning framework	Pytorch (Torch 1.11.0, torchvision 0.12.0)

Table 2. Training protocols for Reference module: CPS of TransUnet and Efficientnet DeeplabV3+

Network initialization	Random initialization
Batch size	2 (labeled) + 2 (unlabeled)
Patch size	512 × 512
Total iterations	50000
Optimizer	AdamW
Initial learning rate (lr)	0.0001
Lr decay schedule	Multiplied by 0.5 for every iteration at [40000, 45000]
Training time	48 h
Loss functions	Dice Loss + Cross-Entropy Loss
Number of model parameters	105M (TransUnet Resnet50) + 11M (Efficientnet DeeplabV3+)[a]
Number of flops	108G (TransUnet Resnet50) + 1,3 G (Efficientnet DeeplabV3+)[b]

[a] Pytorch
[b] Pytorch

Table 3. Training protocols for Propagation module: STCN with Resnet backbone

Network initialization	Random initialization
Batch size	8
Patch size	512 × 512
Total iterations	50000
Optimizer	AdamW
Initial learning rate (lr)	0.0001
Lr decay schedule	multiplied by 0.5 for every iteration at $[40000, 45000]$
Training time	48 h
Loss functions	OhemCE Loss + Lovasz Loss
Number of model parameters	54,416,065[a]

[a] Pytorch

Training Protocols. Currently, we find that using only simple 2D transform functions such as horizontal/vertical flipping or rotating might be enough for both modules to generalize. In the training stage, the Reference module follow traditional training process, in which two models are concurrently trained. For the Propagation module, we inherit the same process as in [8] which samples 3 neighboring slices at a time.

Table 2 and Table 3 mention the training protocols for Reference module and Propagation module, respectively. In both settings, we use the original-sized images, which is $[512, 512]$ for the training and inference phases.

4   Results and Discussion

Quantitative Results. Here we present both quantitative and qualitative results of our proposed method. We also include the ablation study (Table 5) to further analyze the effectiveness of each of our modules.

Some interesting insights can be spotted in Table 4. Overall, we can see that using the pseudo-labeled data for training, helps boost the performance of the model by a great amount. Unfortunately, we have yet to fully explore every unlabeled sample (only 700 samples were used for training in our submission), but intuitively, the number of used unlabeled samples is likely to be directly proportional to the evaluation result. Another notable observation is that the DSC for some small human organs (gallbladder and adrenal glands) can hardly be improved because of the class imbalance problem (as referred in Sect. 4).

Table 5 shows that each module contributes to the final score of our submission. The baseline model that is reported in the first row is TransUnet. The Cross Pseudo Supervision (CPS) refers to using both DeeplabV3+ and TransUnet as training models. The third and fourth rows where both CPS and Uncertainty Estimation (UE) is used mean that pseudo-labels that are qualified by UE are used as supervised inputs in CPS workflow, whereas the remaining unlabeled data are used as unsupervised inputs. Noticeably, in the fourth row, with the

Table 4. Comparison between using and not using the pseudo labels as supervised training data. The model that is used for the report is TransUnet on public test set. The highlighted figures emphasize the highest values in each row.

Number of pseudo-labeled samples	0	200	700
Liver	0.9215	0.9555	**0.9604**
Right Kidney (RK)	0.6548	0.7944	**0.8014**
Spleen	0.8159	0.9144	**0.9255**
Pancreas	0.6235	0.7309	**0.7567**
Aorta	0.8794	0.9272	**0.9335**
Inferior Vena Cava (IVC)	0.7145	0.7967	**0.8207**
Right Adrenal Gland (RAG)	0.4688	0.6507	**0.6545**
Left Adrenal Gland (LAG)	0.4209	**0.6179**	0.6138
Gallbladder	0.4798	**0.5889**	0.5885
Esophagus	0.7086	**0.7784**	0.7783
Stomach	0.7446	0.8403	**0.8424**
Duodenum	0.4387	0.5617	**0.5679**
Left Kidney (LK)	0.6763	**0.8112**	0.8026
Mean DSC	0.6575	0.7668	**0.7728**

Table 5. Ablation experiment on each proposed modules and techniques.

No.	Positional encoding	CPS	Uncertainty estimation	Mask propagation	Mean DSC
1					0.6419
2	✓				0.6575
3	✓	✓			0.762
4	✓	✓	✓		0.7728
5	✓	✓	✓	✓	**0.784**

Mask propagation (MP) applied, DSC score is enhanced substantially. It is surprising that MP only looks upon the minority of the slices to fully propagate through the whole volume. The detailed evaluation for our best submission is shown in Table 6.

Qualitative Results. Looking at examples that are well-predicted by our approach in Fig. 6 (1b, 2b, 3b), it demonstrates good segmentation masks with clear and smooth mask boundaries. Some small organs can also be seen segmented successfully and precisely meaning that both proposed modules can work effectively with organs having various sizes.

Table 6. The final evaluation score for our final submission.

Classes/Metrics	DSC	NSD
Liver	0.974 ± 0.036	0.963 ± 0.063
Right Kidney (RK)	0.883 ± 0.233	0.868 ± 0.241
Spleen	0.9494 ± 0.115	0.935 ± 0.134
Pancreas	0.772 ± 0.147	0.877 ± 0.145
Aorta	0.96 ± 0.045	0.976 ± 0.06
Inferior Vena Cava (IVC)	0.86 ± 0.123	0.86 ± 0.143
Right Adrenal Gland (RAG)	0.735 ± 0.138	0.855 ± 0.144
Left Adrenal Gland (LAG)	0.69 ± 0.171	0.816 ± 0.2
Gallbladder	0.75 ± 0.313	0.733 ± 0.328
Esophagus	0.783 ± 0.147	0.88 ± 0.143
Stomach	0.86 ± 0.113	0.84 ± 0.142
Duodenum	0.6 ± 0.2	0.79 ± 0.215
Left Kidney (LK)	0.877 ± 0.22	0.863 ± 0.23
Mean	0.8233	0.8668

On the other hand, our models suffer from various difficult cases where organs are missing. Generally, there are two cases that negatively affects our approach:

1. Relatively small organs (adrenal glands (Fig. 6(1e)), gallbladder (Fig. 6(1e)), and esophagus (Fig. 6(3e))) account for the lowest DSC since they usually are failed to be identified by the Reference module.
2. Other organs (pancreas (Fig. 6(1e)) and duodenum (Fig. 6.(2e))) despite having larger size, yet their lengths on the axial plane are short and sometimes occluded by many surrounding organs, which can affects how the information propagating through the slices, causing class confusion in the result.

Furthermore, due to the our two-staged pipeline, for the results of the second stage to be good really relies on the first stage' performance. If the reference stage miss-segments any organ, that one will be missed during the entire propagation process. Having said that, this issue mostly just occurs to organs that have short-size length on the axial plane.

Efficiency Results. Segmentation efficiency results are reported in Table 7. GPU memory and GPU utilization is recorded every 0.1 s. The Area under GPU memory-time curve and Area under CPU utilization-time curve are the cumulative values along running time.

Table 7. Efficiency evaluation from official report.

Running times (s)	AUC GPU	AUC CPU
140.73	647605	3729

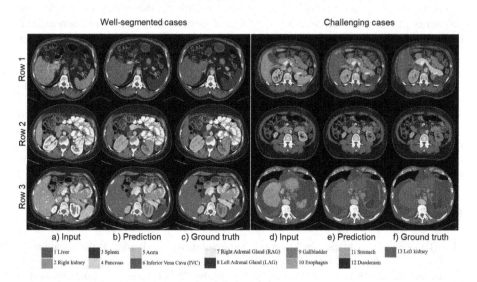

Fig. 6. Qualitative results from the validation set. We illustrate both well-segmented and challenging examples for our proposed segmentation pipeline

Limitation and Future Work. Apparently, although our proposed method has yet to achieve the high result, we believe it can be further improved if these limitation that we identify here are solved. First of all, the problem of imbalanced dataset has arisen because we perceive this as a 2D problem. Due to the slices splitting process, small organs (such as pancreas, gallbladder or adrenal glands) only appear in a small amount of slices, while larger objects have wider range of appearance. Therefore, it leads to the problem of imbalanced dataset. We tried some ways to tackle the problem, for instance: smart sampling, or imbalanced loss, however only slightly improvement was seen. Secondly, the proposed approach is a two-stage method, the second stage is undoubtedly dependent of the first one. If there are any organs that are missed by the Reference module, it definitely cannot be recovered in the Propagation phase. Thus, more attention is needed for the Reference module. In the future, it is encouraged to focus on boosting the performance of the Reference module by fully exploiting the temporal information.

5   Conclusion

In summary, with new advancements in technology, there are endless possibilities for what can be achieved. In the medical field, one of the most common problems that doctors face is accurately segmenting 3D objects from 2D images or volume sequences. Recently, we propose a novel two-stage pipeline that can leverage the strength of many state-of-the-art 2D deep learning algorithms and techniques in videos and images, into the task of 3D object segmentation. This proposal aims to introduce a novel and inspirational approach to solving one of the most common problems in the medical field. In addition, to break the barrier of differences in medical pipeline processes, our solution is able to transfer and exploit the power of multiple domain data in datasets creating more accurate results.

Acknowledgements. This research is funded by Vietnam National University Ho Chi Minh City (VNU-HCM) under grant number DS2020-42-01.

The authors of this paper declare that the segmentation method they implemented for participation in the FLARE 2022 challenge has not used any pre-trained models nor additional datasets other than those provided by the organizers.

Furthermore, no manual intervention has been made in the contribution to the results of the proposed method.

References

1. NIH Pancreas. https://wiki.cancerimagingarchive.net/display/Public/Pancreas-CT (2020). Accessed Aug 2020
2. Baba, Y., Murphy, A.: Windowing (CT) (March 2017). https://doi.org/10.53347/rid-52108. http://dx.doi.org/10.53347/rID-52108
3. Berman, M., Triki, A.R., Blaschko, M.B.: The lovász-softmax loss: a tractable surrogate for the optimization of the intersection-over-union measure in neural networks. In: 2018 IEEE Conference on Computer Vision and Pattern Recognition, CVPR 2018, Salt Lake City, UT, USA, 18–22 June 2018, pp. 4413–4421. Computer Vision Foundation / IEEE Computer Society (2018). https://doi.org/10.1109/CVPR.2018.00464, http://openaccess.thecvf.com/content_cvpr_2018/html/Berman_The_LovaSz-Softmax_Loss_CVPR_2018_paper.html
4. Bilic, P., et al.: The liver tumor segmentation benchmark (LITS). arXiv preprint arXiv:1901.04056 (2019)
5. Chen, J., et al.: Transunet: transformers make strong encoders for medical image segmentation. CoRR abs/2102.04306 (2021., https://arxiv.org/abs/2102.04306
6. Chen, L.-C., Zhu, Y., Papandreou, G., Schroff, F., Adam, H.: Encoder-decoder with Atrous separable convolution for semantic image segmentation. In: Ferrari, V., Hebert, M., Sminchisescu, C., Weiss, Y. (eds.) ECCV 2018. LNCS, vol. 11211, pp. 833–851. Springer, Cham (2018). https://doi.org/10.1007/978-3-030-01234-2_49
7. Chen, X., Yuan, Y., Zeng, G., Wang, J.: Semi-supervised semantic segmentation with cross pseudo supervision. In: IEEE Conference on Computer Vision and Pattern Recognition, CVPR 2021, virtual, June 19–25, 2021. pp. 2613–2622. Computer Vision Foundation / IEEE (2021). https://openaccess.thecvf.com/content/CVPR2021/html/Chen_Semi-Supervised_Semantic_Segmentation_With_Cross_Pseudo_Supervision_CVPR_2021_paper.html
8. Cheng, H.K., Tai, Y., Tang, C.: Rethinking space-time networks with improved memory coverage for efficient video object segmentation. In: Ranzato, M., Beygelzimer, A., Dauphin, Y.N., Liang, P., Vaughan, J.W. (eds.) Advances in Neural Information Processing Systems 34: Annual Conference on Neural Informa-

tion Processing Systems 2021, NeurIPS 2021(December), pp. 6–14, 2021. virtual. pp. 11781–11794 (2021). https://proceedings.neurips.cc/paper/2021/hash/61b4a64be663682e8cb037d9719ad8cd-Abstract.html

9. Clark, K., et al.: The cancer imaging archive (TCIA): maintaining and operating a public information repository. J. Digit. Imaging **26**(6), 1045–1057 (2013)

10. Heller, N., et al.: The state of the art in kidney and kidney tumor segmentation in contrast-enhanced CT imaging: Results of the kits19 challenge. Med. Image Anal. **67**, 101821 (2021)

11. Heller, N., et al.: An international challenge to use artificial intelligence to define the state-of-the-art in kidney and kidney tumor segmentation in ct imaging. Proc. Am. Soc. Clin. Oncol. **38**(6), 626–626 (2020)

12. Isensee, F., Jaeger, P.F., Kohl, S.A., Petersen, J., Maier-Hein, K.H.: nnU-Net: a self-configuring method for deep learning-based biomedical image segmentation. Nat. Methods **18**(2), 203–211 (2021)

13. Luo, X., Hu, M., Song, T., Wang, G., Zhang, S.: Semi-supervised medical image segmentation via cross teaching between CNN and transformer. CoRR abs/2112.04894 (2021), https://arxiv.org/abs/2112.04894

14. Ma, J., Chen, J., Ng, M., Huang, R., Li, Y., Li, C., Yang, X., Martel, A.L.: Loss odyssey in medical image segmentation. Med. Image Anal. **71**, 102035 (2021)

15. Ma, J., Zhang, Y., Gu, S., Zhu, C., Ge, C., Zhang, Y., An, X., Wang, C., Wang, Q., Liu, X., Cao, S., Zhang, Q., Liu, S., Wang, Y., Li, Y., He, J., Yang, X.: Abdomenct-1k: Is abdominal organ segmentation a solved problem? IEEE Trans. Pattern Anal. Mach. Intell. **44**(10), 6695–6714 (2022)

16. Ronneberger, O., Fischer, P., Brox, T.: U-Net: convolutional networks for biomedical image segmentation. In: International Conference on Medical Image Computing and Computer-Assisted Intervention, pp. 234–241 (2015)

17. Roth, H., Farag, A., Turkbey, E., Lu, L., Liu, J., Summers, R.: Data from pancreas-CT. The Cancer Imaging Archive (2016)

18. Roth, H.R., Lu, L., Farag, A., Shin, H.-C., Liu, J., Turkbey, E.B., Summers, R.M.: DeepOrgan: multi-level deep convolutional networks for automated pancreas segmentation. In: Navab, N., Hornegger, J., Wells, W.M., Frangi, A.F. (eds.) MICCAI 2015. LNCS, vol. 9349, pp. 556–564. Springer, Cham (2015). https://doi.org/10.1007/978-3-319-24553-9_68

19. Simpson, A.L., et al.: A large annotated medical image dataset for the development and evaluation of segmentation algorithms. arXiv preprint arXiv:1902.09063 (2019)

20. Wang, J., Chen, Z., Wang, L., Zhou, Q.: An active learning with two-step query for medical image segmentation. In: 2019 International Conference on Medical Imaging Physics and Engineering (ICMIPE), pp. 1–5. IEEE (2019)

21. Wu, Z., Shen, C., van den Hengel, A.: High-performance semantic segmentation using very deep fully convolutional networks. CoRR abs/1604.04339 (2016), http://arxiv.org/abs/1604.04339

Revisiting nnU-Net for Iterative Pseudo Labeling and Efficient Sliding Window Inference

Ziyan Huang[1,2], Haoyu Wang[1,2], Jin Ye[2], Jingqi Niu[1,2], Can Tu[1,2], Yuncheng Yang[1,2], Shiyi Du[2,3], Zhongying Deng[2,4], Lixu Gu[1], and Junjun He[2(✉)]

[1] Shanghai Jiao Tong University, Shanghai, China
{ziyanhuang,small_dark}@sjtu.edu.cn
[2] Shanghai AI Lab, Shanghai, China
hejunjun@pjlab.org.cn
[3] Sichuan University, Sichuan, China
[4] University of Surrey, Guildford, UK

Abstract. nnU-Net serves as a good baseline for many medical image segmentation challenges in recent years. It works pretty well for fully-supervised segmentation tasks. However, it is less efficient for inference and cannot effectively make full use of unlabeled data, both of which are vital in real clinical scenarios. To this end, we revisit nnU-Net and find the trade-off between efficiency and accuracy in this framework. Based on the default nnU-Net settings, we design a co-training framework consisting of two strategies to generate high-quality pseudo labels and make efficient inference respectively. Specifically, we first design a resource-intensive nnU-Net to iteratively generate high-quality pseudo labels for unlabeled data. Then we train another light-weight 3D nnU-Net using labeled data and selected unlabeled data, with high-quality pseudo labels used for the latter to achieve efficient segmentation. We conduct experiments on the FLARE22 challenge. Our resource-intensive nnU-Net achieves the mean DSC of 0.9064 on 13 abdominal organ segmentation tasks and ranks first on the validation leaderboard. Our light-weight nnU-Net shows the mean DSC of 0.8773 on the validation leaderboard but it makes a better trade-off between accuracy and efficiency. On the test set, it shows the mean DSC of 0.8864, the mean NSD of 0.9465, and the average inference time of 14.59s and wins the championship of the FLARE22 challenge. Our code is publicly available at https://github.com/Ziyan-Huang/FLARE22.

Keywords: Segmentation · Semi-supervised learning · Computational efficiency

1 Introduction

Abdominal organ segmentation is an important prerequisite of many clinical applications. In recent years, deep learning based methods are widely used to

J. Ma and B. Wang (Eds.): FLARE 2022, LNCS 13816, pp. 178–189, 2022.
https://doi.org/10.1007/978-3-031-23911-3_16

segment abdominal organs automatically. One of the most important baselines among these methods is nnU-Net [5] and many top solutions for medical image segmentation challenges in recent years are built based on it. Although nnU-Net can achieve state-of-the-art performance in a fully supervised manner, two distinct issues are observed: (1) the default nnU-Net has quadratic computation complexity to volume shape due to sliding-window inference; (2) the default nnU-Net does not support semi-supervised training. However, both the time budget for model inference and the number of labeled data are limited in real clinical scenarios. So, there is a great need for a framework that can make use of unlabeled data and make efficient inference simultaneously.

The Fast and Low-resource Semi-supervised Abdominal Organ Segmentation Challenge 2022 (FLARE22) is a competition that aims at efficiently segmenting 13 organs in CT images from 20+ medical groups. In addition to evaluating the abdominal organ segmentation accuracy, it also takes model efficiency into consideration. By studying the top methods in FLARE21 [7], we find that although the nnU-Net based method [4] can achieve the best DSC and NSD scores, all the top-5 methods do not use nnU-Net. This is probably due to its high resource consumption and low inference speed, making it only rank ninth. We summarized the main efficiency takeoffs from the winning methods in FLARE21: (1) use a small model and low-resolution images; (2) input whole volume image and use two-stage segmentation. Obviously, nnU-Net can also benefit from a small model and low-resolution input. However, inputting the whole volume images will lose the spacing information of medical images. We thus argue that keeping the spacing information and using the sliding-window strategy in nnU-Net is still necessary. The goal of two-stage segmentation is to first locate the region of interest (ROI) with a small computational cost and then conduct fine segmentation only on the ROI to achieve high efficiency. However, the default sliding window inference strategy in nnU-Net spends too much time on the background area, which heavily increases the inference time, especially in whole-body CT images.

The distinction between FLARE22 and FLARE21 is that challenge this year is the semi-supervised learning (SSL) task. In addition to 50 well-annotated images, 2000 unlabeled images are also provided. This setting is reasonable as the pixel-wise annotation is expensive and laborious especially when each pixel of thousands of CT images needs to be annotated into 13 different abdominal organs. Semi-supervised learning method, as a solution to such a dilemma, can be mainly divided into two types: (1) consistency-regularization-based method; (2) pseudo-label-based method. We pick the pseudo-label-based method and combine it with the nnU-Net framework for its simplicity. To achieve high performance, the quality and reliability of pseudo labels are essential. However, we can hardly achieve both efficiency and accuracy using only one model. Thus, we use an efficient small model for inference, while adopting a large model to generate high-quality pseudo labels to train such a small model.

In this paper, we design a framework consisting of two modified 3D nnU-Net to generate high-quality pseudo labels and make inference efficiently respectively.

Specifically, we design a resource-intensive nnU-Net to iteratively generate high-quality pseudo labels for 2000 unlabeled data. Then we conduct image-level selection based on the stability of different re-training iterations and filter out the pseudo labels that are less reliable. To achieve high inference efficiency, we first train a lightweight nnU-Net using the union of labeled images and selected unlabeled images with pseudo labels. Then, we further propose an efficient sliding window strategy based on the prior knowledge of the abdomen to reduce the number of inference windows. Furthermore, we also rewrite the implementation code of the time-consuming part in nnU-Net such as crop and resample.

Our main contributions are summarized as follows:

- We design a pseudo labeling framework based on nnU-Net that can generate high-quality pseudo labels and make inference efficiently simultaneously.
- We propose an image-level pseudo label selection method based on the stability of the pseudo labels during different re-training iterations. Models trained using our selected pseudo labels perform better.
- We propose an efficient sliding-window inference strategy by considering the prior knowledge of the abdominal organ volume. This strategy can greatly reduce the number of inference windows.
- We optimize the time-consuming parts of the code in nnU-Net such as crop and resample.

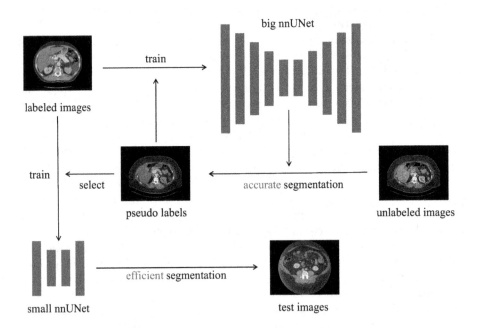

Fig. 1. Overview of our proposed framework.

Table 1. Comparison of different segmentation strategies. The first two rows evaluate model designs and the remaining rows are for inference strategies. The order of axes of input patch size and spacing is (z,y,x).

Settings	Default	Accurate	Efficient
Channels in the first stage	32	32	16
Convolution number per stage	2	3	2
Downsampling times	5	5	4
Input patch size	(40, 224, 192)	(48, 224, 224)	(32, 128, 192)
Input spacing	(2.5, 0.8, 0.8)	(2.5, 0.8, 0.8)	(4.0, 1.2, 1.2)
Test time augmentation	yes	yes	no

2   Method

As illustrated in Fig. 1, our framework contains two 3D nnU-Net to achieve high-quality pseudo labeling and efficient inference respectively.

2.1   Accurate Segmentation vs Efficient Segmentation

As revealed by EfficientNet [10], deeper and wider networks trained with higher resolution images always have better performance but also cost more computational resources. The default 3D nnU-Net prefers to keep the original resolution of images for better accuracy and resample the spacings of all images to the median spacings of the dataset (10th percentile of the spacings for anisotropic axis). However, the default nnU-Net also makes a compromise on the size of the network and input patch to make the network trainable within 10 GB GPU memory.

Based on the default setting of nnU-Net, we design a set of accurate but resource-intensive settings and a set of efficient settings. In the accurate settings, we use a bigger model and a bigger input patch size. In the efficient setting, we not only use a smaller model and smaller input patch size but also resample images to larger spacing. That also means the input images are with lower resolutions for efficient settings. Test time augmentation is applied in the default nnU-Net and our accurate setting, but we do not use it in our efficient setting as it will cost about 8× inference time. The detailed configurations and the comparison with default nnU-Net are listed in Table 1.

For image prepossessing, both of our accurate settings and efficient settings follow the default nnU-Net that clips CT images to 0.5 and 99.5 percentiles of foreground voxels and normalizes images by subtracting the mean then divides by the standard deviation calculated on all images. We do not conduct any postprocessing in our settings.

2.2   Iterative Pseudo Labeling by Accurate Segmentation

We adopt pseudo labeling, a simple but effective method, to leverage the unlabeled data for training model. Considering the unsatisfactory performance of the efficient segmentation strategy mentioned above, which may degrade the quality of pseudo labels, we use the accurate segmentation strategy to generate high-quality pseudo labels for the efficient segmentation strategy.

Simple Pseudo Labeling Scheme. Our pseudo labeling strategy includes the following steps:

1. Train 5 big nnU-Net models by 5-fold cross-validation on the labeled data.
2. Predict one-hot hard pseudo labels on unlabeled data using our designed accurate inference setting with a 5-fold ensemble of big nnU-Net.
3. Iterative re-train a big nnU-Net on the union of labeled data and unlabeled data with pseudo labels and then generate new one-hot hard pseudo labels for the next round.
4. Select pseudo labels based on the stability of pseudo labels during different training rounds.
5. Train a small nnU-Net on the union of labeled data and selected unlabeled data with pseudo labels for final evaluation.

Here we use the summation between Dice loss and cross-entropy loss because compound loss functions have been proven to be robust in various medical image segmentation tasks [6].

Pseudo Label Selection. As the trained big nnU-Net may not perform well in all the unlabeled images, some unreliable pseudo labels may harm the training of small nnU-Net. We design a simple method to filter the unreliable pseudo labels based on the stability during different training iterations. We assume that the generated pseudo labels should be stable during iterative training. If some pseudo labels vary greatly in different iterations, it indicates that the model is very uncertain about these pseudo labels and we should not use them for training. We calculate the uncertainty of pseudo labels using the following equation:

$$u = \frac{1}{K-1} \sum_{i=2}^{K} \frac{SUM(y_i \neq y_{i-1})}{SUM(y_i > 0)} \tag{1}$$

where u is the uncertainty and K is the total number of iterations, y_i is the pseudo label generated in iteration i.

2.3 Efficient Sliding Window Inference

Due to the high resolution of volumetric medical images, nnU-Net adopts the sliding-window strategy for inference. In this strategy, the total inference time depends on the number of windows and the inference time per window. Given input size (x, y, z), window size (p_x, p_y, p_z) and inference step size s, the number of sliding window N can be calculated as below:

$$N = \lceil \frac{x - p_x}{s * p_x} \rceil * \lceil \frac{y - p_y}{s * p_y} \rceil * \lceil \frac{z - p_z}{s * p_z} \rceil \tag{2}$$

where $s \in (0, 1]$ and $\lceil \cdot \rceil$ means round up operation.

Lower Resource Consumption for Each Window. In our efficient inference setting, we use a small model and small patch size as in Table 1 to accelerate the inference speed for each window and also reduce the GPU memory.

Reduce Total Number of Sliding Window. The default window sliding strategy designs steps for axis x, y, and z separately and uses three layers of for loop to traverse the whole image. However, the abdominal area occupies a small percentage of the entire image, especially in whole-body CT images. With prior knowledge of human anatomy, the region of abdominal organs is expected to have a limited volume and locate in the middle of each transverse section. So we propose to use 3 × 3 windows for each transverse section with 50% overlapping. In addition, we first do inference in the middle window, if this window has no foreground area, we can skip surrounding windows.

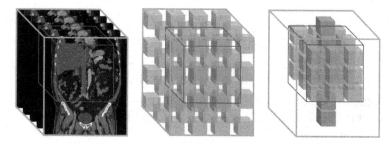

Fig. 2. Illustration of our proposed efficient sliding window strategy and comparison with nnU-Net. The red box indicates the region of interest for abdominal organs. The middle figure is the original sliding window strategy used in nnU-Net. The right figure is our proposed strategy that uses the middle window (brown) for every transverse section first to determine whether to do inference for surrounding windows (blue). (Color figure online)

3   Experiments

3.1   Dataset and Evaluation Measures

The FLARE2022 dataset is collected from more than 20 medical groups under the license permission, including MSD [9], KiTS [2,3], AbdomenCT-1K [8], and TCIA [1]. The training set includes 50 labeled CT scans with pancreas disease and 2000 unlabelled CT scans with liver, kidney, spleen, or pancreas diseases. The validation set includes 50 CT scans with liver, kidney, spleen, or pancreas diseases. The testing set includes 200 CT scans where 100 cases have liver, kidney, spleen, or pancreas diseases and the other 100 cases have uterine corpus endometrial, urothelial bladder, stomach, sarcomas, or ovarian diseases. All the CT scans only have image information and the center information is not available.

The evaluation measures consist of two accuracy measures: Dice Similarity Coefficient (DSC) and Normalized Surface Dice (NSD), and three running efficiency measures: running time, area under GPU memory-time curve, and area under CPU utilization-time curve. All the measures will be used to compute the ranking. Moreover, the GPU memory consumption has a 2 GB tolerance.

3.2 Implementation Details

The development environments and requirements are presented in Table 2. The training protocols of big nnU-Net and small nnU-Net are listed in Table 3 and 4 respectively. We adopt data augmentation of additive brightness, gamma, rotation, scaling, and elastic deformation on the fly during training. It is noticeable that we use mirror data augmentation for the big model but abandons it for the small model as the small model does not do test time augmentation (TTA) of flipping during inference.

Table 2. Development environments and requirements.

System version	CentOS Linux release 7.6.1810
CPU	Dual AMD Rome 7742@3.4 GHz
RAM	32×32GB; 3200MT/s
GPU (number and type)	8x NVIDIA A100 80GB Tensor Core GPUs
CUDA version	11.2
Programming language	Python 3.8.0
Deep learning framework	Pytorch (Torch 1.10.1)
Specific dependencies	nnU-Net 1.7.0
Code	https://github.com/Ziyan-Huang/FLARE22

Table 3. Training protocols for big nnU-Net.

Network initialization	"He" normal initialization
Batch size	2
Patch size	48×224×224
Total epochs	1000
Optimizer	SGD with nesterov momentum ($\mu = 0.99$)
Initial learning rate (lr)	0.01
Lr schedule	Poly learning rate policy: $(1 - epoch/1000)^{0.9}$
Training time	24 h
Loss function	Dice loss and cross entropy loss
Number of model parameters	82 M
Number of flops	776 G
CO_2eq	34.01 Kg

Table 4. Training protocols for small nnU-Net.

Network initialization	"He" normal initialization
Batch size	2
Patch size	32×128×192
Total epochs	1500
Optimizer	SGD with nesterov momentum ($\mu = 0.99$)
Initial learning rate (lr)	0.01
Lr schedule	Poly learning rate policy: $(1 - epoch/1500)^{0.9}$
Training time	12 h
Loss function	Dice loss and cross entropy loss
Number of model parameters	5.4 M
Number of flops	136 G
CO_2eq	11.08 Kg

4   Results and Discussion

4.1   Quantitative Results on Validation Set

For iterative pseudo labeling, we repeatedly generate pseudo labels for three iterations by using the big nnU-Net and then filter out 76 unreliable pseudo labels in the final iteration. The 76 unreliable pseudo labels is chosen by Eq. 1 when the threshold of μ is set to 0.1. That is, we have 50 labeled images and 1924 images with reliable pseudo labels in the end. We compare the performance of both big nnU-Net and small nnU-Net trained with or without 1924 reliable pseudo labels. We report the results of DSC on the validation leaderboard[1] in Table 5.

Table 5. DSC of accurate segmentation and efficient segmentation with and without selected pseudo labels on online validation leaderboard.

Model	Training Images	Liver	RK	Spleen	Pancreas	Aorta	IVC	RAG	LAG
Big nnU-Net	Labeled Only	0.9707	0.8894	0.9228	0.8688	0.9576	0.8950	0.8105	0.8414
Big nnU-Net	With Pseudo Labels	0.9802	0.9508	0.9696	0.8965	0.9731	0.9088	0.8481	0.8469
Small nnU-Net	Labeled Only	0.9564	0.8655	0.9134	0.8011	0.9292	0.8632	0.7466	0.7005
Small nnU-Net	With Pseudo Labels	0.9708	0.9382	0.9537	0.8764	0.9529	0.8909	0.7740	0.8038

Model	Training Images	Gallbladder	Esophagus	Stomach	Duodenum	LK	Mean
Big nnU-Net	Labeled Only	0.8375	0.8696	0.9067	0.7755	0.8903	0.8797
Big nnU-Net	With Pseudo Labels	0.8459	0.8894	0.9142	0.8363	0.9233	0.9064
Small nnU-Net	Labeled Only	0.6556	0.7931	0.8483	0.7077	0.8485	0.8176
Small nnU-Net	With Pseudo Labels	0.7660	0.8653	0.8949	0.8052	0.9127	0.8773

---

[1] https://flare22.grand-challenge.org/evaluation/challenge/leaderboard/.

As shown in Table 5, training models with labeled data and selected data with pseudo labels can improve models' performance compared to training models with only labeled data. Moreover, the improvement is more significant for small models with an efficient inference strategy.

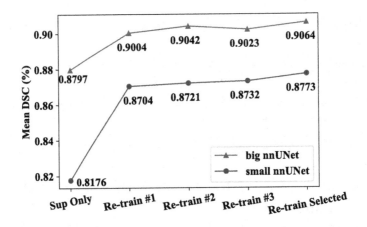

Fig. 3. Effectiveness of iterative training and label selection

We examine the effectiveness of iterative training and model selection in Figure 3. We can see that retraining models for more iteration can help improve performance but the performance gain is gradually flattening. We also observe that filtering out some noisy labels can further improve the models' performance.

4.2   Qualitative Results on Validation Set

Figure 4 shows 4 representative segmentation results of our small nnU-Net trained on 50 labeled data and 1924 selected pseudo labels for final submission. For Case #21 and Case #35, the network successfully identifies all organs with high accuracy. For Case #42 and Case # 48, it is easy to see that some under-segmentation and over-segmentation errors occurred. We argue that this is due to the small nnU-Net lack of reprehensibility and images after resampling to low resolution lose some important details.

4.3   Segmentation Efficiency Results

We build our small nnU-Net with an efficient inference strategy as a docker image for final submission. In Table 6, we report the efficiency evaluation results on our personal computer with 32 GB RAM, CPU i7-8700 and GPU 1070 using the official evaluation code[2].

---

[2] https://github.com/JunMa11/FLARE/tree/main/FLARE22/Evaluation.

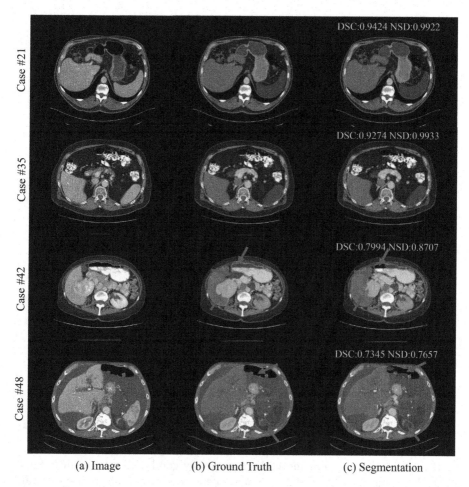

(a) Image   (b) Ground Truth   (c) Segmentation

Fig. 4. Qualitative results of our small nnU-Net on two easy cases (Case #21 and Case #35) and two hard cases (Case #42 and Case #48).

Table 6. Efficiency evaluation results of our submitted docker. All metrics reported are the average values on 50 validation cases

Time	GPU memory	AUC GPU Time	CPU Utilization	AUC CPU Time
12.8s	1762MiB	15990	71.8%	242

4.4   Results on Final Testing Set

Our method wins the championship among 47 submissions on the final testing set. Tables 7 and 8 shows the detail evaluation metrics of our method on final testing set.

Table 7. Testing results of our proposed method. All metrics reported are the average values on 200 testing cases.

DSC	NSD	Time	AUC GPU Time	AUC CPU Time
0.8864	0.9465	14.59s	14307	295

Table 8. Evaluation metrics of average±standard deviation of DSC and NSD per substructure on 200 testing cases.

Substructure	Mean DSC	Mean NSD
Liver	0.9743±0.0110	0.9863±0.0243
Right Kidney	0.9466±0.1179	0.9700±0.1161
Spleen	0.9432±0.1288	0.9624±0.1370
Pancreas	0.8528±0.1042	0.9537±0.1009
Aorta	0.9559±0.0239	0.9884±0.0289
Inferior Vena Cava	0.9040±0.0619	0.9224±0.0688
Right Adrenal Gland	0.8280±0.0941	0.9568±0.1020
Left Adrenal Gland	0.8286±0.0929	0.9591±0.0830
Gallbladder	0.8340±0.2548	0.8486±0.2631
Esophagus	0.8122±0.1174	0.9176±0.1183
Stomach	0.9237±0.0746	0.9609±0.0757
Duodenum	0.7904±0.1325	0.9236±0.1106
Left Kidney	0.9291±0.1396	0.9539±0.1397

It is noticeable that our method achieves very good performance in terms of NSD. We argue that the sliding window inference strategy plays an important role in boundary segmentation.

4.5 Limitation and Future Work

Pseudo labeling is a simple and conventional method for semi-supervised learning, but the pseudo label can still be noisy even after the uncertainty-based pseudo label selection. We will refer to the updated research progress to improve the quality of pseudo labels in our future work.

5 Conclusion

In this paper, we design a framework based on nnU-Net to use the unlabeled data for training and make inference efficiently. We believe that our proposed framework can serve as a good baseline for semi-supervised learning and efficient inference for medical image segmentation.

Acknowledgements. The authors of this paper declare that the segmentation method they implemented for participation in the FLARE 2022 challenge has not used any pre-trained models nor additional datasets other than those provided by the organizers. The proposed solution is fully automatic without any manual intervention.

References

1. Clark, K., et al.: The cancer imaging archive (TCIA): maintaining and operating a public information repository. J. Digital Imaging **26**(6), 1045–1057 (2013)
2. Heller, N., et al.: The state of the art in kidney and kidney tumor segmentation in contrast-enhanced CT imaging: results of the kits19 challenge. Med. Image Anal. **67**, 101821 (2021)
3. Heller, N., et al.: An international challenge to use artificial intelligence to define the state-of-the-art in kidney and kidney tumor segmentation in CT imaging. Am. Soc. Clin. Oncol. **38**(6), 626 (2020)
4. Huang, Z., Wang, Z., Yang, Z., Gu, L.: AdwU-Net: adaptive depth and width u-net for medical image segmentation by differentiable neural architecture search. In: Medical Imaging with Deep Learning (2022). https://openreview.net/forum?id=kF-d1SKWJpS
5. Isensee, F., Jaeger, P.F., Kohl, S.A., Petersen, J., Maier-Hein, K.H.: nnU-Net: a self-configuring method for deep learning-based biomedical image segmentation. Nat. Methods **18**(2), 203–211 (2021)
6. Ma, J., et al.: Loss odyssey in medical image segmentation. Med. Image Anal. **71**, 102035 (2021)
7. Ma, J., et al.: Fast and low-GPU-memory abdomen CT organ segmentation: the flare challenge. Med. Image Anal. **82**, 102616 (2022). https://doi.org/10.1016/j.media.2022.102616
8. Ma, J., et al.: Abdomenct-1k: Is abdominal organ segmentation a solved problem? In: IEEE Transactions on Pattern Analysis and Machine Intelligence (2021). https://doi.org/10.1109/TPAMI.2021.3100536
9. Simpson, A.L., et al.: A large annotated medical image dataset for the development and evaluation of segmentation algorithms. arXiv preprint arXiv:1902.09063 (2019)
10. Tan, M., Le, Q.: EfficientNet: rethinking model scaling for convolutional neural networks. In: International Conference on Machine Learning, pp. 6105–6114. PMLR (2019)

A Simple Mean-Teacher UNet Model for Efficient Abdominal Organ Segmentation

Zixiao Zhao$^{(\boxtimes)}$ and Jiahua Chu

AI Innovation and Commercialisation Centre, NUSRI, Suzhou, China
{zixiao.zhao,jiahua.chu}@nusri.cn

Abstract. One inevitable barrier to deep learning-based medical image segmentation algorithms is that for such tasks requiring high accuracy, all models must be trained using large datasets annotated by experts, and this process is exceptionally time-consuming and laborious. For abdominal organ segmentation, this problem becomes more prominent as the image size becomes larger. To address this problem, we design a classical UNet model using the Mean-Teacher strategy to obtain relatively satisfactory segmentation (58.93% DSC and 59.54% NSD)results on a semi-supervised abdominal segmentation dataset. The core idea is to use labeled data to improve the segmentation performance of the model itself, while introducing noise on unlabeled data to improve the generalization of the model. Inspired by nnUNet, we use as simple a model structure as possible, thus ensuring the efficiency during training and inference phases ($< 2\,\mathrm{GB}$ VRAM consumption and $\sim 10\,\mathrm{s}$ inference time).

Keywords: Medical image segmentation · Abdominal organ segmentation · Semi-supervised · UNet · Mean-Teacher

1 Introduction

In recent years, Convolutional Neural Networks (CNNs) and Transformers-based approaches have achieved state-of-the-art results in the field of medical image segmentation, e.g. [1,19]. However, with the development of such methods, the structure of the model becomes more and more complex, the parameters of the model increase dramatically, and the size of the annotated data required to train such complex models becomes larger and larger [8]. For medical image segmentation tasks, the annotation of the dataset implies expert labeling at pixel or voxel level, a process that is often extremely time-consuming and laborious [18]. For abdominal organ segmentation, this problem becomes more serious because the organs or diseases contained in this region are more complex, and the size and resolution of the images become larger [10].

In this context, semi-supervised segmentation methods become more practical due to their properties of requiring only a small amount of fine annotation and more unlabeled data instead. In the last three years, a large number of

J. Ma and B. Wang (Eds.): FLARE 2022, LNCS 13816, pp. 190–201, 2022.
https://doi.org/10.1007/978-3-031-23911-3_17

semi-supervised segmentation methods have achieved satisfactory results in their respective domains. One of the most widely used methods is the Mean-Teacher model [15] and its many variants [12,17,18]. Other commonly used strategies include pseudo labeling [16], adversarial learning [6], contrastive learning [11] and etc.

Despite advances in semi-supervised learning benchmarks, previous methods still face several major challenges: **Domain variation:** Most of these methods are based on 2D natural images and require additional learning costs if migrated to medical images. **Generalization:** Considering the limited amount of training data, training deep models is usually deficient due to over-fitting and co-adapting [17].

In this work, we propose a simple and effective semi-supervised scheme that is also based on the Mean Teacher [15] idea. This framework takes labeled and unlabeled images as input and introduces random noise for contamination, respectively. The uncontaminated original input images will predict the results by a Student model composed of an ordinary UNet [13], while the contaminated data will predict the other set of results by a Teacher model with exactly the same structure. For the labeled data, the Student model is supervised by ground truth on the one hand and by the consistency constraint of the predicted results of the contaminated data on the other hand, while for the unlabeled data, only their consistency loss is used for supervision. The parameters of the Teacher model are then periodically updated from the M_S by exponential moving average (EMA).

The main contribution of this work are two-fold: 1) Inspired by nnUnet [7], our approach uses only the classical UNet model for segmentation, making the training and prediction process cheap (<5 GB RAM and <2 GB VRAM) and efficient (6 s/image). 2) Still inspired by nnUnet [7], we use proper preprocessing methods (and multiple augmentation methods during training phase), which enables our model to achieve stable results even on data with inconsistent distribution.

2   Method

2.1   Preprocessing

Thanks to the rich transformation API provided by MONAI framework [3], we applied many pre-processing methods that can increase the reusability of the model.

General Preprocessing: General preprocessing represents transforms that are applied in the training, validation and prediction phases.

- Orientation matching: Based on the orientation of training data, all input images are uniformly adjusted to the "LPI" orientation.
- Resampling method for anisotropic data: After orientation matching we resample the image to the spacing of (4, 4, 10) to reduce the size of the input data.

- Intensity normalization method: For the intensity of the data, we only reserve the voxels whose intensity is inside the interval [-1000, 500], and then adjusted the value range to [0.0, 1.0].

2.2 Proposed Method

For general semi-supervised learning, the training set always consists of two parts. The labeled dataset D_l with N annotated images and the unlabeled dataset D_u, where there are M raw images ($M >> N$). The whole training set is $D_{N+M} = D_l \cup D_u$. For an image $x_i \in D_l$, its ground truth is available. Conversely, if $x_j \in D_u$, its ground truth is not provided [9]. Our Mean Teacher UNet model is shown in Fig. 1. For both D_l and D_u, they will be used for the calculation of consistency loss, corresponding to L_{c1} and L_{c2} in the figure. For D_l, it is additionally used to compute the common supervised segmentation loss L_s to update the model parameters.

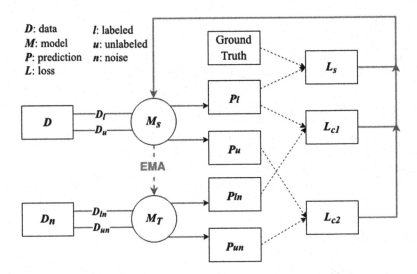

Fig. 1. Network architecture: Student and Teacher model are both randomly initialized, which receive uncontaminated and contaminated data respectively. Teacher model's parameter will be gradually updated from Student model by EMA.

In fact, we followed the exact same strategy as Mean Teacher. The overall architecture of the network consists of two parts, Student model M_S and Teacher model M_T. In our design, these two models are composed of two identical initialized UNet models.

$$\theta_T' = \alpha\theta_T + (1-\alpha)\theta_S \tag{1}$$

The update of M_T's parameters is obtained by exponentially moving average from M_S's parameters, depicted in Eq. 1. At the beginning of training phase, since model comes from random initialization, the parameters of M_S are definitely incorrect. M_T should be based on what M_S learns, so α should start from zero. As the network is being trained, after M_S reaches a certain accuracy, the ensemble can eventually be used, which means α can come to the value of 0.99 in the end. The network parameters of the M_S are updated by the gradient descent of the loss function. The loss function includes two categories: first the supervised Dice loss, which ensures the model has the basic segmentation ability, the second part is the unsupervised loss function, or consistency loss, and here we use MSE loss, which mainly ensures that the prediction of M_S is as similar as possible to the one of M_T between the contaminated and uncontaminated data (the contamination applied here is the additive Gaussian white noise). Because the parameters of M_T are the moving average of M_S, the prediction should not have too much jitters for any fluctuations. If the model is correct, the predicted labels of the two models Student and Teacher should be close. Then tuning the model in the direction that makes the prediction of the two models close is equal to move the model towards predicting the correct labels.

2.3 Post-processing

Due to the nature of the dataset, we did not use specific post-processing methods.

3 Experiments

3.1 Dataset and Evaluation Measures

The FLARE2022 dataset is curated from more than 20 medical groups under the license permission, including MSD [14], KiTS [4,5], AbdomenCT-1K [10], and TCIA [2]. The training set includes 50 labelled CT scans with pancreas disease and 2000 unlabelled CT scans with liver, kidney, spleen, or pancreas diseases. The validation set includes 50 CT scans with liver, kidney, spleen, or pancreas diseases. The testing set includes 200 CT scans where 100 cases has liver, kidney, spleen, or pancreas diseases and the other 100 cases has uterine corpus endometrial, urothelial bladder, stomach, sarcomas, or ovarian diseases. All the CT scans only have image information and the center information is not available.

The evaluation measures consist of two accuracy measures: Dice Similarity Coefficient (DSC) and Normalized Surface Dice (NSD), and three running efficiency measures: running time, area under GPU memory-time curve, and area under CPU utilization-time curve. All measures will be used to compute the ranking. Moreover, the GPU memory consumption has a 2 GB tolerance.

3.2 Implementation Details

Environment Settings. The development environments and requirements are presented in Table 1.

Table 1. Development environments and requirements.

Windows/Ubuntu version	Ubuntu 18.04.4 LTS
CPU	Intel(R) Xeon(R) Gold 6226 CPU @ 2.70GHz
RAM	12×32GB; 2.67MT/s
GPU (number and type)	8× NVIDIA GeForce RTX 2080Ti
CUDA version	11.1
Programming language	Python 3.6.10
Deep learning framework	Pytorch (Torch 1.7.0, torchvision 0.8.0)
Specific dependencies	monai 0.8.0
(Optional) Link to code	https://github.com/SeanCho1996/MeanTeacher3dUNet

Training Protocols. A refined training parameters are shown in Table 2.

In the training phase we perform a series of augmentation on the input data to improve the robustness of the model.

- Random Affine: In this stage we add random rotation and scale transformation.
- Cropping strategy: The cropping strategy is different for labeled and unlabeled training data: for labeled data, the foreground patches are randomly cropped according to the value of the labels, and conversely for unlabeled data, a completely random cropping is used. Patch size is fixed to (128, 128, 16)
- Other augmentation methods: random Gaussian noise as well as random flip in the three axes.

Table 2. Training protocols.

Network initialization	"he" normal initialization
Batch size	8 * 3 samples per image
Patch size	128×128×16
Total epochs	1000
Optimizer	Adam
Initial learning rate (lr)	1e–4
Lr decay schedule	/
Training time	15 h
Number of model parameters	3.5 M[7]
Number of flops	30.27 G[8]
CO_2eq	1 Kg[9]

4   Results and Discussion

4.1   Quantitative Results on Validation Set

The overall quantitative results are shown in Table 3.

Table 4 illustrates the results of either using the unlabeled data or not. It can be easily seen that the semi-supervised model outperforms the fully supervised model using only labeled data on all other classes except Pancreas and Duodenum with a subtle advantage of ∼0.6%. The generalization of the model is greatly enhanced due to the use of unlabeled data, coupled with a wide variety of data augmentations.

Table 3. Quantitative results on validation set.

Organ	DSC(%)	NSD (%)
Liver	81.56 ± 17.07	72.48 ± 19.02
Right Kidney	69.03 ± 24.96	61.02 ± 24.81
Spleen	76.03 ± 19.49	67.03 ± 20.68
Pancreas	54.87 ± 14.79	65.90 ± 14.47
Aorta	79.94 ± 12.27	76.32 ± 14.21
Inferior Vena Cava	68.10 ± 14.09	58.75 ± 14.45
Right Adrenal Gland	38.55 ± 17.90	51.25 ± 19.69
Left Adrenal Gland	35.97 ± 20.06	47.41 ± 23.77
Gallbladder	32.81 ± 27.87	24.31 ± 21.31
Esophagus	54.05 ± 15.88	65.11 ± 16.99
Stomach	57.32 ± 19.91	53.76 ± 19.39
Duodenum	46.20 ± 15.99	66.54 ± 17.25
Left Kidney	71.78 ± 22.57	64.17 ± 24.43
Mean	58.93 ± 18.68	59.54 ± 19.27

4.2   Qualitative Results on Validation Set

At the image level, we find that our model performs well in processing test images that are isotropic with labeled data, as shown in Figs. 2 and 3. The dimensions of these two images are (512, 512, 96) and (512, 512, 89), respectively, while the average size of the labeled data is approximately (512, 512, 100). Conversely, for images anisotropic with labeled data, as shown in Figs. 4 and 5, our model performs relatively poorly in this case. The dimensions of these two images are (512, 512, 203) and (512, 512, 171), respectively, and the scale in the coronal direction is almost twice of the labeled data. The reason for this situation is that in order to reduce the resource consumption of the model, we set the spacing of preprocessing relatively large, and in the process of downsampling, too much information is lost from these large scale images, resulting in their features not being easily computed.

Table 4. DSC(%) comparison on validation set.

Organ	With unlabeled data	without unlabeled data
Liver	**85.58**	80.81
Right Kidney	**71.69**	67.66
Spleen	**76.07**	72.87
Pancreas	53.93	**54.30**
Aorta	**79.62**	77.67
Inferior Vena Cava	**68.40**	66.84
Right Adrenal Gland	**38.06**	37.05
Left Adrenal Gland	**37.91**	33.03
Gallbladder	**34.22**	29.86
Esophagus	**57.83**	53.67
Stomach	**61.89**	50.18
Duodenum	45.41	**46.04**
Left Kidney	**72.22**	63.82
Mean	**60.22**	56.44

At the organ level, for targets with fixed shapes and large volumes, such as the right and left kidneys, the liver, and the spleen, it can be seen that our model performs well. In addition our model performs well for targets with fixed positions, such as the aorta and inferior vena cava. By observing the images we found that our model does not perform well when dealing with smaller scale targets, especially for (left and right) adrenal glands and gallbladder. This is fully explainable because as we set a large spacing, the feature representation would inevitably be weakened of small-scale targets.

4.3   Quantitative Results on Test Set

The overall quantitative results on test set are shown in Table 5.

4.4   Segmentation Efficiency Results

For the efficiency of segmentation, our model predicted 50 validation images using about 5 min, which we think is a relatively acceptable time. For the majority of validated images, the time used to predict individual results was within 11 s (the mean inference time on the validation set of our method is 11.56 s), but for images with large scales, our method used up to 45.45 s Although we increased the spacing of the input data to make the image array size smaller, we had to sacrifice the patch size to reduce the GPU memory usage (with a mean of 2036.04 MB and a max of 2067 MB), resulting in a larger number of patches, so our final prediction time is similar to the performance of nnUnet.

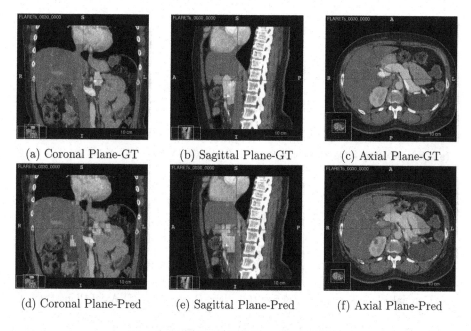

(a) Coronal Plane-GT   (b) Sagittal Plane-GT   (c) Axial Plane-GT

(d) Coronal Plane-Pred   (e) Sagittal Plane-Pred   (f) Axial Plane-Pred

Fig. 2. Standard Validation Case 00030

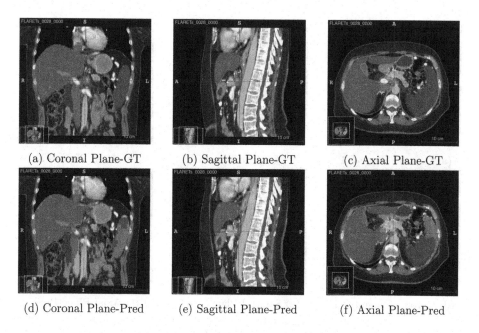

(a) Coronal Plane-GT   (b) Sagittal Plane-GT   (c) Axial Plane-GT

(d) Coronal Plane-Pred   (e) Sagittal Plane-Pred   (f) Axial Plane-Pred

Fig. 3. Standard Validation Case 00028

198   Z. Zhao and J. Chu

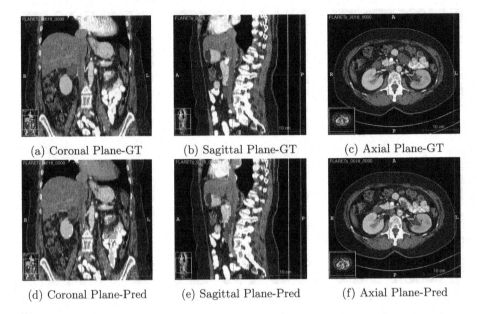

(a) Coronal Plane-GT   (b) Sagittal Plane-GT   (c) Axial Plane-GT

(d) Coronal Plane-Pred   (e) Sagittal Plane-Pred   (f) Axial Plane-Pred

Fig. 4. Bias Validation Case 00018

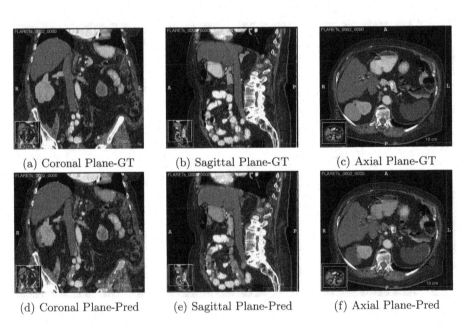

(a) Coronal Plane-GT   (b) Sagittal Plane-GT   (c) Axial Plane-GT

(d) Coronal Plane-Pred   (e) Sagittal Plane-Pred   (f) Axial Plane-Pred

Fig. 5. Bias Validation Case 00002

Table 5. Quantitative results on test set.

Organ	DSC(%)	NSD (%)
Liver	80.12 ± 10.56	68.61 ± 14.39
Right Kidney	64.59 ± 24.25	55.27 ± 24.22
Spleen	73.44 ± 22.86	65.14 ± 22.52
Pancreas	50.61 ± 16.43	63.11 ± 17.45
Aorta	78.00 ± 14.41	74.46 ± 16.35
Inferior Vena Cava	67.08 ± 15.68	59.61 ± 16.41
Right Adrenal Gland	41.91 ± 15.82	56.39 ± 19.22
Left Adrenal Gland	38.44 ± 19.45	51.00 ± 23.74
Gallbladder	35.14 ± 26.80	25.82 ± 19.69
Esophagus	52.70 ± 15.39	64.44 ± 16.50
Stomach	52.73 ± 19.33	48.11 ± 18.38
Duodenum	41.87 ± 15.75	62.04 ± 16.08
Left Kidney	68.61 ± 14.39	60.38 ± 23.44
Mean	58.14 ± 18.47	58.03 ± 19.11

4.5   Limitations and Future Work

As mentioned in Sects. 4.2 and 4.4, our model had to compromise the spacing after resampling and the size of the patches entering the neural network in order to improve the computational speed and reduce the computational consumption, which resulted in our model's ability to handle small-scale targets becoming extremely poor.

To solve this problem, our subsequent work has two general directions: one is to reduce the spacing appropriately to find the optimal parameter settings to balance the computational consumption and accuracy (we have tried smaller spacing, which will undoubtedly improve the segmentation accuracy significantly), and the other is to use a cascade model following nnUNet's practice to add an additional neural network structure for small-size targets.

In addition to optimization in terms of network structure, we can also do more experiments in data augmentation methods. At this stage, we have only used conventional and simple data augmentation methods. Due to time constraints, we did not have time to implement more complex enhancement methods such as CutOut or CutMix.

5   Conclusion

In conclusion, this work uses the classical Unet model and the Mean Teacher strategy to implement a semi-supervised abdominal organ segmentation task. We do not use complex model structures or difficult-to-deploy usage methods for unlabeled data because we adhere to the idea that for medical images, which usually have relatively fixed structures, good results should be obtained even using simple designs. This idea is also in line with the core idea of the nnUnet model [7], which has been most widely used in recent years. In addition, we slightly sacrifice the accuracy of small target segmentation to obtain a smaller model size and less computational resources.

Acknowledgements. The authors of this paper declare that the segmentation method they implemented for participation in the FLARE 2022 challenge has not used any pre-trained models nor additional datasets other than those provided by the organizers.

References

1. Chen, J., et al.: Transunet: transformers make strong encoders for medical image segmentation. arXiv preprint arXiv:2102.04306 (2021)
2. Clark, K., et al.: The cancer imaging archive (tcia): maintaining and operating a public information repository. J. Digit. Imaging **26**(6), 1045–1057 (2013)
3. Consortium, M.: MONAI: medical open network for AI (2020). https://doi.org/10.5281/zenodo.4323058. https://github.com/Project-MONAI/MONAI
4. Heller, N., et al.: The state of the art in kidney and kidney tumor segmentation in contrast-enhanced CT imaging: results of the kits19 challenge. Med. Image Anal. **67**, 101821 (2021)
5. Heller, N., et al.: An international challenge to use artificial intelligence to define the state-of-the-art in kidney and kidney tumor segmentation in CT imaging. Proc. Am. Soc. Clin. Oncol. **38**(6), 626 (2020)
6. Hu, X., et al.: Coarse-to-fine adversarial networks and zone-based uncertainty analysis for NK/T-cell lymphoma segmentation in CT/pet images. IEEE J. Biomed. Health Inform. **24**(9), 2599–2608 (2020)
7. Isensee, F., Jaeger, P.F., Kohl, S.A., Petersen, J., Maier-Hein, K.H.: nnU-net: a self-configuring method for deep learning-based biomedical image segmentation. Nat. Methods **18**(2), 203–211 (2021)
8. Luo, X.: SSL4MIS. https://github.com/HiLab-git/SSL4MIS (2020)
9. Luo, X., Hu, M., Song, T., Wang, G., Zhang, S.: Semi-supervised medical image segmentation via cross teaching between CNN and transformer. arXiv preprint arXiv:2112.04894 (2021)
10. Ma, J., et al.: Abdomenct-1k: Is abdominal organ segmentation a solved problem? IEEE Trans. Pattern Anal. Mach. Intell. (2021). https://doi.org/10.1109/TPAMI.2021.3100536
11. Peng, J., Wang, P., Desrosiers, C., Pedersoli, M.: Self-paced contrastive learning for semi-supervised medical image segmentation with meta-labels. In: Advances in Neural Information Processing Systems 34 (2021)
12. Reiß, S., Seibold, C., Freytag, A., Rodner, E., Stiefelhagen, R.: Every annotation counts: Multi-label deep supervision for medical image segmentation. In: Proceedings of the IEEE/CVF Conference on Computer Vision and Pattern Recognition, pp. 9532–9542 (2021)
13. Ronneberger, O., Fischer, P., Brox, T.: U-net: Convolutional networks for biomedical image segmentation. In: International Conference on Medical image computing and computer-assisted intervention, pp. 234–241 (2015)

14. Simpson, A.L., et al.: A large annotated medical image dataset for the development and evaluation of segmentation algorithms. arXiv preprint arXiv:1902.09063 (2019)

15. Tarvainen, A., Valpola, H.: Mean teachers are better role models: weight-averaged consistency targets improve semi-supervised deep learning results. In: Advances in Neural information processing systems 30 (2017)

16. Wang, G., et al.: Semi-supervised segmentation of radiation-induced pulmonary fibrosis from lung CT scans with multi-scale guided dense attention. In: IEEE Transactions on Medical Imaging (2021)

17. You, C., Zhou, Y., Zhao, R., Staib, L., Duncan, J.S.: SimcCVD: simple contrastive voxel-wise representation distillation for semi-supervised medical image segmentation. In: IEEE Transactions on Medical Imaging (2022)

18. Yu, L., Wang, S., Li, X., Fu, C.-W., Heng, P.-A.: Uncertainty-aware self-ensembling model for semi-supervised 3D left atrium segmentation. In: Shen, D., et al. (eds.) MICCAI 2019. LNCS, vol. 11765, pp. 605–613. Springer, Cham (2019). https://doi.org/10.1007/978-3-030-32245-8_67

19. Zhou, Z., Rahman Siddiquee, M.M., Tajbakhsh, N., Liang, J.: UNet++: a nested U-net architecture for medical image segmentation. In: Stoyanov, D., et al. (eds.) DLMIA/ML-CDS -2018. LNCS, vol. 11045, pp. 3–11. Springer, Cham (2018). https://doi.org/10.1007/978-3-030-00889-5_1

Cascade Dual-decoders Network for Abdominal Organs Segmentation

Ershuai Wang⬡, Yaliang Zhao, and Yajun Wu[✉]

Department of Research and Development, ShenZhen Yorktal DMIT Co. LTD,
Beijing, China
wuyj@yorktal.com

Abstract. In order to make full use of unlabeled images, we developed a pseudo-label based localization-to-segmentation framework for efficient abdominal organs segmentation. To reduce the target region, we locate the abdomen by a U-Net, then we train a fine organ segmentation model, which reduce the maximum usage of RAM memory. Segmentation with Dual-decoders is designed to improve the stability and cross supervise each other by pseudo labels. We also propose a class-weighted loss to pay more attention on the small organs like gallbladder, pancreas, which improve the mean DSC. Finally, we test the models on the public validation set, the total running time for the 50 CT images is 6676 s, the mean DSC is 0.8830 and the mean NSD is 0.9189.

Keywords: U-Net · Segmentation · Semi-supervised learning

1 Introduction

In recent years, deep supervised learning methods have made excellent achievements in computer vision, especially in computer-aided diagnosis [2], such as lesion detection [3], tumor benign and malignant diagnosis [4], organ segmentation [6] and so on. Abdominal organ segmentation involves organ quantification, surgical planning, disease diagnosis and so on. On the one hand, there are many organs, including liver, kidneys, pancreas, spleen, stomach and other organs [8]. Each organ has different sizes and shapes, for example, the shape of stomach in different time varies a lot even for the same person, these make accurate pixel segmentation very difficult. On the other hand, manual labeling is expensive and time consuming. Besides, labeling medical images requires professional medical knowledge and rich experience, which makes it much more difficult to achieve the needs of practical application by using supervised learning method. Therefore, semi-supervised learning, which makes effective use of a large number of unlabeled data and less labeled data, has become a research hotspot in the field of deep learning.

This paper proposes a cascade abdominal organ segmentation model follow the semi-supervised learning. Our framework based on the famous nnU-Net [5], and we trained a prime model using the 50 labeled CTs with the default

J. Ma and B. Wang (Eds.): FLARE 2022, LNCS 13816, pp. 202–213, 2022.
https://doi.org/10.1007/978-3-031-23911-3_18

parameters. To expand the training dataset [10], we generate the pseudo labels for 2000 unlabeled training cases using the trained model. Then we develop a cascade coarse-to-fine framework based on the provided labels and the pseudo labels. The first coarse model aims to obtain the rough location of the abdominal regions and the second fine model aims to segment the organs correctly. The fine model adopts cross pseudo training method [1,9], which reduces the feature noise influence and improves the stability.

The main contributions of this work are summarized as follows:

- We propose a cascade coarse-to-fine framework to make a trade-off of resource and precision.
- We design a dual-decoder model based on nn-UNet to make full use of unlabeled examples.
- We propose a class-weighted loss to improve the DSC of small organs.

2 Method

To expand the training dataset, we train a prime segmentation network based on nnU-Net with 50 provided labels first, then generate the pseudo labels for the unlabeled images. Finally, we train our coarse-to-fine framework using the all images and fine-tuning the segmentation model with the class-weighted loss. In this work, we do not optimize the segmentation efficiency of cascade framework.

2.1 Preprocessing

The preprocessing method in this paper refers to the fingerprint features of dataset proposed by nnU-Net [5], including the following steps:

- CT scans shape normalization   According to the average voxel spacing distance of the training data, the nearest neighbor interpolation is performed on the training data, that is, the CT's voxel spacing are rescale to $1.93 \times 1.50 \times 1.50$ mm for localization model and $1 \times 0.78 \times 0.78$ mm for segmentation model.
- Voxel intensity normalization   The mean value, variance and values of 0.5% and 99.5% of all training samples are counted, then the voxel intensity is normalized. Concretely, the voxel intensity is truncated to $[-973, 295]$, then minus the mean value 79.492 and divide the variance 142.997.

2.2 Pseudo Labeling

The objective of pseudo-labeling is to generate proxy labels to enhance the learning process [11,12]. Pseudo-labeling was successfully applied to a variety of tasks, such as image classification, semantic segmentation , text classification, machine translation and when learning from noisy data [12]. Therefore, we adopt pseudo labeling to enhance the abdominal organs segmentation.

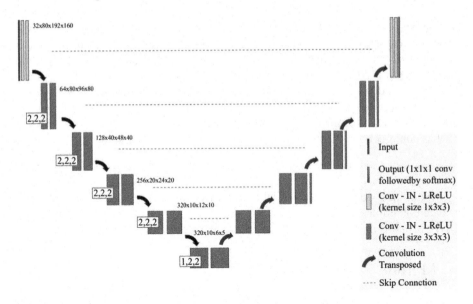

Fig. 1. Basic nnU-Net

To our best knowledge, nnU-Net has very good segmentation performance on many tasks even if we use the default parameters, such as number of layers, number of filters per layer, number of pooling layers. So, we train a prime nnU-Net model with the provided 50 labeled cases at first. Concretely, the model has 5 stages in encoder and decoder as showed in Fig. 1, and there are 2 convolution layers in each stage. The input patch-size is $80 \times 192 \times 160$, the number of filters are [32, 64, 128, 256, 320], the stride of first 4 stages and the last stage are [2, 2, 2] and [1, 2, 2] respectively.

After 2000 epochs training, we test the model on the pubic validation set which got a 0.8671 mean DSC. Therefore, we believe that this model can segment the abdominal organs well. Then, we generate the 2000 unlabeled training cases on 2 computers with this model. In this way, we expand the training set a lot. However, we find that this model takes about very large RAM especially for cases imaging whole body. Also, this basic model is very slow, it takes about 5 days to generate 1000 cases.

2.3 Proposed Method

To reduce the memory usage and inference time, we propose a cascade framework. As shown in the Fig. 2, the cascade framework consists of a localization model and a segmentation model, where the first localization model is used to determine the region of interest(ROI) before employing a segmentation model based on nn-UNet.

In a word, we locate the abdomen in low resolution space, then we segment the ROI in high resolution space.

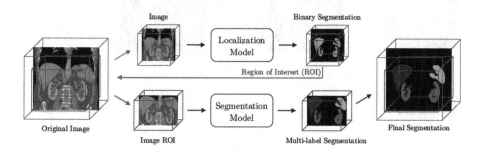

Fig. 2. Cascade framework

Localization Model. Our localization model is implemented as a coarse binary segmentation U-Net where all labeled organs are treated as the foreground label and which is trained using the full image content after greatly downsampling the raw image. The localization model can generate binary segmentation for each input image, which are used to compute the bounding box of abdominal region which we define as the ROI. The network architecture was adapted from the U-Net and trained using the generalized dice loss, i.e.,

$$L_l = L_{GD}(p, t) \tag{1}$$

where L_{GD} represents dice loss, p and t represent the predict label and the ground truth label. Our input size is $96 \times 160 \times 160$, spacing are $1.93 \times 1.50 \times 1.50$ mm.

Segmentation Model. The proposed segmentation network consists of one encoder and two decoders, as shown in Fig. 3. Each encoding block is composed of two **Conv->BN->LReLU** sequences, as shown in Fig. 4. Each decoding block consists of a up-sampling layer and an encoding block. We concatenate the feature channels between the decoder and the encoder with the same shape to reuse features and improve the ability of network feature extraction.

Specifically, the encoder includes five stages, in which the stride of the first convolution block of the coding block in the first and the last stage are [1, 2, 2], the stride for the other stages are [2, 2, 2], and the number of filters are [32, 64, 128, 256, 320]. The parameters for decoders are similar to the encoder but in the reverse direction. In this paper, the convolution kernel size are fixed as $3 \times 3 \times 3$.

For inference, we can use both decoders to predict which behaves like ensemble to get a better segmentation. Alternatively, we can use any one of the decoders to predict for saving time. During this competition, we only use the first decoder branch.

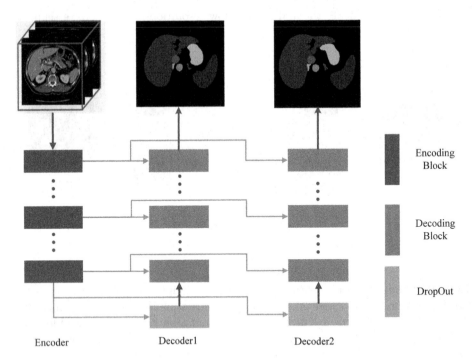

Fig. 3. Schematic of segmentation network

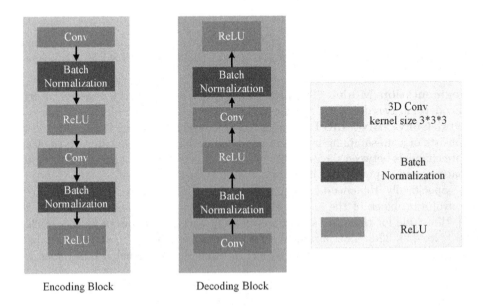

Fig. 4. Encoding and decoding blocks

Loss Function. The training objective contains two parts: supervision loss and cross pseudo supervision loss:

$$L = l_s + \lambda l_{cps} \tag{2}$$

where λ is the trade-off weight, we set $\lambda = 0.25$. The supervision loss l_s is formulated using the standard pixel-wise cross-entropy loss l_{cs} and dice similarity coefficient l_{dsc} on the training CT scans over the two decoder paths:

$$l_s = \frac{1}{|T|} \sum_T \frac{1}{DHW} \sum_{i=1}^{DHW} \sum_{k=0}^{1} l_{ce}(p_{i,k}, t_i, w_c) + w l_{dsc}(\hat{t}_{i,k}, t_i, w_c) \tag{3}$$

where T is the training dataset consists of manual labeled part and pseudo label part, l_{ce} is the cross-entropy loss function, $p_{i,k}$ is the predicted probability of the k_{th} decoder, t_i is the label, $\hat{t}_{i,k}$ is generate label, w_c is the class weight based on the previous dice similarity coefficient and $w = 1$ is the trade-off weight between cross entropy and dice similarity. Specifically, the higher the dice score of a category, the more accurate the prediction of that category is. Therefore, more attention should be paid to the prediction of the other categories in subsequent training. Based on this, we adopt the form of dice reciprocal as the original class weight, then we normalized the weights by the sum. In the training process, the class weights are updated in a way similar to momentum optimization.

$$w_{ci} = \frac{1}{dsc_i + \epsilon} \tag{4}$$

$$w_{ci} = \frac{w_{ci}}{\sum_{i=1}^{13} w_{ci}} \tag{5}$$

$$w_{ci}^k = 0.5 w_{ci}^{k-1} + 0.5 w_{ci}^k \tag{6}$$

where dsc_i is the dice score of the $i-th$ organ, ϵ=1e-6 is added to avoid the error of division by zero, w_*^k is the weight of the $k-th$ epoch and we set $w_{ci}^0 = \frac{1}{13}$.

2.4   Post-processing

Connected component-based post-processing is commonly used in medical image segmentation. Especially in organ image segmentation, it often helps to eliminate the detection of spurious false positives by removing all but the largest connected component. So we compare the mean DSC between the prime predict and the post-processing. We find that the post-processing improve the DSC for liver, kidneys, spleen and aorta but degrade the DSC for small organs, especially for pancreas, gallblader and esophagus. Finally, we decide to do post-processing only on the liver, kidneys, spleen and aorta, thus improve the mean DSC by 0.0008.

3   Experiments

3.1   Dataset and Evaluation Measures

Dataset. The FLARE 2022 is an extension of the FLARE 2021 [7] with more segmentation targets and more diverse abdomen CT scans. The FLARE2022 dataset is curated from more than 20 medical groups under the license permission, including MSD [10], KiTS [3,4], AbdomenCT-1K [8], and TCIA [2]. The training set includes 50 labelled CT scans with pancreas disease and 2000 unlabelled CT scans with liver, kidney, spleen, or pancreas diseases. The validation set includes 50 CT scans with liver, kidney, spleen, or pancreas diseases.

The testing set includes 200 CT scans where 100 cases has liver, kidney, spleen, or pancreas diseases and the other 100 cases has uterine corpus endometrial, urothelial bladder, stomach, sarcomas, or ovarian diseases. All the CT scans only have image information and the center information is not available.

Evaluation Measures. The evaluation measures consist of two accuracy measures: Dice Similarity Coefficient (DSC) and Normalized Surface Dice (NSD), and three running efficiency measures: running time, area under GPU memory-time curve, and area under CPU utilization-time curve. All measures will be used to compute the ranking. Moreover, the GPU memory consumption has a 2 GB tolerance.

3.2   Implementation Details

Data Augmentation. We run the augmentations on the fly and with associated probabilities to obtain a never ending stream of unique examples the same as nnU-Net [5]. Concretely, we apply rotation, scaling, mirror, Gaussian noise, brightness variation and contrast variation on the sampled patches.

Environment Settings. The development environments and requirements are presented in Table 1.

Table 1. Development environments and requirements.

Windows/Ubuntu version	Windows 10 pro
CPU	Intel(R) Core(TM) i7-10700kF CPU@3.80GHz
RAM	16×4 GB; 2.67 MT/s
GPU (number and type)	One NVIDIA RTX 3090 24 G
CUDA version	11.1
Programming language	Python 3.8
Deep learning framework	Pytorch (Torch 1.10, torchvision 0.9.1)
Link to code	https://github.com/Shenzhen-Yorktal/flare22

Training Protocols. In the training process, the batch size is 2 and 500 patches are randomly selected from the training set per epoch, the patch size is fixed as 56 * 160 * 192. For optimization, we train it for 1500 epochs using SGD with a learning rate of 0.01 and a momentum of 0.9. During training, the learning rate is annealed following the poly learning rate policy, where at each iteration, the base learning rate is multiplied by .

Table 2. Training protocols.

Network initialization	"he" normal initialization
Batch size	2
Patch size	$56 \times 160 \times 192$
Total epochs	1500
Optimizer	SGD with nesterov momentum ($\mu = 0.99$)
Initial learning rate (lr)	0.01
Lr decay schedule	poly learning rate policy $lr = 0.01 * (1 - \frac{e}{m})^2$
Training time	104.5 h
Number of model parameters	41.22 M
Number of flops	59.32 G

4 Results and Discussion

4.1 Quantitative Results on Validation Set

We perform controlled experiments with the same training configurations as described in Sect. 3.2. As the baseline, we train a U-Net-like model with the 50 labeled data only. Then we generate the pseudo labels for the 2000 unlabeled data, and re-train the same model with the labeled data and pseudo labeled data. After that, we fine-tune the model with class-weighted loss. Finally, we obtain 3 models with different mean DSC: 0.8671, 0.8749, 0.8890.

Table 3 illustrates the detailed results on validation set. It's obvious that the pseudo label improves the baseline DSC for most organs except RAG and LK . We think that the pseudo label behaves like the augmentation, which enlarges the training set 40 times and improving the mean DSC. The degradation of RAG and LK come from the over-fitting of the baseline model. Class-weighted loss, assign larger weights for organs with poor DSC, improves the DSC a lot for RAG, LAG, gallbladder and LK. We think that the class-weighted loss is similar to the attention mechanism, which degrades the extreme high DSC slightly but improves the others.

We choose the class-weighted model for the FLARE22, and the all followings are based on this.

Table 3. Segmentation DSC of abdominal organs.

DSC	Labeled only	All	Class-weighted loss
Liver	0.9721	0.9807	0.9790
Right Kidney(RK)	0.9140	0.9257	0.9387
Spleen	0.9569	0.9727	0.9580
Pancreas	0.8505	0.8882	0.8701
Aorta	0.9560	0.9674	0.9601
IVC	0.8833	0.9026	0.9018
RAG	0.8367	0.8226	0.8603
LAG	0.8345	0.8367	0.8603
Gallbladder	0.7279	0.7401	0.7650
Esophagus	0.8263	0.8690	0.8754
Stomach	0.8673	0.8952	0.8941
Duodenum	0.7584	0.7764	0.7915
Left Kidney(LK)	0.8890	0.8722	0.9027
Mean	**0.8671**	**0.8749**	**0.8890**

4.2 Qualitative Results on Validation Set

Both DSC and NSD scores vary greatly in abdominal organs segmentation between different case. For example, the mean DSC for validation case21 and case48 are 0.967 and 0.686, the mean NSD are 0.995 and 0.716.

Figure 5 presents some well-segmented and challenging cases in the validation set. It can be observed that for the well-segmented cases, the predictions are almost the same with the ground truths. We think that the satisfying segmentation come from the clear boundaries and good contrast of the organs. In contrast with the well-segmented cases, the challenging cases are poor, which missing some organs part or all, as shown in Fig. 5(b). We think that the bad segmentation come from the heterogeneous lesions and the unclear boundaries.

4.3 Segmentation Efficiency Results on Validation Set

We run our models on a docker with NVIDIA 1080 GPU(12 GB) and 64 GB RAM for the 50 validation cases. The mean running time per case is 133.5 s, the maximum GPU memory used is 3041 MB and the maximum RAM used is 27466 MB. We find that the large RAM consumption are during the prediction of validation Case 10 and 50 which are scans of full body. The average AUC of GPU and CPU are 252158 and 2422 respectively, which is really high because of the long inference time.

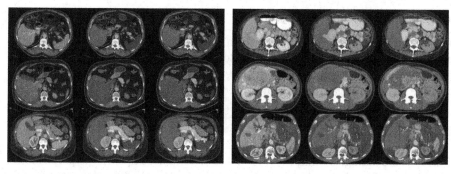

(a) Well-segmented cases (b) Challenging cases

Fig. 5. Well-segmented and challenging cases from validation sets

Table 4. Results on final testing set.

	DSC	NSD
Liver	0.9820 ± 0.0137	0.9843 ± 0.0288
Right Kidney(RK)	0.9488 ± 0.1505	0.9466 ± 0.1520
Spleen	0.9716 ± 0.0618	0.9732 ± 0.0751
Pancreas	0.8569 ± 0.1257	0.9431 ± 0.1257
Aorta	0.9649 ± 0.0352	0.9811 ± 0.0415
IVC	0.9063 ± 0.0855	0.9063 ± 0.0954
RAG	0.8934 ± 0.0753	0.9768 ± 0.0738
LAG	0.8774 ± 0.1117	0.9612 ± 0.1059
Gallbladder	0.8266 ± 0.2903	0.8355 ± 0.2988
Esophagus	0.8220 ± 0.1530	0.9032 ± 0.1511
Stomach	0.9133 ± 0.1048	0.9317 ± 0.1118
Duodenum	0.7741 ± 0.1741	0.8978 ± 0.1401
Left Kidney(LK)	0.9385 ± 0.1506	0.9363 ± 0.1411
Mean	**0.8981**	**0.9367**

4.4 Results on Final Testing Set

According to the requirement, we submit the docker to FLARE22 and the organizer run the model on the hidden test set, which consists of 200 CT scans. The final mean DSC is 0.8981 and the mean NSD is 0.9367, which are close to the result on validation set. The detail showed in Table 4. We can see that most organs have very high DSC except gallbladder, esophagus and duodenum. We think it due to the relatively smaller volume of these organs.

4.5 Limitation and Future Work

As showed in Sect. 4.3, our model use large RAM for some cases and the GPU memory used is higher than 2048 MB. Besides, the DSC of gallbladder and some tiny organs are much poorer than liver. Therefore, we will focus on the speed and the specified organ segmentation in the future.

5 Conclusion

During the training, we find that the unlabeled images improve the performance which proves the data-driven of deep learning again. And we use cross pseudo supervise to improve the model further, which shows the Semi-Supervised-Learning power in computer vision. It would also be interesting to adapt and examine the effectiveness of SSL in other visual tasks and learning settings.

Acknowledgements. We declare that the segmentation method they implemented for participation in the FLARE 2022 challenge has not used any pre-trained models nor additional datasets other than those provided by the organizers. The proposed solution is fully automatic without any manual intervention.

References

1. Chen, X., Yuan, Y., Zeng, G., Wang, J.: Semi-supervised semantic segmentation with cross pseudo supervision. In: Proceedings of the IEEE/CVF Conference on Computer Vision and Pattern Recognition (CVPR), pp. 2613–2622 (2021)
2. Clark, K., et al.: The cancer imaging archive (tcia): maintaining and operating a public information repository. J. Digit. Imaging **26**(6), 1045–1057 (2013)
3. Heller, N., et al.: The state of the art in kidney and kidney tumor segmentation in contrast-enhanced CT imaging: results of the kits19 challenge. Med. Image Anal. **67**, 101821 (2021)
4. Heller, N., et al.: An international challenge to use artificial intelligence to define the state-of-the-art in kidney and kidney tumor segmentation in CT imaging. Proc. Am. Soc. Clin. Oncol. **38**(6), 626 (2020)
5. Isensee, F., Jaeger, P.F., Kohl, S.A., Petersen, J., Maier-Hein, K.H.: nnU-net: a self-configuring method for deep learning-based biomedical image segmentation. Nat. Methods **18**(2), 203–211 (2021)
6. Ma, J., et al.: Loss odyssey in medical image segmentation. Med. Image Anal. **71**, 102035 (2021)
7. Ma, J., et al.: Fast and low-GPU-memory abdomen CT organ segmentation: the flare challenge. Med. Image Anal. **82**, 102616 (2022). https://doi.org/10.1016/j.media.2022.102616
8. Ma, J.: Abdomenct-1k: Is abdominal organ segmentation a solved problem? IEEE Trans. Pattern Anal. Mach. Intell. (2021). https://doi.org/10.1109/TPAMI.2021.3100536
9. Ouali, Y., Hudelot, C., Tami, M.: Semi-supervised semantic segmentation with cross-consistency training. IEEE (2020)
10. Simpson, A.L., et al.: A large annotated medical image dataset for the development and evaluation of segmentation algorithms. arXiv preprint arXiv:1902.09063 (2019)

11. Yang, X., Song, Z., King, I., Xu, Z.: A survey on deep semi-supervised learning. CoRR abs/2103.00550 (2021). https://arxiv.org/abs/2103.00550
12. Zoph, B., et al.: Rethinking pre-training and self-training. CoRR abs/2006.06882 (2020). https://arxiv.org/abs/2006.06882

Semi-supervised 3D U-Net Learning Based on Meta Pseudo Labels

Chuda Xiao[1,2], Zhuo Chen[2], Haoyu Li[1], Dan Li[2], Rashid Khan[1], Jinyu Tian[2], Weiguo Xie[2(✉)], and Liyilei Su[1,3(✉)]

[1] College of Big data and Internet, Shenzhen Technology University, Shenzhen 518188, China
{2070416011,2100411010}@stumail.sztu.edu.cn,
Rashidkhan@mail.ustc.edu.cn, suliyilei@sztu.edu.cn
[2] Wuerzburg Dynamics Inc.,
Shenzhen 518118, China
{zhuo.chen,dan.li,jinyu.tian,weiguo.xie}@wuerzburg-dynamics.com
[3] Guangdong Key Laboratory for Biomedical Measurements and Ultrasound Imaging, National-Regional Key Technology Engineering Laboratory for Medical Ultrasound, School of Biomedical Engineering, Shenzhen University Medical School, Shenzhen 518060, China

Abstract. Deep learning models have demonstrated promising performance for segmenting medical images and are significantly dependent on a huge amount of well-annotated data. However, it is difficult to get a large amount of data, particularly in clinical practices. Likewise, high-performance deep learning models have an enormous model size, restricting their use in actual applications. In order to reduce the burden of both expensive annotations and computational expenses, we designed the semi-supervised knowledge-based method on top of 3D U-Net and Meta Pseudo Labels. We train the teacher network with labelled data to generate the pseudo labels. And then we train the student network on the pseudo labels, and give the training feedback to the teacher network. The student network on FLARE2022 grand challenge Dataset achieved 81.19 % of DSC and 85.20% of NSD. As for the network inference speed, it needs 50.59 s for a single case.

Keywords: Meta pseudo labels · Semi-supervise · One-step gradient

1 Introduction

Abdomen organ segmentation is essential and plays an important role in artificial intelligence-based clinical diagnosis and treatment such as organ quantification and surgical planning etc. [1]. In order to accelerate such research and developments, Fast and Low-resource semi-supervised Abdominal oRgan sEgmentation in CT (FLARE 2022) challenge has been introduced, that uses semi-supervised

---

C. Xiao, Z. Chen and H. Li—These authors contributed equally to this work.

J. Ma and B. Wang (Eds.): FLARE 2022, LNCS 13816, pp. 214–222, 2022.
https://doi.org/10.1007/978-3-031-23911-3_19

settings and focuses on the usage of unlabeled data. Though it is not easy to segment multiple organs automatically. For instance, multiple organs may vary in shape and size, and thus, organ lesions lead to abnormal segmentation. Similarly, multi-center data with different scan ranges, and high computing resource are required. However, it is also not easy to collect large amount of annotated data. Thus, semi-supervised learning techniques are efficient to generate labeled data from unlabeled data. Therefore, we propose a 3D U-Net Meta pseduo labels (MPL) method [2], which is a semi-supervise learning approach for segmenting multiple abdominal organs. The proposed method has the following features.

1. Using the MPL semi-supervise method with 3D U-Net [3] can perform automatic segmentation of multiple organs in abnormal CTs.
2. Combine the nnU-Net [4] framework, a surpervise learning framework, with the semi-supervise learning.

2   Method

We proposed a pair of networks entails a teacher and student network based on Meta Pseudo Labels. In the proposed network, teacher module generates pseudo labels from unlabeled data. Further, the pseudo labels and labeled images are utillized for training the student module. The teacher network receives feedback from the student network regarding their performance for the improvement of their predictions. The schematic diagram of teacher-student network is depicted in Fig. 1.

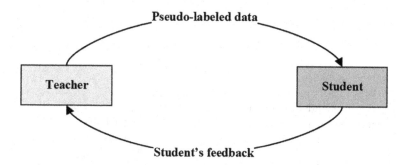

Fig. 1. The teacher-student semi-supervised network. When training the models, teacher model would inference the unlabeled data and use the pseudo-labeled data from teacher model to train the student model. The student model provides the feedback to teacher model.

2.1   Pre-processing

Our preprocessing approach is the same as the nn U-Net. In the preprocessing step, the computed tomography (CT) images were left uncropped. However, for anisotropic images (maximum axis spacing > 3), in-plane resampling is performed with third order spline whereas out of plane interpolation is performed with nearest neighbor interpolation. Furthermore, we use 0.5 and 99.5 percentiles of the foreground voxels for clipping as well as the global foreground mean (a standard deviation) for normalization on all images.

2.2   Proposed Method

One-step Gradient. For the proposed method we formulate our model as follows. Where T and S refer to teacher and student networks, respectively, whereas w_T and w_s refer to their parameters. Let (x_l, y_l) is a batch of images and their labels, and define x_u as a batch of unlabeled images. p denotes the soft prediction and L for the loss function. In our method, the loss function is cross-entropy loss and dice loss.

Algorithm 1. One-step gradient on MPL

1: Input: Labeled data x_l, y_l and unlabeled data x_u
2: Initialization:$w_t^{(0)}, w_s^{(0)}, t \leftarrow 0$
3: **repeat**
4:    Sample a labeled example x_l, y_l and an unlabeled example x_u
5:    Put x_l, x_u into teacher network get soft prediction p_l^T, p_u^T:

$$p_l^T = T(x_l; \omega_T^{(t)}), p_u^T = T(x_u; \omega_T^{(t)})$$

6:    Generate pseudo label $\hat{y}_u$:$\hat{y}_u = Argmax(Softmax(p_u^T))$
7:    Feed x_l, x_u into student network get soft prediction p_l^S, p_u^S:

$$p_l^S = S(x_l; \omega_S^{(t)}), p_u^S = S(x_u; \omega_S^{(t)})$$

8:    Update the student using the pseudo label $\hat{y}_u$:

$$\omega_S^{(t+1)} = \omega_S^{(t)} - \alpha_s \nabla_{\omega_S} L(\hat{y}_u, p_u^S)$$

9:    Feed x_l into student network get soft prediction: $p_l^{S'} = S(x_l; \omega_S^{(t+1)})$
10:   Compute the teacher's gradient $g_T^{(t)}$ from student's feedback:

$$g_T^{(t)} = \nabla_{\omega_T}(L(\hat{y}_u, p_l^{S'}) - L(\hat{y}_u, p_l^S) \cdot L(p_u^T, \hat{y}_u))$$

11:   Compute the teacher's gradient on labeled data:

$$g_{T,supervised}^{(t)} = \nabla_{\omega_T} L(p_l^T, y_l)$$

12:   Update the teacher: $\omega_T^{(t+1)} = \omega_T^{(t)} - \alpha_T(g_T^{(t)} + g_{(T,supervised)}^{(t)})$
13:   Update epoch: $t \leftarrow t + 1$
14: **until** $t > N - 1$
Output: Teacher model ω_T^{N-1},Student model ω_S^{N-1}

The Backbone Network. Our backbone network utilizes 3D U-Net, which has four upsampling and downsampling layers. Each layer is composed of 3D convolutions, ReLU activations and batch normalization. The first level of the 3D U-Net extracts 32 feature maps and each downsampling process maximizes the extracted feature maps up to 512. The 3D U-Net backbone network is depecited in Fig. 2.

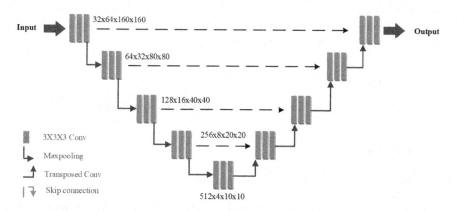

Fig. 2. The 3D U-Net network architecture.

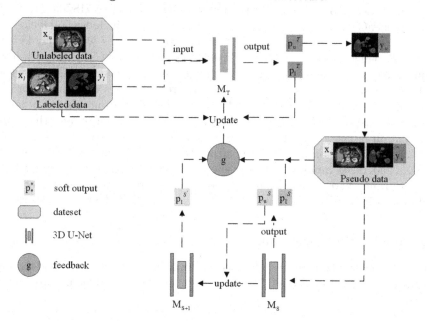

Fig. 3. Our proposed semi-supervised method based on the Meta pseudo labels where the backbone model is a 3D U-Net. x denotes the input, y denotes the label or the output, M represents the model, and p denotes the softmax output.

Proposed Semi-supervised Method. Our semi-supervised learning method is based on MPL and 3D U-Net as shown in Fig. 3 and their symbolic representation described in One-step gradient(Sect. 2.2), which having the detail of the method. In the proposed method, the teacher's model (M_t) is trained only by the labeled data which generates the pseudo data. After that, student's model (M_s) uses the pseudo data and unlabel data to train student model and uses the pseduo labels again by utilizing the gradient descent and update M_s to a new student model i.e., M_{s+1}. Finally, we use the output from M_s and M_{s+1} to calculate the student's model feedback which is used as a reward to train the teacher for generating better pseudo labels.

2.3 Post-processing

As for post-processing, we just resample the data to its original size.

3 Experiments

3.1 Dataset and Evaluation Measures

The FLARE 2022 is an extension of the FLARE 2021 [5] with more segmentation targets and more diverse abdomen CT scans. The dataset is curated from more than 20 medical groups under the license permission including MSD [6], KiTS [7, 8], AbdomenCT-1K [9], and TCIA [10]. The training set includes 50 labeled CT scans with pancreas disease and 2000 unlabeled CT scans with liver, kidney, spleen, or pancreas diseases. The validation set includes 50 CT scans with liver, kidney, spleen, or pancreas diseases. The testing set includes 200 CT scans where 100 cases have liver, kidney, spleen, or pancreas diseases and the other 100 cases have uterine corpus endometrial, urothelial bladder, stomach, sarcomas, or ovarian diseases. All the CT scans only have image information and the center information is not available. The evaluation measures consist of two accuracy measures i.e., Dice Similarity Coefficient (DSC) and Normalized Surface Dice (NSD), and three running efficiency measures: running time, area under GPU memory-time curve (lower than 2048 MB is preferred), and area under CPU utilization-time curve. All measures are used to compute the ranking score.

3.2 Implementation Details

Our implementation details with respect to configured environments and requirements are provided in Table 1. Training protocols for our model are provided in Table 2.

Table 1. Development environments and requirements.

Windows/Ubuntu version	Ubuntu 20.04.1 LTS
CPU	AMD EPYC 7742 64-Core Processor
RAM	1.8TB
GPU (number and type)	NVIDIA A100 40 G($\times$8)
CUDA version	11.4
Programming language	Python 3.8
Deep learning framework	Pytorch (1.10)

Table 2. Training and Inference protocols.

Data augmentation	scaling, rotation, random crop, mirror
Network initialization	"He" normal initialization
Batch size	8
Patch size	$32 \times 64 \times 160 \times 160$
Total epochs	1000
Optimizer	SGD with nesterov momentum(μ=0.99)
Weight decay	3e–5
Initial learning rate (lr)	0.01
Lr scheduler	ReduceLROnPlateau
Training time	113 h
Loss function	Dice Loss + Cross Entropy Loss

4 Results and Discussions

4.1 Quantitative Results on Validation Set

For ablation study to analyze the effect of unlabeled data and semi-supervised learning, the validation set we used was the official data of 50 abdominal CT cases. For labeled data, 50 cases of data were used to train a 3D U-Net model as the baseline segmentation model. For unlabeled data, all of the data were used to train the semi-supervised data model, and the MPL student's model was used to segment organs. The ablation study results are provided in the Table 3, containing the Dice of MPL and baseline method for 13 organs and mean Dice for all classes. Baseline is the 3D U-Net method using all labeled data belonging to supervised learning and MPL is the 3D U-Net method based on proposed MPL, belonging to semi-supervised-based learning. The results show that MPL is better than baseline method.

Table 3. Quantitative results on 50 cases of validation set.

Method	Baseline(Dice)	Baseline+MPL(Dice)
Liver	0.9651	0.9752
RK	0.8643	0.8840
Spleen	0.8580	0.9390
Pancreas	0.8530	0.8777
Aorta	0.9510	0.9624
IVC	0.8777	0.8909
RAG	0.8083	0.8076
LAG	0.8100	0.8066
Gallbladder	0.7143	0.7540
Esophagus	0.8794	0.8781
Stomach	0.8633	0.8824
Duodenum	0.7220	0.7520
LK	0.8712	0.8499
mean	0.8491	0.8661

4.2   Qualitative Results

Figure 4 shows successful segmentation of 4 cases including case0002 and case0006 which are easy cases and the two other cases are challenging. The results show that the proposed method can not segment similar organs and organ boundaries well. For example, the left kidney of case0033 was not well segmented, and some of the organ boundaries in case0038 are incomplete.

4.3   Segmentation Efficiency Results

According to official information, If the GPU memory is less than 2 GB when segmenting the organs, the participants would get the prefect score on the AUC_GPU_Time metric, but our model actually used GPU memory which is nearly with 7 GB memory. So it indicated that the nnU-Net framework has the defect of too high GPU memory and leads to a relatively large AUC_GPU_Time. The main reason is that model trained by nnU-Net framework is too large, which leads to a long running time and high GPU occupancy. And we did not have any optimization at segmentation efficiency.

4.4   Results on Final Test Set

As shown in Table 4, we validate our model on the test set from Flare22 and we achieve the Dice score of 0.8119 and the NSD score of 0.8520. As for the efficiency, it costs an average of 50.59 s for each case. The AUC_GPU_Time is 178242 and the AUC_CPU_Time is 1221 where infered a case from the official result.

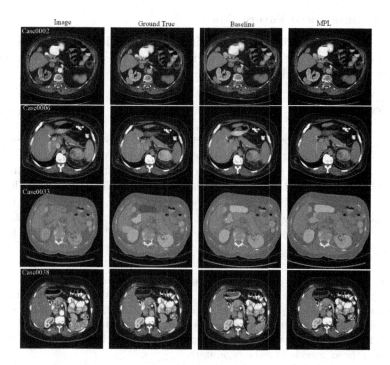

Fig. 4. Qualitative results on challenging and easy cases. The case2 and case6 are the easy inference cases , the case33 and case38 are the challenging cases.

Table 4. the result of testing on the testing set.

Method	Dice	NSD
Liver	0.93106	0.89955
RK	0.83242	0.79604
Spleen	0.85300	0.84863
Pancreas	0.80521	0.89282
Aorta	0.90872	0.92650
IVC	0.82243	0.82277
RAG	0.82164	0.93450
LAG	0.77253	0.88452
Gallbladder	0.74526	0.74285
Esophagus	0.75769	0.84470
Stomach	0.83977	0.85271
Duodenum	0.68229	0.83226
LK	0.78296	0.79772
mean	0.8119	0.8520

4.5   Limitation and Future Work

Our method shows great performance. However, it has limitations, such as high GPU memory usage and long inference time. In the future, we will make efforts to lower GPU usage and speed up the inference.

5   Conclusion

In this paper, we proposed a 3D U-Net semi-supervised approach based on Meta Pseudo Labels (MPL) for training the neural networks with limited labeled data and a large number of unlabeled images for medical image segmentation. We trained baseline method using labeled data and 3D U-Net MPL on labeled data and unlabeled data. DSC are used to assess the accuracy. Three different running computational efficiency measures were also computed which proved the effectiveness of our semi-supervised approach experimentally compared to baseline method.

Acknowledgements. We are thankful to the School-Enterprise Graduate Student Cooperation Fund of Shenzhen Technology University, and the Project of Educational Commission of Guangdong Province of China (No. 2022ZDJS113). The authors of this paper declare that the segmentation method they implemented for participation in the FLARE 2022 challenge has not used any pre-trained models nor additional datasets other than those provided by the organizers.

References

1. Gibson, E., et al.: Automatic multi-organ segmentation on abdominal CT with dense V-networks. IEEE Trans. Med. Imaging **37**(8), 1822–1834 (2018)
2. Pham, H., Dai, Z., Xie, Q., Le, Q. V.: Meta pseudo labels. In Proceedings of the IEEE/CVF Conference on Computer Vision and Pattern Recognition, pp. 11557–11568 (2021)
3. Ronneberger, O., Fischer, P., Brox, T.: U-net: convolutional networks for biomedical image segmentation. arXiv:1505.04597
4. Isensee, F., et al.: nnU-net: self-adapting framework for U-net-based medical image segmentation. arXiv preprint arXiv:1809.10486 (2018)
5. Ma, J., et al.: Fast and low-GPU-memory abdomen CT organ segmentation: the flare challenge. Med. Image Anal. **82**, 102616 (2022)
6. Simpson, A.L., et al.: A large annotated medical image dataset for the development and evaluation of segmentation algorithms. arXiv preprint arXiv:1902.09063 (2019)
7. Heller, N., et al.: The state of the art in kidney and kidney tumor segmentation in contrast-enhanced CT imaging: results of the kits19 challenge. Med. Image Anal. **67**, 101821 (2021)
8. Heller, N., et al.: An international challenge to use artificial intelligence to define the state-of-the-art in kidney and kidney tumor segmentation in CT imaging. Amer. Soc. Clin. Oncol. **38**(6), 626 (2020)
9. Ma, J., et al.: Abdomenct-1k: Is abdominal organ segmentation a solved problem? In: IEEE Transactions on Pattern Analysis and Machine Intelligence (2021)
10. Clark, K., et al.: The cancer imaging archive (tcia): maintaining and operating a public information repository. J. Digit. Imaging **26**(6), 1045–1057 (2013)

Coarse to Fine Automatic Segmentation of Abdominal Multiple Organs

Yi Lv[1,2] , Yu Ning[2] , and Junchen Wang[2,3](✉)

[1] North China Research Institute of Electro-optics, Beijing 100015, China
[2] School of Mechanical Engineering and Automation, Beihang University,
Beijing 100191, China
wangjunchen@buaa.edu.cn
[3] Beijing Advanced Innovation Center for Biomedical Engineering,
Beihang University, Beijing, China

Abstract. Abdominal multi-organ segmentation is fast becoming a key instrument in preoperative diagnosis. Using the results of abdominal CT image segmentation for three-dimensional reconstruction is an intuitive and accurate method for surgical planning. In this paper, we propose a stable three-stage fast automatic segmentation method for abdominal 13 organs: liver, spleen, pancreas, right kidney, left kidney, stomach, gallbladder, esophagus, aorta, inferior vena cava, right adrenal gland, left adrenal gland, and duodenum. Our method includes preprocessing the CT data, segmenting the multi-organ and post-processing the segmentation outputs. The results on the test set show that the average DSC performance is about 0.766. The average time and GPU memory consumption for each case is 81.42 s and 1953 MB.

Keywords: Medical image segmentation · Deep learning · Neural network

1 Introduction

Abdominal multi organ segmentation is of great significance in medical diagnosis and research. Through pixel level segmentation of CT or MRI and three-dimensional reconstruction of the segmentation results, doctors can obtain more intuitive information of patients' abdominal organs [3,4,10,17,20]. In recent years, medical image automatic segmentation algorithm has made a great breakthrough. Methods based on deep learning has achieved excellent performance in this task [9,12,18,19]. The deep learning technology based on neural networks can achieve fast segmentation, and effectively solve the problem of low accuracy and long time-consuming image segmentation [8,15]. The research in recent years mainly focuses on the network structure and segmentation framework. At present, the most widely used network structure is the encoding-decoding shaped structure similar to U-Net [14], such as 3D U-Net [1] and V-Net [13], and nnU-Net [7] has also achieved excellent results in the field of segmentation framework.

J. Ma and B. Wang (Eds.): FLARE 2022, LNCS 13816, pp. 223–232, 2022.
https://doi.org/10.1007/978-3-031-23911-3_20

For example, in the MICCAI challenge 2019 kits19 competition, the accuracy of nnU-Net using 3D U-Net in the task of kidney segmentation is very close to that of human, but the required time to complete a segmentation is far less than that of manual segmentation. The deep learning-based methods not only surpass the traditional algorithms, but also approach the accuracy of manual segmentation. However, previous published studies are limited to be used on low-configuration devices.

In this paper, we propose a stable three-stage automatic segmentation method for abdominal 13 organs: liver, spleen, pancreas, right kidney, left kidney, stomach, gallbladder, esophagus, aorta, inferior vena cava, right adrenal gland, left adrenal gland, and duodenum. Our method can complete the segmentation task, including preprocessing the CT data, segmenting the multi-organ and finally post-processing the segmentation outputs, with low GPU memory occupation.

2   Methods

2.1   Preprocessing

In the preprocessing stage, we first standardize the spacing of CT. Due to the amount of available GPU memory, the patch size that can be processed in 3D CNNs is typically quite limited. Thus, the target spacing, which directly impacts the total size of the images in voxels, also determines how much contextual information the CNN can capture in its patch size. We reshape all the data with the voxel spacing of $4.4 \times 2.5 \times 2.5$ mm for the first step and $3.0 \times 1.6 \times 1.6$ mm for the second step. After spacing standardization, we set the maximum in-plain resolution to 128×176 pixels for the first step and 230×300 pixels for the second step, so as to prevent data with high original spacing from being too large after the standardization of spacing and resulting in a significant increase in segmentation time.

2.2   Proposed Method

To verify the impact of segmentation pipeline strategy on the results, we used an improved 3D U-Net as the segmentation network. The network architecture is illustrated in Fig. 1. The network includes an encoding path and a decoding path, each of which has four resolution levels. Each level of the encoding path contains two $3 \times 3 \times 3$ convolution layers, and the convolution layers followed by a ReLu layer and a $2 \times 2 \times 2$ Maximum pool layer with step size of 2. In the decoding path, each level also contains two $3 \times 3 \times 3$ convolution layers , and the convolution layers followed by a ReLu layer and an upsampling layer.The summation between Dice loss and cross entropy loss is chosen as the loss function. We used adaptive moment estimation (Adam) as the optimizer. The batch size was set to be 2. The networks were initialized using Kaiming normal initialization. We set the learning rate to be 1e-3 and reduced the learning rate by a multiplier of 0.99 after every 5 epochs until it reached 1e-6.

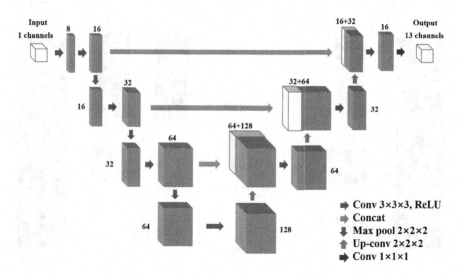

Fig. 1. The network architecture. Gray cuboids represent feature maps. The number of channels is denoted next to the feature map.

The pipeline of our method consists of three stages: global locating, organ locating and organ segmentation. Each stage of our method will generate a segmentation result for the complete CT, and the operation of the second and the third steps are based on the previous result. As shown in Fig. 2, in the global locating stage, we first cut the original CT into several ROIs, and then segment each ROI with the first trained neural network. In the organ locating stage, we first locate the region of abdominal organs in the whole CT according to the results of the first step, and then we save this region with a higher resolution and segment it with the second trained network. In the stage of organ segmentation, we locate and crop each organ according to the results of the second step, and then use the corresponding network to fine segment each organ. Finally, we superimpose the segmentation results of each organ to the corresponding position and then generate the feature map of final segmentation result.

In order to further improve the robustness of the network on different data, we adopt the training strategy of semi-supervised learning.Since no research has proved that more unlabeled data in semi supervised learning is better, we set the unlabeled data as much as the number of labeled data. In the training process, we use 40 labeled data and 50 randomly selected unlabeled data as the training set used in the stage of global locating and organ locating. We use the labeled data to train the model in the first 50 epochs, and then introduce the unlabeled data.We use the trained model to segmentation the unlabeled dataset after each five epochs, and we use the results as the label for training. As the first two stages are the segmentation of complete CT, which is different from the third stage, we only use the semi-supervised learning strategy for the first two stages.

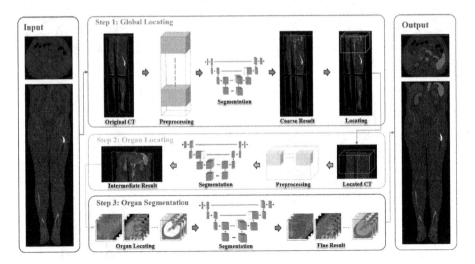

Fig. 2. The pipeline of our proposed method.

2.3 Post-processing

In the post-processing stage, we splice the results of the network segmentation. We keep the region with the largest volume and remove the rest to eliminate isolated incorrectly predicted labels. To improve the segmentation efficiency of our method, we clear the cache and delete the used feature map and the model from the GPU after each step. Finally, the maximum GPU memory we use is 1953MB.

3 Experiments

3.1 Dataset and Evaluation Measures

The FLARE2022 dataset is curated from more than 20 medical groups under the license permission, including MSD [16], KiTS [5,6], AbdomenCT-1K [11], and TCIA [2]. The training set includes 50 labelled CT scans with pancreas disease and 2000 unlabelled CT scans with liver, kidney, spleen, or pancreas diseases. The validation set includes 50 CT scans with liver, kidney, spleen, or pancreas diseases. The testing set includes 200 CT scans where 100 cases has liver, kidney, spleen, or pancreas diseases and the other 100 cases has uterine corpus endometrial, urothelial bladder, stomach, sarcomas, or ovarian diseases. All the CT scans only have image information and the center information is not available.

The evaluation measures consist of two accuracy measures: Dice Similarity Coefficient (DSC) and Normalized Surface Dice (NSD), and three running efficiency measures: running time, area under GPU memory-time curve, and area under CPU utilization-time curve. All measures will be used to compute the ranking. Moreover, the GPU memory consumption has a 2 GB tolerance.

3.2   Implementation Details

Environment Settings. The environments and requirements are presented in Table 1.

Table 1. Environments and requirements.

Windows/Ubuntu version	Windows 10
CPU	AMD Ryzen 7 5800X
RAM	8GB × 4
GPU (number and type)	One RTX8000 48G
CUDA version	10.2
Programming language	Python 3.7.9
Deep learning framework	Pytorch(Torch 1.8.0, torchvision 0.9.0)
Average inference time	81.42s
GPU memory consumption	1953 MB

Training Protocols. The Training protocols are presented in Table 2.

Table 2. Training protocols.

Network initialization	Kaiming normal initialization
Data augmentation methods	Scaling, rotations, brightness, contrast, gamma
Batch size	8
Patch size	$64 \times 128 \times 176$
Total epochs	100
Optimizer	Adam
Initial learning rate (lr)	0.01
Lr decay schedule	multiplied by 0.99 every 5 epochs
Training time	5.9 h
Number of model parameters	1.328M
Number of flops	33.263 G
Loss function	Combination of Dice loss and WCE loss

3.3   Resource Consumption

The Resource consumption during inference is presented in Table 3.

Table 3. Resource consumption during inference.

Total Running Time on Validation Set	67.85 mins
Maximum RAM consumption	< 8 GB
Maximum GPU memory consumption	1953 MB

4   Results and Discussion

As the accuracy metrics, the average DSC between the predicted mask and the ground truth mask were employed. Assume A and B are two masks, the metric is given by (1).

$$DSC = \frac{2(A \cap B)}{A + B} \tag{1}$$

4.1   Quantitative Results on Validation Set

Table 4 compares the experimental data on the segmentation results on 13 organs in the three stages. In the stage of global locating, organ locating and organ segmentation, our method achieves average DSC of 0.63, 0.73 and 0.77 respectively. The highest DSC between the three stages are highlighted in Table 4. It is apparent from this table that the DSC results in stage 3 is significantly higher than the previous stages.

Table 4. Comparison on 13 Structures on official validation and testing results.

	Official Validation			Testing
	Stage 1	Stage 2	Stage 3	Result
Liver	0.902	0.868	0.903	0.866
Right Kidney	0.798	0.864	0.896	0.885
Spleen	0.802	0.898	0.926	0.910
Pancreas	0.497	0.708	0.683	0.676
Aorta	0.837	0.911	0.930	0.915
Inferior Vena Cava	0.710	0.802	0.846	0.836
Right Adrenal Gland	0.490	0.600	0.653	0.695
Left Adrenal Gland	0.354	0.528	0.610	0.653
Gallbladder	0.393	0.463	0.562	0.569
Esophagus	0.573	0.652	0.671	0.666
Stomach	0.672	0.780	0.799	0.807
Duodenum	0.379	0.577	0.593	0.589
Left Kidney	0.789	0.856	0.867	0.893
Average	0.630	0.731	0.765	0.766

As the models used in the first and the second stage were semi-supervised trained with unlabeled data, we also test the effect of unlabeled data. Table 5 shows the DSC comparison of our method with and without using unlabeled data. It can be observed that the accuracy of our method using unlabeled data has been improved.

Table 5. Comparison of our method with and without using unlabeled data.

	Average DSC	Standard Deviation of DSC
With Unlabeled Data	0.731	0.142
Without Unlabeled Data	0.678	0.186

4.2   Qualitative Results on Validation Set

Figure 3 shows three examples with good segmentation results on CT slices in validation set. Figure 4 shows the results with voxel-based rendering from three examples in the validation set. In these results, the performance of our method is generally stable.

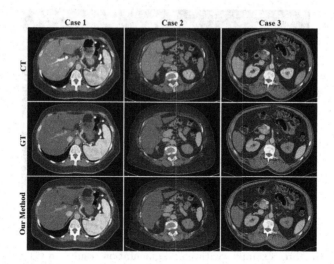

Fig. 3. Three examples with good segmentation results on CT slices.

As shown in Fig. 5, there also have examples with bad segmentation results on CT slices in validation set. In the first case of the bad results, part of the right kidney tumor and pancreas were not correctly recognized. This is because there is not much data with kidney tumors in the training set, and the characteristic boundary between pancreas and surrounding tissues is not particularly obvious. In the second case, our method performs bad on spleen and stomach. The gray

230   Y. Lv et al.

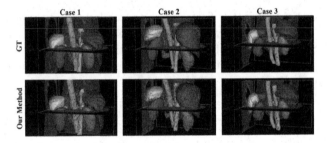

Fig. 4. Segmentation results with voxel-based rendering from three examples in the evaluation dataset. For each example, the ground truth and the segmentation results are given for visual comparison.

value of stomach is abnormally high in CT image, which not only led to the wrong recognition of the stomach, but also covered the correct label of spleen. In the third case, a typical liver recognition error occurred. Due to the rarity of such features in training data, the network habitually takes the lung boundary as the criterion for judging the region of liver.

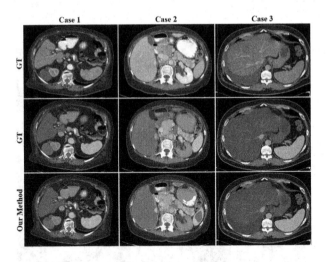

Fig. 5. Three examples with bad segmentation results on CT slices.

5   Conclusion

We propose a three-stage automatic segmentation method for abdominal 13 organs based on improved 3D U-Net. The results show that the average dice of our method is 0.77 on the official validation leaderboard. The results show that the accuracy of our method on massive organs is better than that for small organs. The speed of three-stage method is fast, but it is difficult to achieve higher accuracy due to the limitation of feature map size. Future work will focus on promoting accuracy based on less stage methods, in which the segmentation speed can be further improved.

Acknowledgements. The authors of this paper declare that the segmentation method they implemented for participation in the FLARE 2022 challenge has not used any pre-trained models nor additional datasets other than those provided by the organizers. The proposed solution is fully automatic without any manual intervention. This work was supported by Natural Science Foundation of China (Grant No. 62173014) and Natural Science Foundation of Beijing Municipality (Grant No. L192057).

References

1. Çiçek, Ö., Abdulkadir, A., Lienkamp, S.S., Brox, T., Ronneberger, O.: 3D U-Net: learning dense volumetric segmentation from sparse annotation. In: Ourselin, S., Joskowicz, L., Sabuncu, M.R., Unal, G., Wells, W. (eds.) MICCAI 2016. LNCS, vol. 9901, pp. 424–432. Springer, Cham (2016). https://doi.org/10.1007/978-3-319-46723-8_49
2. Clark, K., et al.: The cancer imaging archive (TCIA): maintaining and operating a public information repository. J. Digit. Imaging **26**(6), 1045–1057 (2013)
3. Couteaux, V., et al.: Kidney cortex segmentation in 2D CT with U-Nets ensemble aggregation. Diagn. Interv. Imaging **100**(4), 211–217 (2019)
4. Fu, Y., et al.: A novel MRI segmentation method using CNN-based correction network for MRI-guided adaptive radiotherapy. Med. Phys. **45**(11), 5129–5137 (2018)
5. Heller, N., et al.: The state of the art in kidney and kidney tumor segmentation in contrast-enhanced CT imaging: results of the KiTS19 challenge. Med. Image Anal. **67**, 101821 (2021)
6. Heller, N., et al.: An international challenge to use artificial intelligence to define the state-of-the-art in kidney and kidney tumor segmentation in CT imaging **38**(6), 626 (2020)
7. Isensee, F., Jäger, P.F., Kohl, S.A., Petersen, J., Maier-Hein, K.H.: Automated design of deep learning methods for biomedical image segmentation. arXiv preprint arXiv:1904.08128 (2020)
8. Kim, D.Y., Park, J.W.: Computer-aided detection of kidney tumor on abdominal computed tomography scans. Acta Radiol. **45**(7), 791–795 (2004)
9. LeCun, Y., Bengio, Y., Hinton, G.: Deep learning. Nature **521**(7553), 436–444 (2015)
10. Li, J., Zhu, S.A., Bin, H.: Medical image segmentation techniques. J. Biomed. Eng. **23**(4), 891–894 (2006)
11. Ma, J., et al.: Abdomenct-1k: Is abdominal organ segmentation a solved problem. In: IEEE Transactions on Pattern Analysis and Machine Intelligence (2021)
12. Micheli-Tzanakou, E.: Artificial neural networks: an overview. Netw. Comput. Neural Syst. **22**(1–4), 208–230 (2011)
13. Milletari, F., Navab, N., Ahmadi, S.A.: V-net: fully convolutional neural networks for volumetric medical image segmentation. In: 2016 Fourth International Conference on 3D Vision (3DV), pp. 565–571. IEEE, Stanford, CA, USA (2016)
14. Ronneberger, O., Fischer, P., Brox, T.: U-Net: convolutional networks for biomedical image segmentation. In: Navab, N., Hornegger, J., Wells, W.M., Frangi, A.F. (eds.) MICCAI 2015. LNCS, vol. 9351, pp. 234–241. Springer, Cham (2015). https://doi.org/10.1007/978-3-319-24574-4_28

15. Shelhamer, E., Long, J., Darrell, T.: Fully convolutional networks for semantic segmentation. IEEE Trans. Pattern Anal. Mach. Intell. **39**(4), 640–651 (2017)
16. Simpson, A.L., et al.: A large annotated medical image dataset for the development and evaluation of segmentation algorithms. arXiv preprint arXiv:1902.09063 (2019)
17. Yang, Y., Jiang, H., Sun, Q.: A multiorgan segmentation model for CT volumes via full convolution-deconvolution network. BioMed. Res. Int. **2017**, 6941306 (2017)
18. Zarándy, Á., Rekeczky, C., Szolgay, P., Chua, L.O.: Overview of CNN research: 25 years history and the current trends. In: 2015 IEEE International Symposium on Circuits and Systems (ISCAS), pp. 401–404. IEEE, Lisbon, Portugal (2015)
19. Zhang, J., Zong, C., et al.: Deep neural networks in machine translation: an overview. IEEE Intell. Syst. **30**(5), 16–25 (2015)
20. Zhao, C., Carass, A., Lee, J., He, Y., Prince, J.L.: Whole brain segmentation and labeling from CT using synthetic MR images. In: Wang, Q., Shi, Y., Suk, H.-I., Suzuki, K. (eds.) MLMI 2017. LNCS, vol. 10541, pp. 291–298. Springer, Cham (2017). https://doi.org/10.1007/978-3-319-67389-9_34

MTSegNet: Semi-supervised Abdominal Organ Segmentation in CT

Shiman Li[1,2], Siqi Yin[1,2], Chenxi Zhang[1,2], Manning Wang[1,2],
and Zhijian Song[1,2(✉)]

[1] Digital Medical Research Center, School of Basic Medical Sciences,
Fudan University, Shanghai 200032, China
`zjsong@fudan.edu.cn`
[2] Shanghai Key Laboratory of Medical Imaging Computing and Computer Assisted
Intervention, Shanghai 200032, China

Abstract. Multi-organ segmentation from CT scan is useful in clinical applications. However, difficulties in data annotation impede its practical usage. In this work, we propose MTSegNet for multi-organ segmentation task in semi-supervised way. Total number of 13 organs in chest and abdomen are included. For network architecture, Attention U-Net serves as basic structure to guarantee segmentation performance and usage of context information. For those unlabeled data, Mean Teacher Model, which is a commonly used semi-supervised structure, is added to the pipeline to facilitate better use of unlabeled data. Besides, class-aware weight and post-process are used as auxiliary methods to further improve performance of model. Experiments on validation set and test set got averaged Dice Similarity Coefficient (DSC) of 0.6743 and 0.7034, respectively.

Keywords: Semi-supervised · Multi-organ · Abdominal segmentation

1 Introduction

Multi-organ segmentation from CT scan has many important practical applications in clinical scene. However, due to manually annotation is time-consuming and labor-intensive, supervised methods are no longer satisfied. In this paper, we focus on semi-supervised learning method for multi-organ segmentation task. There are several challenges. 1) Labels includes 13 organs in chest and abdomen, which has varying size, shape and contour. 2) Besides, according to human body internal structure, organs have complicated context relationship, without regard to its normal and abnormal conditions. 3) Additionally, a large proportion of unlabeled data requires a better way to get fully use of it. 4) The trade-off between model structure and limited GPU memory size.

In this work, we propose a semi-supervised multi-organ segmentation model MTSegNet to effectively and efficiently tackle challenges mentioned above.

S. Li and S. Yin—Contribute equally to this work.

J. Ma and B. Wang (Eds.): FLARE 2022, LNCS 13816, pp. 233–244, 2022.
https://doi.org/10.1007/978-3-031-23911-3_21

Attention U-Net serves as basic structure to guarantee segmentation performance and usage of context information. For those unlabeled data, Mean Teacher Model, which is a commonly used semi-supervised structure, is added to the pipeline to facilitate better use of unlabeled data. Besides, class-aware weight and post-process are used as auxiliary methods to further improve performance of model.

The main contributions of this work are summarized as follows:

1. We propose MTSegNet for 13 labels multi-organ segmentation task using CT scans, which based on Attetion U-Net's attention and statistics information to exploit contextual information in a better way.
2. We designs Mean Teacher's consistency structure to make fully use of the given unlabeled data. An auxiliary class-aware weight are setting to abridge the differences of labels
3. Post-process are given to improve the performance of model further, based on statistic prior information.

2   Method

For the task of segmenting 13 organs of interest in the abdomen of FLARE2022, we propose MTSegNet, which is based on Mean Teacher's [8] semi-supervised method to segment organs using Attention U-Net on sliding patches. The details of the method will be described as follows.

2.1   Preprocessing

The baseline method includes the following pre-processing strategies:

- *Reorienting images.* Reordering original images' direction to left-posterior-inferior view.
- *Resampling images* Two options are given. We use shape resampling in our work.
  - Resampling by space. Resampling image to 1mm spacing in each axis to increase the comparability of images and restore the real physical locations.
  - Resampling by size. Resize images to pre-defined size of inputs (i.e. [160, 160, 160].
- *Intensity normalization.* The image in normalized by specific values of window width and window level, which is 400 and 40, respectively.

2.2   Proposed Method

Our proposed MTSegNet contains three effective methods: Mean Teacher's consistency regularization, Attetion U-Net's attention mechanism, and class-aware weight setting.

The main framework of our approach is shown in Fig. 1 We input labelled data into the student network and unlabeled data into the student and teacher networks at the same time. We averages the weights of the student model to the teacher model, which ensuring the stability of the model.

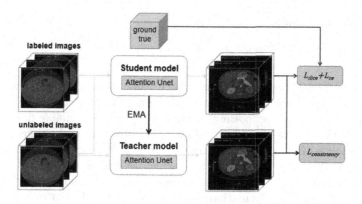

Fig. 1. Network architecture

Among them, we use Dice loss and cross entropy loss for the labeled images, because compound loss functions have been proved to be robust in various medical image segmentation [5]. In order to supervise the unlabeled data, we calculate the consistency loss using the prediction results of the teacher and student model for regularization as a way to improve the model generalization.

For the segmentation of multi-organs, there are often many irrelevant regions in the image for the segmentation of one type of organs, and the resulting redundant information will affect the segmentation results. Therefore, we use the Attention U-Net as the basic backbone network, and its Attention Gate attention mechanism can help the network learn the spatial location and other features of different organs.

In addition, the segmentation difficulty of different organs varies, and in order to better improve the overall segmentation results, we set class-aware weights and set higher weights for the more difficult segmented organs in calculating the loss to help the network learn the difficult organs for segmentation. The class-aware weights is set as a super-parameter, which is manually adjusted before training. The specific implementation is in the form of multiplication of loss and class weights. We set the weight as 1.0, 1.0, 1.0, 1.0, 1.5, 1.0, 1.5, 2.0, 2.0, 1.5, 2.0, 2.0, 2.0, 1.0 for background and classes 1 to 13. The Dice loss is formulated as follow:

$$\text{Loss}_{\text{Dice}} = 1 - \sum_{i=0}^{c=13} \frac{2\,|P_i \cap Y_i|}{|P_i| + |Y_i|} \times W_i \tag{1}$$

236   S. Li et al.

where, P_i and Y_i indicate the prediction and ground truth of class i, respectively. And W_i indicates the weight of the class. Based on the solution of nnUnet [4], we recommend using Float16 as the tensor type to improve inference speed and reduce resource consumption.

2.3 Post-processing

To refine the segmentation output, several post-processing methods are considered.

Statistic Information. Since basic structure of human body is similar between individuals, we stat the volume, location information of each label in the given labeled cases (after pro-processing) to make fully use of available data.

Figure 2 shows labels location information after uniformly resized to same size. For each label, box plot includes six boxes corresponding to minimal and maximal coordinates along z/y/x axis, which reflects a general locations and deviation of labels in labeled cases. Histogram in Fig. 3 shows each labels volume statistics. All the information collected from labeled data may utilize as a reference for incoming unlabeled data in post-processing process.

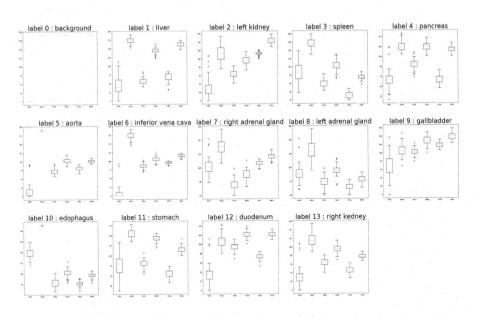

Fig. 2. Labels location statistics

Based on statistics information, post-processing includes two steps: First, Connected Component Analysis-Labeling is applied on the model output. Additionally, some small isolated prediction regions are removed based on the statistic information on each labels.

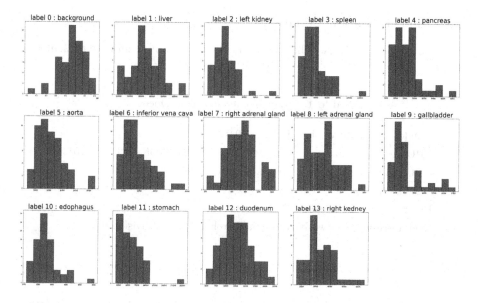

Fig. 3. Labels volume statistics

3   Experiments

3.1   Dataset and Evaluation Measures

Description of dataset: The FLARE2022 dataset is curated from more than 20 medical groups under the license permission, including MSD [7], KiTS [2,3], AbdomenCT-1K [6], and TCIA [1].

Description of data: The training set includes 50 labelled CT scans with pancreas disease and 2000 unlabelled CT scans with liver, kidney, spleen, or pancreas diseases. The validation set includes 50 CT scans with liver, kidney, spleen, or pancreas diseases. The testing set includes 200 CT scans where 100 cases has liver, kidney, spleen, or pancreas diseases and the other 100 cases has uterine corpus endometrial, urothelial bladder, stomach, sarcomas, or ovarian diseases. All the CT scans only have image information and the center information is not available.

The total number of cases is 50 labeled data and 2000 unlabeled data. K-fold ($k = 5$) training strategy are used for labeled data for train/validate/test splitting. Unlabeled data are chosen for training only.

The evaluation measures consist of two accuracy measures: Dice Similarity Coefficient (DSC) and Normalized Surface Dice (NSD), and three running efficiency measures: running time, area under GPU memory-time curve, and area under CPU utilization-time curve. All measures will be used to compute the ranking. Moreover, the GPU memory consumption has a 2 GB tolerance.

3.2   Implementation Details

Environment Settings. The environments and requirements are presented in Table 1.

Table 1. Environments and requirements.

Windows/Ubuntu version	Ubuntu 20.04
CPU	Intel(R) Core(TM) i5-9600K CPU @ 3.70 GHz
GPU (number and type)	Nvidia GeForce 2080Ti ($\times 2$)
CUDA version	11.4
Programming language	Python 3.6
Deep learning framework	Pytorch (Torch 1.10.2, torchvision 0.4.0)

Training Protocols. As for the training protocols, we introduce some details by the form of table as follow (Table 2):

Table 2. Training protocols.

Network initialization	"he" normal initialization
Batch size	4
Labelled number in Batch size	2
Patch size	$96 \times 96 \times 96$
Stride x/y/z	$48 \times 48 \times 48$
Total epochs	1000
Optimizer	SGD with nesterov momentum ($\mu = 0.9$)
Initial learning rate (lr)	0.01
Lr decay schedule	Linear decay
Training time	14–16 hours
Number of model parameters	6.17M[a]
Number of flops	59.02G[b]

[a] https://github.com/sksq96/pytorch-summary.
[a] https://github.com/facebookresearch/fvcore.

To be more specific, the patch sampling strategy in the training phase is the random crop, while in the validating phase we slide the patch by the stride in the table.

4   Results and Discussion

Unlabeled data are used in Mean Teacher Model and consistency loss calculation. 2000 cases of unlabeled data ease the problem of annotation lacking and could help model to be more robust.

To further improve model performance, class-aware weight are added, which balance the internal differences between labels to a great extent. Meanwhile, Attention U-Net has the ability to focus on context information and make fully use of anatomy structural locations.

However, dice score and some measurements are not satisfied now, possible reasons are: 1) unsuitable input patch size, which may mislead model with inadequate input information. 2) abnormal cases may confuse model. How to identify special cases and let the model rely more on high confidence cases are remain unsolved.

4.1   Quantitative Results on Validation Set

We randomly divide the 50 labeled data into training and validation sets in a 4:1 ratio and use the k-fold approach for validation. Result are shown in Table 3.

Table 3. Performance on validation set.

Organ	Liver	RK	Spleen	Pancreas	Aorta	IVC	RAG
DSC	0.9202	0.8149	0.8298	0.611	0.8673	0.7783	0.4905
Organ	LAG	Gallbladder	Esophagus	Stomach	Duodenum	LK	Mean
DSC	0.4033	0.4162	0.6432	0.7462	0.5046	0.7406	0.6743

The use of unsupervised data improves the performance of the model. However, with the modification of the model, we lost the original Ablation Experiment on the effect of unlabeled data, and no new ablation experiment has been carried out.

Firstly, Table 4 show the effectiveness of preprocessing on the training dataset, which lead to better evaluation result in most labels, especially for pancreas, right adrenal gland and left adrenal gland.

Table 4. Ablation study of preprocess.

	Label 1		Label 2		Label 3		Label 4		Label 5		Label 6		Label 7	
	dice_score	hd95	dice_score	hd95	dice_score	hd95	dice_score	hd95	dice_score	hd95	dice_score	hd95	dice_score	hd95
W/o preprocess	0.9716	1.5890	0.8684	10.0501	0.9505	2.8849	0.7255	5.4089	0.9381	3.9550	0.8387	3.6709	0.7350	2.0953
Preprocess	0.9690	3.6099	0.8714	10.9476	0.9271	3.8832	0.7749	4.5959	0.9321	1.2472	0.8618	4.0251	0.8168	1.4988
	Label 8		Label 9		Label 10		Label 11		Label 12		Label 13		Average	
	dice_score	hd95	dice_score	hd95	dice_score	hd95	dice_score	hd95	dice_score	hd95	dice_score	hd95	dice_score	hd95
W/o preprocess	0.6757	5.8350	0.8731	7.5368	0.7629	2.13278	0.8562	6.2145	0.7221	6.0233	0.9276	6.5980	0.8343	4.9607
Preprocess	0.7332	3.2363	0.8937	4.3394	0.7243	4.4726	0.8825	8.1836	0.7217	5.7623	0.9461	10.1733	0.8303	5.0753

Table 5. Ablation study of class-aware weight.

	Label 1		Label 2		Label 3		Label 4		Label 5		Label 6		Label 7	
	dice_score	hd95	dice_score	hd95	dice_score	hd95	dice_score	hd95	dice_score	hd95	dice_score	hd95	dice_score	hd95
W/o class-aware weight	0.9624	5.0721	0.8659	9.8311	0.9330	3.1310	0.7246	4.7754	0.9232	4.6414	0.8204	3.8115	0.7173	4.6115
Class-aware weight	0.9716	1.5890	0.8684	10.0501	0.9505	2.8849	0.7255	5.4089	0.9381	3.9550	0.8387	3.6709	0.7350	2.0953

	Label 8		Label 9		Label 10		Label 11		Label 12		Label 13		Average	
	dice_score	hd95	dice_score	hd95	dice_score	hd95	dice_score	hd95	dice_score	hd95	dice_score	hd95	dice_score	hd95
W/o class-aware weight	0.7220	4.5190	0.8764	2.4145	0.7748	2.3610	0.8300	8.1811	0.6284	6.3779	0.9206	8.8114	0.8230	5.2722
Class-aware weight	0.6757	5.8350	0.8731	7.5368	0.7629	2.6278	0.8562	6.2145	0.7221	6.0233	0.9276	6.5980	0.8343	4.9607

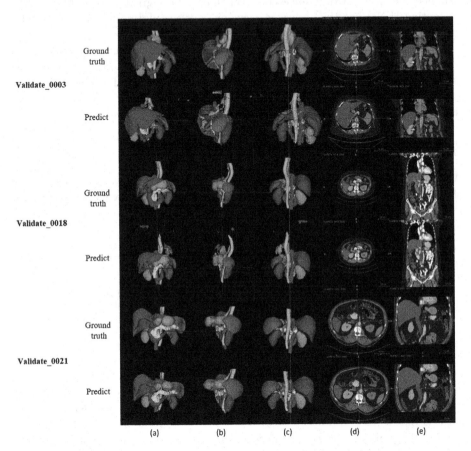

Fig. 4. Visualization of cases with satisfying result. (a) Front view. (b) Side view. (c) Back view. (d) Axial view. (E) Coronal view.

Besides, we explore the effectiveness of class-aware weight on training data in Table 5. Similar to the effect of preprocessing, most labels' measurement has increased.

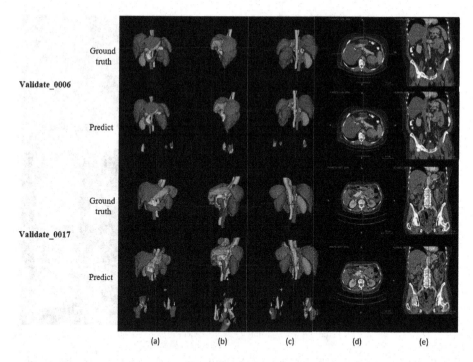

Fig. 5. Visualization of Unsatisfactory results. (a) Front view. (b) Side view. (c) Back view. (d) Axial view. (E) Coronal view

4.2   Visualization

To give an further analyze to the result in an more intuitive way, we visualize several cases, including its prediction mask and ground truth label.

Figure 4 shows some examples with satisfactory result. Due to the quantity of labels, We visualize each case from multi-view as show in the first three columns. Tubular lumen-like organ (i.e. Aorta and IVC) has considerably good result, which shows the effectiveness of attention module. When observing the details of predictions, the edge and surface is not as smooth as the ground truth, indicating that a powerful post-processing method is needed to further improve the performance.

Figure 5 shows several cases with unsatisfactory result. The possible reason of the performance degradation is that the original input has large range in z-axis. In another words, ground truth labels are located in just few slices, which may introduce nuisance information and increase the difficulties for trained network to predict the coarse location of organs and its final segmentation mask. Thus, although the main slices have ground truth-like prediction, those extra area shows in the lower part (i.e. hip) are definitely wrong. To reduce the impact of input size, a location network or post-process method may be helpful to give a coarse suggestions on alternative slices, or re-fine the prediction result through prior knowledge of anatomy.

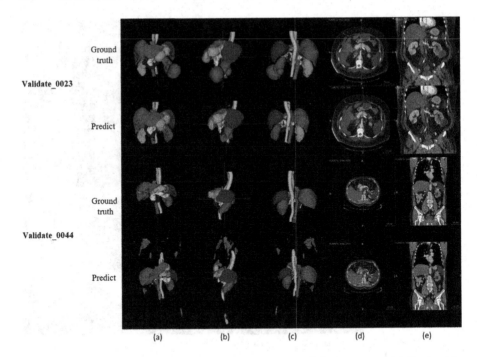

Fig. 6. Visualization of difficult cases. (a) Front view. (b) Side view. (c) Back view. (d) Axial view. (E) Coronal view

Unknown disease is also challenging, as it increase the variation of organs between cases. Figure 6 shows several failed prediction, which possibly caused by abnormal organs, such as liver in validate case 0044 and left kidney in validate case 0023. Moreover, organ like stomach has a disappointed result as the anatomical variability are comparably large between cases, such as validate case 0003 and validate 0012 shown in Fig. 4. Similarly, pancreas is easy to be misclassified, due to its contrast and variable shape. Since 14 organs has mutual constraints, mining relative position between organs and anatomical structure should be considered in the future.

4.3 Quantitative Results on Test Set

Results on test set are shown in Table 6. Including average score (AVG) and standard deviation (STD) of DSC and NSD of each organ and final mean result of all

4.4 Efficiency of the Method

The max GPU memory is 2395M and the AUC of CPU varies from 500 to 4800 in validation set.

Table 6. Performance on test set.

	Name	Liver	RK	Spleen	Pancreas	Aorta	JVC	RAG
DSC	AVG	0.9483505	0.8618665	0.875381	0.5917635	0.9080215	0.825371	0.524265
	STD	0.037949668	0.207216528	0.206019203	0.241541075	0.086333642	0.133338821	0.254396351
		LAG	Gallbladder	Esophagus	Stomach	Duodenum	LK	Mean
DSC	AVG	0.4540385	0.43166	0.578257	0.770988	0.527637	0.8462805	0.703375385
	STD	0.288194299	0.3657501	0.24846958	0.170715222	0.214083741	0.198379682	0.204029839
		Liver	RK	Spleen	Pancreas	Aorta	rvc	RAG
NSD	AVG	0.904239	0.8239195	0.8553155	0.71848	0.9305165	0.818754	0.6904825
	STD	0.100097309	0.224250366	0.217654229	0.242036863	0.109057073	0.148377794	0.282271853
		LAG	Gallbladder	Esophagus	Stomach	Duodenum	LK	Mean
NSD	AVG	0.592652	0.3834735	0.712121	0.7552445	0.755684	0.7963375	0.749016885
	STD	0.328952015	0.330597739	0.264299128	0.185882842	0.199104964	0.211049075	0.218740865

5 Conclusion

The main finding and results show that, MTSegNet shows its ability in multi-organ segmentation tasks. Both labeled and unlabeled data contributes to model training by using Mean Teacher model and Attention U-Net Model. Besides, preprocessing and class-aware weight helps further improvement in model performance. However, there are still many drawbacks need to be completed in the future.

Acknowledgements. The authors of this paper declare that the segmentation method they implemented for participation in the FLARE 2022 challenge has not used any pre-trained models nor additional datasets other than those provided by the organizers.

References

1. Clark, K., et al.: The cancer imaging archive (TCIA): maintaining and operating a public information repository. J. Digit. Imaging **26**(6), 1045–1057 (2013)
2. Heller, N., et al.: The state of the art in kidney and kidney tumor segmentation in contrast-enhanced CT imaging: results of the kits19 challenge. Med. Image Anal. **67**, 101821 (2021)
3. Heller, N., et al.: An international challenge to use artificial intelligence to define the state-of-the-art in kidney and kidney tumor segmentation in CT imaging. Proc. Am. Soc. Clin. Oncol. **38**(6), 626–626 (2020)
4. Isensee, F., Jaeger, P.F., Kohl, S.A., Petersen, J., Maier-Hein, K.H.: NNU-net: a self-configuring method for deep learning-based biomedical image segmentation. Nat. Methods **18**(2), 203–211 (2021)
5. Ma, J., et al.: Loss odyssey in medical image segmentation. Med. Image Anal. **71**, 102035 (2021)
6. Ma, J., et al.: Abdomenct-1k: is abdominal organ segmentation a solved problem? IEEE Trans. Pattern Anal. Mach. Intell. (2021). https://doi.org/10.1109/TPAMI. 2021.3100536

7. Simpson, A.L., et al.: A large annotated medical image dataset for the development and evaluation of segmentation algorithms. arXiv preprint arXiv:1902.09063 (2019)
8. Tarvainen, A., Valpola, H.: Mean teachers are better role models: weight-averaged consistency targets improve semi-supervised deep learning results. In: NIPS (2017)

Uncertainty-aware Mean Teacher Framework with Inception and Squeeze-and-Excitation Block for MICCAI FLARE22 Challenge

Hui Meng[1]($\boxtimes$), Haochen Zhao[2], Ziniu Yu[2], Qingfeng Li[2], and Jianwei Niu[2,3]

[1] School of Intelligent Science and Technology, Hangzhou Institute for Advanced Study, University of Chinese Academy of Sciences, 1 Sub-lane Xiangshan, Hangzhou 310024, China
huimeng@ucas.ac.cn
[2] Research center of Big Data and Computational Intelligence, Hangzhou Innovation Institute of Beihang University, Hangzhou 310051, China
[3] State Key Laboratory of Virtual Reality Technology and Systems, School of Computer Science and Engineering, also with the Beijing Advanced Innovation Center for Big Data and Brain Computing (BDBC), Beihang University, Beijing 100191, China

Abstract. Semi-supervised learning has attracted extensive attention in the field of medical image analysis. However, as a fundamental task, semi-supervised segmentation has not been investigated sufficiently in the field of multi-organ segmentation from abdominal CT. Therefore, we propose a novel uncertainty-aware mean teacher framework with inception and squeeze-and-excitation block (UMT-ISE). Specifically, the UMT-ISE consists of a teacher model and a student model, in which the student model learns from the teacher model by minimizing segmentation loss and consistency loss. Additionaly, we adopt an uncertainty-aware algorithm to make the student model learn accurate and reliable targets by making full use of uncertainty information. To capture multi-scale features, the inception and squeeze-and-excitation block are incoporated into the UMT-ISE. It is worth noting that abdominal CT of test cases are first extracted before multi-organ segmentation in the inference phase, which significantly improves segmentation accuracy. We implement experiments on the FLARE22 challenge. Our method achieves mean DSC of 0.7465 on 13 abdominal organ segmentation tasks.

Keywords: Semi-supervised learning · Multi-organ segmentation · Uncertainty estimation · Multi-scale features

1 Introduction

Accurate segmentation of medical images is essential for many clinical applications, such as disease diagnosis and tumor localization [4]. Nowadays, manual segmentaion results given by radiologists are widely regarded as gold standards.

© The Author(s), under exclusive license to Springer Nature Switzerland AG 2022
J. Ma and B. Wang (Eds.): FLARE 2022, LNCS 13816, pp. 245–259, 2022.
https://doi.org/10.1007/978-3-031-23911-3_22

However, manual segmentation is tedious and time consuming. Additionally, manual segmentation heavily depends on radiologists' experience and suffers from intra- and inter-observer variabilities. Therefore, many researchers have developed different automatic segmentation methods [16], which are supposed to assist radiologists to make accurate diagnosis.

For abdominal organ segmentation, most research work focus on single organ segmentation, such as kidney [6] or blood vessels [9]. Compared with single-organ segmentation, multi-organ segmentation faces two major challenges. The first one is that large morphological differences between multiple organs limit accurate segmentation of all organs. The second one is that it's difficult to obtain large dataset with accurate annotations for multi-organ segmentation. Therefore, it is necessary to make full use of unlabeled medical images to improve the multi-organ segmentation accuracy [5].

To utilize unlabeled medical images effectively, we propose a novel UMT-ISE for segmenting multiple organs from 3D abdominal CT. The UMT-ISE is constructed based on conventional teacher-student model [3], which consists of a teacher model and a student model. For the same unlabeled data under different perturbations, the segmentation predictions of the teacher model and the student model are constrained to be consistent [17]. Different from the conventional teacher-student model, the UMT-ISE adopts framework of uncertainty-aware mean teacher (UA-MT) [17]. The teacher model in the UMT-ISE generates multiple predictions for each target under Monte Carlo sampling and gives uncertainty evaluation. The predictions with high uncertainty are filtered out and the predictions with low uncertainty are retained to compute consistency loss. Based on the design of the uncertainty evaluation, the teacher model tends to generate high-quality predictions and the student model can be constantly optimized. Considering multiple organs have different sizes, the inception and squeeze-and-excitation (ISE) block are incoporated into the UMT-ISE to capture multi-scale features.

2 Method

2.1 Preprocessing

The preprocessing operations can be divided into coarse segmentation and conventional data processing. Noted that the coarse segmentation is achieved by cropping CT-scans in z-axis, x-axis and y-axis directions, respectively. The detailed information of preprocessing operations are listed as follows:

– Cropping strategy in z-axis direction:
  The range of CT scans varies depending on the situation. For example, some patients may have CT scans not only of abdominal area, but of entire chest, lower abdomen and even legs. In some cases, only the abdominal region containing target organs is presented. Therefore, it is necessary to filter out some irrelevant and redundant slices in CT scans. In this study, we train an

uncertainty-aware mean teacher (UA-MT) network to perform coarse abdominal segmentation.

To extract CT scans only containing abdominal region, we implement different cropping strategies in z direction. For training data with labels, we tailor them according to the range of target organs in annotations. For training data without labels, validation data and test data, we first implement coarse segmentation of target organs based on the trained UA-MT network and then crop CT scans according to the scope of segmentated organs.

During reference, we adopt specific preprocessing for large samples containing more than 800 slices and with z-axis spacing of 1. For these samples, we first equally divide the whole CT scans into three parts. Then, the coarse segmentation of target organs is implemented for each part. Finally, the CT scans containing target organs are extracted based on the segmentation results.

- Cropping strategy in x-axis and y-axis directions:
  According to observations, different samples have different proportions of target region to CT images in x-axis and y-axis directions. In some samples, the target organs only occupy a small region in CT images. It is necessary to cropping redundant background in x-axis and y-axis direction to enlarge the target organs. Conversely, the target organs in some samples occupy a large region in CT images. The target organs in these samples are close to the edge of the CT images, which resulting in mis-segmentation of target organs. For these samples, we pad the CT images with zero in x-axis and y-axis directions to ensure appropriate proportions of the target region to the corresponding CT images.

- Adjusting window level and window width:
  In order to achieve high contrast between the target organs and the background area, we adjust window width and window level of the original CT images. According to doctor's experience, the window width and window level of the CT images are adjusted to 40 and 255, respectively.

- Image Resampling:
  In this study, the network input of UMT-ISE is randomly cropped patches from whole CT images. The input size of the UMT-ISE is $112 \times 112 \times 80$, while the size of the whole CT images is much larger than $112 \times 112 \times 80$. To ensure the cropped patches contain efficient information, we resample all CT images to $192 \times 192 \times 96$ after the above preprocessing.

- Image normalization:
  After the above preprocessing, we implement z-score normalization on CT images based on the mean and standard deviation of the intensity values.

- Data augmentation:
  In this study, we implement random cropping on the whole CT images to obtain network input. Additionally, horizontal flipping are performed to achieve data augmentation.

2.2 Proposed Method

Strategies to use the unlabelled cases:

The input of teacher model and student model are the same CT images with different noises, and the output of the two models are constrained by unsupervised loss function.

Network architecture details:

The network architecture of the UMT-ISE is shown in Fig. 1. The UMT-ISE is composed of two modified V-Net models, i.e. the teacher model and the student model, and the two models share the network structure. We update the teacher's weights as an exponential moving average (EMA) [17] of the student's weights to ensemble the information in different training step. Referring to the UA-MT [17], we estimate the uncertainty with the Monte Carlo Dropout [17]. In multi-organ segmentation, different organs have different size and the segmentation accuracy of small organs is low. In order to improve the accuracy of multi-organ segmentation, we insert ISE blocks in V-Net to obtain the modified V-Net. The ISE block mainly contains inception block and squeeze-and-excitation (SE) block, which can obtain multi-scale feature maps with channel attention. The network structure of the modified V-Net is shown in Fig. 2.

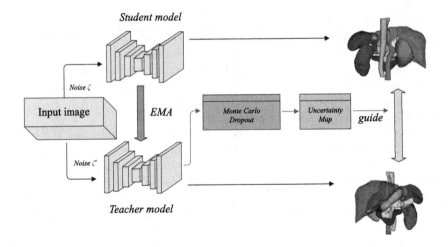

Fig. 1. Network architecture of the UMT-ISE. The network is constructed of a student model, a teacher model, and an uncertainty estimation module. The backbone of the student model and the teacher model is V-Net equipped with ISE blocks. The estimated uncertainty from the teacher model guides the student model to learn from the more reliable targets.

The structure of the ISE block is shown in Fig. 3. The ISE block integrates the residual block, Inception block, and a SE block. Multiple convolution layers with different convolution kernels are used in the Inception block to obtain multiple feature maps with different receptive fields. Then, the feature maps are fused to generate multi-scale features to alleviate the impact of size diversity in multi-organ segmentation. The structure of the Inception block is shown in Fig. 4(a).

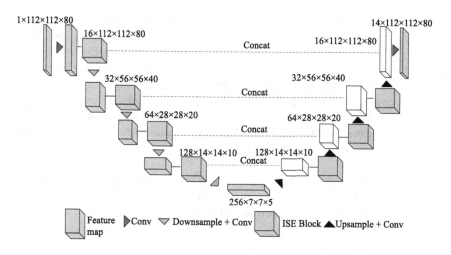

Fig. 2. Network architecture of the modified V-Net. The network is constructed of an encoder and a decoder, where four ISE blocks are inserted at the encoder and three ISE blocks are inserted at the decoder.

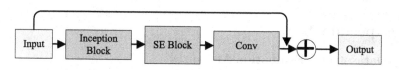

Fig. 3. The detailed architecture of the ISE block.

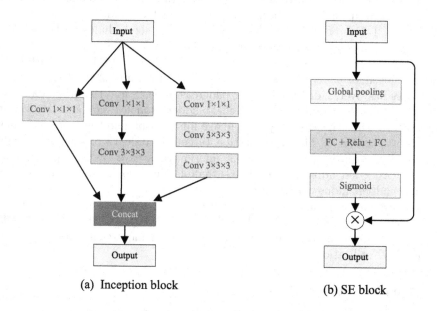

(a) Inception block   (b) SE block

Fig. 4. The detailed architecture of the Inception block (a) and the SE block (b).

Although the Inception block can enhance features of targets with different size, the redundant features in the multi-scale feature map reduce the discriminability of the network. Thus, a SE block is adopted to recalibrate the importance of the multi-scale features obtained by the Inception block. The structure of the SE block is illustrated in Fig. 4(b). In the SE block, a global average pooling layer is used to aggregate the global information, which is followed by two fully connected (FC) layers to capture the channel-wise relationships. Then, the features given by the Inception block is recalibrated by the channel-wise relationships through point-wise multiplication.

Loss function:

In this study, we adopt Dice loss and cross entropy loss to calculate supervised loss on labeled data. Additionally, consistency loss on both unlabelled data and labeled data are calculated to optimize the network.

2.3 Post-processing

The post-processing operation used in this study is removing small connected areas to reduce false positive islands. Specifically, the largest connected area of each segmented organ is retained, and the other connected areas are removed.

3 Experiments

3.1 Dataset and Evaluation Measures

The FLARE 2022 is an extension of the FLARE 2021 [10] with more segmentation targets and more diverse images. The dataset is curated from more than 20 medical groups under the license permission, including MSD [14], KiTS [7,8], AbdomenCT-1K [11], and TCIA [2]. The training set includes 50 labeled CT scans with pancreas disease and 2000 unlabelled CT scans with liver, kidney, spleen, or pancreas diseases. The validation set includes 50 CT scans with liver, kidney, spleen, or pancreas diseases. The testing set includes 200 CT scans where 100 cases has liver, kidney, spleen, or pancreas diseases and the other 100 cases has uterine corpus endometrial, urothelial bladder, stomach, sarcomas, or ovarian diseases. All the CT scans only have image information and the center information is not available. The segmentation targets include 13 organs: liver, right kidney (RK), spleen, pancreas, aorta, inferior vena cava (IVC), right adrenal gland (RAG), left adrenal gland(LAG), gallbladder, esophagus, stomach, duodenum, and left kidney (LK).

The evaluation measures consist of two accuracy measures: Dice Similarity Coefficient (DSC) and Normalized Surface Dice (NSD), and three running efficiency measures: running time, area under GPU memory-time curve, and area under CPU utilization-time curve.

3.2 Implementation Details

Environment Settings. The environments and requirements are presented in Table 1.

Table 1. Environments and requirements.

Windows/Ubuntu version	Windows 10
CPU	Intel(R) Core(TM) i9-9900K CPU @ 3.60GHz
RAM	16×2 GB;
GPU (number and type)	1 NVIDIA Tesla V100 GPU (48G)
CUDA version	11.1
Programming language	Python 3.6
Deep learning framework	Pytorch (Torch 1.7.0, torchvision 0.8.0)
Specification of dependencies	None
(Optional) Link to code	

Training Protocols. In the training process, the batch size is set as 16, and the patch size is fixed as $80 \times 112 \times 112$. For optimization, we train our network for 2000 epochs using stochastic gradient descent (SGD) algorithm with an initial learning rate of 0.05 and a momentum of 0.9. During training, we use the poly scheduling to decay the learning rate. The calculation of the learning rate is as follows:

$$lr = lr_{base} \times (1 - \frac{epoch}{total\_epochs})^{0.9}$$

where lr denotes the learning rate, and lr_{base} is the initial learning rate. $epoch$ and $total\_epochs$ are current training epoch and the total training epochs, respectively.

Referring to the UA-MT [17], we use dice loss and the cross-entropy loss to calculate supervised loss. The consistency loss is adopted to calculate unsupervised loss. The total loss of our method is the weighted sum of the supervised loss and the unsupervised loss, which is defined as follows:

$$Loss_{total} = Loss_{CE} + Loss_{Dice} + \lambda * Loss_{consist}$$

where $Loss_{total}$ denotes total loss. $Loss_{CE}$, $Loss_{Dice}$ and $Loss_{consist}$ are the cross-entropy loss, Dice loss, and the consistency loss, respectively. λ is an ramp-up weighting coefficient that controls the trade-off between the supervised and unsupervised loss (Table 2).

4   Results

In this section, we assess the performance of the UMT-ISE using FLARE22 dataset. This section is arranged as follows: First, an ablation study for attention modules is implemented to verify the effectiveness of the ISE block. Second, we conduct ablation studies for improvement strategies including utilizing unlabelled data, coarse segmentation and post processing. Third, we evaluate our method on different backbones by replacing our backbone with V-Net [12], 3D U-Net [1], and Attention U-Net [13]. Fourth, we compare our method with baselines including mean teacher (MT) model [15] and the UA-MT model. Last,

Table 2. Training protocols.

Network initialization	"he" normal initialization
Batch size	16
Patch size	$80 \times 112 \times 112$
Total epochs	2000
Optimizer	SGD with nesterov momentum ($\mu = 0.99$)
Initial learning rate (lr)	0.05
Lr decay schedule	lr = Initial learning rate $\times (1 - \frac{epoch}{total\_epochs})^{0.9}$
Training time	48 h
Loss function	cross entropy loss + Dice loss+λ *consistency loss
Number of model parameters	9.44M[a]
Number of flops	41.40G[b]
CO_2eq	1 Kg[c]

[a] https://github.com/sksq96/pytorch-summary.
[b] https://github.com/facebookresearch/fvcore.
[c] https://github.com/lfwa/carbontracker/.

the segmentation results on test set and qualitive results of our method are presented.

4.1   Ablation Study for Attention Modules

The ablation study is implemented to evaluate the effectiveness of the ISE block. The baseline of the ablation study is the UA-MT network with our proposed preprocessing and post-processing operations. Table 3 lists quantitative results of different networks on validation set. Compared with the baseline, employing the SE block individually yields a result of 0.7259 in mean DSC, which represents 4.33% improvement. Additionally, the network with only the inception block achieves 0.7446 in mean DSC, which outperforms the baseline by 6.2%. Furthermore, integration of the inception block and the SE block (i.e., UMT-ISE) yields the highest mean DSC (0.7465). These comparisons illustrate that the inception block and the SE block have potential to improve the accuracy of multi-organ segmentation.

4.2   Ablation Study for Improvement Strategies

To validate the superiority of our method in utilizing unlabelled data, we trained two models based on our method using different data. The first one is trained with only labeled data, and the second one is trained with both labeled and unlabelled data. The two models are tested on validation set, and the DSCs given by the two models are listed in Table 4. Compared with the first model, the DSCs of most organs given by the second model are higher. Additionally, the mean DSC given by the second model is 0.7465, which outperforms that of

Table 3. Quantitative results of ablation experiments for attention modules.

Attention module	None	SE block	Inception block	ISE block
Liver	0.9260	0.9338	0.9527	0.9549
RK	0.8278	0.8357	0.8493	0.8499
Spleen	0.8588	0.8616	0.8650	0.8890
Pancreas	0.6493	0.6944	0.7099	0.7155
Aorta	0.8467	0.8377	0.8367	0.8490
IVC	0.6499	0.7444	0.7738	0.7687
RAG	0.5107	0.5832	0.5723	0.6115
LAG	0.5076	0.4919	0.5716	0.5168
Gallbladder	0.5916	0.6297	0.6475	0.6431
Esophagus	0.5760	0.6663	0.6712	0.6822
Stomach	0.6065	0.7855	0.7911	0.8160
Duodenum	0.4770	0.5322	0.6274	0.5472
LK	0.8454	0.8408	0.8115	0.8602
Mean DSC	0.6826	0.7259	0.7446	0.7465

Table 4. Comparison results of our models trained with and without unlabelled data.

Training data	Only labeled data	Labeled and unlabeled data
Liver	0.9221	0.9549
RK	0.8280	0.8499
Spleen	0.8118	0.8890
Pancreas	0.7148	0.7155
Aorta	0.8020	0.8490
IVC	0.7331	0.7687
RAG	0.6158	0.6115
LAG	0.5473	0.5168
Gallbladder	0.5677	0.6431
Esophagus	0.6548	0.6822
Stomach	0.7629	0.8160
Duodenum	0.5748	0.5472
LK	0.7465	0.8602
Mean DSC	0.7193	0.7465

the first model by 2.72%. These results demonstrate that the utilization of the unlabelled data can improve the segmentation performance in our method.

To evaluate the effectiveness of the coarse segmentation and the post processing, we implemented inference experiments on validation set with different strategies. The baseline is our model tested without coarse segmentation and post processing. Table 5 lists quantitative results of our model tested with different inference strategies. Compared with the baseline, conducting the coarse segmentation individually yields a significantly higher result of 0.7461 in mean DSC, which represents 12.85% improvement. Additionally, inference with only the post processing obtains higher mean DSC (0.6275) than that of the baseline (0.6176). Furthermore, implementing both the coarse segmentation and the post processing achieves the highest mean DSC (0.7465). All these comparisons demonstrate that the coarse segmentation and the post processing can effectively improve accuracy of multi-organ segmentation.

Table 5. Quantitative results of ablation study for coarse segmentation and post processing.

Inference strategy	None	Only coarse segmentation	Only post processing	Coarse segmentation and post processing
Liver	0.9116	0.9514	0.9136	0.9549
RK	0.7408	0.8370	0.7942	0.8499
Spleen	0.8218	0.8841	0.7911	0.8890
Pancreas	0.5801	0.7150	0.6356	0.7155
Aorta	0.7592	0.8459	0.7056	0.8490
IVC	0.6967	0.7809	0.6849	0.7687
RAG	0.5014	0.6107	0.3799	0.6115
LAG	0.2595	0.5180	0.3969	0.5168
Gallbladder	0.4275	0.6296	0.6002	0.6431
Esophagus	0.5803	0.7029	0.5457	0.6822
Stomach	0.6081	0.8106	0.5802	0.8160
Duodenum	0.3814	0.5540	0.4581	0.5472
LK	0.7606	0.8595	0.6711	0.8602
Mean DSC	0.6176	0.7461	0.6275	0.7465

4.3 Experiments on Different Backbones

To evaluate the performance of the UMT-ISE over different backbones, we replaced backbones of the teacher model and the student model with V-Net [12], 3D U-Net [1], and attention U-Net [13], respectively. The proposed preprocessing and post-processing operations are conducted for all models in comparison experiments. Table 6 lists quantitative results of different networks on validation set. Compared with the network with the V-Net as the backbone, our method achieves significantly higher mean DSC. Additionally, the 3D U-Net and the attention U-Net obtain higher mean DSC than the V-Net. Furthermore, our method achieves the highest mean DSC (0.7465). These comparisons further indicate the efficiency of the UMT-ISE in multi-organ segmentation.

Table 6. Quantitative results of networks with different backbones on validation set.

Backbone	V-Net	3D U-Net	Attention U-Net	V-Net+ISE block
Liver	0.9260	0.9542	0.9487	0.9549
RK	0.8278	0.8521	0.8269	0.8499
Spleen	0.8588	0.9106	0.8686	0.8890
Pancreas	0.6493	0.6523	0.7070	0.7155
Aorta	0.8467	0.8574	0.8532	0.8490
IVC	0.6499	0.6592	0.7090	0.7687
RAG	0.5107	0.4695	0.5710	0.6115
LAG	0.5076	0.5499	0.5961	0.5168
Gallbladder	0.5916	0.6703	0.6236	0.6431
Esophagus	0.5760	0.6538	0.6498	0.6822
Stomach	0.6065	0.7243	0.7180	0.8160
Duodenum	0.4770	0.4339	0.4648	0.5472
LK	0.8454	0.8659	0.8511	0.8602
Mean DSC	0.6826	0.7118	0.7222	0.7465

4.4   Comparison Experiments with Baselines

The UMT-ISE is constructed based on the UA-MT model, which is generated by modifying the MT model [15]. To validate the superiority of the UMT-ISE over the UA-MT and the MT model, we trained and tested the conventional UA-MT and MT model using FLARE22 dataset. Tabel 7 lists quantitative results of different methods on validation set. Compared with the MT model, the UA-MT model obtains higher mean DSC (0.5905). Additionally, the UMT-ISE achieves the highest mean DSC (0.7465), which outperforms the MT and the UA-MT by 16.21% and 15.60%, respectively. These results verify the effectiveness of the uncertainty-aware scheme, the ISE block, the coarse segmentation and the post processing in our method.

4.5   Segmentation Results of Our Method

Table 8 lists quantitative results of our method on testing set. The mean DSC and NSD are 0.7104 and 0.7763, respectively. Consistent with the validation results, the segmentation of liver achieves the highest DSC (0.9501) and the segmentation of LAG obtains the lowest DSC (0.5201).

Figure 5 and Fig. 6 show examples with good segmentation results and bad segmentation results, respectively. As for the bad segmentation cases, we think there are three reasons. The first one is that the low imaging quality of the CT images causes the bad segmentation. Specifically, there are dark holes in some organs which results in broken segmentation results of the organs. As shown in Case#0048 and Case#0042 (Fig. 6), the segmentation results of stomach are incomplete because of interference of dark holes. The second one is that our

Table 7. Quantitative results of different methods on validation set.

Method	MT	UA-MT	UMT-ISE
Liver	0.8834	0.8982	0.9549
RK	0.7110	0.7319	0.8499
Spleen	0.7388	0.7754	0.8890
Pancreas	0.5254	0.4783	0.7155
Aorta	0.7849	0.7960	0.8490
IVC	0.5868	0.6487	0.7687
RAG	0.4268	0.3712	0.6115
LAG	0.3638	0.2846	0.5168
Gallbladder	0.4996	0.4641	0.6431
Esophagus	0.5322	0.5835	0.6822
Stomach	0.4612	0.5173	0.8160
Duodenum	0.3741	0.3935	0.5472
LK	0.7095	0.7336	0.8602
Mean DSC	0.5844	0.5905	0.7465

Table 8. Quantitative results of our method on testing set.

Organ	DSC	NSD
Liver	0.9501	0.9495
RK	0.8444	0.8647
Spleen	0.8243	0.8364
Pancreas	0.6535	0.7732
Aorta	0.7988	0.8411
IVC	0.7132	0.7191
RAG	0.6036	0.7818
LAG	0.5201	0.6593
Gallbladder	0.6094	0.5911
Esophagus	0.6273	0.7472
Stomach	0.7885	0.8038
Duodenum	0.4674	0.6675
LK	0.8348	0.8564
Mean	0.7104	0.7763

model is not robust enough for accurate segmentation of small organs. As shown in Case#0048 (Fig. 6), the left kidney is not segmented. The last one is that the target organs only occupy a small region in some CT images (Case#0028),

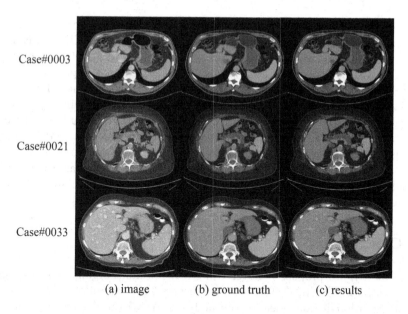

(a) image   (b) ground truth   (c) results

Fig. 5. Well-segmented examples from validation sets.

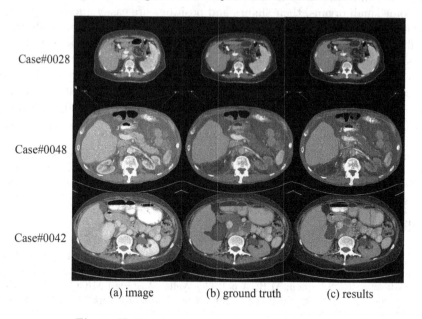

(a) image   (b) ground truth   (c) results

Fig. 6. Challenging examples from validation sets.

which increases the difficulty of segmentation. Although the coarse segmentation can enlarge abdominal region in CT images, the image quality is decreased.

To optimize inference efficiency of our method, we adopt coarse segmentation to crop redundant slices, which reduces calculation of the UMT-ISE during inference. Additionally, we use CT scans resampled to $96 \times 192 \times 192$ during inference rather than using original CT scans. Furthermore, patch-based segmentation is implemented in inference which optimizes inference efficiency. To evaluate the inference efficiency of our method, we run our trained model on a docker with NVIDIA 2080Ti GPU(12 GB) and 32 GB RAM for the 50 validation cases. The average inference time is 56.11 s, and the maximum GPU memory used is 2.98 GB. Noted that validation Case 10 and 50 are scans of full body, which consume 103.31 and 237.89 s, respectively. The average area under GPU memory-time curve and area under CPU utilization-time curve are 152226 and 951, respectively.

5   Conclusion

In this study, we propose a novel UMT-ISE for multi-organ segmentation in abdominal CT. The UMT-ISE achieves fast and accurate multi-organ segmentation. Additionally, our method can be tested on CPU, which is convenient to complete some clinical tasks. However, our method still has some limitations. For some small organs, their shapes and positions are easily affected by tumors and edema. Our method is not robust enough for segmentation of small organs. Additionally, it is difficult to extract abdominal regions for the cases with many CT slices, and the segmentation results of these cases are not satisfied. Furthermore, the coarse segmentation improves the final segmentation accuracy, but increases inference time to some extent. Our future work will focus on the accurate segmentation of small organs in multi-organ segmentation and develop more fast and accurate segmentation methods.

Acknowledgment. The authors of this paper declare that the segmentation method they implemented for participation in the FLARE22 challenge didn't use any pretrained models or additional datasets other than those provided by the organizers.

References

1. Çiçek, Ö., Abdulkadir, A., Lienkamp, S.S., Brox, T., Ronneberger, O.: 3D U-net: learning dense volumetric segmentation from sparse annotation. In: Ourselin, S., Joskowicz, L., Sabuncu, M.R., Unal, G., Wells, W. (eds.) MICCAI 2016. LNCS, vol. 9901, pp. 424–432. Springer, Cham (2016). https://doi.org/10.1007/978-3-319-46723-8_49
2. Clark, K., et al.: The cancer imaging archive (TCIA): maintaining and operating a public information repository. J. Digit. Imaging 26(6), 1045–1057 (2013)
3. Cui, W., et al.: Semi-supervised brain lesion segmentation with an adapted mean teacher model. In: Chung, A.C.S., Gee, J.C., Yushkevich, P.A., Bao, S. (eds.) IPMI 2019. LNCS, vol. 11492, pp. 554–565. Springer, Cham (2019). https://doi.org/10.1007/978-3-030-20351-1_43

4. Fu, Y., et al.: A novel MRI segmentation method using CNN-based correction network for MRI-guided adaptive radiotherapy. Med. Phys. **45**(11), 5129–5137 (2018)

5. Ganaye, P.-A., Sdika, M., Benoit-Cattin, H.: Semi-supervised learning for segmentation under semantic constraint. In: Frangi, A.F., Schnabel, J.A., Davatzikos, C., Alberola-López, C., Fichtinger, G. (eds.) MICCAI 2018. LNCS, vol. 11072, pp. 595–602. Springer, Cham (2018). https://doi.org/10.1007/978-3-030-00931-1_68

6. Heimann, T., et al.: Comparison and evaluation of methods for liver segmentation from CT datasets. IEEE Trans. Med. Imaging **28**(8), 1251–1265 (2009)

7. Heller, N., et al.: The state of the art in kidney and kidney tumor segmentation in contrast-enhanced CT imaging: results of the kits19 challenge. Med. Image Anal. **67**, 101821 (2021)

8. Heller, N., et al.: An international challenge to use artificial intelligence to define the state-of-the-art in kidney and kidney tumor segmentation in CT imaging. Proc. Am. Soc. Clin. Oncol. **38**(6), 626–626 (2020)

9. Kirbas, C., Quek, F.: A review of vessel extraction techniques and algorithms. ACM Comput. Surv. (CSUR) **36**(2), 81–121 (2004)

10. Ma, J., et al.: Fast and low-GPU-memory abdomen CT organ segmentation: the flare challenge. Med. Image Anal. **82**, 102616 (2022). https://doi.org/10.1016/j.media.2022.102616

11. Ma, J., et al.: Abdomenct-1k: is abdominal organ segmentation a solved problem? IEEE Trans. Pattern Anal. Mach. Intell. **44**(10), 6695–6714 (2022)

12. Milletari, F., Navab, N., Ahmadi, S.-A.: V-net: fully convolutional neural networks for volumetric medical image segmentation. In: 2016 Fourth International Conference on 3D Vision (3DV), pp. 565–571 (2016)

13. Oktay, O., et al.: Attention u-net: learning where to look for the pancreas. arXiv preprint arXiv:1804.03999 (2018)

14. Simpson, A.L., et al.: A large annotated medical image dataset for the development and evaluation of segmentation algorithms. arXiv preprint arXiv:1902.09063 (2019)

15. Tarvainen, A., Valpola, H.: Mean teachers are better role models: weight-averaged consistency targets improve semi-supervised deep learning results. In: Advances in Neural Information Processing Systems 30 (2017)

16. Wang, Y., Zhou, Y., Shen, W., Park, S., Fishman, E.K., Yuille, A.L.: Abdominal multi-organ segmentation with organ-attention networks and statistical fusion. Med. Image Anal. **55**, 88–102 (2019)

17. Yu, L., Wang, S., Li, X., Fu, C.-W., Heng, P.-A.: Uncertainty-aware self-ensembling model for semi-supervised 3D left atrium segmentation. In: Shen, D., et al. (eds.) MICCAI 2019. LNCS, vol. 11765, pp. 605–613. Springer, Cham (2019). https://doi.org/10.1007/978-3-030-32245-8_67

Self-pretrained V-Net Based on PCRL for Abdominal Organ Segmentation

Jiapeng Zhang[✉] (iD)

University of Shanghai for Science and Technology, Shanghai, China
201440057@st.usst.edu.cn

Abstract. Abdomen organ segmentation has many important clinical applications. However, the manual annotating process is time-consuming and labor-intensive. In the "Fast and Low-resource semi-supervised Abdominal oRgan sEgmentation in CT" challenge, the organizer provide massive unlabeled CT images. To effectively utilize unlabeled cases, we propose a self-pretrained V-net. Inspired by the preservational contrastive representation learning (PCRL), the proposed method consists of two steps: 1) using a large amount of unlabeled data to obtain a pretrained model, 2) using a small amount of labeled data to perform fully supervised fine-tuning on the basis of the former. The feature extraction part used in both stages uses the same backbone network. The difference is that the pre-training stage introduces the additional image reconstruction branch and the corresponding momentum branch to construct image reconstruction and contrastive learning, and the fully-supervised model downstream uses a fully convolutional network for segmentation prediction. In the pre-training stage, by incorporating diverse image reconstruction tasks into the contrastive learning, the representation ability of the backbone network for specific image data during the upstream feature extraction process is enhanced. Besides, the half-precision (Float16) is used in the prediction stage, which reduces the GPU load by about 36% without losing the prediction accuracy and the maximum used GPU memory is 1719 MB. Quantitative evaluation on the FLARE2022 validation cases, this method achieves the average dice similarity coefficient (DSC) of 0.4811 and average normalized surface distance (NSD) of 0.4513.

Keywords: Self-supervised learning · Self-transfer learning · Organ segmentation

1 Introduction

Abdominal organ segmentation plays an important role in clinical practice, the state-of-the-art methods have achieved inter-observer performance in several benchmark datasets. However, most of the existing abdominal datasets only contain single-center, single-phase, single-vendor, or single-disease cases, and it is unclear whether the excellent performance can be generalized on more diverse datasets. Some SOTA methods have good general applicability. However, when

J. Ma and B. Wang (Eds.): FLARE 2022, LNCS 13816, pp. 260–269, 2022.
https://doi.org/10.1007/978-3-031-23911-3_23

the training data is limited and the task is complex, it is difficult for the model to be fully trained. Moreover, many SOTA methods use model ensembles to boost performance, but these solutions usually have a large model size and cost extensive computational resources, which are impractical to be deployed in clinical practice.

Compared with labeled data, unlabeled data is usually easier to obtain because the manual labeling process is omitted. To make full use of the massive unlabeled cases, self-supervised learning has been widely adopted [2]. Based on the massive unlabeled data provided by the Fast and Low-resource semi-supervised Abdominal oRgan sEgmentation in CT challenge, we attempted to design our method based on V-Net [7], and PCRL [12].

Specifically, the backbone uses the encoder-decoder style architecture with skip connection [8]. The vast majority of successful algorithms for image segmentation in the medical domain such as V-net [7] and Dense U-net [10] are based on this U-shape structure. For unlabeled data, we use the method of retaining contrastive representation learning to obtain a pre-training weight through self-supervised learning. Then, perform full supervision finetuning through limited annotated data. Note that this pre-trained model was trained from the unlabeled cases provided by the challenge, and no additional pre-trained models were used in the process. Compared with methods that only use contrastive learning, PCRL can generate stronger representations of image information in the upstream feature extraction network by reconstructing different contexts. Besides, to take into account the use of GPU memory and the preservation of information between multiple organs and backgrounds, we adopt a horizontal plane scaling and vertical sliding window strategy to train the model. Meanwhile, due to the limitation of GPU resources, we use a smaller input size to reduce resource consumption.

The main contributions of this work are summarized as follows:

1) We propose a PCRL-based self-pretrained multi-organ segmentation framework to make full use of the massive unlabeled cases.
2) To reduce resource consumption and speed up the inference process, we compress the input size and utilize a smaller width for the network.

2 Method

As mentioned in Fig. 1, this whole segmentation framework is composed of a selfsupervised pretrain stage and a full-supervised finetuning stage. The detail description of the method is as follows.

2.1 Preprocessing

The proposed method includes the following preprocessing steps:

– Cropping strategy: Crop the training dataset to the non-zero region.

- Resampling method for anisotropic data: First, the images are reoriented
  to a unified direction. To obtain a larger receptive field during the training
  process, we tend to use a relatively complete patch for training. In this way
  the model can capture better relative relationship between the various organs.
  Constrained by hardware conditions, the original image is downsampled to
  160 × 160 for clises in the transverse section, and the spacing of inferior-
  superior axis is unified to 2.5. Both in-plane and out-of-plane with third-order
  spline interpolation.
- Intensity normalization method: First, the images is clipped to the range
  [−320, 320]. Then a z-score normalization is applied based on the mean and
  standard deviation of the intensity values [11].

2.2   Proposed Method

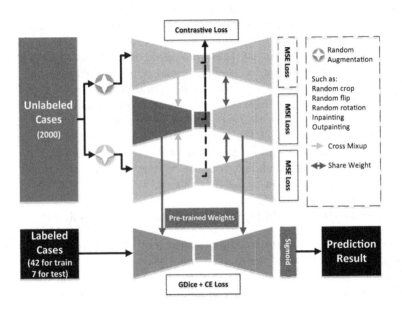

Fig. 1. Self-supervised pretrain and full-supervised fine-tuning framework

The unlabeled data are used to construct a self-supervised learning process to
obtain a pre-trained model for augmenting the fully supervised training process.
The encoder and the decoder in both pretarin stage and finetuning stage are
connected via a U shape architecture.

For the pretrain stage, the PCRL contains three different encoders and one
shared decoder. The three different encoders are ordinary encoder, momentum
encoder, and cross-mixup encoder, where the momentum encoder is obtained

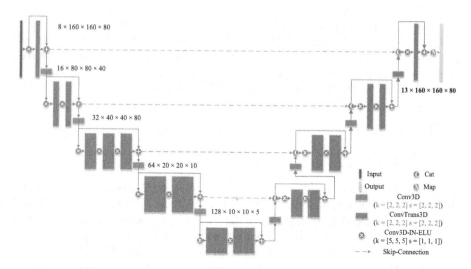

Fig. 2. V-Net backbone, where the input size and the number of network layers are modified accordingly to this task.

from the exponential moving average to the ordinary encode, and the cross-mixup encoder is the hybrid encoder mixed by both former encoders. Following Zhou et al. [12], for a batch of input image, different data augmentation methods, such as random crop, random flip and random rotation are first applied to generate three batches of images corresponding to three encoders which are set as the ground truth targets of the MSE loss after decoder. Then low-level processing operations, including inpainting, outpainting are performed randomly to generate the original encoder and the momentum encoder inputs. And the input of the cross-mixup encoder is the mixup of these two inputs. The feature maps output from the original encoder and the last layer of the momentum encoder are deposited into the sequence K after global average pooling encoding to construct the constructive learning [2].

For the fintuning stage, the weights from the pre-training phase are used. And the difference is that a sigmoid layer is utilized after the decoder to perform the downstream task of segmentation.

The detail of each layer, hyper-parameters, such as stride, weight size, etc. of the backbone are shown in Fig. 2

Loss function: During self-pretrain stage, the contrastive loss and MSE loss are used; During the fine-tuning stage, we use the summation between generalized Dice loss and cross entropy loss because it has been proved to be robust [5] in medical image segmentation tasks.

To reduce resource consumption, a smaller input size to reduce resource consumption. Besides, existing network frameworks (such as PyTorch) usually use full precision (Float64) for prediction. However, for intensive prediction tasks such as 3D image segmentation, the use of full-precision model parameters will greatly increase the hardware burden in the deduction process. In this work, the half-precision (Float32) is used in the prediction stage, which reduces the GPU load by about 36% without losing the prediction accuracy.

3   Experiments

3.1   Dataset and Evaluation Measures

The FLARE2022 dataset is curated from more than 20 medical groups under the license permission, including MSD [9], KiTS [3,4], AbdomenCT-1K [6], and TCIA [1]. The training set includes 50 labelled CT scans with pancreas disease and 2000 unlabelled CT scans with liver, kidney, spleen, or pancreas diseases. The validation set includes 50 CT scans with liver, kidney, spleen, or pancreas diseases. The testing set includes 200 CT scans where 100 cases has liver, kidney, spleen, or pancreas diseases and the other 100 cases has uterine corpus endometrial, urothelial bladder, stomach, sarcomas, or ovarian diseases. All the CT scans only have image information and the center information is not available.

The evaluation measures consist of two accuracy measures: Dice Similarity Coefficient (DSC) and Normalized Surface Dice (NSD), and three running efficiency measures: running time, area under GPU memory-time curve, and area under CPU utilization-time curve. All measures will be used to compute the ranking. Moreover, the GPU memory consumption has a 2 GB tolerance.

3.2   Implementation Details

Environment Settings. The development environments and requirements are presented in Table 1.

Table 1. Development environments and requirements.

Windows/Ubuntu version	Ubuntu 16.04.5 LTS
CPU	Intel(R) Xeon(R) CPU E5-2640 V3 @2.60 GHz
RAM	8×4 GB; 2.4MT/s
GPU (number and type)	4 Nvidia Geforce RTX 2080 (8G)
CUDA version	11.1
Programming language	Python 3.9
Deep learning framework	Pytorch (Torch 1.8.1, torchvision 0.9.0)
Specific dependencies	V-Net[a]/PCRL[b]

[a]https://github.com/mattmacy/vnet.pytorch
[b]https://github.com/Luchixiang/PCRL

Table 2. Training protocols.

Network initialization	"he" normal initialization
Batch size	4
Patch size	80 × 160 × 160
Total epochs	2000
Optimizer	Adam
Initial learning rate (lr)	0.0001
Learning rate decay schedule	MultiStepLR: milestones = [100, 200, 500], gamma = 0.5
Training time	11.4 day (self-pretrain) + 22.5 h (fine-tuning)
Loss	Contrast Loss + MSE Loss (self-pretrain); GDice Loss + CE Loss (fine-tuning)
Number of model parameters	43.60M[a]
Number of flops	218.7G[b]

[a]https://github.com/sksq96/pytorch-summary
[b]https://github.com/facebookresearch/fvcore

Training Protocols. The training protocols of the baseline method is shown in Table 2. During self-supervised pretraining, random crop, random flip, random rotation, inpainting, outpainting and gaussian blur are used for constraction of contrastive learning. During the full-supervised fine-tuning, an area with a length of 80 on the axis is randomly cropped to obtain a 3D input patch of height 80 pixels, note that each patch contains at least one foreground class.

4   Results and Discussion

4.1   Quantitative Results on Validation Set

Table 3. Quantitative results on validation set in terms of DSC. The 1st row represents the method without self-pretrained, and the 2nd row represents the method with self-pretrained. (where the Liv., RK, Spl., Pan., Aor, IVC, RAG, LAG, Gal., Eso., Sto., Duo, and LK are Liver, Right Kidney, Spleen, Pancreas, Aorta, inferior vena cava, right adrenal gland, left adrenal gland, gallbladder, esophagus, stomach, duodenum, and left kidney, respectively.)

Organ	Liv	RK	Spl	Pan	Aor	IVC	RAG	LAG	Gal	Eso	Sto	Duo	LK	Mean
DSC (%)	**83.10**	**67.97**	**69.26**	**49.44**	**76.14**	**64.45**	2.00	4.00	**40.03**	39.02	**55.45**	**40.46**	**68.65**	50.77
DSC (%)	73.89	59.06	61.14	34.64	74.31	59.32	**40.50**	**32.06**	26.56	41.63	41.58	32.09	57.75	48.67

Table 3 illustrate the quantitative results on the provided validation set. Including the mean DSC and individual DSC for liver (Liv.), right kidney (RK), spleen(Spl.), pancreas (Pan.), aorta (Aor.), inferior vena cava (IVC), right adrenal gland (RAG), left adrenal gland (LAG), gallbladder (Gal.), esophagus (Eso.), stomach (Stm.), duodenum (Duo.) and left kidney (LK). Although all

Table 4. Ablation study on provided validation cases. The 1st row and the 3rd row represent the methods without self-pretrained, and the 2nd and 4th rows represent the methods with self-pretrained. (where the Liv., RK, Spl., Pan., Aor, IVC, RAG, LAG, Gal., Eso., Sto., Duo, and LK are Liver, Right Kidney, Spleen, Pancreas, Aorta, inferior vena cava, right adrenal gland, left adrenal gland, gallbladder, esophagus, stomach, duodenum, and left kidney, respectively.)

	Liv	RK	Spl	Pan	Aor	IVC	RAG	LAG	Gal	Eso	Sto	Duo	LK	Mean
DSC (%)	84.28	61.01	70.49	50.87	77.94	67.23	0.00	0.00	27.41	46.85	48.95	39.47	71.79	49.71
DSC (%)	77.20	55.59	64.83	37.81	72.39	61.86	37.45	32.11	18.50	39.74	41.33	25.85	60.82	48.11
NSD (%)	70.53	48.56	59.41	56.08	77.41	61.38	0.00	0.00	21.23	56.16	46.94	58.73	66.18	47.89
NSD (%)	60.74	42.31	48.48	43.42	63.33	52.52	48.76	40.30	12.74	51.03	36.48	38.32	48.30	45.13

other metrics were higher than the method using the self-pretrained model. left and right adrenals were barely predictable when self-pretrained model was not used.

Table 4 illustrate the ablation study on provided 50 validation cases. Overall, the proposed method performs well on large organs such as liver and spleen, while it performs poorly on small organs such as esophageal islets and left and right adrenal glands. In addition, it can be seen that the performance of the segmentation model is significantly improved on the right and left adrenal glands after self-pretraining with unlabeled data.

Due to memory limitations, our method uses a smaller raw input size of the network as well as a smaller channel size, which exacerbates the risk of the model losing contextual information when dealing with small targets. The process of pretraining on unlabeled data improves the upstream feature extraction part of the model for feature representation under specific data distribution, which can effectively mitigate the risk of small organ loss.

4.2   Qualitative Results on Validation Set

Figure 3 present some examples on our splitted validation set. It can be found that the method using pretrained model from unlabeled data performs better for the prediction of small organs such as left and right adrenal glands compared to the method that does not utilize unlabeled data. Also, due to the use of sliding windows in our method and the preprocessing strategy of uniform spacing, there may be a certain degree of missing prediction when the input scan interval is too large or when the scan spacing differs too much from the standard spacing, which is a major reason for the decrease in evaluation metrics.

4.3   Results on Final Testing Set

Our final results on the test set are shown in Table 5. The final mean DSC value is 46.26%, and the mean NSD is 40.09%. The results show that the model also responds well to small targets that are difficult to segment, such as adrenal glands. The results on the test set are consistent with those of the validation set.

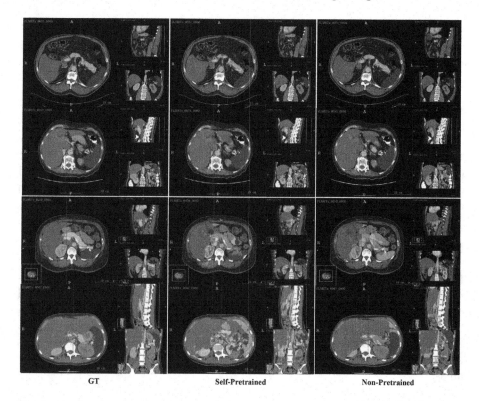

GT   Self-Pretrained   Non-Pretrained

Fig. 3. Qualitative results on some examples. First two columns are some good cases and the last two columns are some worse cases.

Table 5. Overview of DSC and NSD metrics on test set (where the Liv., RK, Spl., Pan., Aor, IVC, RAG, LAG, Gal., Eso., Sto., Duo, and LK are Liver, Right Kidney, Spleen, Pancreas, Aorta, inferior vena cava, right adrenal gland, left adrenal gland, gallbladder, esophagus, stomach, duodenum, and left kidney, respectively.)

Organ	Liv	RK	Spl	Pan	Aor	IVC	RAG	LAG	Gal	Eso	Sto	Duo	LK	Mean
DSC (%)	61.68	56.55	53.04	35.05	72.17	60.38	43.97	35.42	27.30	34.85	35.77	26.42	58.54	46.24
NSD (%)	41.18	36.67	33.50	35.37	60.77	48.89	56.96	45.05	16.90	44.19	26.31	34.08	41.27	40.09

4.4   Segmentation Efficiency Results on Validation Set

To balance performance and resource consumption, We perform a scaling operation on the slicer in the transverse section, while taking a random sliding window in the Inferior-Superior axis direction to obtain a uniform size input patch. Also, the images are stretched to a fixed axis spacing of 2.5 before processing. This means that the model prediction efficiency will be greatly reduced for long range CT scans where the extent of the abdominal cavity cannot be determined (e.g., some cases in the validation set), while it is efficient for CT data where the extent of the abdominal cavity is more certain (e.g., 50 cases in the training set).

4.5 Limitation and Future Work

As mentioned before, although the sliding window strategy can effectively reduce the resource burden compared to the overall processing, it may also lead to more time-consuming and unnecessary resource wastage on CT data with larger scan ranges, and can also result in incorrect segmentation results in non-target (abdominal) intervals. In addition, the predictive power of the model for small organs remains limited. In the future, we will focus on addressing these two aspects and exploring more possibilities for unlabeled data.

5   Conclusion

In this work, we proposed a method based on PCLR and V-Net to segment abdomial organs fast and cost low-resource. The self-supervised pre-trained model obtained from a large amount of unlabeled data effectively improves the prediction ability of the segmentation model for small organs such as adrenal glands. It performs well on healthy data with well-defined target intervals, however, it performs poorly and is relatively time-consuming for CT data with large scan areas.

Acknowledgements. The authors of this paper declare that the segmentation method they implemented for participation in the FLARE 2022 challenge has not used any pre-trained models nor additional datasets other than those provided by the organizers. The proposed solution is fully automatic without any manual intervention.

References

1. Clark, K., et al.: The cancer imaging archive (TCIA): maintaining and operating a public information repository. J. Digit. Imaging **26**(6), 1045–1057 (2013)
2. He, K., Fan, H., Wu, Y., Xie, S., Girshick, R.B.: Momentum contrast for unsupervised visual representation learning. In: 2020 IEEE/CVF Conference on Computer Vision and Pattern Recognition, CVPR 2020, Seattle, WA, USA, 13–19 June 2020, pp. 9726–9735. Computer Vision Foundation/IEEE (2020). https://doi.org/10.1109/CVPR42600.2020.00975
3. Heller, N., et al.: The state of the art in kidney and kidney tumor segmentation in contrast-enhanced CT imaging: results of the KiTS19 challenge. Med. Image Anal. **67**, 101821 (2021)
4. Heller, N., et al.: An international challenge to use artificial intelligence to define the state-of-the-art in kidney and kidney tumor segmentation in CT imaging. Proc. Am. Soc. Clin. Oncol. **38**(6), 626–626 (2020)
5. Ma, J., et al.: Loss odyssey in medical image segmentation. Med. Image Anal. **71**, 102035 (2021)

6. Ma, J., et al.: AbdomenCT-1K: is abdominal organ segmentation a solved problem? IEEE Trans. Pattern Anal. Mach. Intell. (2021). https://doi.org/10.1109/TPAMI. 2021.3100536

7. Milletari, F., Navab, N., Ahmadi, S.A.: V-net: fully convolutional neural networks for volumetric medical image segmentation. In: 2016 Fourth International Conference on 3D Vision (3DV), pp. 565–571 (2016). https://doi.org/10.1109/3DV.2016. 79

8. Ronneberger, O., Fischer, P., Brox, T.: U-net: convolutional networks for biomedical image segmentation. In: International Conference on Medical Image Computing and Computer-Assisted Intervention, pp. 234–241 (2015)

9. Simpson, A.L., et al.: A large annotated medical image dataset for the development and evaluation of segmentation algorithms. arXiv preprint arXiv:1902.09063 (2019)

10. Wang, Z., Zou, N., Shen, D., Ji, S.: Non-local U-Nets for biomedical image segmentation. In: AAAI, pp. 6315–6322 (2020)

11. Zhang, F., Wang, Y., Yang, H.: Efficient context-aware network for abdominal multi-organ segmentation. arXiv preprint arXiv:2109.10601 (2021)

12. Zhou, H., Lu, C., Yang, S., Han, X., Yu, Y.: Preservational learning improves self-supervised medical image models by reconstructing diverse contexts. In: 2021 IEEE/CVF International Conference on Computer Vision, ICCV 2021, Montreal, QC, Canada, 10–17 October 2021, pp. 3479–3489. IEEE (2021). https://doi.org/ 10.1109/ICCV48922.2021.00348

Abdominal Multi-organ Segmentation Using CNN and Transformer

Rui Xin[ID] and Lisheng Wang[✉][ID]

Institute of Image Processing and Pattern Recognition, Department of Automation,
Shanghai Jiao Tong University, Shanghai, China
lswang@sjtu.edu.cn

Abstract. In this paper, we combine the advantages of convolution local correlation and translation invariance in CNN with Transformer's ability to effectively capture long-term dependencies between pixels to produce high-quality pseudo labels. In order to segment images efficiently and quickly, we select nnU-Net [2] as the final segmentation network and use pseudo labels, unlabeled data and labeled data together to train the network, and then we use Generic U-Net [2], the backbone network of nnU-Net, as final prediction network. The mean DSC of the prediction results of our method on validation set of FLARE2022 Challenge [3] is 0.7580.

Keywords: Medical segmentation · Pseudo label · Semi-supervision learning

1 Introduction

Accurate segmentation of organs or lesions from medical images plays an important role in many clinical applications, such as diagnosis, treatment and postoperative planning. With the increase of annotation data, deep learning has achieved great success in image segmentation. However, for medical images, the acquisition of annotation data is often expensive because of the expertise and time required to generate accurate annotations, especially in 3D images.

In order to reduce labeling cost, many methods have been proposed in recent years to develop high-performance medical image segmentation models to reduce labeling data. A small amount of labelled data and a large amount of unlabeled data are more consistent with the actual clinical scenarios. The semi-supervised learning framework obtains high-quality segmentation results by learning directly from limited labeled data and a large amount of unlabeled data.

In this paper, a semi-supervised method for abdominal multi-organ image segmentation is proposed, which combines CNN and Transformer [1] to generate a large amount of pseudo labels, and uses pseudo labels, unlabeled data and labeled data to train the network, which is equivalent to dataset augmentation and improving the performance of the network.

© The Author(s), under exclusive license to Springer Nature Switzerland AG 2022
J. Ma and B. Wang (Eds.): FLARE 2022, LNCS 13816, pp. 270–280, 2022.
https://doi.org/10.1007/978-3-031-23911-3_24

2 Method

This chapter focuses on two network frameworks used to generate high-quality pseudo labels, and the entire process of using the pseudo label to improve the performance of the backbone network.

2.1 nnU-Net

Preprocessing. We first crop the non-zero regions of the image and resample the cropped data, and then we use Z-Score standardization to normalize the data. The Z-Score standardized formula is as follows:

$$z = \frac{x - \mu}{\sigma} \tag{1}$$

μ is the average value of the CT value of the image label, σ is the variance of the CT value of the image label.

Network. We use 3D U-Net [8] at full resolution for training. As shown in Fig. 1, this 3D U-Net is Generic U-Net, the backbone network of nnU-Net, which is also used as the final prediction network.

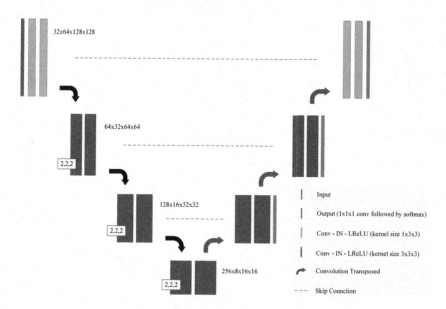

Fig. 1. Generic U-Net, the backbone network of nnU-Net.

Training. We use the sum of dice loss and cross entropy loss as our total loss function:

$$\mathcal{L}_{\text{total}} = \mathcal{L}_{\text{dc}} + \mathcal{L}_{\text{ce}} \qquad (2)$$

The dice loss function is formulated as follows:

$$\mathcal{L}_{\text{dc}} = -\frac{2}{|K|} \sum_{k \in K} \frac{\sum_{i \in I} u_i^k v_i^k}{\sum_{i \in I} u_i^k + \sum_{i \in I} v_i^k} \qquad (3)$$

where u is softmax output and v is one hot encoding ground and truth. K is the number of categories. The formula of cross entropy loss function is as follows:

$$\mathcal{L}_{\text{ce}} = -\sum_x p(x) \log q(x) \qquad (4)$$

The probability distribution p is the expected output, and the probability distribution q is the actual output.

Testing. The whole testing process is based on the patch size and we use TTA for data augmentation.

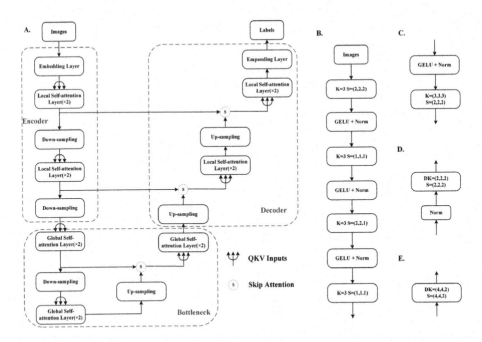

Fig. 2. The overall structure of nnFormer. A shows the architecture of nnFormer. B, C, D and E are the specific details of embedding layer, down-sampling layer, up-sampling layer and expanding layer, respectively. K represents the convolutional kernel size. S represents the stride. DK represents the deconvolutional kernel size. Norm is the normalization strategy.

2.2   nnFormer [9]

Network. As shown in Fig. 2, the backbone structure of nnFormer is mainly composed of encoder, bottleneck layer and decoder.

The encoder includes an embedding layer, two local self-attention layer blocks and two down-sampling layers. The input image is transformed into features that can be processed by the network through the convolution structure.

The decoding part symmetrically includes two local self-attention layer blocks, two up-sampling layers and the last patch expanding layer for mask prediction. nnFormer uses a local 3D image block-based self-attention calculation called V-MSA [9]. Compared with the traditional voxel self-attention calculation method, V-MSA can greatly reduce the computational complexity.

The bottleneck layer consists of a down-sampling layer, an up-sampling layer, and three global self-attention layer blocks to provide a large receive domain to support the decoder. At the same time, adding skip attention [9] connections in a symmetrical manner between the corresponding feature pyramids of the encoder and decoder helps to recover fine-grained details in the prediction.

Training and Testing. In nnFormer, we use the same training and testing strategy as nnU-Net.

2.3   Proposed Method

The overall architecture of the approach is shown in Fig. 3, which consists of the generation of pseudo label and the prediction network. In pseudo label generation stage, nnU-Net and nnFormer network models are mainly used. In the final prediction part, we adopt Generic U-Net, the basic network model of nnU-Net.

Pseudo Label Generation. Specifically, in the generation stage of pseudo label, we mainly adopt two network models, nnU-Net and nnFormer. We first train the two models with only 50 cases of labeled data, and then predicted the unlabeled data respectively, and generated the final prediction result by means of prediction probability fusion. This method combine the advantages of local correlation of convolution to spatial information encoding in CNN and long-term dependency capturing in Transformer [4].

After the prediction results are obtained, we use the connected domain analysis for data selection, only the largest part of the connected domain results of each label were saved. Finally, the pseudo label containing each organ is obtained, as shown in Fig. 4. We use ITK-SNAP [7] for visualization.

Predictive Network. To improve the segmentation efficiency, we use simple network structure for final prediction. We adopt the backbone network Generic U-Net in nnU-Net method as our predictive network. After obtaining pseudo label, the original label and generated pseudo label are trained through nnU-Net, and finally Generic U-Net, the basic network of nnU-Net, is used as the final prediction network.

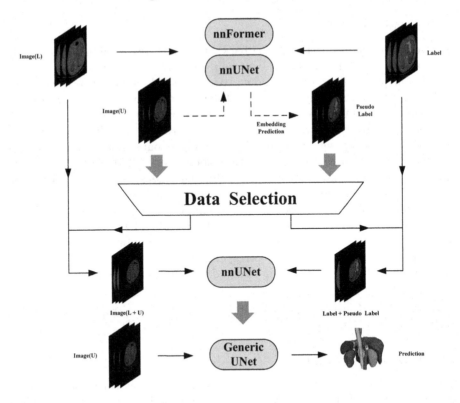

Fig. 3. The overall architecture. Images(L) represents the labeled image. Images(U) represents the unlabeled image. Images(L+U) represents the labeled and unlabeled image mixed together.

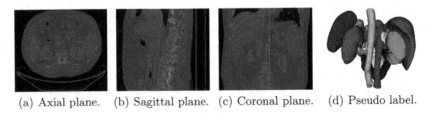

(a) Axial plane.   (b) Sagittal plane.   (c) Coronal plane.   (d) Pseudo label.

Fig. 4. Three planes of an unlabeled CT image and corresponding generated pseudo label.

Post-processing. In some computer vision tasks, it is necessary to do some post-processing on the output of the model to optimize the visual effect, and connected domain is a common post-processing method. Especially for segmentation tasks, sometimes there are some false positives in the output mask. Finding independent contours with small area through 3D connected domain and removing them can effectively improve the visual effect. We use connected domain principal component analysis to remove 3D small connected domains and retain the largest part of each label connected domain.

3 Experiments

Dataset. The FLARE 2022 is an extension of the FLARE 2021 [5] with more segmentation targets and more diverse abdomen CT scans. The FLARE2022 Challenge [3] provides a small amount of labeled cases and a large amount of unlabeled cases regarding abdominal organs. The training set includes 50 labeled CT images and organ of patients with pancreatic disease and 2000 unlabeled CT images of patients with pancreatic disease. The organs to be segmented include 13 organs, including liver, spleen, pancreas, right kidney, left kidney, stomach, gallbladder, esophagus, aorta, inferior vena cava, right adrenal gland, left adrenal gland and duodenum. The validation set includes 50 CT images from patients with liver, kidney, spleen, or pancreas disease. The test set includes 100 CT images of patients with liver, kidney, spleen, and pancreas diseases and 100 CT images of patients with endometrial, bladder, stomach, sarcoma, and ovarian diseases [6].

Evaluation Measures. The evaluation indexes of this competition include dice similarity coefficient, normalized surface dice, running time, area under GPU memory time curve and area under CPU utilization time curve.

The dice similarity coefficient is a statistic used to evaluate the similarity of two samples, essentially measuring the overlap of two samples. The formula is as follows:

$$DSC = \frac{2|X \cap Y|}{|X| + |Y|} \tag{5}$$

$|X|$ and $|Y|$ represent the number of elements in each set, respectively. It is used to measure how similar the prediction result is to the original label. Normalized surface dice is a boundary-based evaluation method used to describe the boundary error between the prediction result and the original label. In addition, the GPU memory and GPU utilization are recorded every 0.1s, and the area under the GPU memory-time curve and the area under the CPU utilization-time curve are cumulative values of running time.

Implementation Details. The development environments and requirements are presented in Table 1.

We use the same training strategy for nnU-Net and nnFormer. The training protocol is presented in Table 2.

Table 1. Development environments and requirements.

Ubuntu version	Ubuntu 18.04.5 LTS
CPU	Intel(R) Core(TM) i9-10920X CPU@3.50 GHz
RAM	126 GB
GPU	1 NVIDIA GeForce RTX 3090(24G)
CUDA version	11.4
Programming language	Python 3.6
Deep learning framework	Pytorch (Torch 1.9.1, torchvision 0.10.1)

Table 2. Training protocol.

Batch size	2
Patch size	$64 \times 128 \times 128$
Total epochs	1000
Optimizer	SGD with nesterov momentum ($\mu = 0.99$)
Initial learning rate(lr)	0.01
Network initialization	"he" normal initialization
Lr decay schedule	"poly" strategy 6
Training time	90 h
Loss function	Sum of cross entropy loss and dice loss

Before training, we resample all images to the same spacing. In the process of training, we use data augmentation methods such as rotation, scaling, Gaussian noise, Gaussian blur, gamma enhancement and mirror image.

$$lr = initial\_lr \times \left(1 - \frac{epoch\_id}{max\_epoch}\right)^{0.9} \tag{6}$$

4   Results

4.1   Quantitative Results on Validation Set

This method combines the advantages of CNN and Transformer to produce a high-quality pseudo label. We use 50 labeled data for training and test on the validation set. This produces a higher quality result than using either model alone, and their respective dice score metrics on the validation set are shown in Table 3.

We compare the prediction results of this method with those of directly transferring to Generic U-Net after training without using pseudo label. The dice score of the predicted results on the validation set without and with pseudo label training are shown in Table 4. The results show that using pseudo label can greatly improve network segmentation performance.

Table 3. The dice metrics of the prediction results of nnU-Net and nnFormer on the validation set and The dice metrics of their embedding prediction results on the validation set. RK, IVC, RAG, LAG and LK represent right kidney, inferior vena cava, right adrenal gland, left adrenal gland and left kidney respectively.

Methods	Average	Liver	RK	Spleen	Pancreas	Aorta	IVC	RAG
nnU-Net	0.8310	0.9512	0.8640	0.8734	0.8494	0.9377	0.8747	0.7972
nnFormer	0.8008	0.9550	0.7936	0.8867	0.8244	0.9208	0.8093	0.7358
nnU-Net+nnFormer	0.8500	0.9631	0.8926	0.9080	0.8709	0.9475	0.8674	0.8049

Methods	LAG	Gallbladder	Esophagus	Stomach	Duodenum	LK
nnU-Net	0.7820	0.6456	0.8079	0.8502	0.7164	0.8530
nnFormer	0.7383	0.8441	0.7308	0.8562	0.6467	0.8189
nnU-Net+nnFormer	0.7807	0.7168	0.8185	0.8992	0.7363	0.8441

Table 4. The dice metrics of the prediction results of nnU-Net and nnFormer on the validation set and The dice metrics of their embedding prediction results on the validation set. RK, IVC, RAG, LAG and LK represent right kidney, inferior vena cava, right adrenal gland, left adrenal gland and left kidney respectively.

Methods	Average	Liver	RK	Spleen	Pancreas	Aorta	IVC	RAG
w/ pseudo label	0.7580	0.9540	0.7972	0.8265	0.6980	0.9233	0.8662	0.6560
w/o pseudo label	0.6376	0.8891	0.6112	0.7384	0.6207	0.8285	0.7015	0.5012

Methods	LAG	Gallbladder	Esophagus	Stomach	Duodenum	LK
w/ pseudo label	0.6276	0.6547	0.7334	0.7333	0.6012	0.7832
w/o pseudo label	0.5089	0.5529	0.6184	0.6829	0.4356	0.6004

This shows the value of large amounts of unlabeled data. A large amount of unlabeled image data is used to generate pseudo labels, which can get high-quality data after selection, which can make up for the shortage of labels to some extent and improve the prediction ability of the model. For prediction on the validation set, some results and their corresponding labels are shown in Fig. 5. The structure of prediction network is simple and it is difficult to learn deeper features, so the prediction results of some unseen CT images are bad.

4.2 Segmentation Efficiency Results on Validation Set

In this paper, we adopt Generic U-Net, the backbone network of nnU-Net, as the final prediction network. Because the size of some images is too large, nnU-Net or nnFomer consumes too much RAM, which exceeds the required maximum limit. nnU-Net or nnFomer can not be used as the final predictive framework. Compared with nnU-Net or nnFormer, this method can greatly reduce RAM, GPU memory consumption and running time because of the simple predictive

Table 5. The average efficiency results of this method on validation set. The efficiency results include running time, maximum memory consumed by GPU, area under GPU memory-time curve and area under CPU utilization-time curve.

Time	GPU (Max Memory)	AUC (GPU-Time)	AUC (CPU-Time)
111.18 s	2433 MiB	256444.39 $MiB \times s$	2023.45 $MiB \times s$

framework. The efficiency indicators in the validation set are shown in Table 5. Beyond that, we do not optimize the segmentation efficiency.

4.3 Results on Final Testing Set

The DSC index of the results on final testing set is shown in Table 6, and the NSD index of the results on final testing set is shown in Table 7.

Table 6. The DSC index of the results on final testing set. RK, IVC, RAG, LAG and LK represent right kidney, inferior vena cava, right adrenal gland, left adrenal gland and left kidney respectively.

	Liver	RK	Spleen	Pancreas	Aorta	IVC	RAG	LAG
AVG	0.9360	0.7050	0.7471	0.6114	0.8698	0.8314	0.6374	0.5206
STD	0.0636	0.3774	0.3356	0.2760	0.2081	0.1788	0.2840	0.3357

	Gallbladder	Esophagus	Stomach	Duodenum	LK
AVG	0.5574	0.6480	0.5956	0.4902	0.6727
STD	0.4052	0.2592	0.3648	0.2943	0.3953

Table 7. The NSD index of the results on final testing set. RK, IVC, RAG, LAG and LK represent right kidney, inferior vena cava, right adrenal gland, left adrenal gland and left kidney respectively.

	Liver	RK	Spleen	Pancreas	Aorta	IVC	RAG	LAG
AVG	0.8907	0.6958	0.7239	0.6887	0.8779	0.8259	0.7366	0.6043
STD	0.1183	0.3688	0.3447	0.2844	0.2150	0.1841	0.2995	0.3684

	Gallbladder	Esophagus	Stomach	Duodenum	LK
AVG	0.5290	0.7430	0.6039	0.6410	0.6752
STD	0.4085	0.2683	0.3581	0.3088	0.3849

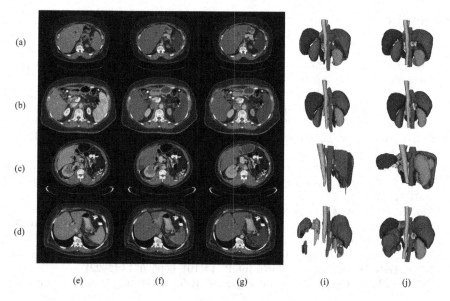

Fig. 5. Some visualized results on the validation set and corresponding labels. Row (a) and row (b) are good predicted results and corresponding labels. Row (c) and row (d) are bad predicted results and corresponding labels. Column (f) are predicted results of axial slices and column (g) are corresponding labels of axial slices. Column (i) are 3D results of predicted results and column (j) are 3D results of corresponding labels.

4.4 Limitation and Future Work

The method proposed in this paper only adopts CNN in the final prediction network, and the limited receptive field leads to the failure to capture global information. In the future, it is hoped to design a lightweight network combining the characteristics of CNN and Transformer for efficient inference of images.

5 Conclusion

In this paper, we combine the advantages of CNN and Transformer to establish a long-term dependency relationship, and produce high-quality pseudo labels to enhance the performance of network segmentation. Moreover, we adopt Generic U-Net, the backbone network of nnU-Net, as the final prediction network. The results show that the combination of the two methods produce a high-quality pseudo label compared to using CNN or Transformer alone, and the method achieves effective semi-supervised segmentation performance in the FLARE2022 Challenge.

References

1. Dosovitskiy, A., et al.: An image is worth 16x16 words: transformers for image recognition at scale (2020). https://doi.org/10.48550/ARXIV.2010.11929. https://arxiv.org/abs/2010.11929
2. Isensee, F., Jaeger, P.F., Kohl, S.A., Petersen, J., Maier-Hein, K.H.: nnU-Net: a self-configuring method for deep learning-based biomedical image segmentation. Nat. Methods 18(2), 203–211 (2021)
3. Ma, J., Wang, B., Bharadwaj, S.: FLARE2022 challenge (2022). https://flare22.grand-challenge.org/
4. Liu, Z., et al.: Swin transformer: hierarchical vision transformer using shifted windows (2021). https://doi.org/10.48550/ARXIV.2103.14030. https://arxiv.org/abs/2103.14030
5. Ma, J., et al.: Fast and low-GPU-memory abdomen CT organ segmentation: the flare challenge. Med. Image Anal. 82, 102616 (2022). https://doi.org/10.1016/j.media.2022.102616
6. Ma, J., et al.: AbdomenCT-1K: is abdominal organ segmentation a solved problem? IEEE Trans. Pattern Anal. Mach. Intell. 44(10), 6695–6714 (2022)
7. Yushkevich, P., Gerig, G., Bharadwaj, S.: ITK-SNAP (2022). http://www.itksnap.org/
8. Ronneberger, O., Fischer, P., Brox, T.: U-net: convolutional networks for biomedical image segmentation. In: International Conference on Medical Image Computing and Computer-Assisted Intervention, pp. 234–241 (2015)
9. Zhou, H.Y., Guo, J., Zhang, Y., Yu, L., Wang, L., Yu, Y.: nnFormer: interleaved transformer for volumetric segmentation (2021). https://doi.org/10.48550/ARXIV.2109.03201. https://arxiv.org/abs/2109.03201

Combining Self-training and Hybrid Architecture for Semi-supervised Abdominal Organ Segmentation

Wentao Liu[1], Weijin Xu[1], Songlin Yan[1], Lemeng Wang[1], Haoyuan Li[1], and Huihua Yang[1,2(✉)]

[1] School of Artificial Intelligence, Beijing University of Posts and Telecommunications, Beijing 100876, China
`yhh@bupt.edu.cn`
[2] School of Computer Science and Information Security, Guilin University of Electronic Technology, Guilin 541004, China

Abstract. Abdominal organ segmentation has many important clinical applications, such as organ quantification, surgical planning, and disease diagnosis. However, manually annotating organs from CT scans is time-consuming and labor-intensive. Semi-supervised learning has shown the potential to alleviate this challenge by learning from a large set of unlabeled images and limited labeled samples. In this work, we follow the self-training strategy and employ a high-performance hybrid architecture (PHTrans) consisting of CNN and Swin Transformer for the teacher model to generate precise pseudo labels for unlabeled data. Afterward, we introduce them with labeled data together into a two-stage segmentation framework with lightweight PHTrans for training to improve the performance and generalization ability of the model while remaining efficient. Experiments on the validation set of FLARE2022 demonstrate that our method achieves excellent segmentation performance as well as fast and low-resource model inference. The average DSC and NSD are 0.8956 and 0.9316, respectively. Under our development environments, the average inference time is 18.62 s, the average maximum GPU memory is 1995.04 MB, and the area under the GPU memory-time curve and the average area under the CPU utilization-time curve are 23196.84 and 319.67. The code is available at https://github.com/lseventeen/FLARE22-TwoStagePHTrans.

Keywords: Abdominal organ segmentation · Semi-supervised learning · Hybrid architecture

1 Introduction

Medical image segmentation aims to extract and quantify regions of interest in biological tissue or organ images. Among them, abdominal organ segmentation has many important clinical applications, such as organ quantification, surgical planning, and disease diagnosis. However, manually annotating organs from CT

J. Ma and B. Wang (Eds.): FLARE 2022, LNCS 13816, pp. 281–292, 2022.
https://doi.org/10.1007/978-3-031-23911-3_25

scans is time-consuming and labor-intensive. Thus, we usually cannot obtain a huge number of labeled cases. As a potential alternative, semi-supervised semantic segmentation has been proposed to learn a model from a handful of labeled images along with abundant unlabeled images to explore useful information from unlabeled cases. The organizer of FLARE2022 curated a large-scale and diverse abdomen CT dataset, including 2300 CT scans from 20+ medical groups. There are 50 labeled data and 2000 unlabeled data available. Compared with FLARE 2021, the challenge for FLARE 2022 is how to leverage the large amount of unlabeled data to improve the segmentation performance while taking into account efficient inference.

Self-training [8] via pseudo labeling is a conventional, simple, and popular pipeline to leverage unlabeled data, where the retrained student is supervised with hard labels produced by the teacher trained on labeled data, which is commonly regarded as a form of entropy minimization in semi-supervised learning [17]. The performance of the model of teacher and student in it is crucial. Benefiting from the excellent representation learning ability of deep learning, convolutional neural networks [1,13] (CNNs) have achieved tremendous success in medical image analysis. In spite of achieving extremely competitive results, CNN-based methods lack the ability to model long-range dependencies due to inherent inductive biases such as locality and translational equivariance. Transformer [3,10,16], relying purely on attention mechanisms to model global dependencies without any convolution operations, has emerged as an alternative architecture that has delivered better performance than CNNs in computer vision on the condition of being pre-trained on large-scale datasets. Therefore, many hybrid architectures derived from the combination of CNN and Transformer have emerged, which offer the advantages of both and have gradually become a compromise solution for medical image segmentation without being pre-trained on large datasets.

In previous work [9], we proposed a parallel hybrid architecture (PHTrans) for medical image segmentation where the main building blocks consist of CNN and Swin Transformer to simultaneously aggregate global and local representations. PHTrans can independently construct hierarchical local and global representations and fuse them in each stage, fully exploiting the potential of CNN and the Transformer. Extensive experiments on BCV [7] demonstrated the superiority of PHTrans against other competing methods on abdominal multi-organ segmentation. In this work, we propose a solution combining the hybrid architecture PHTrans with self-training for the FLARE2022 challenge. Firstly, we employ a high-performance PHTrans with the nnU-Net frame as the teacher model to generate precise pseudo-labels for unlabeled data. Secondly, the labeled data and pseudo-labeled data are fed together into a two-stage segmentation framework with lightweight PHTrans for training, which locates the regions of interest (ROIs) first and then finely segments them. Experiments on the validation set of FLARE2022 demonstrate that our method achieves excellent segmentation performance as well as fast and low-resource model inference.

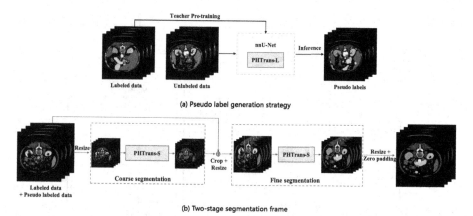

Fig. 1. Overview of our proposed semi-supervised abdominal organ segmentation method based on self-training and PHTrans.

2   Method

We propose a semi-supervised abdominal organ segmentation method based on self-training [19] and PHTrans [9], as shown in Fig. 1, which is a three-stage two-network (teacher and student) pipeline, i.e., (1) train a teacher model using labeled data, (2) generate pseudo labels for unlabeled data and (3) train a separate student model using labeled data and pseudo-labeled data. We employ one high-performance PHTrans and two lightweight PHTrans as teacher and student models, respectively. (1) and (2) are performed in the nn-UNet [6] framework with the default configuration except that UNet is replaced by PHTrans. Some of the cases in the validation set include other tissues or organs in addition to the abdomen, such as the neck, buttocks, and legs. For instance, the last case in the validation set has 1338 slices, but only about 250 of those slices belong to the abdomen. Motivated by the solutions of Flare2021's champion and third winner [15,18], we adopt a two-stage segmentation framework and whole-volume-based input strategy in the student to improve the computational efficiency. We introduce the labeled data and the pseudo-labeled data together into the two-stage segmentation framework for training. The coarse segmentation model aims to obtain the rough location of the target organ from the whole CT volume. The fine segmentation model achieves precise segmentation of abdominal organs based on cropped ROIs from the coarse segmentation result. Finally, the segmentation result is restored to the size of the original data by resampling and zero padding. The method is described in detail in the following subsections.

2.1   Preprocessing

The preprocessing strategy for labeled data and pseudo-labeled data in the two-stage segmentation framework is as follows:

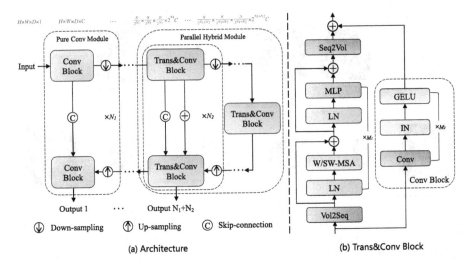

Fig. 2. (a) The architecture of PHTrans; (b) Parallel hybird block consisting of Transformer and convolution (Trans&Conv block).

- Image reorientation to the target direction
- Resampling images to uniform sizes. We use small-scale images as the input of the two-stage segmentation to improve the segmentation efficiency. Coarse input: [64, 64, 64]; Fine input: [96, 192, 192].
- We applied a z-score normalization based on the mean and standard deviation of the intensity values in the input volume.
- Considering that the purpose of coarse segmentation is to roughly extract the locations of abdominal organs, we set the voxels whose intensity values are greater than 1 in the resampled ground truth to 1, which converts the multi-classification abdominal organ segmentation into a simple two-classification integrated abdominal organ segmentation.

2.2 Proposed Method

An overview of the PHTrans [9] is illustrated in Fig. 2(a). PHTrans follows the U-shaped encoder and decoder design, which is mainly composed of pure convolution modules and parallel hybrid ones. Given an input volume $x \in \mathbb{R}^{H \times W \times D}$, where H, W and D denote the height, width, and depth, respectively, we first utilize several pure convolution modules to obtain feature maps $f \in \mathbb{R}^{\frac{H}{2^{N_1}} \times \frac{W}{2^{N_1}} \times \frac{D}{2^{N_1}} \times 2^{N_1}C}$, where N_1 and C denote the number of modules and base channels, respectively. Afterwards, parallel hybrid modules consisting of Transformer and CNN were applied to model the hierarchical representation from the local and global feature. The procedure is repeated N_2 times with $\frac{H}{2^{N_1+N_2}} \times \frac{W}{2^{N_1+N_2}} \times \frac{D}{2^{N_1+N_2}}$ as the output resolutions and $2^{N_1+N_2}C$ as the channel number. Corresponding to the encoder, the symmetric decoder is similarly built based on pure convolution modules and parallel hybrid modules, and fuses

semantic information from the encoder by skip-connection and addition operations. Furthermore, we use deep supervision at each stage of the decoder during
the training, resulting in a total of $N_1 + N_2$ outputs, where joint loss consisting of
cross entropy and dice loss is applied. The architecture of PHTrans is straightforward and changeable, where the number of each module can be adjusted according to medical image segmentation tasks, i.e., N_1, N_2, M_1 and M_2. Among them,
M_1 and M_2 are the numbers of Swin Transformer blocks and convolution blocks
in the parallel hybrid module.

The parallel hybrid modules are deployed in the deep stages of PHTrans,
where the Trans&Conv block, as its heart, achieves hierarchical aggregation
of local and global representations by CNN and Swin Transformer. The scale-
reduced feature maps are fed into Swin Transformer (ST) blocks and convolution (Conv) blocks, respectively. We introduce Volume-to-Sequence (V2S) and
Sequence-to-Volume (S2V) operations at the beginning and end of ST blocks,
respectively, to implement the transform of volume and sequence, making it
concordant with the dimensional space of the output that Conv blocks produce.
Specifically, V2S is used to reshape the entire volume (3D image) into a sequence
of 3D patches with a window size. S2V is the opposite operation. As shown in
Fig. 2(b), an ST block consists of a shifted window based multi-head self attention (MSA) module, followed by a 2-layer MLP with a GELU activation function
in between. A LayerNorm (LN) layer is applied before each MSA module and
each MLP, and a residual connection is applied after each module [10]. In M_1
successive ST blocks, the MSA with regular and shifted window configurations,
i.e., W-MSA and SW-MSA, is alternately embedded into ST blocks to achieve
cross-window connections while maintaining the efficient computation of non-
overlapping windows.

For medical image segmentation, we modified the standard ST block into
a 3D version, which computes self-attention within local 3D windows that are
arranged to evenly partition the volume in a non-overlapping manner. Supposing
$x \in \mathbb{R}^{H \times W \times S \times C}$ is the input of ST block, it would be first reshaped to $N \times L \times C$,
where N and $L = W_h \times W_w \times W_s$ denote the number and dimensionality of
3D windows, respectively. The convolution blocks are repeated M_2 times with a
$3 \times 3 \times 3$ convolutional layer, a GELU nonlinearity, and an instance normalization
layer (IN) as a unit. Finally, we fuse the outputs of the ST blocks and Conv blocks
by an addition operation. The computational procedure of the Trans&Conv block
in the encoder can be summarized as follows:

$$y_i = S2V(ST^{M_1}(V2S(x_{i-1}))) + Conv^{M_2}(x_{i-1}), \qquad (1)$$

where x_{i-1} is the down-sampling results of the encoder's $i - 1^{th}$ stage. In the
decoder, besides skip-connection, we supplement the context information from
the encoder with an addition operation. Therefore, the Trans&Conv block in the
decoder can be formulated as:

$$z_i = S2V(ST^{M_1}(V2S(x_{i+1} + y_i)) + Conv^{M_2}([x_{i+1}, y_i]), \qquad (2)$$

where x_{i+1} is the up-sampling results of the decoder's $i + 1^{th}$ stage and y_i is
output of the encoder's i^{th} stage. The down-sampling contains a strided convo-

lution operation and an instance normalization layer, where the channel number is halved and the spatial size is doubled. Similarly, the up-sampling is a strided deconvolution layer followed by an instance normalization layer, which doubles the number of feature map channels and halved the spatial size.

2.3 Post-processing

Connected component-based post-processing is commonly used in medical image segmentation. Especially in organ image segmentation, it often helps to eliminate the detection of spurious false positives by removing all but the largest connected component. We applied it to the output of the coarse and fine models.

3   Experiments

3.1 Dataset and Evaluation Measures

The FLARE 2022 is an extension of the FLARE 2021 [11] with more segmentation targets and more diverse abdomen CT scans. The FLARE2022 dataset is curated from more than 20 medical groups under the license permission, including MSD [14], KiTS [4,5], AbdomenCT-1K [12], and TCIA [2]. The training set includes 50 labeled CT scans with pancreas disease and 2000 unlabeled CT scans with liver, kidney, spleen, or pancreas diseases. The validation set includes 50 CT scans with liver, kidney, spleen, or pancreas diseases. The testing set includes 200 CT scans where 100 cases has liver, kidney, spleen, or pancreas diseases and the other 100 cases has uterine corpus endometrial, urothelial bladder, stomach, sarcomas, or ovarian diseases. All the CT scans only have image information and the center information is not available.

The evaluation measures consist of two accuracy measures: Dice Similarity Coefficient (DSC) and Normalized Surface Dice (NSD), and three running efficiency measures: running time, area under GPU memory-time curve, and area under CPU utilization-time curve. All measures will be used to compute the ranking. Moreover, the GPU memory consumption has a 2 GB tolerance.

3.2 Implementation Details

We employ two different configurations of PHTrans for pseudo-label generation and two-stage segmentation, respectively. In order to achieve high-precision pseudo-label generation, PHTrans-L adopted a high-performance configuration with large model parameters and computational complexity. In PHTrans-L, we empirically set the hyper-parameters $[N_1, N_2, M_1, M_2]$ to $[2, 2, 2, 2]$ and adopted the stride strategy of nnU-Net [6] for down-sampling and up-sampling. Moreover, the base number of channels C is 36, and the numbers of heads of multi-head self-attention used in different encoder stages are $[3, 6, 12, 24]$. We set the size of 3D windows $[W_h, W_w, W_s]$ to $[4, 5, 5]$ in ST blocks. However, PHTrans-S is configured as a lightweight architecture to meet efficient model inference, where the

Table 1. The parameter setting of PHTrans-L and PHTrans-S.

Model	PHTrans-L	PHTrans-S
Hyper-parameters $[N_1, N_2, M_1, M_2]$	[2, 4, 2, 2]	[2, 3, 2, 2]
Base channel number	36	16
Down-sampling number	5	4
Heads number of self-attention	[3, 4, 12, 24]	[4, 4, 4]
3D windows size	[4, 5, 5]	[4, 4, 4]/[3, 4, 4]
MLP-ratio	4	1

Table 2. Development environments and requirements.

Windows/Ubuntu version	Ubuntu 20.04.3 LTS
CPU	Intel(R) Xeon(R) Silver 4214R CPU @ 2.40 GHz
RAM	32 × 4 GB; 2933 MT/s
GPU (number and type)	One NVIDIA 3090 24G
CUDA version	11.6
Programming language	Python 3.8.13
Deep learning framework	Pytorch (Torch 1.11, torchvision 0.12.0)
Specific dependencies	nn-UNet

Table 3. The training protocols of two-stage segmentation model.

Model	Coarse model/Fine model
Network initialization	"he" normal initialization
Batch size	64/4
Patch size	64 × 64 × 64/96 × 192 × 192
Total epochs	300
Optimizer	AdamW
Initial learning rate (lr)	0.01
Lr decay schedule	Cosine Annealing LR
Loss function	Cross entropy + Dice
Training time (hours)	0.5/19.75
Number of model parameters	6.66 M[a]
Number of flops	18.60/251.19 G[b]
CO_2eq	0.0856/1.7688 kg kg[c]

[a] https://github.com/sksq96/pytorch-summary
[b] https://github.com/facebookresearch/fvcore
[c] https://github.com/lfwa/carbontracker/

base number of channels is 16 and the number of up-sampling and down-sampling is 4. Other model hyperparameter settings are detailed in Table 1. The development environments and requirements are presented in Table 2. The training protocols for coarse and fine segmentation are presented in Table 3. In the training phase, we train on all 50 labeled data and random 450 pseudo-labeled data at each epoch. To alleviate the over-fitting of limited training data, we employed online data argumentation, including random rotation, scaling, adding white Gaussian noise, Gaussian blurring, adjusting rightness and contrast, simulation of low resolution, Gamma transformation, and elastic deformation.

4   Results and Discussion

4.1   Quantitative Results on Validation Set

Using the default nnU-Net as the baseline, we employ PHTrans instead of U-Net for comparative experiments. Table 4 shows that the average DSC on the validation set of "nnU-Net+PHTrans" is 0.8756, which is 0.0237 higher than that of nnU-Net, fully demonstrating PHTrans's excellent medical image segmentation ability. Although "nnU-Net+PHTrans" has achieved impressive segmentation results without using unlabeled data, nnU-Net is not conducive to the "Fast and Low-resource" of the FLARE challenge due to low-spacing resampling and sliding window inference. However, the segmentation results of "Two-stage+PHTrans" (TP) were less than satisfactory, with an average DSC of only 0.6889. We consider the reason is that the whole-volume based input strategy greatly reduces the resolution of the image and thus the segmentation accuracy is lost. In addition, the resampling volume of fixed size has a large difference in spacing, and it is difficult for the model to learn general representations in the limited labeled data, resulting in poor generalization ability. In contrast, we introduce pseudo-labeled data generated by the "nnU-Net+PHTrans" teacher model to further improve the segmentation performance and generalization ability. The results of "Two-stage+PHTrans+PD" (TPP) demonstrate that the original segmentation framework produces significant performance gains after training on 2000 pseudo-labeled data (PD). In spite of the fact that there is wrong label information in the pseudo labels, the average DSC improved from 0.6889 to 0.8956. Furthermore, Table 5 shows that the TPP achieved an average NSD of 0.9316 on the validation set.

Table 4. Ablation study on validation set. (PD: pseudo-labeled data participated in the training.)

Methods	Mean DSC	Liver	RK	Spleen	Pancreas	Aorta	IVC
nnU-Net	0.8519	0.9693	0.8662	0.9107	0.8433	0.9604	0.8813
nnU-Net+PHTrans	0.8756	0.9693	0.8997	0.9488	0.8601	0.9583	0.9161
Two-stage+PHTrans	0.6889	0.8930	0.7840	0.8307	0.5886	0.8828	0.8111
Two-stage+PHTrans+PD	**0.8956**	**0.9761**	**0.9368**	**0.961**	**0.8728**	**0.9613**	**0.9165**

Methods	RAG	LAG	Gallbladder	Esophagus	Stomach	Duodenum	LK
nnU-Net	0.8268	0.7806	0.7022	0.8558	0.8743	0.7384	0.8653
nnU-Net+PHTrans	**0.8496**	0.8178	0.7313	**0.8777**	0.9073	0.7822	0.8649
Two-stage+PHTrans	0.5774	0.4229	0.5535	0.6651	0.6782	0.5053	0.7632
Two-stage+PHTrans+PD	0.8132	**0.835**	**0.8346**	0.8737	**0.9194**	**0.8045**	**0.9377**

Table 5. Quantitative results of NSD on validation set. (PD: pseudo-labeled data participated in the training.)

Methods	Mean NSD	Liver	RK	Spleen	Pancreas	Aorta	IVC
Two-stage+PHTrans+PD	0.9316	0.9761	0.9198	0.9572	0.9422	0.9863	0.9138
Methods	RAG	LAG	Gallbladder	Esophagus	Stomach	Duodenum	LK
Two-stage+PHTrans+PD	0.9273	0.9125	0.8659	0.9258	0.9485	0.9158	0.9192

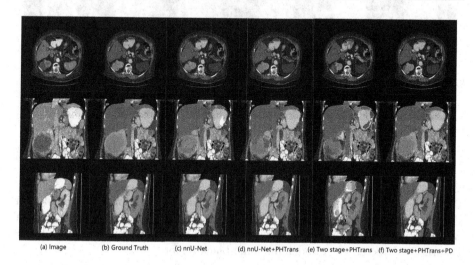

(a) Image   (b) Ground Truth   (c) nnU-Net   (d) nnU-Net+PHTrans   (e) Two stage+PHTrans   (f) Two stage+PHTrans+PD

Fig. 3. Visualization of segmentation results of abdominal organs.

4.2   Qualitative Results on Validation Set

We visualize the segmentation results of the validation set. The representative samples in Fig. 3 demonstrate the success of identifying organ details by TPP, which is the closest to the ground truth compared to other methods due to retaining most of the spatial information of abdominal organs. In particular, it outperforms TP significantly by leveraging unlabeled data, which enhances the robustness of the segmentation model. Furthermore, we show representative examples of poor segmentation, as shown in Fig. 4. The first row demonstrates that TP and TPP only detect part of the spleen (blue region), which can be inferred from the flat edge on the right that the first-stage coarse segmentation did not accurately locate the entire abdominal organ. The second row shows a case with a large tumor inside the liver (red region), where the pathological changes pose an extreme challenge for the abdominal organ segmentation. In this case, nnU-Net shows poor segmentation performance. PHTrans improves this result with the global modeling capabilities of the Transformer. In contrast, benefiting from the strategy of whole-volume based input, TP segments a relatively complete liver. However, the performance of TPP to segment livers with pathological changes degrades when training with more pseudo-labeled data. We consider that pseudo labels generated by training on labeled data without liver

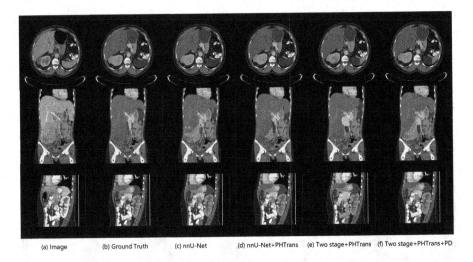

Fig. 4. Challenging examples from validation set. (Color figure online)

disease tend to produce a large amount of erroneous label information in liver disease cases, resulting in a degraded performance of TPP for segmenting liver disease cases. The third row shows another case where none of the methods accurately detected the duodenum (blue-black region).

4.3 Segmentation Efficiency Results on Validation Set

In the official segmentation efficiency evaluation under development environments shown in Table 2, the average inference time of 50 cases in the validation set is 18.62 s, the average maximum GPU memory is 1995.04 MB, and the area under the GPU memory-time curve and the average area under the CPU utilization-time curve are 23196.84 and 319.67, respectively.

4.4 Results on Final Testing Set

We submitted the docker of our solution, which was evaluated by the challenge official on the test set, and the results are shown in Tables 6 and 7.

Table 6. The DSC of the test set from the official evaluation.

Mean	Liver	RK	Spleen	Pancreas	Aorta	IVC
0.8941	0.9786	0.9567	0.9377	0.828	0.9607	0.9269
RAG	LAG	Gallbladder	Esophagus	Stomach	Duodenum	LK
0.8749	0.861	0.8444	0.8075	0.9281	0.7835	0.9358

Table 7. The NSD of the test set from the official evaluation.

Mean	Liver	RK	Spleen	Pancreas	Aorta	IVC
0.9395	0.9844	0.9615	0.9416	0.9316	0.9834	0.9395
RAG	LAG	Gallbladder	Esophagus	Stomach	Duodenum	LK
0.9668	0.9516	0.8556	0.8954	0.954	0.9078	0.9409

4.5 Limitation and Future Work

We used a simple but effective self-training strategy for pseudo-label generation. Theoretically, the accuracy of pseudo labels can be further improved by multiple iterative optimization of the teacher and the student [12] or by performing selective re-training via prioritizing reliable unlabeled datas [17]. In addition, we did not use model deployment in inference. In future work, we plan to use ONNX and TensorRT to further accelerate inference and reduce GPU memory.

5 Conclusion

In this work, we follow the self-training strategy and employ a high-performance PHTrans with the nnU-Net frame for the teacher model to generate precise pseudo-labels. After that, we introduce them with labeled data into a two-stage segmentation framework with lightweight PHTrans for training to improve the performance and generalization ability of the model while remaining efficient. Experiments on the validation set of FLARE2022 demonstrate that our method achieves excellent segmentation performance and computational efficiency. In the future, we will optimize the self-training strategy and apply model deployment to further improve the segmentation performance and fast and low-resource inference.

Acknowledgements. The authors of this paper declare that the segmentation method they implemented for participation in the FLARE 2022 challenge has not used any pre-trained models nor additional datasets other than those provided by the organizers. The proposed solution is fully automatic without any manual intervention.

References

1. Çiçek, Ö., Abdulkadir, A., Lienkamp, S.S., Brox, T., Ronneberger, O.: 3D U-Net: learning dense volumetric segmentation from sparse annotation. In: Ourselin, S., Joskowicz, L., Sabuncu, M.R., Unal, G., Wells, W. (eds.) MICCAI 2016, Part II. LNCS, vol. 9901, pp. 424–432. Springer, Cham (2016). https://doi.org/10.1007/978-3-319-46723-8_49
2. Clark, K., et al.: The cancer imaging archive (TCIA): maintaining and operating a public information repository. J. Digit. Imaging **26**(6), 1045–1057 (2013)

3. Dosovitskiy, A., et al.: An image is worth 16x16 words: transformers for image recognition at scale. In: 9th International Conference on Learning Representations, ICLR 2021, Virtual Event, Austria, 3–7 May 2021. OpenReview.net (2021). https://openreview.net/forum?id=YicbFdNTTy

4. Heller, N., et al.: The state of the art in kidney and kidney tumor segmentation in contrast-enhanced CT imaging: results of the KiTS19 challenge. Med. Image Anal. **67**, 101821 (2021)

5. Heller, N., et al.: An international challenge to use artificial intelligence to define the state-of-the-art in kidney and kidney tumor segmentation in CT imaging. Proc. Am. Soc. Clin. Oncol. **38**(6), 626–626 (2020)

6. Isensee, F., Jaeger, P.F., Kohl, S.A., Petersen, J., Maier-Hein, K.H.: nnU-Net: a self-configuring method for deep learning-based biomedical image segmentation. Nat. Methods **18**(2), 203–211 (2021)

7. Landman, B., Xu, Z., Igelsias, J., Styner, M., Langerak, T., Klein, A.: MICCAI multi-atlas labeling beyond the cranial vault–workshop and challenge. In: Proceedings of MICCAI Multi-Atlas Labeling Beyond Cranial Vault–Workshop Challenge, vol. 5, p. 12 (2015). https://www.synapse.org/#!Synapse:syn3193805/wiki/217789

8. Lee, D.H., et al.: Pseudo-label: the simple and efficient semi-supervised learning method for deep neural networks. In: Workshop on Challenges in Representation Learning, ICML, vol. 3, p. 896 (2013)

9. Liu, W., et al.: PHTrans: parallelly aggregating global and local representations for medical image segmentation. In: Wang, L., Dou, Q., Fletcher, P.T., Speidel, S., Li, S. (eds.) MICCAI 2022. LNCS, pp. 235–244. Springer, Cham (2022). https://doi.org/10.1007/978-3-031-16443-9_23

10. Liu, Z., et al.: Swin transformer: hierarchical vision transformer using shifted windows. In: Proceedings of the IEEE/CVF International Conference on Computer Vision, pp. 10012–10022 (2021)

11. Ma, J., et al.: Fast and low-GPU-memory abdomen CT organ segmentation: the flare challenge. Med. Image Anal. **82**, 102616 (2022). https://doi.org/10.1016/j.media.2022.102616

12. Ma, J., et al.: AbdomenCT-1K: is abdominal organ segmentation a solved problem? IEEE Trans. Pattern Anal. Mach. Intell. **44**(10), 6695–6714 (2022)

13. Ronneberger, O., Fischer, P., Brox, T.: U-Net: convolutional networks for biomedical image segmentation. In: Navab, N., Hornegger, J., Wells, W.M., Frangi, A.F. (eds.) MICCAI 2015, Part III. LNCS, vol. 9351, pp. 234–241. Springer, Cham (2015). https://doi.org/10.1007/978-3-319-24574-4_28

14. Simpson, A.L., et al.: A large annotated medical image dataset for the development and evaluation of segmentation algorithms. arXiv preprint arXiv:1902.09063 (2019)

15. Thaler, F., Payer, C., Bischof, H., Stern, D.: Efficient multi-organ segmentation using spatialconfiguration-net with low GPU memory requirements. arXiv preprint arXiv:2111.13630 (2021)

16. Vaswani, A., et al.: Attention is all you need. In: Advances in Neural Information Processing Systems, vol. 30 (2017)

17. Yang, L., Zhuo, W., Qi, L., Shi, Y., Gao, Y.: ST++: make self-training work better for semi-supervised semantic segmentation. In: Proceedings of the IEEE/CVF Conference on Computer Vision and Pattern Recognition, pp. 4268–4277 (2022)

18. Zhang, F., Wang, Y., Yang, H.: Efficient context-aware network for abdominal multi-organ segmentation. arXiv preprint arXiv:2109.10601 (2021)

19. Zhu, Y., et al.: Improving semantic segmentation via efficient self-training. IEEE Trans. Pattern Anal. Mach. Intell. (2021). https://doi.org/10.1109/TPAMI.2021.3138337

Semi-supervised Multi-organ Segmentation with Cross Supervision Using Siamese Network

Dengqiang Jia(✉)

School of Naval Architecture, Ocean and Civil Engineering,
Shanghai Jiao Tong University, Shanghai, China
wangxifeng004@163.com

Abstract. Numerous unlabeled data is useful for supervised medical image segmentation, if the labeled data is limited. To leverage all the unlabeled images for efficient abdominal organ segmentation, we developed semi-supervised framework with cross supervision using siamese network, i.e., SemiSeg-CSSN. Cross supervision enables the two networks to optimize the network using pseudo-labels generated by the other. Moreover, we applied the cascade strategy for the task because of the large and uncertain locations of the abdomen regions. To validate the effects of unlabeled data, we employed an unlabeled image filtering strategy to select the unlabeled image and their pseudo label images with low uncertainty. On the FLARE2022 validation cases, with the help of unlabeled data, our method obtained the average dice similarity coefficient (DSC) of 77.7% and average normalized surface distance (NSD) of 82.0%, which is better than the supervised method. The average running time is 12.9 s per case in inference phase and maximum used GPU memory is 2052 MB.

Keywords: Semi-supervised · Cross supervision · Label filtering

1 Introduction

For supervised learning, few labeled data tend to leading the over-fitting problem. In the task of medical image analysis, however, manual voxel-level labeling is expensive and time-consuming because of the professional domain knowledge.

Semi-supervised learning (SSL) aims to solve the learning problem in scenario of sparsely labeled images and a large number of auxiliary unlabeled images. These learning methods have been studied in classification problems [8,15].

Currently, semi-supervised segmentation has raised attention. Self-training strategy tries to learn from unlabeled data by imputing the labels for samples predicted with high confidence [1,2,14].

There are many datasets of natural images datasets available for semi-supervised segmentation, such as Pascal VOC 2012 [7] and Cityscapes [6]. For medical image segmentation, FLARE2022 challenge has a large-scale abdominal datasets that contains 50 labeled images and 2000 unlabeled images. Besides, the challenge has at most 13 organs are annotated, which belongs to the standard closed-set SSL [4]. The difficulty of this challenge is to segment both large and small organs given a scenario with less labeled data.

The multi-organ segmentation have three main difficulties.

- Class imbalance problem.As shown in Fig. 1, RAG and LAG have small class ratios, which leads to the class imbalance problem.
- Large shape variations and pathology influence. Some organs, e.g., Gallbladder (brown), Pancreas (yellow) and Duodenum (blue) shown in Fig. 2, have large variation on shapes, and some organs are diseased, such as liver and kidney tumors (see Fig. 3).
- Non-uniform images. Some images have incomplete abdominal regions, and the image information are not normalized.

In this paper, we proposed a siamese network with cross supervision to train the semi-supervised segmentation network. Two networks, which have the same architecture and the same number of parameters, are introduced, and they are

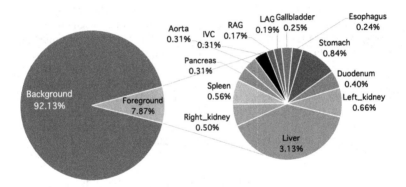

Fig. 1. Class ratio in the 50 labeled images in FLARE2022.

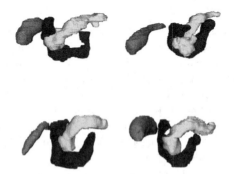

Fig. 2. Four selected examples in FLARE2022. Large shape variations of Gallbladder (brown), Pancreas (yellow) and Duodenum (blue). (Color figure online)

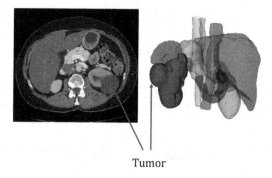

Tumor

Fig. 3. A selected examples in FLARE2022. The left kidney has a tumor.

initialized differently at the beginning of training. These two segmentation networks can generate pseudo label images, and supervise each other's training in the manner of cross supervision. Moreover, we employed a filtering strategy for unlabeled images. These selected unlabeled images have pseudo label images with low uncertainty, which can ensure the stability of training.

The main contributions of our work are summarized as follows:

- To leverage the unlabeled data, we use cross supervision strategy, which is achieved via a siamese network.
- To improve the efficiency, we use anisotropic convolution block and strip pooling module.
- We also employ a filtering strategy to improve the performance.
- The effectiveness and efficiency of the proposed semi-supervised framework are demonstrated on FLARE2022 challenge dataset, where we achieve the top 10 with low time cost and less memory usage.

2 Method

Figures 4 and 5 show our approach using cross supervision with labelled and unlabelled data, respectively.

2.1 Preprocessing

The labeled images are cropped using their corresponding labels, which avoid selecting the patch without any labels. For the unlabeled images, we use the trained coarse segmentation model to crop the abdominal regions. All the images are re-sampled for a fixed spacing, i.e., $1\,\mathrm{mm} \times 1\,\mathrm{mm} \times 3\,\mathrm{mm}$.

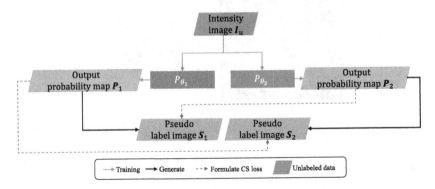

Fig. 4. Cross supervision framework when using unlabeled data. The siamese network contains two sub-networks, denoted as P_{θ_1} and P_{θ_2}, whose architectures are the same, and the two sub-networks are initialized differently at the beginning of training. When using unlabeled images, two segmentation probability maps P_1 and P_2 for the given intensity image I_u. The two probability maps can be transformed to two different pseudo label images S_1 and S_1 for the input image. Thus, these two segmentation sub-networks can generate pseudo label images, and supervise each other's training in the manner of cross supervision.

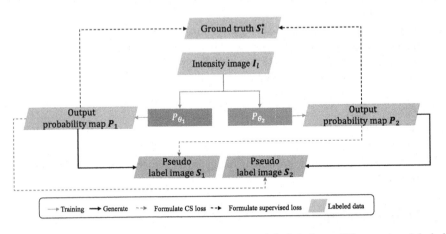

Fig. 5. Cross supervision framework when using labeled data. When using labeled images, two loss functions are constructed, i.e., the cross supervision loss and supervision loss. The two subnetworks can also generate the pseudo label images for intensity image I_l. The two subnetworks can be supervised based on these pseudo label images in the cross-supervision manner. Besides, the label images can be considered as ground truth of segmentations, therefore, the output probability maps can be also supervised with the ground truth of the segmentation.

2.2 Proposed Method

We propose a semi-supervised segmentation framework for multi-organ segmentation task, which can leverage large number of unlabeled data. The framework consists of two sub-networks, which have the same structures. We separately optimize the sub-networks, and simultaneously use them to predict the pseudo labels of unlabeled data. We train the two networks in a cross-supervised manner [3].

Besides, we employed a cascade strategy, which aims to segmenting the abdomen organs via coarse-to-fine procedure [18]. Because the region of interest, i.e., ROI, of abdominal organs is large, we can not efficiently segment all the organs in a single-stage network. Therefore, we first segmented the organs from downsampling images, which can be seen as a coarse segmentation. With the help of the coarse segmentation, we segmented the organs from the original images in the second stage.

We can also train a semi-supervised network via selected unlabeled images, which is based on the uncertainty metric of their pseudo label images.

2.3 Cross Supervision Using Siamese Network (CSSN)

Let $\mathcal{L} = \{(I_1, S_1^*), (I_2, S_2^*), ..., (I_N, S_N^*)\}$ and $\mathcal{U} = \{I_{N+1}, I_{N+2}, ..., I_M\}$ denote the labeled data and unlabeled data. I and S^* denote the intensity image and label image. The aim of the semi-supervised segmentation is to obtain a segmentation plan that can leverage $\mathcal{L}$ and $\mathcal{U}$. We can use the segmentation plan to predict a probability map P for I as:

$$P = P_\theta(I). \tag{1}$$

In particular, we introduce two sub-networks, i.e., P_{θ_1} and P_{θ_2}, to obtain two probability maps for a fixed image I:

$$\begin{aligned} P_1 &= P_{\theta_1}(I), \\ P_2 &= P_{\theta_2}(I). \end{aligned} \tag{2}$$

The siamese networks (P_{θ_1} and P_{θ_1}) have the same structures and the same number of parameters but are initialized differently at the beginning of training. As in Eq. 2, we can obtain two different predictions for one input image because of the two sub-networks with different parameters. Since we use label information for supervision, we can use any supervised loss functions, e.g., cross-entropy loss, dice loss and combination of them, which we denote as ℓs in this work.

As shown in Fig. 4, for unlabeled data $\mathcal{L}$, we employ a bidirectional consistent strategy for supervision. For example, sub-network P_{θ_1} can be supervised by the pseudo label images generated by the frozen subnetwork P_{θ_2}. For voxel i of an unlabeled image, we can calculate the loss as:

$$\ell_s\left(p_{i|\theta_1}, s_{i|\theta_2}\right), \tag{3}$$

where $p_{i|\theta_1}$ denotes the predicted probability for voxel i using sub-network P_{θ_1}, and $s_{i|\theta_2}$ is the label for voxel i generated by P_{θ_2}. The sub-network P_{θ_2} can be supervised in the similar manner.

Thus, the cross-supervised (CS) loss function for $\boldsymbol{I}_u \in \mathcal{U}$ can be formulated as follows:

$$\mathcal{C}_u^u = \frac{1}{V_u} \sum_{i \in I_u} \left(\ell_s \left(p_{i|\theta_1}, s_{i|\theta_2} \right) + \ell_s \left(p_{i|\theta_2}, s_{i|\theta_1} \right) \right), \tag{4}$$

where V_u is the number of voxels in $\boldsymbol{I}_u$.

As shown in Fig. 5, for labeled data $\boldsymbol{I}_l \in \mathcal{L}$, we first employ supervised loss functions for the two sub-networks:

$$\mathcal{C}_s = \frac{1}{V_l} \sum_{i \in I_l} \left(\ell_s \left(p_{i|\theta_1}, s_i^* \right) + \ell_s \left(p_{i|\theta_2}, s_i^* \right) \right), \tag{5}$$

where s_i^* is the voxel i in the label image $\boldsymbol{S}^*$. The number of voxels in $\boldsymbol{I}_l$ is denoted as V_l.

As shown in Fig. 5, using the pseudo label images, we can also formulate the CS loss for labeled data in the same manner as Eq. (4), i.e., $\mathcal{C}_u^l$.

The training loss function can be formulated as:

$$\mathcal{C} = \mathcal{C}_s + \mathcal{C}_u^u + \mathcal{C}_u^l. \tag{6}$$

2.4   Unlabeled Image Filtering (UIF) Based on Uncertainty

Unlabeled images may contain cases with different distributions than labeled images. Although we used pseudo-label images inject strong data augmentations, some pseudo-label images with high uncertainty were still prone to accumulate and degrade the performance. To solve this problem, we prioritized reliable unlabeled images based on holistic prediction-level stability.

To obtain reliable unlabeled images, we employed UIF on the pseudo-labeled images, as the selection approach of Yang et al. [17]. We selected 200 (top 10%) unlabeled images and their pseudo-labeled images with the lowest uncertainty from the 2000 unlabeled images. For an unlabeled image $\boldsymbol{I}_l$, we can compute the uncertainty as:

$$U_l = 1 - \frac{1}{9} \sum_{j=1}^{9} \mathrm{DSC}(\boldsymbol{S}_{l|\mathcal{M}_{j*100}}, \boldsymbol{S}_{l|\mathcal{M}_{1000}}), \tag{7}$$

where $\boldsymbol{S}_{l|\mathcal{M}_{j*100}}$ denotes the pseudo label image of $\boldsymbol{I}_l$ generated by trained model $\mathcal{M}_{j*100}$. The trained model $\mathcal{M}_{j*100}$ is saved to the disk in epoch $j*100$ during training the supervised segmentation network.

After we have selected 200 unlabeled images, we can train a new SemiSeg-CSSN with a new mixed dataset containing both labeled and unlabeled images. We embedded CSSN during training the network.

2.5 Strategies to Improve Inference Speed and Reduce Resource Consumption

We take the whole image as input and output a segmentation result of the whole image size, which is more efficient than using a patchwork segmentation result based on patches. Besides, we employed the strategies from efficientSegNet [18] to reduce the resource consumption. An anisotropic convolution with a $k \times k \times 1$ intra-slice convolution and a $1 \times 1 \times k$ inter-slice convolution are used in the decoder module. In addition, the low-level and high-level feature maps are aggregated by addition rather than concatenation due to the low GPU memory footprint.

2.6 Post-processing

For the results of segmentations, we used the maximal union region selection as post-processing steps. We selected the unique region which has the maximal areas from the candidate regions for each class.

3 Experiments

3.1 Dataset and Evaluation Measures

The FLARE2022 dataset is curated from more than 20 medical groups under the license permission, including MSD [16], KiTS [9,10], AbdomenCT-1K [13], and TCIA [5]. It is an extension of the FLARE 2021 [12] with more segmentation targets and more diverse abdomen CT scans. The training set includes 50 labelled CT scans with pancreas disease and 2000 unlabelled CT scans with liver, kidney, spleen, or pancreas diseases. The validation set includes 50 CT scans with liver, kidney, spleen, or pancreas diseases. The testing set includes 200 CT scans where 100 cases has liver, kidney, spleen, or pancreas diseases and the other 100 cases has uterine corpus endometrial, urothelial bladder, stomach, sarcomas, or ovarian diseases. All the CT scans only have image information and the center information is not available.

The evaluation measures consist of two accuracy measures: Dice Similarity Coefficient (DSC) and Normalized Surface Dice (NSD), and three running efficiency measures: running time, area under GPU memory-time curve, and area under CPU utilization-time curve. All measures will be used to compute the ranking. Moreover, the GPU memory consumption has a 2 GB tolerance.

3.2 Implementation Details

Environment Settings. The environments and requirements for training are presented in Table 1.

Table 1. Environments and requirements for training.

Windows/Ubuntu version	Ubuntu 20.04.4 LTS
CPU	Platinum 82 series (72vCPU) v5@2.5 GHz
RAM	16×4 GB; 2.67 MT/s
GPU (number and type)	NVIDIA V100 16×32 G
CUDA version	11.1
Programming language	Python 3.6
Deep learning framework	Pytorch (Torch 1.8.0, torchvision 0.9.0)
Code is publicly available at	SemiSeg-CSSN

Training Protocols. We implemented the proposed framework using EfficientSegNet network used in FLARE21 challenge. The patch-based Unet such as nnUnet [11] also can be used as the basic segmentation, however, we found it consumes large RAM when prediction. Brightness, crop, random rotation, random transition and random elastic deformation were used for data augmentation. We random resampled the data with size described in Table 2. Besides, we trained the coarse model with the 50 labeled images.

Table 2. Training protocols for SemiSeg-CSSN.

Network initialization	Kaiming normal initialization
Batch size	8(coarse), 1(fine)
Input size (coarse)	160×160×160
Input size (fine)	192×192×192
Total epochs	500(coarse), 200(fine)
Optimizer	Adam with betas (0.9, 0.99), L2 penalty: 0.00001
Loss	Dice loss and focal loss (alpha = 0.5, gamma = 2)
Initial learning rate (lr)	0.01
Training time (coarse)	6 (coarse), 300(fine) hours

4 Results and Discussion

4.1 Quantitative Results on Validation Set

We used 50 labeled and 2000 unlabeled images to train the network in cross-supervised manner. The results show that the method using unlabeled data improve the dice score of the method with only 50 labeled images.

Table 3. Quantitative results of supervised and semi-supervised methods in terms of DSC and NSD on the validation dataset. The symbol 50(L)+ 2000(U) denotes the method, which used 50 labeled and 2000 unlabeled images. We reported the mean and standard deviation in parentheses.

Organ	Supervised 50(L) DSC(%), NSD(%)	SemiSeg-CSSN 50(L)+2000(U) DSC(%), NSD(%)	SemiSeg-CSSN+UIF 50(L)+200(U) DSC(%), NSD(%)	SemiSeg – CSSN* 50(L)+2000(U) DSC(%), NSD(%)
Liver	90.8(7.3),85.4(13.0)	93.7(5.4), 91.3(10.7)	96.3(2.0),96.7(4.7)	92.5(14.1),90.6(15.4)
RK	79.3(33.6) ,77.93(32.8)	80.5(32.8),79.0(32.5)	79.8(31.9), 79.5(31.9)	87.3(26.2),86.7(26.3)
Spleen	92.5(7.4),90.0(12.3)	89.8(21.9),89.0(23.4)	87.6(18.7), 88.6(18.5)	91.6(19.8),91.7(20.9)
Pancreas	68.8(12.3),76.2(14.5)	73.3(13.8),81.1(14.6)	78.4(15.3), 88.8(13.8)	75.4(15.8),82.8(16.9)
Aorta	90.6(4.0),91.8(6.6)	94.5(2.6),96.3(3.9)	93.8(2.6), 96.5(3.2)	91.8(14.5),93.6(15.2)
IVC	83.5(11.7),80.4(12.3)	87.7(8.6),87.0(8.9)	87.0(11.6),87.1(10.6)	82.4(16.2),80.5(17.0)
RAG	54.1(31.6),63.0(35.0)	64.1(33.2),72.6(37.1)	77.3(14.6),89.9(10.0)	64.8(31.7),74.5(36.0)
LAG	24.4(29.6),48.1(34.8)	51.7(32.0),71.6(27.8)	72.1(20.7),82.4(21.7)	47.5(32.9),70.0(30.8)
Gallbladder	42.3(40.0),39.3(39.3)	60.3(38.0),57.6(38.1)	63.9(41.4),61.9(42.2)	68.0(34.8),66.1(35.7)
Esophagus	75.1(17.1),84.8(18.2)	82.4(9.8),91.7(9.5)	76.7(12.9),86.5(14.2)	76.0(21.3),84.1(23.2)
Stomach	71.0(29.0),71.0(29.3)	83.0(18.8),84.8(17.9)	74.2(28.7),78.5(28.1)	80.8(24.2),82.4(24.4)
Duodenum	61.7(26.0),76.9(26.0)	64.0(23.8),78.2(22.0)	59.1(26.8),74.8(24.9)	63.3(23.1),77.0(22.7)
LK	88.2(22.2),87.2(22.5)	88.6(21.1),85.4(22.2)	81.7(25.1), 82.3(25.0)	88.6(19.9),85.4(21.5)
Avg.	70.9(31.0) ,74.8(29.4)	78.0(26.6),82.0(25.3)	79.1(24.5),84.1(23.7)	77.7(13.1),82.0(7.9)

Table 4. Quantitative.

Mean runtime (s)	Maximum used GPU memory (MB)	AUC GPU time	AUC CPU time
12.9	2052	13776.9	250.6

Table 3 shows the results of the proposed methods. The results of our submitted solution (docker container), which is evaluated by the organizers of FLARE2022, are reported in the last two columns in Table 3, i.e., SemiSeg – CSSN*. The other results are evaluated on the 20 selected validation cases, whose ground truth are send by the organizers.

Compared to the supervised method, the average DSC of the semi-supervised method (SemiSeg-CSSN) improves from 70.9% to 78.0%, while the average NSC improves from 74.8% to 82.0%. The results show that LAG, Gallbladder and RAG segmentation is the three difficult organs and Liver, Spleen and Aorta is the three easy organs for abdominal organ segmentation. The difficulties may be due to unclear boundaries and class imbalance issues. Besides, the standard deviations of Gallbladder segmentation are relative large, which demonstrates the method achieves disappointed robustness for Gallbladder. As shown in Fig. 6, Case #0047 has a complete Gallbladder, while Case #0048 does not have one. Moreover, as shown in Fig. 6, the pathologies, such as the tumor in Liver in Case #0047, have negative effects on the segmentation.

Besides, for 2000 unlabeled images, we generated their pseudo label images using trained supervised segmentation network. Then, we used UIF to select 200 unlabeled images and their pseudo label images with low uncertainty, and trained a new segmentation network via SemiSeg-CSSN. As shown in Table 3, the DSC of semi-supervised segmentation network improves from 78.0% to 79.1%.

Table 5. Quantitative results SemiSeg-CSSN in terms of DSC and NSD on the test dataset. We used 50 labeled and 2000 unlabeled images for training. We reported the mean and standard deviation in parentheses.

Organ	DSC(%)	NSD(%)
Liver	4.3(5.2)	92.7(8.8)
RK	89.1 (21.6)	87.6 (22.3)
Spllen	90.6(20.3)	90.7(21.3)
Pancreas	71.2(17.9)	79.8(19.3)
Aorta	93.3(8.2)	95.1(9.0)
IVC	83.6(15.1)	83.1(16.3)
RAG	75.2(20.4)	86.2(22.1)
LAG	48.7(31.9)	74.8(28.7)
Gallbladder	66.5(36.3)	65.0(36.2)
Esophagus	69.0(22.4)	77.5(25.3)
Stomach	83.4(17.8)	84.8(17.7)
Duodenum	65.1(17.3)	79.0(18.0)
LK.	86.4(21.7)	82.3(23.0)
Avg.	78.2(13.0)	83.0(7.7)

Table 6. Quantitative results of the good (Case #0006 and Case #0035) and bad (Case #0047 and Case #0048) examples.

Organ	Case #0006 DSC(%), NSD(%)	Case #0035 DSC(%), NSD(%)	Case #0047 DSC(%), NSD(%)	Case #0048 DSC(%), NSD(%)
Liver	96.8, 93.2	96.7, 96.8	82.2, 67.0	87.1, 82.2
RK	96.5, 96.7	97.3, 97.1	95.7, 93.4	84.8, 77.6
Spleen	97.9, 97.9	98.0, 99.6	85.8, 76.4	63.6, 50.0
Pancreas	83.6, 90.5	87.9, 99.0	60.9, 68.0	66.6, 75.7
Aorta	95.8, 97.6	96.4, 99.8	92.3, 96.8	86.9, 85.2
IVC	94.5, 97.5	93.5, 94.4	86.0, 84.7	53.5, 57.7
RAG	90.9, 97.6	70.2, 85.8	0.0,0.0	63.7, 66.0
LAG	87.1, 95.2	75.3, 80.6	11.5, 61.5	15.0, 63.9
Gallbladder	100.0, 100.0	53.9, 52.9	52.7, 55.0	0.0, 0.0
Esophagus	85.4, 92.9	88.52, 96.6	87.2, 99.0	57.6, 70.8
Stomach	89.9, 88.6	92.8, 97.7	76.4, 76.8	40.3, 41.0
Duodenum	72.9, 82.67	85.0, 96.8	4.8, 15.3	59.5, 76.4
LK	95.1, 88.2	97.6, 98.3	98.1, 98.2	93.8, 89.4
Avg.	91.3, 93.6	87.2, 91.6	64.1, 68.3	59.4, 63.9

4.2 Segmentation Efficiency Results on Validation Set

Table 4 presents the segmentation efficiency results. The mean runtime is 12.9 s per case in prediction step, maximum used GPU memory is 2052 MB, AUC GPU time is 13776.9, and AUC CPU time 250.6.

4.3 Quantitative Results on Test Set

Table 5 shows the quantitative result of SemiSeg-CSSN on test dataset. The average DSC of 13-organ segmentation is 78.2 ± 13.0%, and the average NSD is 83.0 ± 7.8%. The organs with the highest and lowest DSC were Liver and LAG, respectively. The gallbladder has the largest standard deviation (Table 6).

Intensity image   SemiSeg-CSSN   Ground truth

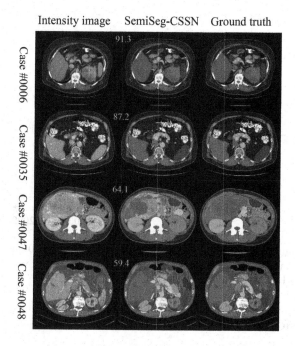

Fig. 6. Qualitative results on good (Case #0006 and Case #0035) and bad (Case #0047 and Case #0048) examples. First column is the image, second column is the results achieved by our propose method, and third column is the ground truth of the segmentation. The DSC of each case is presented at the top-left corner.

4.4 Ablation Study: Influence of Different Number of Unlabeled Data

To further validate the effect unlabeled images, different numbers of unlabeled images from the training set were selected. For each case, we trained the SemiSeg-CSSN model using 50 labeled images and different number, i.e., ranging from 0 to 2000, of unlabeled images. Note that supervised model used 0 unlabeled images. Figure 7 shows the segmentation results. With the number of unlabeled images increases, the performance of SemiSeg-CSSN models are increased, and all the models with unlabeled images perform better than the supervised method. Moreover, it is clear that the SemiSeg-CSSN model tends to converge when trained with more than 1000 unlabeled images.

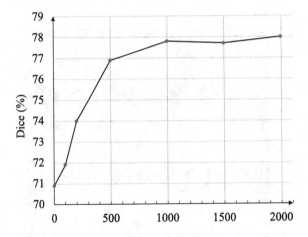

Fig. 7. Performance plot of our semi-supervised approach with 50 labeled images and different number (from 0 to 2000) of unlabeled images. Note the case with 0 unlabeled images denotes the fully supervised method.

5   Discussion and Conclusion

Using unlabeled data, the proposed semi-supervised method achieved better results than the results of the supervised method. Whether using supervised or semi supervised methods, the segmentation of some organs is still challenging. LAG segmentation obtained disappointing performance because of unclear boundaries and class imbalance issues. The existence of seriously pathology-affected organs, such as Livers and Kidneys, are critical factor for the poor segmentation performance. Besides, further research is needed to identify accurate boundaries and suppress pathological effects.

SemiSeg-CSSN+UIF model only used 200 unlabeled images, which achieved higher DSC and NSD than the model with un-filtering 2000 unlabeled images. It means the quality counts more than quantity when using unlabeled images. However, because UIF can be used in any trained segmentation network to select unlabeled images, there is a progressive training strategy, which is needed to explore in the future.

5.1   Limitation and Future Work

We summarize the limitations and potential improvement as follows:

- Address the difficulties of multi-organ segmentation with class imbalance problem.
- Robust algorithms for shape variation of organs and presence of pathologies.
- Normalization of ROI and image information.
- The quality of pseudo labels needs more attention than quantity.

Acknowledgements. The authors of this paper declare that the segmentation method they implemented for participation in the FLARE 2022 challenge has not used any pre-trained models nor additional datasets other than those provided by the organizers.

References

1. Blum, A., Mitchell, T.: Combining labeled and unlabeled data with co-training. In: Proceedings of the Eleventh Annual Conference on Computational Learning Theory, pp. 92–100 (1998)
2. Chen, L.-C., Lopes, R.G., Cheng, B., Collins, M.D., Cubuk, E.D., Zoph, B., Adam, H., Shlens, J.: Naive-student: leveraging semi-supervised learning in video sequences for urban scene segmentation. In: Vedaldi, A., Bischof, H., Brox, T., Frahm, J.-M. (eds.) ECCV 2020. LNCS, vol. 12354, pp. 695–714. Springer, Cham (2020). https://doi.org/10.1007/978-3-030-58545-7_40
3. Chen, X., Yuan, Y., Zeng, G., Wang, J.: Semi-supervised semantic segmentation with cross pseudo supervision. In: Proceedings of the IEEE/CVF Conference on Computer Vision and Pattern Recognition, pp. 2613–2622 (2021)
4. Chen, Y., Mancini, M., Zhu, X., Akata, Z.: Semi-supervised and unsupervised deep visual learning: a survey. IEEE Trans. Pattern Anal. Mach. Intell. **2022**, 1–23 (2022). https://doi.org/10.1109/TPAMI.2022.3201576
5. Clark, K., et al.: The cancer imaging archive (TCIA): maintaining and operating a public information repository. J. Digit. Imaging **26**(6), 1045–1057 (2013)
6. Cordts, M., et al.: The cityscapes dataset for semantic urban scene understanding. In: Proceedings of the IEEE Conference on Computer Vision and Pattern Recognition, pp. 3213–3223 (2016)
7. Everingham, M., Eslami, S., Van Gool, L., Williams, C.K., Winn, J., Zisserman, A.: The pascal visual object classes challenge: A retrospective. Int. J. Comput. Vision **111**(1), 98–136 (2015)
8. Fralick, S.: Learning to recognize patterns without a teacher. IEEE Trans. Inf. Theory **13**(1), 57–64 (1967)
9. Heller, N., et al.: The state of the art in kidney and kidney tumor segmentation in contrast-enhanced CT imaging: results of the kits19 challenge. Med. Image Anal. **67**, 101821 (2021)
10. Heller, N., et al.: An international challenge to use artificial intelligence to define the state-of-the-art in kidney and kidney tumor segmentation in ct imaging. Proc. Am. Soc. Clin. Oncol. **38**(6), 626–626 (2020)
11. Isensee, F., Jaeger, P.F., Kohl, S.A., Petersen, J., Maier-Hein, K.H.: NNU-net: a self-configuring method for deep learning-based biomedical image segmentation. Nat. Methods **18**(2), 203–211 (2021)
12. Ma, J., et al.: Fast and low-GPU-memory abdomen CT organ segmentation: the flare challenge. Med. Image Anal. **82**, 102616 (2022). https://doi.org/10.1016/j.media.2022.102616
13. Ma, J., et al.: Abdomenct-1k: is abdominal organ segmentation a solved problem? IEEE Trans. Pattern Anal. Mach. Intell. **44**(10), 6695–6714 (2022)
14. Mittal, S., Tatarchenko, M., Brox, T.: Semi-supervised semantic segmentation with high-and low-level consistency. IEEE Trans. Pattern Anal. Mach. Intell. **43**(4), 1369–1379 (2019)
15. Scudder, H.: Probability of error of some adaptive pattern-recognition machines. IEEE Trans. Inf. Theory **11**(3), 363–371 (1965)

16. Simpson, A.L., et al.: A large annotated medical image dataset for the development and evaluation of segmentation algorithms. arXiv preprint arXiv:1902.09063 (2019)

17. Yang, L., Zhuo, W., Qi, L., Shi, Y., Gao, Y.: St++: make self-training work better for semi-supervised semantic segmentation. In: Proceedings of the IEEE/CVF Conference on Computer Vision and Pattern Recognition, pp. 4268–4277 (2022),

18. Zhang, F., Wang, Y., Yang, H.: Efficient context-aware network for abdominal multi-organ segmentation. arXiv preprint arXiv:2109.10601 (2021)

Efficient Semi-supervised Multi-organ Segmentation Using Uncertainty Rectified Pyramid Consistency

Meng Han[(✉)], Yijie Qu, and Xiangde Luo

School of Mechanical and Electrical Engineering, University of Electronic Science and
Technology of China, Chengdu, China
ginkgo7777@163.com

Abstract. To meet the problems that great dependence on fully annotated data and spatio-temporal inefficiency of remaining automatic
multi-organ segmentation methods, an efficient semi-supervised framework with uncertainty rectified pyramid consistency regularization is
introduced. Specifically, inspired by the fact that the predictions of the
same input should be similar under different disturbance, this work uses
an extending backbone to produce different-scale predictions for unlabeled images and encourage them to be consistent. In order to avoid
lost of fine detail or model collapse when directly encouraging the multi-
scale predictions to be consistent, a rectified scale-level uncertainty-aware
module is introduced to enable the framework to gradually learn from
reliable prediction regions. To deal with the domain gaps among multi-
center datasets, a number of prepocessing methods are utilized, such
as resampling the multi-center CT volumes to the same spacing and
adjusting the window level and width. Quantitative evaluation on the
FLARE2022 20 validation cases given the labels, this method achieves
the average dice similarity coefficient (DSC) of 0.793 and average normalized surface distance (NSD) of 0.852.

Keywords: Semi-supervised learning · Multi-organ segmentation ·
Uncertainty rectifying · Pyramid consistency

1 Introduction

Whole abdominal organ segmentation plays an important role in the diagnosis of
abdominal lesions, radiotherapy and follow-up. Manual organ delineation is time-
consuming and error-prone [7]. Although many automatic segmentation methods
based on deep learning have achieved good performances in abdominal organ
segmentation, most of them rely heavily on large-scale fully annotated data,
which is often difficult to obtain due to cost and privacy issues. Additionally,
these methods are often difficult to be implemented into clinical practice due to
the large model size and the extensive computational resources.

To meet the needs of fast inference and low computational cost while only
use a small number of labeled cases, we introduce an efficient semi-supervised

© The Author(s), under exclusive license to Springer Nature Switzerland AG 2022
J. Ma and B. Wang (Eds.): FLARE 2022, LNCS 13816, pp. 307–317, 2022.
https://doi.org/10.1007/978-3-031-23911-3_27

framework with uncertainty rectified pyramid consistency to fully make use of the unlabeled data referring to the work of [6]. Concretely, we extend a U-Net [9] backbone to produce pyramid predictions at different scales and encourages these multi-scale predictions to be consistent for a given input. A standard supervised loss is used for learning from labeled data. For unlabeled cases, we encourages the pyramid predictions to be consistent, which served as a regularization. Since the predictions of the unlabeled cases are not necessarily reliable because of its insufficient supervision information, which may cause the model to collapse and lose details [6], we introduce to estimate the uncertainty via the prediction discrepancy among multi-scale predictions. Different from those that estimate the uncertainty of each target prediction with Monte Carlo sampling [5], which needs massive computational costs as it requires multiple forward passes to obtain the uncertainty in each iteration, this work just needs a single forward pass. Under the guidance of the estimated uncertainty, the model strengthens the consistent learning of reliable regions and weakens that of unreliable ones. Meanwhile, to further improve the utilization of unlabeled data information and increase the segmentation efficiency, we introduce the uncertainty minimization [11] to reduce the prediction variance during training.

To address the domain gaps among FLARE2022 training, validation, and test sets, we employ a series of data preprocessing methods. For instance, resampling the images' spacing to $2 \times 2 \times 2.5\,\mathrm{mm}$, adjusting the window level and window width of the CT images, data augmentation with CLAHE, gamma correction, random noise, random rotate and random flip.

2 Method

The overview of the proposed semi-supervised segmentation network is illustrated in Fig. 1, which consists of a 3D U-Net [9] backbone with a pyramid prediction structure at the decoder and an uncertainty rectifying module.

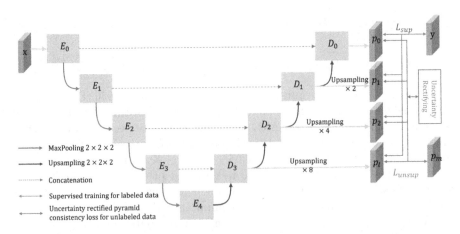

Fig. 1. Network architecture.

2.1   Multi-scale Prediction Network with Pyramid Consistency

Firstly, we introduce pyramid prediction network (PPNet) [6] for the multi-organ segmentation task, which can produce prediction at different decoder layers. In this work, a 3D U-Net is employed as backbone and is modified to produce pyramid predictions by adding $1 \times 1 \times 1$ convolution followed by a softmax layer as the prediction layer after each upsampling block. A dropout layer and a feature-level noise addition layer are inserted before the prediction layer to introduce more perturbations to the network.

For an input image x_i, the PPNet generates a series of multi-scale predictions $[p'_0, p'_1, \cdots, p'_l, \cdots, p'_{L-1}]$, where L denotes the number of decoder layers, and p'_l are the corresponding prediction at decoder layer l. In this work, we set $L = 4$ for the multi-organ segmentation. Then, the multi-scale predictions are rescaled to the input size, and the the corresponding results are denoted as $[p_0, p_1, \cdots, p_l, \cdots, p_{L-1}]$. For the labeled data, we use a combination of Dice and cross-entropy loss at multiple scales as the supervised loss:

$$\mathcal{L}_{sup} = \frac{1}{L} \sum_{l=0}^{L-1} \frac{\mathcal{L}_{dice}(p_l, y_i) + \mathcal{L}_{ce}(p_l, y_i)}{2} \tag{1}$$

where $y_i, \mathcal{L}_{dice}, \mathcal{L}_{ce}$ denote the ground truth of input x_i, the Dice loss and the cross entropy loss, respectively.

To efficiently leverage unlabeled data, we use a pyramid consistency loss to encouraging the multi-scale predictions to be consistent by minimizing their discrepancy(i.e., variance) with L_2 distance:

$$\mathcal{L}_{pc} = \frac{1}{L} \sum_{l=0}^{L-1} \|p_l - p_m\|_2 \tag{2}$$

where p_m is the average prediction across scales, which is denoted as:

$$p_m = \frac{1}{L} \sum_{l=0}^{L-1} p_l \tag{3}$$

2.2   Uncertainty Rectified Pyramid Consistency Loss

As the pyramid predictions have different spatial resolutions, imposing voxel-level consistency directly between these predictions may lead to problems due the different spatial frequencies, such as lost of fine detail or model collapse. Inspired by existing works [1,11], a scale-level uncertainty-aware method is introduced to address these problems, which only requires a single forward pass and thus need less computational cost and running time than exiting methods [5].

We use the KL-divergence between the prediction at decoder layer l and the mean prediction as the uncertainty measurement:

$$\mathcal{U}_l \approx \sum_{j=0}^{C} p_l^j \cdot \log \frac{p_l^j}{p_m^j} \tag{4}$$

where $C = 14$ is the class(i.e., channel) number in this work, and p_l^j is the jth channel of p_l. We can get a set of uncertainty maps $\mathcal{U}_0, \mathcal{U}_1, \cdots, \mathcal{U}_l, \cdots, \mathcal{U}_{L-1}$, where $\mathcal{U}_l$ represents the uncertainty of p_l. A larger value of $\mathcal{U}_l$ indicates the prediction for that pixel at scale l has high uncertainty, which means the prediction is unreliable and may be ignored for stable unsupervised learning.

Based on the uncertainty maps, we automatically select reliable voxels(with low uncertainty) to rectify the pyramid consistency loss for better using the information of unlabeled data:

$$\mathcal{L}_{unsup} = \frac{1}{L} \underbrace{\frac{\sum_{l=0}^{L-1} \sum_v (p_l^v - p_m^v)^2 \cdot w_l^v}{\sum_{l=0}^{L-1} \sum_v w_l^v}}_{uncertainty \quad rectification} + \underbrace{\frac{1}{L} \sum_{l=0}^{L-1} \|\mathcal{U}_l\|_2}_{uncertainty \quad minimization} \tag{5}$$

where p_l^v and $\mathcal{U}_l^v$ are the corresponding prediction and uncertainty values for voxel v at decoder layer l. Rather than use the threshold-based cut off approaches which is hard to determine [1], we follow the policy in [11] to use a voxel- and scale-wise weight w_l^v to automatically rectify the MSE loss, which is defined as: $w_l^v = e^{-\mathcal{U}_l^v}$, where a higher uncertainty leads to lower weight. Meanwhile, in order to encourage the PPNet to produce more consistent predictions at different scales, we use the uncertainty minimization term as a constraint.

2.3 The Overall Loss Function

The proposed semi-supervised segmentation network learns form both labeled data and unlabeled data by minimizing the following combined objective function:

$$\mathcal{L}_{total} = \mathcal{L}_{sup} + \lambda \cdot \mathcal{L}_{unsup} \tag{6}$$

where λ is a widely-used time-dependent Gaussian warming up function [5] to control the balance between the supervised loss and the unsupervised loss. The formula of $\lambda(t)$ is: $\lambda(t) = w_{max} \cdot e^(-5(1 - \frac{1}{t_{max}})^2$, where w_{max} means the final regularization weight, t denotes the current training step and t_{max} is the maximal training step.

2.4 Preprocessing

To reduce the domain gaps between multi-center data, the following preprocessing techniques are employed:

- Resampling the anisotropic data:
    Due to differences in scanners or acquisition protocols, data from different centers usually have different spacing. The convolution operation of CNN requires the image to be isotropic for better feature extraction. So all data, including training, validation and test data, need to be resampled to keep the image isotropic. Observing the resolution information of the training data, combined with the consideration of the trade-off between the amount of contextual information in the networks patch size and the details retained in the

image data, the sampling layer spacing is set to 2.5 mm. To save memory overhead and speed up training, the intra-layer resolution is resampled to 2 mm × 2 mm.

- Adjusting window level and window width:
  The method of adjusting the window width and window level was leveraged to improve the contrast of abdominal CT images. And the window level and width were adjusted 50 and 400, respectively.
- Intensity normalization method:
  The data were normalized with z-score normalization based on the mean and standard deviation of the intensity to avoid the problem of data being compressed after normalization.
- Data augmentation method:
  Due to the lack of label data and to avoid the problem of overfitting, channel-wise gamma correction, random noise, random flip, random rotate were used to augment the training data.

2.5 Post-processing

A connected component analysis of segmentation mask is applied on the outputs to remove small connected areas. And then the results are resampled back to original spacing for the convenience of the following evaluation.

3 Experiments

3.1 Dataset and Evaluation Measures

The FLARE2022 dataset is curated from more than 20 medical groups under the license permission, including MSD [10], KiTS [3,4], AbdomenCT-1K [8], and TCIA [2]. The training set includes 50 labelled CT scans with pancreas disease and 2000 unlabelled CT scans with liver, kidney, spleen, or pancreas diseases. The validation set includes 50 CT scans with liver, kidney, spleen, or pancreas diseases. The testing set includes 200 CT scans where 100 cases has liver, kidney, spleen, or pancreas diseases and the other 100 cases has uterine corpus endometrial, urothelial bladder, stomach, sarcomas, or ovarian diseases. All the CT scans only have image information and the center information is not available.

The evaluation measures consist of two accuracy measures: Dice Similarity Coefficient (DSC) and Normalized Surface Dice (NSD), and three running efficiency measures: running time, area under GPU memory-time curve(AUC GPU-Time), and area under CPU utilization-time curve(AUC CPU-Time). Moreover, the GPU memory consumption has a 2 GB tolerance.

3.2 Implementation Details

Environment Settings. The development environments and requirements are presented in Table 1.

Table 1. Development environments and requirements.

Windows/Ubuntu version	Ubuntu 20.04.4 LTS
CPU	Intel(R) Xeon(R) CPU E5-2678 v3 @ 2.50 GHz
RAM	16×4 GB; 2.67MT/s
GPU (number and type)	Four NVIDIA Corporation TU102(2080Ti) 10G
CUDA version	11.4.48
Programming language	Python 3.7.13
Deep learning framework	Pytorch (Torch 1.11.0, torchvision 0.12.0)
Specific dependencies	None

Training Protocols. The training protocols of the baseline method is shown in Table 2.

Table 2. Training protocols.

Network initialization	"he" normal initialization
Batch size	4
Patch size	80×96×96
Total epochs	100
Optimizer	Adam with momentum ($\mu = 0.9$)
Initial learning rate (lr)	0.001
Lr decay schedule	halved by 20 epochs
Training time	24 h
Number of model parameters	15.3M
Number of flops	59.32G

Testing Protocols. In the inference stage, we only use the output of the last layer as prediction, without using the deep supervision.

4   Results and Discussion

4.1   Quantitative Results on Validation Set

Table 3 shows the results of this work on the total 50 validation cases from the leaderboard, while Table 4 illustrates the results on the 20 validation cases whose ground truth are publicly provided by FLARE2022. Large-volume organs like liver, Aorta, spleen and kidney have relatively good performance. However, the poor performance on small organs and diseased organs reduces the overall average performance. Indeed, the segmentation results have the problem of organ disappearance, that is, the segmentation results of some organs, especially small organs, are not predicted on some cases. Another problem is that due to the deformation of some diseased organs as well as the lack training of model on such data, the segmentation prediction of diseased organs is completely wrong. The above two situations are the main reasons that lead to the corresponding DSC and NSD of some cases' organs segmentation valuing 0, which is also a part to be further explored and sovled. It is noted that the values of NSD are generally better than that of DSC, where NSD can reflect edge segmentation to a certain extent while DSC can reflect region segmentation, indicating that the method proposed in this paper has a relatively better performance on organ boundary segmentation.

Table 3. Quantitative results of this work comparing with those of baseline on 50 validation cases. RK, IVC, RAG, LAG and LK represent right kidney, inferior vena cava, right adrenal gland, left adrenal gland and left kidney respectively.

Organs	DSC(ours, %)	DSC(baseline,%)
Liver	94.06	94.71
RK	85.02	83.17
Spleen	89.41	80.08
Pancreas	73.44	65.11
Aorta	90.09	90.97
IVC	79.90	76.97
RAG	63.17	63.56
LAG	66.31	53.13
Gallbladder	72.71	54.09
Esophagus	74.07	66.04
Stomach	78.54	75.81
Duodenum	65.44	55.69
LK	81.56	79.14
Mean	77.98	72.19

We set a plain 3D-UNet, like Fig. 1, without deep supervision and pyramid consistency as baseline. Comparing segmentation results of baseline using only label data with our proposal under the same experimental conditions on 20 validation cases whose ground truth are publicly given, as shown in Table 4, the semi-supervised method proposed in this paper is improved both on DSC by about 8.76% and NSD by about 9.06%, which directly demonstrate that effective utilization of unlabeled data can improve segmentation performance. On the total validation set, as shown in Table 3, our method also obtains an average DSC score of 77.8%, which is also 5.79% higher than the baseline of 72.19%, showing the effectiveness of this work. The poor results using only labeled data also demonstrate the importance of the distribution of training data to model performance. That is, data from different centers will directly affect the generalization of the model. Especially in the data of FLARE2022, there is the problem

Table 4. Quantitative results of this work comparing with those of baseline on 20 validation cases(best) that ground truth given. RK, IVC, RAG, LAG and LK represent right kidney, inferior vena cava, right adrenal gland, left adrenal gland and left kidney respectively.

Organs	DSC(ours, %)	NSD (ours, %)	DSC (baseline, %)	NSD (baseline, %)
Liver	93.73	91.30	95.04	93.62
RK	87.49	86.44	77.96	77.24
Spleen	92.78	91.40	79.95	79.66
Pancreas	76.94	87.52	66.20	76.71
Aorta	91.55	95.96	91.09	95.40
IVC	81.27	82.04	75.86	75.44
RAG	68.84	85.49	60.33	75.81
LAG	68.51	84.03	58.02	69.60
Gallbladder	69.19	71.00	42.50	40.56
Esophagus	75.16	84.87	65.46	76.80
Stomach	78.49	82.98	70.36	74.56
Duodenum	64.95	79.93	52.62	72.39
LK	81.94	83.68	81.67	81.98
Mean	79.30	85.17	70.54	76.11

of different organ lesions between the training set and validation set, making their distributions vary and leading to extremely poor segmentation of some organs.

4.2   Qualitative Results on Validation Set

Figure 2 presents the qualitative results on the validation set, where row 1 and 2 show some cases that are relatively easy to segment while row 3 and 4 show cases that are challenging to segment. It can be find that the cases of row 1 and 2 where exist no severe artifacts or lesions in the organs have clear boundaries and good contrast for the segmentation results. Compared with the well-segmented cases, the challenge cases usually have noise(row 3) or organs lesion(row 4), which create difficulties in correctly segmenting the organs and lead to disappointing performance.

4.3   Results on Final Testing Set

Table 5 shows the segmentation quantitative results on testing set, with an average DSC of 77.78% and average NSD of 83.89%. It can be seen that the results on testing set are very similar to those on the validation set, showing the robustness of our method. The running time and resource consumption are represented in Table 6. Compared with the results of each team finally displayed on the

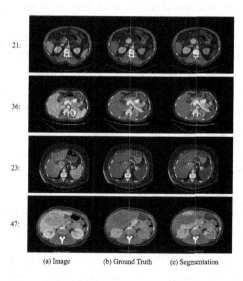

(a) Image   (b) Ground Truth   (c) Segmentation

Fig. 2. Qualitative evaluation of model performance on validation set. Row 1 and 2 are well-segmented examples showing their relatively good segmentation results and corresponding labels. Row 3 and 4 are challenging examples showing bad segmentation performance and corresponding labels. The leftmost number on each row represents the case number.

Table 5. Quantitative results on testing set. RK, IVC, RAG, LAG and LK represent right kidney, inferior vena cava, right adrenal gland, left adrenal gland and left kidney respectively.

Organs	DSC(%)	NSD(%)
Liver	94.04 ± 8.33	93.37 ± 10.72
RK	87.22 ± 24.01	87.73 ± 24.54
Spleen	82.13 ± 28.72	83.14 ± 29.02
Pancreas	70.78 ± 22.99	81.01 ± 24.83
Aorta	91.56 ± 10.60	95.54 ± 11.32
IVC	79.67 ± 19.94	81.14 ± 20.74
RAG	73.67 ± 15. 07	90.76 ± 16.66
LAG	72.17 ± 17.95	87.16 ± 19.88
Gallbladder	69.93 ± 33.71	70.38 ± 34.54
Esophagus	68.93 ± 21.66	78.83 ± 23.77
Stomach	74.31 ± 23.30	76.89 ± 23.19
Duodenum	58.15 ± 25.13	74.25 ± 25.16
LK	88.60 ± 19.38	90.41 ± 19.20
Mean	77.78 ± 11.58	83.89 ± 12.58

Table 6. Segmentation efficiency results on testing set.

Index	Time(s)	AUC CPU-Time($MiB \times s$)	AUC GPU-Time ($MiB \times s$)
	18.70 ± 4.33	398.80 ± 77.67	25774.29 ± 11703.85

official website of the FLARE2022 competition[1], the method in this paper shows a relatively high efficiency.

5 Conclusion

In this work, it can be seen that the segmentation results of small organs is not very good. The deformation of the diseased organ is also not considered in the segmentation process. In the future, further research can be carried out in terms of boundary constraints and attention mechanisms.

Acknowledgements. We declare that the segmentation method that implemented for participation in the FLARE 2022 challenge has not used any pre-trained models nor additional datasets other than those provided by the organizers. The proposed solution is fully automatic without any manual intervention.

References

1. Cao, X., Chen, H., Li, Y., Peng, Y., Wang, S., Cheng, L.: Uncertainty aware temporal-ensembling model for semi-supervised a bus mass segmentation. IEEE Trans. Med. Imaging **40**(1), 431–443 (2020)
2. Clark, K., et al.: The cancer imaging archive (TCIA): maintaining and operating a public information repository. J. Digit. Imaging **26**(6), 1045–1057 (2013)
3. Heller, N., et al.: The state of the art in kidney and kidney tumor segmentation in contrast-enhanced CT imaging: results of the kits19 challenge. Med. Image Anal. **67**, 101821 (2021)
4. Heller, N., et al.: An international challenge to use artificial intelligence to define the state-of-the-art in kidney and kidney tumor segmentation in CT imaging. Proc. Am. Soc. Clin. Oncol. **38**(6), 626–626 (2020)
5. Liu, X., et al.: Weakly supervised segmentation of covid19 infection with scribble annotation on CT images. Pattern Recogn. **122**, 108341 (2022)
6. Luo, X., et al.: Efficient semi-supervised gross target volume of nasopharyngeal carcinoma segmentation via uncertainty rectified pyramid consistency. In: de Bruijne, M., et al. (eds.) MICCAI 2021. LNCS, vol. 12902, pp. 318–329. Springer, Cham (2021). https://doi.org/10.1007/978-3-030-87196-3_30
7. Luo, X., et al.: Word: Revisiting organs segmentation in the whole abdominal region. arXiv preprint arXiv:2111.02403 (2021)
8. Ma, J., et al.: Abdomenct-1k: is abdominal organ segmentation a solved problem? IEEE Trans. Pattern Anal. Mach. Intell. **44**(10), 6695–6714 (2022)

---

[1] https://flare22.grand-challenge.org/testing-results/.

9. Ronneberger, O., Fischer, P., Brox, T.: U-Net: convolutional networks for biomedical image segmentation. In: Navab, N., Hornegger, J., Wells, W.M., Frangi, A.F. (eds.) MICCAI 2015. LNCS, vol. 9351, pp. 234–241. Springer, Cham (2015). https://doi.org/10.1007/978-3-319-24574-4_28
10. Simpson, A.L., et al.: A large annotated medical image dataset for the development and evaluation of segmentation algorithms. arXiv preprint arXiv:1902.09063 (2019)
11. Zheng, Z., Yang, Y.: Rectifying pseudo label learning via uncertainty estimation for domain adaptive semantic segmentation. Int. J. Comput. Vision **129**(4), 1106–1120 (2021)

A Pseudo-labeling Approach
to Semi-supervised Organ Segmentation

Jianwei Gao[✉][iD], Juan Xu, and Honggao Fei

Digital Health China Technologies Co., LTD., Beijing, China
{gaojw,xujuan,feihg}@dchealth.com

Abstract. In this paper, we adopt a "pseudo-labeling" approach to semi-supervised learning based on 50 labeled images and 2000 unlabeled images. This approach yields a model with 0.7496 mean DSC on the validation set, outperforming the 0.6903 mean DSC of the model with only 50 labeled images.

Keywords: Abdominal organ segmentation · Semi-supervised · Pseudo-labeling

1 Introduction

Abdomen organ segmentation has many important clinical applications. Typically, a large number of labeled data is required to train a accurate segmentation model. However, manually annotating organs from CT scans is time-consuming and labor-intensive. This requires us to use appropriate semi-supervised segmentation methods to use unlabeled data, such as disturbance regularization based on data or model [7,8] and consistency constraint based on multitask [6].

FLARE22 provides 50 labeled images and 2000 unlabeled images to train the segmentation model of 13 organs. There are three main difficulties. First, we need to realize the segmentation of 13 organs. Second, more than 97% of the training data are unlabeled. Third, we need to balance model performance and resource consumption.

In order to use unlabeled data as well as labeled data, we adopted a pseudo-labeling approach to develop a segmentation model drawing on the idea of developing a classification model in [5]. Specifically, we first trained a model with labeled data, and then used the model to predict the unlabeled data to give them pseudo-labels. Finally, we fine-tuned the original model using all labeled data and partially filtered pseudo-labeled data.

2 Method

2.1 Preprocessing

We use several pre-processing strategies as follows.

J. Ma and B. Wang (Eds.): FLARE 2022, LNCS 13816, pp. 318–326, 2022.
https://doi.org/10.1007/978-3-031-23911-3_28

- Cropping strategy
  We use the CT scans as the data source to generate the bounding box of foreground, and then crop only the foreground object of the images.
- Resampling method for anisotropic data
  We resample the original data to unify the voxel spacing into $[1.0, 1.0, 1.0]$.
- Intensity normalization method
  We normalize the intensity of $[-300.0, 300.0]$ to $[0.0, 1.0]$ and change those less than -300.0 and those greater than 300.0 to 0.0 and 1.0, respectively.

2.2 Proposed Method

Figure 1 illustrates the applied 3D nnU-Net [4], where a 3D U-Net architecture is adopted. We use the leaky ReLU function with a negative slope of 0.01 as the activation function. Our 3D nnU-Net has 14 out channels, corresponding to the background and 13 organs respectively.

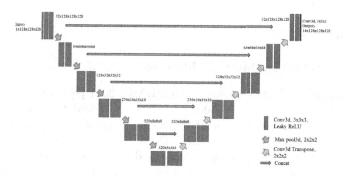

Fig. 1. Our 3D U-Net architecture

Our pseudo-labeling strategy for using unlabeled images is shown in Fig. 2. First, we trained a model with the 50 labeled images. Then we used this model to predict the 2000 unlabeled images to give them pseudo-labels. After that, we picked out 676 pseudo-labeled images with at least 2000 voxels for each organ to ensure that each organ of each pseudo-labeled image is present and not too small, and put them together with the 50 labeled images. At last, we used these 726 images to fine-tune the original model.

We use the sum of Dice loss (after applying a softmax function) and Cross Entropy Loss as the loss function.

When predicting a single image with the trained segmentation model, we first resample it to a voxel spacing of $[1.0, 1.0, 1.0]$, as we did during training, and try to predict. If there is a "CUDA out of memory" error, we resample it to $[2.0, 2.0, 2.0]$ voxel spacing to reduce the size of the resampled image and thus reduce the usage of GPU memory.

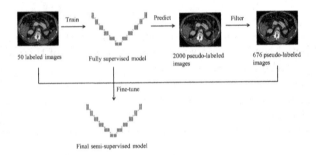

Fig. 2. Pseudo-labeling strategy

2.3 Post-processing

During model prediction, we select the label (from 0 to 13) corresponding to the largest of the 14 outputs for each voxel.

3 Experiments

3.1 Dataset and Evaluation Measures

The FLARE 2022 is an extension of the FLARE 2021 [9] with more segmentation targets and more diverse abdomen CT scans. The dataset is curated from more than 20 medical groups under the license permission, including MSD [11], KiTS [2,3], AbdomenCT-1K [10], and TCIA [1]. The training set includes 50 labelled CT scans with pancreas disease and 2000 unlabelled CT scans with liver, kidney, spleen, or pancreas diseases. The validation set includes 50 CT scans with liver, kidney, spleen, or pancreas diseases. The testing set includes 200 CT scans where 100 cases has liver, kidney, spleen, or pancreas diseases and the other 100 cases has uterine corpus endometrial, urothelial bladder, stomach, sarcomas, or ovarian diseases. All the CT scans only have image information and the center information is not available.

The evaluation measures consist of two accuracy measures: Dice Similarity Coefficient (DSC) and Normalized Surface Dice (NSD), and three running efficiency measures: running time, area under GPU memory-time curve, and area under CPU utilization-time curve. All measures will be used to compute the ranking. Moreover, the GPU memory consumption has a 2 GB tolerance.

3.2 Implementation Details

Environment Settings. The development environments and requirements are presented in Table 1.

Table 1. Development environments and requirements.

Windows/Ubuntu version	Ubuntu 20.04.4 LTS
CPU	Intel(R) Xeon(R) Gold 5218R CPU @ 2.10 GHz
RAM	128 G
GPU (number and type)	2 NVIDIA Tesla T4 (16G)
CUDA version	11.6
Programming language	Python 3.6
Deep learning framework	Pytorch (Torch 1.10.1, torchvision 0.11.2)
Specific dependencies	numpy 1.19.5, SimpleITK 2.0.2, monai 0.8.1

Training Protocols. As described below.

Random flipping strategy (only for initial training stage): each image has a 20% probability of flipping along the x-axis and a 20% probability of flipping along the y-axis.

Random Gaussian smooth (only for initial training stage): each image has a 10% probability of being Gaussian smoothed with sigma in (0.5, 1.15) for every spatial dimension.

Random Gaussian noise (only for initial training stage): each image has a 10% probability of being added with Gaussian noise with mean in (0, 0.5) and standard deviation in (0, 1).

Random intensity change (only for initial training stage): each image has a 10% probability of changing intensity with gamma in (0.5, 2.5).

Random intensity shift (only for initial training stage): each image has a 10% probability of shifting intensity with offsets in (0, 0.3).

Patch sampling strategy: 2 patches of size $[128, 128, 128]$ are randomly cropped from each image. The center of each patch has 50% probability in the foreground and 50% probability in the background.

Optimal model selection criteria: we tried several different training protocols and selected the model with the highest DSC on the validation set.

Some details of the initial training stage and the fine-tuning stage are shown in Table 2 and Table 3 respectively.

4 Results and Discussion

4.1 Quantitative Results on Validation Set

DSC results on validation set are shown in Table 4. It can be seen from the table that the generalization ability of the model is indeed improved by using unlabeled data through the "pseudo-labeling" method.

4.2 Qualitative Results on Validation Set

Two examples of good segmentation are shown in Fig. 3 and two examples of bad segmentation are shown in Fig. 4. Visualization is achieved with ITK-SNAP [12] version 3.8.0.

Table 2. Training protocols (initial training stage).

Network initialization	"he" normal initialization
Batch size	2
Patch size	128×128×128
Total epochs	1600
Optimizer	Adam
Initial learning rate (lr)	0.0001
Lr decay schedule	Initial learning rate$\times(1-epoch/500)^{0.9}$
Training time	77 h
Loss function	The sum of dice loss and cross entropy loss
Number of model parameters	31.42M

Table 3. Training protocols (fine-tuning stage).

Network initialization	Model after initial training
Batch size	2
Patch size	128 × 128 × 128
Total epochs	40
Optimizer	Adam
Initial learning rate (lr)	0.00005
Lr decay schedule	Initial learning rate$\times(1-epoch/500)^{0.9}$
Training time	39 h
Loss function	The sum of dice loss and cross entropy loss
Number of model parameters	31.42 M

Table 4. Results on validation set.

	Without using unlabeled data	Using unlabeled data
Mean DSC	0.6903	0.7496
Liver	0.9312	0.9493
RK	0.7151	0.8098
Spleen	0.8180	0.8962
Pancreas	0.6631	0.7506
Aorta	0.7474	0.7953
IVC	0.7003	0.7692
RAG	0.6792	0.6910
LAG	0.5257	0.5400
Gallbladder	0.6235	0.6543
Esophagus	0.6196	0.6641
Stomach	0.7550	0.8219
Duodenum	0.5261	0.5803
LK	0.6703	0.8225

From the perspective of organs, the segmentation results of organs with fewer surrounding organs are better, such as liver and spleen. From the perspective of images, some potential reasons for the bad-segmentation cases are listed below.

(1) The size of the case is very large, so we have to reduce the size of the case by resampling to avoid GPU memory overflow.
(2) The case is not clear, distorted, or skewed.
(3) There are rare structures in the case that are not in the training set.

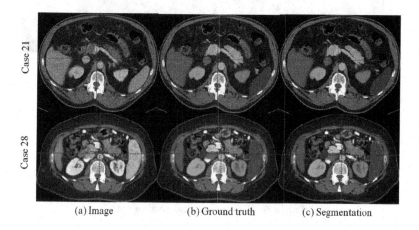

(a) Image   (b) Ground truth   (c) Segmentation

Fig. 3. Good segmentation examples

4.3 Segmentation Efficiency Results on Validation Set

Segmentation efficiency results for the 5th validation submission are shown in Table 5.

Table 5. Results on validation set.

Running time	1538.14 s
Maximal GPU Memory	16327 MB
Area under GPU memory-time curve	11050890
Area under CPU utilization-time curve	26722.79

The running time is relatively short since we didn't use any cascaded framework. In the testing phase, we used the "sliding_window_inference" function of monai to slice the image into several 128×128×128 patches and predict them separately. This can lead to a large GPU memory consumption when the image size is large.

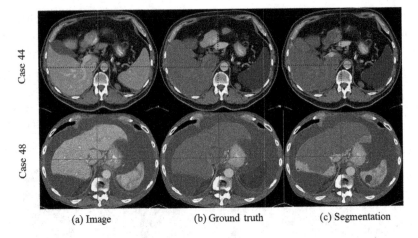

(a) Image   (b) Ground truth   (c) Segmentation

Fig. 4. Bad segmentation examples

4.4   Results on Final Testing Set

DSC and NSD results on final testing set are shown in Table 6.

Table 6. Results on final testing set.

	DSC results	NSD results
Mean	0.7502	0.7779
Liver	0.9402	0.9005
RK	0.8230	0.7567
Spleen	0.8614	0.8052
Pancreas	0.7151	0.8071
Aorta	0.7971	0.8007
IVC	0.7663	0.7480
RAG	0.7484	0.8588
LAG	0.6396	0.7515
Gallbladder	0.6575	0.6231
Esophagus	0.6249	0.7233
Stomach	0.7860	0.7977
Duodenum	0.5739	0.7628
LK	0.8195	0.7769

4.5 Limitation and Future Work

In terms of model accuracy, first, we give pseudo-labels only once for the unlabeled images at present. In the future, we are going to give pseudo-labels and finetune the model for several times. Second, we used the same rules for all organs when filtering the pseudo-labeled images. It is more reasonable to use different rules for different organs. Third, we consider using some post-processing methods, such as largest connected component extraction, hole filling, open operation and closed operation, which are not used at present.

In terms of segmentation efficiency, we consider changing the value of the "device" parameter of the "sliding_window_inference" function of monai from "torch.device('cuda')" to "torch.device('cpu')" to reduce the GPU memory consumption. In addition, we consider using some optimization methods to improve the running speed of the model in the future.

5 Conclusion

Using unlabeled data through "pseudo-labeling" method can improve the performance of the model.

Acknowledgements. The authors of this paper declare that the segmentation method they implemented for participation in the FLARE 2022 challenge has not used any pre-trained models nor additional datasets other than those provided by the organizers. The proposed solution is fully automatic without any manual intervention.

References

1. Clark, K., et al.: The cancer imaging archive (TCIA): maintaining and operating a public information repository. J. Digit. Imaging **26**(6), 1045–1057 (2013)
2. Heller, N., et al.: The state of the art in kidney and kidney tumor segmentation in contrast-enhanced CT imaging: results of the kits19 challenge. Med. Image Anal. **67**, 101821 (2021)
3. Heller, N., et al.: An international challenge to use artificial intelligence to define the state-of-the-art in kidney and kidney tumor segmentation in CT imaging. Proc. Am. Soc. Clin. Oncol. **38**(6), 626–626 (2020)
4. Isensee, F., Jaeger, P.F., Kohl, S.A., Petersen, J., Maier-Hein, K.H.: nnU-net: a self-configuring method for deep learning-based biomedical image segmentation. Nat. Methods **18**(2), 203–211 (2021)
5. Lee, D.H., et al.: Pseudo-label: the simple and efficient semi-supervised learning method for deep neural networks. In: Workshop on challenges in representation learning, ICML, p. 896 (2013)
6. Li, S., Zhang, C., He, X.: Shape-aware semi-supervised 3d semantic segmentation for medical images. In: Martel, A.L., et al. (eds.) MICCAI 2020. LNCS, vol. 12261, pp. 552–561. Springer, Cham (2020). https://doi.org/10.1007/978-3-030-59710-8_54
7. Li, X., Yu, L., Chen, H., Fu, C.W., Heng, P.A.: Semi-supervised skin lesion segmentation via transformation consistent self-ensembling model. arXiv preprint arXiv:1808.03887 (2018)

8. Li, X., Yu, L., Chen, H., Fu, C.W., Xing, L., Heng, P.A.: Transformation-consistent self-ensembling model for semi-supervised medical image segmentation. IEEE Trans. Neural Netw. Learn. Syst. **32**(2), 523–534 (2020)

9. Ma, J., et al.: Fast and low-GPU-memory abdomen CT organ segmentation: the flare challenge. Med. Image Anal. **82**, 102616 (2022)

10. Ma, J., et al.: Abdomenct-1k: is abdominal organ segmentation a solved problem? IEEE Trans. Pattern Anal. Mach. Intell. **44**(10), 6695–6714 (2022)

11. Simpson, A.L., et al.: A large annotated medical image dataset for the development and evaluation of segmentation algorithms. arXiv preprint arXiv:1902.09063 (2019)

12. Yushkevich, P.A., et al.: User-guided 3D active contour segmentation of anatomical structures: significantly improved efficiency and reliability. Neuroimage **31**(3), 1116–1128 (2006)

Author Index

Printed in the United States
by Baker & Taylor Publisher Services